C0-AVZ-476

EDWARD BENLOWES

EDWARD BENLOWES

(1602 - 1676)

BIOGRAPHY OF A MINOR POET

By HAROLD JENKINS

UNIVERSITY OF LONDON
THE ATHLONE PRESS
1952

92
B437j

156749

Published by

THE ATHLONE PRESS

at the Senate House, London, W. C. 1.

Distributed by Constable & Co. Ltd.

12 Orange Street, London, W. C. 2.

Published in the United States of America by

HARVARD UNIVERSITY PRESS

Cambridge, Massachusetts

Printed in The Netherlands by E. J. BRILL, *Leiden*

PREFACE

When Edward Benlowes put before the world in 1652 his big poem, *Theophila*, he commended to the reader "these Intervall *Issues* of spiritual *Recreation*" in these words: "If thou thinkest that I have wanted *Salt* to preserve them to Posterity, know that the very *Subject* It self is *Balsam* enough to make them perpetual." In that was the modesty proper to an author's preface, yet at the same time the boast that his work would enjoy a lasting fame. A lively circle of admirers and flatterers, some at least of whom had known the bounty for which Benlowes was renowned, helped to sustain him in the confidence with which he looked towards posterity. Yet when he died in 1676, Anthony à Wood spoke of him as "a great poet of his time," bearing witness in a single phrase both to Benlowes' fame and to the fact that it was already past. Fifteen years later, in his *Fasti Oxonienses*, Wood repeated his verdict, but, with a significant shift of emphasis, pushed Benlowes a little farther into oblivion with the words: "Much noted in his time, but since not, for the art and faculty of poetry." Benlowes had already, before his death, been excessively ridiculed by Samuel Butler in his Character of "A Small Poet". This was printed among Butler's *Remains* in 1759, and its effect, aided by a gibe of Pope's in *The Dunciad*, was to make Benlowes, in so far as he was heard of at all, an almost legendary example of a bad poet. Yet throughout the nineteenth century his *Theophila*, by reason of its handsome decorations, continued to be a book-collector's prize, and in 1905 Saintsbury, challenging the traditional verdict, ventured to claim attention for the text. *Theophila* and two of Benlowes' shorter poems were included in the first volume of Saintsbury's *Minor Poets of the Caroline Period*. Since then the vogue for "metaphysical" poetry has helped to draw him a little way out of his obscurity and caused him to be spoken of with a certain approbation and even with enthusiasm. [1]

As for the man himself, Anthony à Wood was responsible for

---

[1] Notably in Williamson, *The Donne Tradition*, 1930, pp. 175-181, where, however, the debt to Saintsbury seems clear.

the romantic portrait of a man who squandered a vast fortune and died in destitution. Like most of Wood's portraits, this has a lot of truth in it; but it gives a distorted view because Wood could only guess at details and knew nothing of Benlowes' early and middle life. Yet in Wood's two columns was contained almost all that was known of Benlowes' career for well over two hundred years, as may be seen by comparing his account with that in the *Dictionary of National Biography* and with the accounts by Saintsbury in an article in volume II of *The Bibliographer* (New York, 1903), in the *Minor Poets of the Caroline Period*, and in *The Cambridge History of English Literature*. Nor could the Rev. Andrew Clark add much when he contributed an article on Benlowes to the *Essex Review* in 1909. A return to original sources has nevertheless yielded many new facts. Three articles on Benlowes' life were published in 1936-37, one by Dr. Carl Niemeyer and two by myself. I now attempt the first full-length biography of this minor poet.

I hardly know whether apology is needed for the time and research I have given to a poet who has so long been obscure, though for my part I would sooner write a life which has never yet been written than dress up in new guise one which has been written many times before. A minor poet may sometimes reflect more faithfully than a great one the age which produces them both, merely by reason of that completer submission to circumstance which is part of what makes him "minor." Benlowes, I venture to think, is a useful mirror of a seventeenth-century way of life and one kind of seventeenth-century taste.

One item in this taste was a care for the appearance of a poem on the page. Benlowes was fastidious to a pedantic degree about details of spelling and typography; and in quotation it seems essential to reproduce these. The exact effect of his profuse italics may not be apparent when a full context is not given, but since it is impossible to draw an intermediate line, I have consistently retained his italics even in short phrases. In most cases I have given Benlowes' contemporaries also their original dress. But here complete consistency is not possible—unless indeed, by modernizing everything, one chose the easy way of consistent loss. Although scholarly texts now usually preserve original spelling, there are still a few exceptions among the standard editions to which it is desirable for references to be given; and some seventeenth-century memoirs—as, for example, the *Autobiography* of D'Ewes or the *Memoirs of Colonel Hutchinson* by his wife—have been published only in modernized form. The particular edition I use is indicated, when necessary, on the first occasion but in the case of works which are frequently cited is not usually repeated in subsequent references. It can, however, always be identified by consulting the Bibliography, which will mark it with an asterisk. In order to decrease a little further the cumbersomeness of footnotes, works which are in any case listed in the Bibliography are sometimes referred to in the footnotes by short titles.

I wish to thank all those who have helped me in any way in the preparation of this book. Large parts of it were originally written in South Africa, and only those who have tried it will appreciate the difficulties of working at a distance both from one's primary sources and a well-equipped specialist library. I gladly remember the staffs of the Witwatersrand University Library and the Johannesburg Public Library for all they did to minimize these difficulties for me. I have inevitably incurred many obligations at the British Museum, the Bodleian, the Public Record Office, the Essex County Record Office, and elsewhere. I am grateful to all those English librarians who have allowed me to examine and to all those American ones who have sent me information about copies of Benlowes' works in their custody. I have received particular courtesies from the past and present librarians of Benlowes' own college, St John's College, Cambridge. At one stage the librarian of the Petyt Library at Skipton most generously let me have the Petyt copy of *Theophila* on long loan. Colonel C. H. Wilkinson not only showed me his own copy but gave me notes on other copies he had seen. A good deal of my manuscript was patiently read by Professor J. Y. T. Greig and Professor J. P. R. Wallis, and I have received help both general and particular from Professor C. J. Sisson and Professor Geoffrey Tillotson. My largest creditor, my wife, has given me unstintedly the benefit of her advice, her knowledge, and her time. The editors of the *Modern Language Review* have graciously permitted the use or reproduction of a large part of my article on "Benlowes and Milton" which they published in April 1948. Finally, I thank the University of the Witwatersrand and the University of London for the generous grants which have made publication possible.

H. J.

CONTENTS

EDWARD BENLOWES

CHAPTER ONE

FAMILY TRADITION

Early in the sixteenth century lived a man called Christopher Benlowes, or Bendlowes, as he more often spelled his name.—The *d* was regularly dropped by his great-great-grandson Edward, whose practice will be consistently followed in this book.—This Christopher Benlowes, then, belonged to an established Yorkshire family, but for some reason not now to be discovered, he migrated south to Essex and there, settling at Great Bardfield, collected to himself a number of manors and other smaller properties. Eventually he became a man of sufficient wealth and standing to achieve for himself and his family the dignity of a coat-of-arms. There is record of the grant of his arms and crest by the Garter King-at-Arms, Sir Christopher Barker; [1] and the shield, with its cinquefoil on the bend between two turtle-doves, [2] and the crest, with its centaur with bow and arrow, were later to appear in stained-glass windows or on the covers of books to sustain the renown of somewhat more distinguished representatives of the Benlowes name.

The first of these was Christopher's son William, a celebrated lawyer. His opinion on legal matters long had weight in his profession, and it was the proud boast of his family that he was, for one brief period, at the end of the reign of Mary and the beginning of that of Elizabeth, the only member of the bar to hold the rank of serjeant. Beside this unique distinction the fact that he was a Member of Parliament falls into insignificance. His success in the law enabled him to add considerably to the Benlowes wealth, and he took pride in benefactions, in which a desire to provide monuments to his name mingled with a sense of his duty to man and God. It is recorded that he gave as much as fifty pounds towards the building of the new chapel in Serjeants' Inn. He also gave twenty pounds

[1] British Museum MS. Stowe 692, fol. 12v. Also British Museum MS. Harl. 5846, fol. 12. For the Benlowes genealogy, see *Visitations of Essex* (Harleian Soc.), I, 347.
[2] I do not know why genealogists have followed one another in referring to these as martlets, which they are not.

to the chapel of Corpus Christi College at Cambridge, although he himself had been educated at St. John's. [1]

The care for chapels and churches that became a man of standing who was both grave and pious also showed itself in his own parish of Great Bardfield, where Serjeant Benlowes owned the impropriation of the church together with the advowson of the living. In 1556 he dissolved the impropriation and converted the vicarage into a rectory. Half the money derived from the sale of the tithes, £6. 13s. 4d., was established upon the rector, whom the Serjeant continued to appoint. The other half was used to found a chantry dedicated to the Holy Trinity in Great Bardfield church. The endowment provided that the priest should say prayers for the souls of Queen Mary and King Philip, of the Serjeant's mother and father, his wife and himself, both living and dead, for ever. The day was nearly over for chantries and their Catholic prayers for the dead, and soon they were to be abolished and the chantry lands given to the Crown. One is rather glad, however, that the Serjeant did not live till 1588 to see the revenues that he had dedicated to prayers for souls being granted to Edward Wymark, "a great Chantry-monger." [2]

The Serjeant is said to have remained a devout Catholic all his life. In Mary's reign he had been employed to suppress Lollards and heretics in Essex. But he was a man of genuine piety rather than sectarian zeal. When he was practising at the bar it was his custom at the end of every term to make the sign of the cross and, kneeling down, to kiss the bar solemnly, praying that, if it pleased God, he might be allowed to come back safely after the vacation. [3] His care for ecclesiastical foundations certainly did not cease in a Protestant time. The English parish church maintained the continuity of its tradition through all changes in the official state religion, and the Serjeant's loyalty to a cherished institution rose above any question of creed. In Great Bardfield he continued the pattern of his father, which his greater worldly importance enabled him to engrave the more deeply on the tablet of local history.

---

[1] These facts are taken from Bodleian MS. Rawl. C. 728, fol. 460v; Cole, "Athenae Cantabrigienses," British Museum MS. Addit. 5863 fol. 61v; Venn, *Alumni Cantabrigienses*, I, 132. For the life of Serjeant William Benlowes, see also Cooper, *Athenae Cantabrigienses*, I, 495-497; Woolrych, *Eminent Serjeants-at-Law*, I, 94-100.

[2] Morant, *Essex*, II, 521.

[3] *Cal. S. P., Dom.*, 1595-1597, p. 113.

The records show [1] that Christopher Benlowes had been a prominent figure at Great Bardfield church. He was one of several entrusted with certain church moneys the interest on which had to be used for an annual dinner to the parishioners. He also had charge of some cattle which had been presented to the church so that the profit derived from them might be given to the poor. On one occasion he had the custody of a cross of silver gilt belonging to the church, and this at his death passed into the hands of his son, the Serjeant. In his turn, Serjeant William Benlowes often advanced sums of money to pay for various repairs and furnishings. He also gave a rent of 13s.4d. to help maintain in good repair the church of the adjacent parish of Finchingfield. [2]

In 1574 the Serjeant endowed a chapel at Bardfield Saling, a hamlet to Great Bardfield. The chapel there had been mistakenly disposed of as a chantry in the time of Henry VIII, and the parishioners only recovered it and the priest's house when these were purchased and given back to them by Serjeant Benlowes. His pious munificence thus provided for the preaching of the word of God and the administration of the sacraments in Bardfield Saling. He also gave the priest a stipend of three pounds a year, besides tithes of hay and fruit and livestock. [3] And his care was not confined to consideration for the villagers' souls. He was also interested in their education and their bodily well-being. His will provided for a grammar-school at Great Bardfield and allotted to the schoolmaster a house and garden and an income of ten pounds a year. The schoolmaster was to be a godly, learned, and a virtuous man; he was to be over twenty-four and unmarried; he was to be in holy orders and to assist the rector in the services of the church as well as teaching grammar at the Guildhall. His pupils were to include as many children of the Benlowes family as the head of the family desired to receive his instruction, as well as twelve children from Great Bardfield, four from Little Bardfield, four from Bardfield Saling, and six from Finchingfield. [4] Unfortunately, the Serjeant's provision for the education of the children of the neighbourhood was not maintained by his heirs, who had difficulty in finding a schoolmaster to meet the requirements and allowed the school to lapse. The Serjeant

---

[1] *Transactions of the Essex Archaeological Society*, XI, 310ff.

[2] Finchingfield "Town Book," pp. 3, 17. Morant (*Essex*, II, 369) and others give the amount as £2.13s.4d., but someone seems to have misread the deed.

[3] Morant, *Essex*, II, 522-523.

[4] Particulars from Serjeant Benlowes' will, on which see below.

also indulged largely in a form of charity very fashionable at that time—the endowing of almshouses. Many of the charities of the English villages, with their provision of bread or wood or money for the poor on certain feast-days of the year, date from the sixteenth century. The Serjeant had annual benefactions of that kind running in a host of Essex villages—the Bardfields, Finchingfield, Great Maplestead, Sible Hedingham, Halstead, Bocking, Shalford, Gosfield, Panfield, Wethersfield, Debden, Thaxted—and reaching even into Suffolk at Stoke-by-Clare. In Finchingfield, he gave a house with garden and orchard for the occupation of four poor widows. [1] In other villages, where almshouses already existed, he gave money for their upkeep or for distribution among the poor inhabitants, accompanying his benefactions with the sort of stipulation that often betokened the sixteenth-century gentleman's pious and condescending regard for his worldly inferiors. In Bocking, for example, the people living in the almshouses received from Serjeant Benlowes £5.13s. 4d. a year, divided among them—so long as they were over forty years of age and had no children living with them. This was a common stipulation: children disturbed the peace which was proper for the aged. Any residue of the Bocking grant could be bestowed where the trustees thought fit, provided that the recipients were honest people, not vagrants or idlers. [2]

Many of the Serjeant's charities are listed in his will, a most formidable document preserved at Somerset House, dated November 17, 1584, two days before his death. [3] It charged his heirs to maintain all his charities as he had done during his life. It was difficult for them to do otherwise, for many of the charities were tied to certain

---

[1] Morant, *Essex*, II, 369. Gifts to the poor of Finchingfield were made by a deed delivered over to the townspeople, which was regularly listed as a valuable asset at any stocktaking of parish goods (Finchingfield "Town Book," pp. 3, 17, 71).

[2] Exactly the same stipulations accompanied a gift to the poor of Thaxted. Other charities included 20s. a year to the poor of Halstead, and 20s. to those who dwelt in the almshouses in Alderford Street in Hedingham Sible. The money could be distributed among them, or its value could be given them in wood. There was 6s.8d. a year for the two almshouses at Great Maplestead, and 20s. a year for the poor of Debden, to buy clothes or wood for them or to repair the almshouses near the churchyard in which they lived (Morant, *Essex*, II, 259, 281, 290, 388, 442, 565).

[3] Somerset House, 10 Brudenell. The details that follow do not pretend to offer more than a representative sample of his very numerous bequests. A fuller account of the will is given by C. Fell Smith in the *Essex Review*, XXVII, 117ff. For the date of the Serjeant's death, see Inquisition Post Mortem, Chancery Series II, 207/59.

lands in the Benlowes estates. In fact, the numerous encumbrances were to be a source of great trouble to the Serjeant's great-grandson Edward, the subject of this biography. But the spirit of benevolence was a family heritage, and generations of Benloweses accepted these obligations as a necessary part of their station in life. The good works required of them were sometimes trivial and irksome; for the Serjeant's practical mind perceived the importance of attending to the little things of life. He expected his heirs to send six loads of wood a year to different almshouses at specified times, and to continue his practice of sending herring to the poor widows and "olde maydens" in the Great Bardfield almshouses every week during Lent. Such details did not then seem inconsistent with the dignity of an affluent squire, who, if he believed that God had called him to a place above his neighbours, believed also that he ought to love them next to himself. The duties were not all on one side. The supply of herring was a hint about fasting, and like most benevolent rulers of those simple village communities, the Serjeant thought with charity to purchase holiness. For their almshouses and their twenty-six shillings a year, the poor women were to go twice every week into the chancel of the church and there pray heartily to God for the space of an hour. And every time they defaulted they forfeited a penny of their yearly allowance and some other poor person reaped the benefit.

All parishes which knew the Serjeant's generosity received small sums of money at his death. And fifty poor men and fifty poor women and twenty poor children were to have each a shirt or smock. The Serjeant also desired that any other parishes which were represented at his funeral should have twenty shillings to distribute to their poor. He made numerous small bequests to his servants and dependants and provided for the black clothes which they would need for mourning. All his godchildren were remembered, and the prisoners in Colchester Castle had twenty shillings.

The Serjeant had had a marble tomb made and set up in the chancel in Great Bardfield church, ready to receive his body. And he was buried under this marble tomb by the side of his second wife Alienor. According to his direction their effigies in brass were affixed to it; for he wished after death to have every dignity that was fitting to the degree that God had called him to, but objected to any unnecessary pomp. His own brass is no longer to be seen, but that of Alienor still survives. Alongside it twice over is the Benlowes coat-of-arms, and a brass inscription: "Hic iacet Willihelmus Bendlowes ad legem quondam solus serviens et Alionora uxor eius."

A tablet in honour of the Serjeant was also put up in the chancel. It has a long inscription in Latin verse celebrating his integrity of character and his distinction in the law: he was a faithful pleader and an advocate in whom any client might be happy; he was the only serjeant left who obeyed the law and for seventy-three days he continued alone; he was a great honour to his country while he lived, and all men acknowledged his fame. [1]

Although Christopher Benlowes had acquired the nucleus of the Benlowes estates, it was Serjeant William who really established the family fortunes. His many charities were but thank-offerings for his own riches, a tithe of his wealth consecrated to good works. Most of the money he gained went into lands and property in Essex in his own neighbourhood. When he died the estates included the manors of Brent Hall and Justices and half the manor of Cockfields, all in the parish of Finchingfield; the manor of Priors in Great Bardfield, and that of Fennes in Bocking. Along with Justices went the manor of Hawksells (or Hawkeshall) in Toppesfield; and with Brent Hall went the ownership of Belcumber Hall in Finchingfield. The estates included also numerous houses and cottages, fields and woods and meadows and similar small properties in Finchingfield, Great Bardfield, Little Bardfield, Bardfield Saling, Sible Hedingham, Panfield, Great and Little Sampford, Bocking, Hatfield Peverel, Terling, and Thaxted. [2] The annual income was upwards of a thousand pounds, and the head of the Benlowes family was one of the most important men in all that part of Essex. As an eminent lawyer besides, the Serjeant was an obvious choice for a Justice of the Peace, and he carried out his duties with vigour, whether dominating his fellow-justices at the Chelmsford quarter sessions or dealing with some vagrant or petty malefactor brought before him in his own parish. He was liable, of course, to want his own way: when Finchingfield about 1585 started having three constables instead of two, it was not due to any general desire on the part of the parish-

[1] This inscription is given at length in "A Gentleman", *History of Essex*, II, 295-296, in Wright, *Essex*, II, 65, and in Cooper, *Athenae Cantabrigienses*, I, 496.

[2] An inventory of Serjeant Benlowes' lands may be found in the Inquisition Post Mortem, Chancery Series II, 207/59. For a list of the Benlowes estates in Edward's time (1655), see an unofficial survey preserved in the Essex Record Office at Chelmsford (D/DAc 110). See also Morant's *Essex* for much miscellaneous information about the Benlowes family and their estates, especially II, 367ff., 521.

ioners, but to Serjeant Benlowes' local pride and overbearing will. [1]
But such a human touch of vanity and self-importance was in no
way inconsistent with his character of a benevolent country gentleman. The Serjeant handed on to his descendants a position of authority and a dignified tradition.

Serjeant William had lived in a house at Great Bardfield called
the Place. Some of its original structure still remains, and a beautifully carved corner post abutting on Great Bardfield's main street
has in recent years been re-exposed. Displayed to every passer-by,
as in the Serjeant's own time, are the initials W.B. with the date
1564. Some surviving fragments of sixteenth-century stained glass
have been built into two modern windows, and again one finds
a Latin inscription with the boast that William Benlowes had been
for a time the only serjeant-at-law in England. [2] A love of decoration
and a pride in one's own rank or achievement were part of the in-
heritance of his descendants. With no more pomp than necessary,
yet "accordinge to the degree that god hath called me vnto"—those
were his instructions regarding the brasses on his tomb.

It was not in Great Bardfield that the descendants of the Serjeant
dwelt. After his death the family seat became Brent Hall, in Finchingfield. This manor had been in the family since the time of
Christopher, and perhaps the Serjeant gave the mansion for the
residence of his son William at his marriage. As the family fortunes
rose it was natural that they should move to a more country house,
where they might have what, according to Fynes Moryson, [3] every
gentleman of five hundred or a thousand pounds a year had—
a park enclosed with wooden palings, two or three miles round
and no doubt well stocked with deer. The house was situated not
far from the village, about three-quarters of a mile north-west of
Finchingfield church. It had got its name from the fact that it had
been twice destroyed by fire; and it was an ill-fated house, for it
was to be burnt to the ground a third time during Edward's occupation.

William Benlowes, the Serjeant's son, succeeded to the estates
and all the duties that went with them. His father had charged
him in his will, as he would answer it before Almighty God, "to
lyve and contynue well vertuously and honestly and instantly to

[1] Essex Quarter Sessions Rolls, 94/27.

[2] For a further description and photographs, see C. Fell Smith, "William
Bendlowes of Great Bardfield Place," *Essex Review*, XXVII, 113ff.

[3] *Itinerary* (1907 reprint), IV, 168.

followe vertue good learninge and thryffte all the dayes of his lief." Like his father, he was a devout man, as the world reckons devoutness, and one of his prized possessions was a beautifully illuminated thirteenth-century psalter, now in the Bodleian Library. [1] Bred in the Serjeant's pattern, he had already followed his father to St. John's College, Cambridge, and to Lincoln's Inn. [2] But the son aimed at no distinction in the law and held no extraordinary dignities to add to his position of country squire. What he did inherit from his father along with his estates was a strong sense of family importance and a determination to uphold his rights of property. Like many large landowners, the Benloweses were inevitably involved at times in disputes of ownership, and there was something of a tradition of litigation. In 1576 the Serjeant had quarrelled energetically with a neighbour, Robert Vere, concerning lands in Finchingfield that they both claimed. There had been much erecting and knocking down of fences and driving of one another's cattle in and out of the disputed fields. On one occasion the Serjeant had arrived in person to make a forcible entry over a certain stile, and had instigated a mild affray between his own and Vere's servants. [3] When blows failed, an appeal to Chancery followed. William the son could also resort to force to assert his will, as when, to achieve some unknown purpose, he led a group of men in breaking into a house in Bardfield Saling and assaulting the occupants. [4] And he also got involved in Chancery disputes about the ownership of land. In 1600, for example, he was suing John Wentworth, who claimed rights over the Benlowes manor of Fennes and who had cut down trees and destroyed the gates of enclosed lands which were farmed by one of William Benlowes' tenants. [5] There had been a long quarrel, renewed whenever a tree was felled by either side, and the Serjeant's son naturally stood up for himself.

As the donor of the living of Great Bardfield, William also felt bound to support the parson in a dispute about tithe. He brought an action, therefore, against a prominent landowner, Sir Robert Wrothe, and the hearing, at Brentwood assizes on March 12, 1601, [6]

---

[1] MS. Douce 131.

[2] Baker's note in Wood, *Fasti Oxonienses*, ed. Bliss, II, 358; *Records of the Honourable Society of Lincoln's Inn*, I, 68.

[3] See Chancery Depositions, C24/129/13, 22.

[4] Essex Quarter Sessions Rolls, 96/54.

[5] Chancery Proceedings, Eliz., B26/26; Depositions, C24/288/82; Bodleian MS. Rawl. C. 728, fols. 293ff.

[6] Dates are given throughout in the modern manner which counts the year as beginning on January 1st.

lasted for three hours. William Benlowes got the verdict and recorded it with much glee on a blank page at the end of a case-book of
the Serjeant's. He could afford to smile at Sir Robert Wrothe, who
departed from the courthouse "Greatelye discontented" and "moche
offended" with him, and he thoroughly enjoyed his victory. [1] It
was the more satisfying because these two neighbours had been at
strife ever since William had inherited his father's estates. Sir Robert
Wrothe, as Lord of the Manor of Great Bardfield, had refused to
admit William Benlowes to the tenancy of some small copyhold
property which the Benloweses claimed their right to enjoy. Who
could and who could not lop trees was again a material item in the
dispute, which caused a good deal of interest in the neighbourhood
and also found its way into the law-courts when the Benlowes-
Wrothe quarrel reached a climax in 1601. [2]

These early Benloweses took all this in their stride. Yet prolonged
and involved lawsuits were an inauspicious omen for the birth of
William's grandson, whose fortunes we are to follow and who,
over half a century later, was to entangle himself in Chancery litigation and become overwhelmed by it.

William Benlowes was married to Clare Smyth, of the Smyths
(or Smiths) of Cressing Temple, who afterwards changed their name
to Nevill. He had two sons, Andrew and Francis, each of whom
in their turn married and had children. It is Andrew's son, Edward,
who concerns us in this book.

Andrew, as the elder son, though in fact he was to die before
he could inherit, was given all the gentlemanly advantages that
primogeniture demanded. He had his years at Cambridge, though
he broke precedent in going to King's and not St. John's, and
followed up the university with Lincoln's Inn. [3] Then a suitable
match had to be made for him, and in 1601 he married Phillip, or
Philippa, Gage, who belonged to a well-known Catholic family of
Framfield in Sussex. She was about twenty-five years old at the time
of her marriage, [4] she brought with her a dowry of fifteen hundred
pounds, and a marriage-settlement was made securing the inheri-
tance of the Benlowes estates to the heirs of this marriage. [5] There

[1] Bodleian MS. Rawl. C. 728, fols. 307ff., 314v.

[2] Chancery Depositions, C24/291/6.

[3] Venn, *Alumni Cantabrigienses*, I, 132; *Records of the Honourable Society of
Lincoln's Inn*, I, 123.

[4] She was thirty-eight and more at the death of her father on March 11, 1614
(Inquisition Post Mortem, *Sussex Record Society Publications*, XIV, 98).

[5] Inquisition Post Mortem, Chancery Series II, 343/137; Recovery, Common
Pleas 43/73.

were five sons—Edward, William, Henry, Andrew, and Philip [1]—
and two daughters, Mary and Clare.

The eldest son had been named Edward after his mother's father,
Edward Gage. He was born on July 12, 1602, [2] less than a year before Queen Elizabeth died and, with James I, the troubled Stuart
dynasty began. He lived to grieve for the execution of James's son
and died a dozen years before the grandson abdicated. He was to
show himself no more skilled than they in keeping his own smaller
throne. But before he died he had added to the pursuits of a country
squire an enthusiastic interest in the arts and had become well
known as a literary patron. As a minor poet and religious devotee
he was an interesting example of the intelligentsia of the seventeenth
century, and he did his best to maintain the pursuit of culture and
the habit of devotion amid the political convulsions of that age.

[1] Chancery Proceedings, Collins 140/147.
[2] When he inherited from his grandfather on November 18, 1613, he was
aged 11 years, 4 months, and 6 days (Inquisition Post Mortem, Chancery Series
II, 343/137. Also Wards series, 53/229). The Finchingfield church register,
unfortunately, goes back only to 1617.

CHAPTER TWO

CATHOLIC UPBRINGING

The distinguished heritage that Edward received from his family did not consist in a particularly ancient lineage. There was talk of a pedigree of nineteen descents, which Edward seems to have boasted of to Anthony à Wood; [1] but that was a little touch of vanity that the modern genealogist, who cannot go back beyond Christopher, finds it hard to justify. It is interesting as suggesting a pride in gentle birth, and from the first Edward was very responsive to family tradition. What the family lacked in age it made up for by its conspicuous local influence; and it was not altogether idle for Edward to boast of his extraction.

He inherited great wealth, and with it a sense of the importance that attached to the ownership of land and country-houses. The head of the Benlowes family was accustomed to find fortune kind, to dispose of money freely, and to arrange other people's lives with great goodwill. If fortune were interfered with by a neighbour, it was jealously protected by one's own energy and if necessary assisted by appeal to law.

Nature perhaps had not given Edward great abilities in administration; but his position demanded from him an interest in farms, leases, and tenancies. The Serjeant had taught his descendants to be interested also in their tenants. His numerous precedents were to strengthen in Edward a natural generosity towards social inferiors. The great weight of his personality had impressed itself upon the environment in which Edward was brought up, and it encouraged the young boy to add to a consciousness of family dignity a probity of character and gravity of mind. With this went also an enthusiasm for religion. The young Benlowes was taught to take a serious view of human life. Prayer and the immortal soul were early made realities to him.

This was all the more so because the family, true to tradition, was Catholic. For the good fortune He had bestowed upon them, God

[1] *Life and Times of Anthony Wood*, ed. Clark, II, 361.

asked a special test of faith. As a result of the anti-Catholic legislation of Elizabeth and James I, even their worldly influence
was restricted by their creed. They might assert the rights
of property, but as Catholics they were debarred from holding any
sort of public appointment. One may scan the lists in vain for any
record that the descendants of the Serjeant followed him as a Justice
of the Peace. So the family could not add to its dignity by office.
Driven in upon its own small circle, it maintained its eminence by
its possessions, character, and good works. It took pride in holding
the more staunchly a religion that had become the unpopular creed
of a minority, and of necessity it thought devoutly and felt ardently
about its articles of faith. Though Edward was to abandon the beliefs of his ancestors, this was one of the most important items in
the environment of the young child.

   For long the Catholics had suffered under Elizabeth. For them,
the daughter of Anne Boleyn was not even the legitimate monarch,
and how could they own allegiance to a woman the Pope had ex-
communicated? There were numerous plots against her, and she,
recognizing the papists as a threat to her throne, sought to suppress
their religion. Accordingly, they were commanded to worship in
a church they thought heretical, and recusants were heavily fined. [1]
Their own priests were always being banished or imprisoned and
ran regular risk of martyrdom when they sought surreptitiously to
celebrate the rites of their own religion. The great hope of the Catholics lay in the absence of a direct heir to the Protestant queen.
They had looked longingly to Mary Queen of Scots and the Catholic
power of Spain, and although hope had dwindled after the execution of Mary in 1587 and the defeat of the Armada in 1588, yet
there was still plenty of intriguing and speculation over the succession [2] until James was actually on the throne. In the year of Edward
Benlowes' birth his parents and grandparents would be praying,
along with all truly devout Catholics, that God would grant them
a Catholic ruler, so that their own religion might be restored in
England.

   Andrew Benlowes, Edward's father, had already been in trouble
as a recusant before his marriage. Proceedings had been instituted

---

   [1] See especially the acts of 1581, 1586, and 1593: 23 Eliz., c. 1; 28 & 29 Eliz.,
c. 6; 35 Eliz., c. 2.
   [2] In 1602 Elizabeth issued a proclamation which dealt with the presumption
of the Jesuits in "adventuring" in their writings and speeches to dispose of
her kingdom and crown "at their pleasures" (Dyson, *Proclamations*, p. 397).

against him in or about 1600 and only "stayed" by the intervention of the Earl of Southampton, whose favour he enjoyed along with seven others, including Edward Gage, a cousin of Southampton's mother. [1] This was the Edward Gage whose daughter Andrew Benlowes had since married, and nothing could more clearly reflect an opposition to the orthodox Anglican faith than an alliance with this family. For Edward Gage was one of the most notable recusants in England. The Privy Council had had him committed to the Marshalsea in 1580 for his "obstinacye in Poperye," [2] and his subsequent biography consists largely of the record of his convictions and imprisonments. This was the grandfather after whom Edward Benlowes was named in the last year of Elizabeth's reign.

Catholics expected great relief from the accession of James I in 1603. For if James was himself a Protestant, at least he was the son of Mary. And he had indeed some hope of showing greater tolerance towards the Church of Rome. He took it upon himself to remit the fines which Elizabethan statutes had imposed upon recusant laymen, [3] but at such an invitation to liberty of conscience the Catholics showed themselves to be surprisingly numerous, and Parliament and the orthodox church scented danger. So a bill was passed in 1604 [4] providing that the statutes against recusants should be put into execution. Under Elizabeth it had often been possible to escape conviction; so in many cases the Catholics were worse off than before.

Even under James, however, the law was generally severer than the practice. The letter of the law itself, of course, could be obeyed if you were prepared, while holding Catholic views in silence, to accommodate your conscience to an occasional visit to the Protestant church service. Recusants, though the word is often loosely used to refer to Catholics in general, were, properly speaking, those who refused to go to church.[5] For this they were liable to a fine of twenty

---

[1] S.P., Dom., Eliz., 276/109. It was Gage, no doubt, who was responsible for enlisting Southampton's interest. He was the executor of the will of Southampton's father, and he had been a very active friend of Southampton in all sorts of difficulties about his estates (see Stopes, *Life of Henry, Third Earl of Southampton*).

[2] *Acts of the Privy Council*, n. s., XII, 153.

[3] Gardiner, *History of England... 1603-1642*, I, 116. For the fullest and most authoritative account of James and the Catholics in the early part of the reign, see Gardiner, chs. 3, 5-7.

[4] Statute 1 & 2 Jac. I, c. 4.

[5] It has been estimated that while the total number of recusants in England at the beginning of James's reign was about 8,500, there were probably another

pounds a month. Obviously not very many could afford with equanimity two hundred and sixty pounds per annum for thirteen lunar months, but many of the smaller gentry suffered the alternative penalty of forfeiting two-thirds of their lands to the Crown. Others retained their estates precariously and in fear. But the administration was often lax, and there were many chances of escaping the full penalties. The churchwardens, whose duty it was to report absentees to the Quarter Sessions, were not always anxious to denounce a neighbour, and when they were forced to do so their report was not invariably followed by conviction. Nor was conviction invariably followed by a fine. Debts to the Exchequer were entered on the Recusant Rolls, but these offer overwhelming evidence that fines due were only sporadically recorded and that many of those recorded were not paid. Even so, obviously no recusant could ever feel safe: one never knew when authority would pounce. [1] The amounts, when demanded, were high; and the law provided also for the confiscation of recusants' personal property. The Parliamentary insistence on penalties in the act of 1604 must have given rise to many qualms in Catholic households. And this act was followed early in the next year by a royal command to the same effect. There was a sudden burst of church-going. Nevertheless, some of the members of the Benlowes family, whose ancestors in happier days had taken such pride in the churches of Great Bardfield and Finchingfield and who still held the living of Great Bardfield in their gift, absented themselves from the parish church. Lists of recusants were called for, and a list for Essex was compiled on April 6, 1605, and certified by the Bishop of London. This document reported that among others at Finchingfield Mrs. Clare Benlowes (Edward's grandmother) did not attend church. [2] No reference was made to Edward's grandfather, and it looks therefore as if he conformed. It frequently happened that the Catholic women were more recalcitrant than the men—the

100,000 Catholics who occasionally attended church (Davies, *The Early Stuarts*, pp. 203-204).

[1] Gardiner (*History of England.... 1603-1642*, I, 96) simply says that "all recusants who had sufficient property were liable to a fine of £20 a month." But the statute (23 Eliz., c. 1) makes it clear that all persons over sixteen were "liable" to the fine. Apparently only 16 recusants were regularly paying £20 a month to the Exchequer at the time of Elizabeth's death; but, rash as it is to disagree with Gardiner, I do not think it should be implied that all the rest, if their lands did not happen to be sequestrated, escaped fines altogether. Their names were in most cases well known and if they were often ignored, sometimes they were not.

[2] Historical MSS. Commission, 10th Report, Appendix, pt. 4, p. 488. Essex Quarter Sessions Rolls, 171/60d.

Bishop of Winchester had complained in 1580 that he could persuade the men to come to church but not their wives.[1] There was, of course, good reason for this beyond the feminine character. While the women kept the faith strong on the domestic hearth, the husband's church attendance kept his property from sequestration. The head of the Benlowes family did not endanger the family fortunes more than he could help; but his children, like their mother, stayed away. And so Andrew Benlowes and his wife, Edward's parents, were also named as recusants in the Bishop of London's list in 1605 and were presented as recusants to the Chelmsford Quarter Sessions.[2]

It is not surprising, with this display of official energy, that the recusant roll for the following year[3] suddenly doubles in size. Clare Benlowes, Edward's grandmother, was one of three people in Finchingfield who were to pay forty pounds; and a later list in the same year noted a twenty pound fine for her, and for Andrew Benlowes and his wife as well.

Meanwhile, in 1605 the nation had been shocked by that effort of misguided zeal which we call the Gunpowder Plot. In Parliamentary language it was "that more than barbarous and horrible attempt to have blownen up with Gunpowder the Kinge Queene Prince Lordes and Cōmons in the Howse of Parliament assembled, tending to the utter Subversion of the whole State."[4] Further repressive legislation not unnaturally followed in 1606, and life for Catholics became more unpleasant. Some Catholics, the new act contended, with a glimpse of the obvious, had sometimes gone to church to escape the penalties of the law and to obtain cover for their mischievous designs. It was now made compulsory not only to attend the parish church but to take the sacrament when there. For non-compliance the forfeiture of lands was now more regularly enforced. An existing regulation prohibiting Catholics from travelling more than five miles from their own houses was confirmed. But the most drastic persecution was the institution of a new oath of allegiance, which might be offered to any suspected Catholic at any time, calling on him to repudiate the doctrine that the Pope had authority over the English King and to pledge his assistance to the King in the event of any war caused by a papal sentence of

[1] *Acts of the Privy Council*, n. s., XII, 244.
[2] Historical MSS. Commission, 10th Report, Appendix, pt. 4, p. 488. Essex Quarter Sessions Rolls, 171/60d.
[3] P. R. O., E377/14.
[4] Statute 3 & 4 Jac. I, c. 4.

deposition. This came near to the heart of Catholic belief, and the oath at once provoked a furious controversy which lasted throughout James's reign and which had among its most distinguished participants Cardinal Bellarmine on the one side and Bishop Lancelot Andrewes on the other. Refusal of the oath could lead to new drastic penalties—even to the loss of all property and perpetual imprisonment—but compliance did not remit the usual recusancy fines, which were so valuable an asset to the Exchequer.

Edward's parents and his grandmother were among the many who went on holding out. They were again presented as recusants at the Essex Quarter Sessions in October 1606. [1] His grandmother's name came forward again next year; [2] and again it figured on the recusancy roll—for a debt of £40, and then for a further £120. [3] Andrew, with his Gage connections quite a prominent recusant in official eyes, was treated differently.

What happened in his case was this. The fines collected from recusants and the rents accruing from forfeited lands would sometimes be granted to some courtier or official as a reward for public service. [4] They were assets of the Crown, and could be used by the Crown to pay its obligations. In 1607, when Sir Richard Coningsby was called on to relinquish a royal patent which entitled him to grant licences to merchants dealing in tin in Devon and Cornwall and to collect fourpence for every hundredweight of tin exported, he was granted in compensation the benefits derived from the recusancy of nineteen persons. So much recusancy was valued to Sir Richard at a thousand pounds, and one of the nineteen persons was Andrew Benlowes, gentleman, in the county of Essex. [5] I do not know how much Andrew contributed; as yet only heir apparent to his father, he would have, fortunately, little property of his own. But presumably two-thirds of what he had was sequestrated for the use of Sir Richard Coningsby, and Andrew's status as a recusant was now once and for all established. He seems to have done what he could to justify this in the way of publicly upholding the Catholic religion.

[1] Essex Quarter Sessions Rolls, 177/91, 94.
[2] *Ibid.*, 180/48.
[3] P.R.O., E377/15.
[4] There were instances of the same fines being granted twice over, a fact which perturbed the Lord Treasurer, so that on October 30, 1607, he decided that no grants of recusants' fines should in future be made to private individuals without a proper certificate from the Exchequer (*Cal. S.P., Dom.*, 1603-1610, p. 377).
[5] S.P., Docquets, vol. VIII, Nov. 23, 1607.

He became known as far afield as Cambridge for "a learned Papist." [1]

To the King and his ministers a learned papist was a fair exchange for several tons of tin. A learned papist who valued liberty of conscience sufficiently bought it when he had to; but he would find it mortifiying that the King from whom his church had ventured to expect relief had ended by imposing the abominable oath of allegiance. Doubtless there were many bitter things said against King James in the household at Brent Hall, where the boy Edward Benlowes lived with his parents and his grandparents and an increasing number of brothers and sisters. These early years were quietly spent on the family estates, where the Benloweses were looked up to and where recusancy fines did not easily damage the comfort and distinction of their worldly position. But the atmosphere of any persecution, social or religious, must have its influence early upon a sensitive mind. Edward was surrounded by a persecuted people, whose influence naturally increased the seriousness of his outlook. The hostility their religion met with bred a spirit of intolerance which persisted in Edward even when he had abandoned their faith. He was to take an exaggerated interest in religious controversy and to wage it with a bitterness he showed in nothing else.

A bias towards gravity of mind was enhanced by an early acquaintance with the shock of death. A little before Edward was ten his father died, after a somewhat melodramatic illness. When he was dangerously ill, his family got in touch with John Fortho, a Fellow of Trinity and a doctor of medicine. Fortho went over from Cambridge, to find a man wildly delirious in the "extreamitye of disease." And he was horrified by the "exorbitante speeches" that he heard in the sick room. Mixed with a lot of idle and unintelligible ravings, there kept coming such speeches as "I haue kilde Kinge Jeames.—This daye, I kilde him". And once the dying man exulted, "O meritoriouse deede." One hopes that Andrew Benlowes died happy in his delusion, and Fortho at first thought it all "scarce woorth respecte." Yet the words haunted him and "one more seriouse deliberatione" he "feared such speeches (though idlye spoaken in extreamitye of sicknesse) mighte proceede frome some former treacherouse designe." Andrew Benlowes was beyond the reach of law, but, Fortho wondered, might not others still alive also be involved? This may have been foolishly suspicious, but Fortho's reading of what we might

[1] John Fortho to Earl of Salisbury, S.P., Dom., Jas. I, 63/26.

call the subconscious was correct enough. There had been papist plots against James's life before, and here was a notorious Catholic whose suppressed desire was for the King's assassination. The authorities must be told. And the best man to tell was the Chancellor of the University of Cambridge, who was the Lord Treasurer of England, Robert Cecil, Earl of Salisbury. So when he was back in college, Fortho "with all conueniente speede" sat down and wrote him the whole story. [1] This was in April 1611 or 1612. [2]

In spite of Fortho's informing against Andrew, the surviving members of the Benlowes family were allowed to live fairly peaceably at Brent Hall. His father's death made Edward heir to the estates, and his grandfather William was close on seventy. Before very long—on November 18, 1613—William also died, and Edward at the age of eleven became the head of the family.

At this time the property of a minor passed into the control of the Crown until he should come of age. In practice the Crown delegated its control to one of its subjects. There was no need for this to be a relative of the ward or any guardian appointed by a

---

[1] S.P., Dom., Jas. I, 63/26.

[2] Some difficult discrepancies in the records must here be referred to. Fortho, speaking of Andrew Benlowes as "nowe deade," dated his letter April 11. He gave no year; but at the receiver's end the letter was endorsed "11° Apr. 1611." Yet when William Benlowes died in 1613 the Inquisition Post Mortem (Chancery Series II, 343/137) said that Andrew's death occurred on April 12, 1612. Even conjecture does not easily suppose an error both in the year and the day of the month, and there is more than this. Fortho describes his dying man as "nighe 30 yeare olde," and Andrew Benlowes, who went up to Cambridge in 1592, had certainly turned thirty in 1611. *About* thirty would have done, and Fortho may have meant that, but the *N.E.D.* cites no clear parallel for such a use of "nigh" (as distinct from "nigh about"). This gives an awkward edge to Fortho's reference to "Andrew Bendlowes the younger," which seems to suggest that there were two of the name. Yet Fortho's Andrew was "of Burnt-halle in Essex," and I do not see what Andrew other than Edward's father there could have been there. William Benlowes could not have had two sons Andrew and there was no other descendant of the Serjeant from whom a second Andrew could have sprung. Rather than postulate two Andrew Benloweses living at Brent Hall together, an entirely unknown one who died on April 11, 1611, beside the known one who died on April 12, 1612, I assume an error in dating. Fortho could have been a day behind, and the wrong year in the endorsement would not be a ridiculous slip within three weeks of the new year; or the Inquisition might have been wrong in recording a death two and a half years after its occurrence. Then one sees Fortho's "nighe 30 yeare olde" as the mere estimate it almost certainly was and "the younger" as intended to distinguish Mr. Benlowes the son from Mr. Benlowes the father. I have come across such a usage where father and son did not bear the same name; and of course in this case Fortho might not have known that they did not.

last will and testament. A wardship was a handsome perquisite which the Crown could, if it wished, sell to the highest bidder. If the ward's interests were to be served it was necessary for his friends or relatives to busy themselves in the matter at once. Benlowes' mother had cause for agitation: in this case there were special complications, for recusants were disqualified by law from acting as guardian to a minor. [1] But the State preferred that a Catholic ward should be placed in the care of a Protestant kinsman if he had one, and there were distant relatives available. So Edward Benlowes' wardship was granted to William Smyth of Cressing Temple, the brother of his grandmother. The grant was made on November 17, 1614, and for the privilege of administering his nephew's estates, William Smyth had to pay £266.13s.4d. [2] He was the legal guardian. But it must have been about this time that Francis Benlowes, the younger brother of Edward's father, came back to live at Finchingfield with his wife and family. It would seem that at one time they lived at Brent Hall itself. [3] So presumably it was Francis who mainly took care of the property during Edward's minority.

Things passed fairly quietly. The Benlowes family lived their country life, collected their large rents, paid out their numerous charities, worshipped God after their fashion, and had to go very warily to avoid persecution as Catholics. Edward's mother somehow, though she was well known for a Catholic and throughout her life never wavered in her faith, managed to evade conviction as a recusant. Edward's grandmother, however, was convicted repeatedly, both while living at Brent Hall and in her old age when she had retired to a separate *ménage* of her own with a Catholic manservant to attend her. Between 1610 and 1639 (by which time she must have been well over eighty) her name was presented to the justices at the Essex Quarter Sessions on twenty-nine different occasions. [4] The Exchequer, as I have said, did not always choose to follow up convictions; but whenever the law was specially vigilant Clare Benlowes would be named on the Recusant Roll, to be fined anything up to £140. [5] There is no record that she always paid.

[1] 3 & 4 Jac. I, c. 5.
[2] Wards 9/162; Wards 5/13, no. 2066.
[3] S.P., Dom., Interregnum, G158/315.
[4] Essex Quarter Sessions Rolls, 190/65, 199/151, 207/48, 211/46, 217/36, 219/45, 232/16, 235/43, 237/15, 245/19, 246/8, 250/24, 251/36, 255/39, 263/24, 264/22, 268/27, 269/21, 272/20, 273/15, 274/10, 280/12, 284/10, 293/37, 294/28, 298/37, 301/40, 304/73, 307/38. *Cf.* also S.P., Dom., Interregnum, G158/307.
[5] Recusant Rolls, E377/19, 26, 28, 29, 35 (twice).

Grandmother Clare went on her chosen obstinate way. And from the little I know of Edward's father, I suspect that he too, with the example of Edward Gage before him, would have proved intransigent. But some others of the family took warning from the persecution they saw going on around them. According to the Catholic archpriest of England, this included "the pillaging of property, the squalor of prisons, the terrors of magistrates, the raids of the officials, the snares of false brethren." [1] The Benlowes family did not suffer to this extent. Their general policy was to refrain from doing anything which would jeopardize the estates upon which their social position depended. Some of them certainly became, to use a contemporary phrase, "church papists." But their outward conformity was combined with a staunch inner resistance. The behaviour of Francis Benlowes and his family will illustrate this.

Unlike Edward's father, but like his own father before him, Edward's uncle Francis was never once convicted of recusancy. But he was frequently under suspicion and made a point of safeguarding himself by going openly to church. Later on he could get a most respectable certificate from vicars and churchwardens that all the time he dwelt in Finchingfield he "did.... professe himselfe to be of the Protestant Religion and did often-tymes at least once vppon the Saboth day attend vppon the publique ordinances in the church of ffinchingfeild afforesaid and did once in the yeare at the least receiue the Sacram^t of the Lords Supper there." [2] It was less necessary for his wife Elizabeth to conform, and in fact she was repeatedly denounced as a recusant. During 1610-11, while they were living in Fyfield, she had been four times presented for not going to church; [3] and during their long years at Finchingfield her persistent absence was recorded almost as regularly as that of the grandmother herself. [4] But even she was occasionally seen at

---

[1] *Douay College Diaries, Third, Fourth and Fifth*, I, 386. When Thomas Meynell arrived at Douai in 1631 it was recorded that his grandfather had been imprisoned for the faith fifteen times and his father had paid £4000 in fines (*ibid.*, I, 297-298; and *cf. ibid.*, II, 573ff). For a detailed record of the persecutions suffered by a single Catholic family, the Blundells of Crosby (Lancs.), during this period, see the Chetham Society publication of the *Crosby Records*.

[2] S.P., Dom., Interregnum, G95/429.

[3] Essex Quarter Sessions Rolls, 189/92, 191/81, 192/131, 193/35.

[4] *Ibid.*, 217/36, 232/16, 233/17, 235/43, 237/15, 245/19, 246/8, 251/36. Recusant Rolls, E377/26 (twice), 28, 29. I think it must have been she rather than Edward's mother who was intended when Mrs. Benlowes the younger was named on the Quarter Sessions Roll for Michaelmas 1615 (Q/SR 211/46).

church. [1] And apparently on these occasions Francis and Elizabeth took their children with them. Their daughter Clare afterwards claimed to have been brought up as a Protestant, and although there was some suspicion that she had herself been convicted of recusancy in or about 1626, she and her friends resolutely denied it. [2]

Yet this very Clare made the Catholic alliance that was usual for a Benlowes when "shee was sent vp to London to bee disposed of in Marryage to one Mr. John James," [3] of Smarden in Kent. She thus became known to a certain John Mungeham, a carpenter on her husband's estate, and he, not sharing the loyalty of the Finchingfield folk, years later gave very damaging testimony against her. [4] On one occasion (it would be round about 1630) he was sent across to Finchingfield, where he gossiped with the Brent Hall servants and they compared notes on their popish masters. There was no secret among them of the true sentiments of all the Benlowes family. Mungeham got the impression that Francis Benlowes and his wife had not been to church once in twenty years. And though this was plainly an error, no one can dismiss the tale that Mungeham told in pious horror of how he had himself seen Clare, Mrs. James, and one of her sisters with "crucifixes about their neckes, hanging upon their breasts." This worried him so much that when an opportunity occurred he spoke of it to Clare's brother John. This was not until two years afterwards, when the brother called at Mungeham's house in Smarden on his way home from "Fraunce." Mungeham asked him if he too were a papist, and not only did he admit it but he fell to arguing in support of his religion, so that Mungeham for his pains had to listen to a popish homily, which

[1] S.P., Dom., Interregnum, G95/429, 432.

[2] Ibid., G95/431-434, G158/307-318.

[3] S.P., Dom., Interregnum, G95/431. Incidentally, this marriage proved very unhappy. Very soon grave breaches occurred between Clare and her husband John James, who said that he found her perverse and cross and who suspected her of such offences as a man could not be expected to endure. Either this was because his mind was unhinged or else his mind became unhinged because of it. He was very depressed and attempted suicide. Clare's father was soon on the scene to protect her interests. He had James locked up as a dangerous lunatic with three or four men in constant guard, and made use of James's mental aberration to obtain some control over his property. The result was that James was forced to make a settlement upon Clare, strife between husband and wife was perpetuated, and there began one of the innumerable protracted squabbles about the ownership of lands which disfigure the records of almost all landed families in those times (Chancery Proceedings, 1st series, Chas. I, J33/106).

[4] S.P., Dom., Interregnum, G158/315.

he did not readily forget. No doubt he would have been appalled if he had even suspected where in fact John Benlowes had been to on the Continent. It was not in France that he had stayed, but Flanders, at the English college at Douai. Francis Benlowes might go to Finchingfield church and claim to be a Protestant, but he sent his son abroad to get a Catholic education at the very institution which existed to train priests for the work of converting England back to its old religion. The boy went there when he was seventeen years old in August 1631 and came home for the sake of his health in October 1632. [1] And, had Mungeham only known it, two of the cousins of John and Clare, Edward Benlowes' brothers, had been there too. [2]

[1] *Douay College Diaries*, I, 297, 307.
[2] See below, pp. 36-37.

CHAPTER THREE

EDUCATION

My chief business is with Edward Benlowes, not with his cousin John or his brothers William and Henry. And Edward did not go to Douai. Although the English college there was an object of reverence for all English Catholics as a place where they could send their sons to be educated in their own beliefs, yet there were very good reasons why the eldest son of this Catholic family did not go.

For an English Catholic of the landed class, the path of religious duty led to a conflict with social obligations and cut across the career of a gentleman. The question that Edward's mother and guardian had to decide was whether he should be trained as an English gentleman or as a devout Catholic. There was no system which could fit him to be both; if he succeeded in becoming both it would be in spite of his education and not through it. Edward's mother, one feels, might well have chosen Douai, as she later chose it for her grandson Thomas Peirce, though he too was an eldest son and the heir to large estates. [1] But the family thought otherwise. Upon their decision might very well depend the fortunes of them all. The risk of being fined one hundred pounds for having a son educated abroad meant nothing to people who had always been mulcted for unpopular beliefs; what was serious was that a youth sent beyond the seas for a Catholic education was prohibited from inheriting manors, lands, and tenements within his British Majesty's dominions. [2] Edward Benlowes as the eldest son, the heir whose property was at present under the jurisdiction of the Court of Wards, had to be prepared to swear the hated oath of allegiance and to run no undue risk. Some Catholic families did endanger all their possessions; others tried to protect them and were defied by a wilful heir with ambitions towards martyrdom. The diaries of Douai record two instances, within a couple of months in 1621, of only sons who

[1] *Douay College Diaries*, II, 440. That he was the eldest son is proved by Close Rolls, 1649, part 46, no. 23.
[2] Statute 1 & 2 Jac. I, c. 4.

made their way overseas against their parents' will. [1] But many more families kept their heir at home; nor do I think the choice they made should be held an entirely mercenary one. More than wealth—the whole tradition of their class was involved. The landed gentleman owed a duty to his rank.

The second and third sons could be given to God. So William and Henry Benlowes were destined for a Catholic education. [2] Edward, it was hoped, would never have his faith undermined, but the position in life towards which he had been called directed his course towards Cambridge.

For a Catholic boy, a school in England was all but out of the question. [3] Edward probably received his early education from a private tutor, which would be quite normal for one in his station— though for employing an avowedly Catholic tutor one could be fined as much as forty shillings a day. There might be disadvantages in learning at home, as the boy John Reresby, for example, was forced to admit when he went to school for the first time at the age of fifteen; [4] but that was to some extent a reflection on the home and the tuition. There is nothing to suggest that Edward Benlowes lacked a thorough grounding in the usual learning of those times. It seems unlikely that he ever acquired any great familiarity with modern tongues, and in English his reading was left to chance and his own choice: he had small acquaintance with English authors earlier than the seventeenth century. But he was well-schooled in the important things—was, in fact, acknowledged to be "very carefully educated in grammar learning." [5] The well-taught seventeenth-century boy was begun on the classical languages soon after mastering the alphabet, and from an early age Benlowes read Greek and a very great deal of Latin. Beyond this, since the crown of scholarship lay in the study of the Bible, it was desirable when one grew

---

[1] *Douay College Diaries*, I, 186, 187.

[2] There is no record of what happened to the two youngest sons, Andrew and Philip. They are only known from Chancery Proceedings, Collins 140/147. The absence of their names from the Benlowes pedigree in 1634 (*Visitations of Essex*, Harleian Soc., I, 347) must mean that they were dead by then, and with this footnote I propose to abandon them to a probable death in infancy.

Francis Benlowes, Edward's uncle, had a son Richard (see Francis' will, P.C.C., Fines 81), who does not appear in the Douai records, as well as the John who does. I do not know which was the elder, but this looks rather like another instance of the elder son being educated at home while the younger went abroad.

[3] *Cf.* Mathew, *The Social Structure in Caroline England*, p. 54 and note.

[4] *Memoirs*, ed. Browning, p. 2.

[5] Wood, *Fasti Oxonienses*, II, 358.

up to add a little Hebrew—the holy tongue, as it was called—and there is evidence that Benlowes added it.

An exercise-book preserved in the Bodleian Library [1] is an interesting relic of the schooling that helped to make Benlowes into a fairly accomplished Latinist in an age of Latin scholarship. It contains his fair copies of a series of Latin exercises, and shows him writing solemn compositions on conventional moral maxims—extolling peace over war, praising the man who attains mastery over himself, associating pleasure with grief. There was nothing precocious about this or unduly grave, according to the educational psychology of those days. Edward Herbert claimed that when he was still under nine he filled a sheet of paper with a Latin oration showing how fortune favours the brave, and added fifty or sixty verses to it— all in one day. [2] He was an incorrigible boaster and not an incorrigible truth-teller, but the educational ideal is clear. Simonds D'Ewes, who was exactly of Benlowes' age, was a very competent Latin scholar by the time he was fifteen, able to tackle any Latin author without trouble and to turn out themes and verses to order. [3] The compositions in Benlowes' exercise-book probably belong to his early or middle teens. He wrote studiously in prose on such subjects as "The good of the state is to be set before private convenience"—a proper sentiment for a landed gentleman—"A man's speech is the index of his mind," "Virtue is lasting, wickedness short-lived." He was encouraged to sprinkle his essays with quotations from the authors he had read. Cicero was evidently the favourite; the boy was brought up on the best, though conservative, models. His Latin was thoughtful and correct, but not more original or distinguished than was to be expected of any well-disciplined boy under an earnest classical tutor. Having treated his subject in prose, he was usually set to express the same thoughts rather more concisely in hexameters, and was also introduced to the commoner stanzaic metres. In order to gain facility in them he had occasionally to write a third time on the same theme, and this sort of thing developed in him a remarkable ability as well as liking for expressing a thought in a variety of ways. But he had no great range of idea; new thoughts were less encouraged than new phrases.

In his composition the boy was allowed little break from moral disquisition, but on two occasions he addressed complimentary

[1] MS. Rawl. D. 278.
[2] *Autobiography*, 2nd edn. of Lee [1906], pp. 19-20.
[3] *Autobiography*, I, 95, 102-105.

poems to William Smyth, his great-uncle and guardian, paying the respect required of him and vowing, with much literary hyperbole, that he would never forget his uncle's goodness and generosity. Phoebus himself, if he composed the song, would not be able to do justice to his guardian's merit. A dove would sooner avoid towers, a lion grass, and a ship waters; a salamander would go in terror of flames, a mole flee from the fertile earth sooner than Edward would forget the respect that his uncle deserved or be unmoved in his inmost being by concern for his uncle's welfare. He was at home in classic simile and was learning some of the superficial tricks of rhetoric.

His ordered and somewhat pedantic training was to exaggerate the natural fastidiousness of his mind. Much care was given to penmanship. This was an art then popular, and one which easily lent itself to decoration in an unmechanical age. The regard for the beautiful arrangement of words on a page, the painstaking execution of artistic trivialities which always characterized Benlowes, owed something to the methods of his tutor. He practised various styles of writing, being taught, like his contemporary D'Ewes, "to write a good Roman, secretary, and Greek hand." [1] In the exercises a neat scrivener-like English hand was generally used for prose, with a tall, regular italic for verse. He was taught to admire ornate capitals and his pen easily ran out into splendid flourishes. He was never worried by their meaninglessness; indeed, he was encouraged in a taste for pure design. He would occasionally use red ink for capitals or for titles, and in one piece of verse he picked out in red a single letter in the middle of each line so that the eye, reading down, would catch the title, "Moderata Durant." All this was nothing more than the fashion of his age; but to this early education one traces the delight in anagrams and shaped verses which he never lost. He continued to love the picturesque contrast of types, and later was to print some of his Latin poems in a mixture of black and red. His principal poem, *Theophila*, is still remarkable for the fantastic, but oddly beautiful, printing it received.

When Edward had become tolerably proficient in classical grammar and humanities it was time for him to think about the university. His departure from home was postponed as long as possible—the Catholic boy was not too soon to be flung into a heretic world. But the move to Cambridge had to come, and arrangements were

[1] *Ibid.*, I, 95.

made for him to go up to St. John's, which, though Edward's father
had been at King's, was the traditional Benlowes college. He went
into residence at St. John's in the Easter term of 1620, [1] and matriculated in the university on April 8th. [2] It must have been
round about the same time that his young brother William was
being put to school across the Channel at the flourishing Jesuit
college of St. Omer, ready to go on afterwards to Douai. [3]

By the time Benlowes went to Cambridge, the age of university
undergraduates had certainly risen since the days when Francis Bacon
was nothing out of the ordinary in going up to Trinity at twelve. Even
so, Benlowes, at nearly eighteen, was about two years older than
the average when he entered St. John's as a fellow-commoner. [4]

The fellow-commoners, for the most part sons of the nobility
or the superior landed gentry, paid more for their keep than ordinary
pensioners, bought thereby the privilege of dining at the fellows'
table, and did not need to mix more than they wished with the ordinary crowd—the sons of poor parsons, yeomen, shoemakers,
carpenters, and such like. The pretensions of Benlowes' family had
Edward enrolled among this college aristocracy, and so he presented
St. John's College with the silver goblet expected from one of his
status,[5] and unlike Herrick (who went to St. John's as a fellow-commoner seven years earlier), did not need to worry though the college
was an expensive one. If one may judge by Herrick's complaints,
the house charges alone would come to over twenty pounds a year,
not to mention tutor's fees and books. [6] Simonds D'Ewes, another
fellow-commoner at St. John's, found the fifty pounds a year which
was all his father would give him a "short allowance." [7]

---

[1] Venn, *Alumni Cantabrigienses*, I, 132.

[2] Baker's note in Wood, *Fasti Oxonienses*, II, 358.

[3] *Douay College Diaries*, I, 216. St. Omer had been founded by Father Parsons
in 1592 or 1593 as a school for the sons of English Catholic gentry and it had
by this time well over a hundred pupils.

[4] Among contemporary poets, Cleveland entered Cambridge at fifteen, Milton
and George Herbert at sixteen; on the other hand, Thomas Randolph was
nearly nineteen, and Herrick twenty-two. But *cf*. Mathew, *The Social Structure in
Caroline England*, p. 44n. My statement of the average age is taken from Mullinger,
The University of Cambridge, II, 398. This gives the best *general* account of conditions in the university at this time. The Cambridge chapter in Masson's *Life
of Milton* is also packed with information. See also, especially for curricula,
Morison, *The Founding of Harvard College*, chs. 3-4.

[5] Baker, *History of the College of St. John*, I, 548. Herrick's "College Pot" cost
£5 (Moorman, *Robert Herrick*, p. 34 n.). See also D'Ewes, *Autobiography*, I, 119.

[6] Moorman, *Robert Herrick*, pp. 35-36.

[7] *Autobiography*, I, 119, 147.

The circle into which Benlowes was thrown was naturally the most dashing. The fellow-commoners led the Cambridge fashion, and the Cambridge fashion at that time demanded an exquisite ostentation in the way of enormous cuffs, and roses on the shoes, as well as ruffs and long gay locks of hair. These things were not peculiar to the emptyheaded: according to Walton, even George Herbert, when he was at Trinity, set much store by his clothes as a badge of rank. It is not surprising that Herrick, kept short of money, ran "somewhat deepe into [his] Tailours debt." But Benlowes cannot have lacked the means to enter into competition, and with his weakness for adornment he must have been a pretty addition to the "University-tulips," as the fellow-commoners were called by Joseph Meade of Christ's. [1]

The ways of undergraduates would be something of a revelation to a young gentleman who hitherto had seen little of society. Written rules were strict, but actual discipline was lax. There was a good deal of rowdyism, and brisk business at the taverns. D'Ewes complained of the "swearing, drinking, rioting" of the "debauched and atheistical companions" who "swarmed" in the university. He was horrified to find that "the very sin of lust began to be known and practised by very boys," and, being himself piously inclined, "was fain to live almost a recluse's life." [2] He would have fared no better at Oxford, where Christopher Guise complained of the sirens whose business it was to frequent the tippling-houses and lure the young men on. [3] Benlowes is unlikely to have gone in much for drinking, but no doubt it was at Cambridge that he first grew accustomed to tobacco pipes and the "genuine *Warmth*" of their "active Smoke," which he afterwards celebrated in his verse. Everybody smoked everywhere, students and fellows alike. When King James, who could not abide smoking, visited Cambridge in 1615, tobacco-shops were put out of bounds and it was necessary to insist particularly that no one should smoke in St. Mary's Church. [4]

Among other accomplishments to be acquired at Cambridge were dancing and playing on the viol, while even the studious exercised themselves, as gentlemen should, at things like fencing and tennis. Many did a good deal of riding, and Benlowes, who was later to become a notable horseman, may have been one of those young

---

[1] Masson, *Life of Milton*, I, 104.
[2] *Autobiography*, I, 121, 141.
[3] *Memoirs of the Family of Guise* (Camden 3d. series, vol. XXVIII), pp. 116-117.
[4] Mullinger, *University of Cambridge*, II, 516-517.

gentlemen who hired horses, riding-boots, and whips from Hobson the carrier, and who, being compelled to take whatever mount stood nearest the door, had to submit to the original "Hobson's choice." [1]

The air and poise of a university man were, after all, part of what Benlowes went to Cambridge to acquire. Among the fellow-commoners were many who stayed at the university a year or two, imbibing something of the spirit of the place, pursuing desultory occupations, doing such exercises as their tutors prescribed, but without any desire to complete an academic course. If Benlowes had wished to take a degree, he would have been barred by his religion; [2] but no one need suppose that the thought of a degree was ever in his mind. It was held to be quite inappropriate for the eldest sons of wealthy houses to pursue the ordinary course of study. The instruction given by tutors in the subtleties of logic seemed to Lord Herbert to be all very well for "a mercenary lawyer," but not at all to be commended in "a sober and well-governed gentleman." [3]

Nevertheless, among all the distractions of the university, a "sober and well-governed" mind could not fail to be aware of a great wealth of learning, and there was plenty of encouragement for the lover of books. What Benlowes most valued about Cambridge in later life was the opportunity it had given to develop and extend his reading and to converse with men of scholarly interests. He would take special pride in the reputation of St. John's College as the college of Cheke and Ascham, who had given it the leading place in England in Greek and humanistic studies. While its supremacy was not still unchallenged, especially by Trinity, it was still in the van of classical culture. Among its notables were Andrew Downes, the Regius Professor of Greek, and Robert Metcalfe, a distinguished scholar in Hebrew; and, as the second largest college in Cambridge, with over three hundred students, it offered plenty of scope for Benlowes to make the acquaintance of young men with an enthusiasm for learning not unlike his own. [4]

---

[1] On Hobson, see Steele, *Spectator*, no. 509; and of course Milton's two epitaphs.

[2] James I insisted that all candidates for any degree should subscribe to three articles which proclaimed acceptance of the tenets of the English church. Cambridge, unlike Oxford, held out for a time, but had to succumb in the end (Mullinger, *University of Cambridge*, II, 457-458).

[3] *Autobiography*, p. 26.

[4] Among those in residence when Benlowes went up was John Gauden, who is known to posterity as the reputed author of *Eikon Basilike*. He comes properly in a footnote because, as a sizar, he would be at this time rather outside

Although Benlowes entered college older than most of the other freshmen, there would not be much in that to make him feel humiliated. For his scholastic attainment was little behind his years. The Elizabethan lads of twelve, when they got to the university, were put through the sort of exercise that Benlowes had already done at home. As an example one might cite the Earl of Southampton, Shakespeare's patron, who, at St. John's in his thirteenth year, had written little Latin "themes" to prove that if the studies of youth are arduous, the leisure of age is delightful, and that all men are encouraged in the pursuit of virtue by the hope of reward. [1] Already proficient in this sort of "grammar learning," Benlowes would go on to rhetoric and logic, the regular subjects of the university curriculum, which prepared the student for philosophy proper. He would also acquire some smatterings of mathematics. Logic in particular enjoyed enormous prestige among educated men. It was not merely a discipline of thought, but, as the art of reason, was often regarded—especially among Puritans —as a key bestowed upon man by God to unlock the gateway to God's truth. But this did not prevent the ordinary student from finding it obnoxious—one of the disagreeable necessities which, if you would go to the university, somehow had to be endured. [2] (One suspects that this was

---

Benlowes' orbit; but twenty years later, as Dean of Bocking, he was to become a neighbour of Benlowes in the country, and a friendship between them continued many years (see below, pp. 146-147).

[1] Stopes, *Life of Henry, Third Earl of Southampton*, pp. 24-25.

[2] James Howell found it "clubfisted and crabbed" and "terrible at first sight." Only with patience and practice did he manage to reduce it to the position of a "mere bugbear" (*Familiar Letters*, ed. Jacobs, p. 256). Though his experience admittedly was at Oxford, everything goes to show that the young gentlemen of Cambridge thought the same.

Since some use will be made of Howell's *Familiar Letters* for the light they throw on the seventeenth century, it is as well to remind the reader now that Howell is notoriously unreliable for facts and dates. (The controversy about the authenticity of the letters is well summarized in Jacobs' edition (II, lxiii ff.), and though numerous errors in Jacobs' annotations have been corrected by later work, on this point little, I think, has been added.) But so long as they are not used as evidence for particular events, the *Familiar Letters* do afford valuable evidence for the climate of opinion and the general social background of the period.

I have had much difficulty in deciding what edition to quote from. The early editions tend to the chaotic, and none of the first four is satisfactory by itself. So in the reader's interest I have always given references to Jacobs, and since I do not wish to commit the baffling absurdity—for which there is precedent —of giving references to one edition along with quotations from another, I have used Jacobs' text also, though with some reluctance.

really why Lord Herbert decided that it did not go with gentility.)
Benlowes must have followed pretty much the same routine as
Simonds D'Ewes, who was at St. John's the two years before Benlowes went up. If so, he was taken through Seton's *Dialectica*, the
regular text-book, and then went on to newer authors like Kecker-
mann and Pierre du Moulin. He must certainly have heard of Ramus,
whose reorganization of the traditional logic of Aristotle [1] had
caused great stir at Cambridge in the last decades of the sixteenth
century; but there is little to suggest that the bitter controversies
centering on the Ramist logic had produced any drastic modification
in the traditional character of university studies. D'Ewes had also
read some moral philosophy, history, and physic. In his private
study time he spent many hours on Aristotle, going through the
Ethics, *Politics*, and *Physics*. [2] Benlowes doubtless did the same, and
if one may guess from what in his old age he recommended undergraduates to read, after Aristotle he was taught to respect Duns
Scotus. Perhaps nothing better illustrates the fundamental conservatism of his university environment.

As for the lectures Benlowes attended, again one can only suggest
probabilities. He may well have followed D'Ewes to the Greek
lectures of the famous Downes—D'Ewes heard him on Demos-
thenes [3]—and he probably went sometimes to hear George Herbert's
successor expounding Cicero and Quintilian. He reached Cambridge
just too late to hear Herbert himself lecturing regularly in rhetoric,
though he must have occasionally heard him in the office of university
orator; [4] in later years, when Herbert's poems were being read
everywhere, memories of such occasions would give cause for
pleasurable pride.

The university lectures were for the keener spirits. The students'
exercises were mostly done within the walls of their own colleges.
Their day began early, with chapel at five, and they were kept busy
by their tutors most of the morning. The educational routine at
Cambridge was still largely based on the mediaeval system of disputation, and disputations and declamations were held in the college
chapel, where Benlowes would be expected to attend. Occasionally
he would be called on to take part, answering in Latin, with as much

[1] On this, see Graves, *Peter Ramus and the Educational Reformation of the
Sixteenth Century*; Miller, *The New England Mind*, ch. 5.
[2] For D'Ewes's studies see his *Autobiography*, especially I, 121, 140.
[3] *Ibid.*
[4] *Cf.* Herbert, *Works,* ed. Hutchinson, p. xxix.

display of erudition as he could muster, the arguments of an opponent who would maintain some philosophical thesis. But the amount of his performance cannot have been arduous, and since he was not taking a degree he would never be called upon to do this sort of thing in the public schools of the university.

The elevation of skill in argument to the principal scholarly accomplishment, for the service of which classical authors were ransacked by vastly erudite minds, did a good deal to sharpen the wits of university men, but at the expense of narrowing their outlook. Logic and rhetoric easily became mere techniques of controversy, and when the method was pursued into theology, as it was by the advanced students, it only encouraged the zealous to lay excessive emphasis upon the minutest points of doctrine. The whole system had been denounced as antiquated by Bacon, who objected to the artificiality of the scholars' speeches and thought that at the universities wisdom had degenerated into "childish sophistry and ridiculous affectation." How indeed could it be otherwise when mature subjects like rhetoric and logic had to be fitted to "the capacity of children"?[1] Milton went even further in repeatedly satirizing the "usual method" by which the "unballasted wits" of "poor striplings" were "tost and turmoil'd" in "fadomless and unquiet deeps of controversie." The universities seemed to him "not yet well recover'd from the Scholastick grossness of barbarous ages," and "honest and ingenuous natures comming to the Universities to store themselves with good and solid learning" were "unfortunately fed with nothing else, but the scragged and thorny lectures of monkish and miserable sophistry." Milton hated "the uproar of the noisy School" at Cambridge, and was constantly fretted by the troublesome business of speech-making; he daringly attacked the system even while performing according to its rules.

---

[1] *The Advancement of Learning*, in *Works*, ed Spedding, Ellis, and Heath, III, 326. *Cf.* Peacham, *Compleat Gentleman*, Clarendon Press Reprint, p. 33: "These young things, of twelve, thirteene, or foureteene....have no more care than to expect the next Carrier, and where to sup on Fridayes and Fasting nights: no further thought of study, than to trimme up their studies with Pictures, and place the fairest Bookes in openest view, which, poore Lads, they scarce ever opened, or understand not;...when they come to Logicke, and the crabbed grounds of Arts, there is....a disproportion betweene *Aristotles Categories*, and their childish capacities."

Criticism of the immaturity of undergraduates spread as the century progressed, so that in 1642 James Howell, a fair reflex of ordinary educated opinion, ridiculed the English habit of plunging green wits at the universities into the profundities of mathematics (*Forreine Travell*, Arber reprint, p. 80).

Once, when he had to deliver an oration in the public schools, he chose to attack the whole system of scholastic training, and on another occasion he threw out amid his diligent citations of the usual authorities an appeal to his hearers to be as bored as he was himself. What he wanted and got no opportunity for was to investigate the lives of men and the nature of the physical universe— stones and plants, the winds and the sea, the sun and the stars. By this scientific route the mind might come to know itself, and this was the surest way to the discovery of ultimate truth. This was the only valid approach to the study of divinity itself. [1]

Milton, then, was thoroughly imbued with the new scientific spirit of Bacon. But he found "almost no real companions in study." [2] Few men at Cambridge in the 1620's showed any sign of having heard of Bacon. And there was little awareness of the new world which had been opened up by the Copernican astronomy [3] and the geographical discoveries of the Elizabethan voyagers. Benlowes himself never showed much acquaintance with the "new Philosophy" which called "all in doubt." He was not given to looking forward, and his docile intellect, easily inveigled into metaphysical speculations and captivated by the minutiae of scholarship, was probably well suited to its Cambridge environment. Nor did he find Cambridge so "ill-adapted. . . .to the worshippers of Phoebus" as Milton claimed to do. [4] There were plenty of men in the university who were not only keen versifiers themselves but took a lively interest in contemporary poetry. Benlowes would find that everyone knew Spenser and Sylvester's Du Bartas. The two Cambridge poets, Giles and Phineas Fletcher, who had both but recently left the university after holding fellowships for several years, enjoyed quite a reputation, and Benlowes' admiration for their poems probably dated from his student days.

His reading outside his tutor's program would not be confined to poetry. All the young gentlemen with any intellectual pretensions grappled with divinity. In comparison with that James Howell thought all other knowledge but "Cobweb-learning." [5] Heaven and

---

[1] See especially the *Third Prolusion* (*Works*, Columbia University Press, XII, 171). Quotations and references are from *Of Education* (*Works*, IV, 278-279), *Elegia Prima* (*Works*, I, 169, 175), *The Reason of Church-governement* (*Works*, III, 273), *Prolusions*—Third (*passim*), Fourth, (*Works*, XII, 185), and Seventh (*passim*).

[2] Letter to Alexander Gill, July 2, 1628, *Works*, XII, 13.

[3] For the Copernican theory in the seventeenth century, see pp. 109-110.

[4] *Elegia Prima*, in *Works*, I, 169.

[5] *Familiar Letters*, p. 257.

Hell were much more important than any Baconian theories about the world of matter. Upon a man's theological beliefs his eternity depended. Truth was sought in the scriptures and in the writings of the church. Therefore, in devoting itself to textual exegesis and minute points of doctrine, scholarship was only giving itself to what seemed the most important problems of life and death. The regular course of philosophical study was designed to lead on to theology, which was the ultimate justification of a university's existence. It was a subject that lent itself particularly well to the methods of the schools, and its controversies were many and bitter.

For the first time in his life Benlowes would find himself surrounded by many shades of religious opinion. Though he was used to holding a persecuted faith, in his home Catholic beliefs had been protected. Now they were questioned and argued against by many of his intimate associates. It was impossible—so at least thought James Howell—for a student at the university not to be "somwhat versed in the Controversies 'twixt us and the Church of *Rome*," [1] and as a member of the unpopular church Benlowes had cause to take special interest in such matters. He would often hear it maintained that his church was the whore of Babylon, the Pope antichrist himself. Religious freedom was not, of course, to reach the universities for another two centuries and more, and fellows and office-holders could easily be expelled for theological errors. Things were easier for the obscure, and the situation was not too difficult so long as one did not seek a degree. Still, certain theological formulas had to be subscribed to on entry into college, and one had to be prepared to take the notorious oath of allegiance, which was thorn enough in the consciences of Catholics whose ideals were those of Douai. Many Catholics, however, took the oath when confronted with it, and somehow reconciled their adherence to the Pope with this repudiation of the Pope's authority over the English King. Bitter as it might be, a willingness to swear the oath if necessary was implicit in the family policy which sent Benlowes to Cambridge at all.

At Cambridge Benlowes would soon hear the other side in the matter of the oath. Sooner or later he read the literature of the controversy from the Anglican as well as the Catholic point of view. His sensitive mind could not help responding to the pressure of environment. Nowhere, of course, would he hear anyone sympa-

---

[1] *Forreine Travell*, p. 16.

thetic to his own religion capable of confuting the best brains of the university. The pre-eminence of Cambridge in Anglican theology of a moderately Calvinist trend had been revealed when it provided four of the five English representatives at the Synod of Dort. It was only a year before Benlowes' entry into the university that such distinguished theologians as John Davenant and Samuel Ward had returned to Cambridge with greatly enhanced reputations; and it is difficult to think that Benlowes did not go to hear Davenant, professor of divinity, delivering such lectures as those in which D'Ewes had heard him confuting "the blasphemies of Arminius, Bertius, and the rest of that rabble of Jesuited Anabaptists." [1] In later years the effect of opposition was to drive Benlowes into obstinacy. He became a typical defender of last ditches. But in his young days, suddenly confronted with views different from his own put forward by the learned, he had the exhilarating, if immensely grave, experience of questioning which ditch he ought to choose to defend. In view of what happened later, one may, I think, take it as likely that Benlowes' education at Cambridge had begun to make him restless in his religion beyond anything his family had feared.

He stayed at the university a year or two, which was all that the gentlemen fellow-commoners required before they went on to London to one of the Inns of Court. Lincoln's Inn, the one on which his ancestor the Serjeant had cast distinction and of which his father and grandfather had both been members, was naturally the one chosen for Edward. He was admitted on January 30, 1622. [2] What he did there was no doubt pretty much what all the other young aristocrats did. A few, of course, ended up as barristers and followed the law as a profession, but the majority had no more thought of seeking admission to the bar than of getting their university degree. They were merely finishing their education in the fashionable way. Many simply continued the diversions of the university, spending their time in ordinaries and taverns. The young Christopher Guise, for example, got through the days by taking up dancing and "riding att an academy." [3] But men who had a sober interest in books or perhaps an eye to a career did a fair amount of reading in their chambers. Some instruction in the laws of the land was a seemly

---

[1] *Autobiography*, I, 120.
[2] *Records of the Honourable Society of Lincoln's Inn*, I, 189.
[3] *Memoirs of the Family of Guise*, p. 119.

prelude to any public career, and all but the most frivolous saw it as proper for men of standing to have some training in affairs. The attitude of the most serious-minded may be illustrated in Francis Quarles, another Essex gentleman-poet, later to be a great friend of Benlowes. According to his widow, who wrote a memoir of him, Quarles went from Cambridge to Lincoln's Inn, not to follow the legal profession but rather with the object of fitting himself to compose differences between friends and neighbours. [1] Perhaps this was an extreme example, though it was logical enough for those who thought of rank as obligation. But most men I suppose to have been less altruistic. James Howell justified the custom of learning a little law by the aid it gave a man in preserving his own. For lack of a knowledge of legal practice, many, he said, had "mightily suffered in their estates, and made themselves a prey to their sollicitors and Agents." [2] Unfortunately, to follow Howell's advice was not always to escape the fate he warned against, as the later career of Benlowes will show.

After a fitting period at Lincoln's Inn, Edward Benlowes was ready to enter on the career of a country squire. And very soon, of course, he was to take over the management of the family estates. Eighteen months after his admission to the Inn he reached his majority. On November 18, 1623, a feodary's survey of his lands was made, [3] and these in due course were delivered up to him by the Court of Wards which had granted the administration of them during his minority to his great-uncle.

The education of the gentleman heir, lacking little that would gain him social prestige, had plainly marked him off from his younger brothers. While Edward, in his newly acquired manhood, was enjoying the first flush of pride in his ownership of property and his commanding position in his part of Essex, his brother William was initiated into the Catholic college at Douai. He arrived there in August 1623—having already completed a course of study in the humanities at the Jesuit college of St. Omer [4]—and began a training in some ways parallel to that offered to youths at Cambridge, except that at Douai there was even more direction of all learning towards the ends of theology and that there was inevitably a firm

[1] For this memoir, see Quarles's *Solomons Recantation*. It is quoted at length in the introduction to Grosart's edition of Quarles's *Works*.

[2] *Forreine Travell*, ϼ. 79.

[3] Wards 5/13, no. 2066.

[4] *Douay College Diaries—Third, Fourth and Fifth*, I, 216.

Catholic bias. Though William was never intended for the priest-hood, he was surrounded all the time by those who were and for whose training—not simply as priests but as missionaries—the whole curriculum at Douai was devised. William started at once on logic, and during the next four years he passed through the regular classes in philosophy and got well advanced in theology itself. [1] By this time he had been joined by the next brother, Henry, who had also come from St. Omer. And Henry, though he did not go quite so far as William, also worked his way through the college into the class of theology before he left. [2]

There is no doubt that within the rigid limits of their study these two became much more learned than Edward himself, more skilled in disputation, better disciplined in mind. The Greek and Latin taught at St. Omer were excellent, and at Douai students showed a strict application to the work laid down for them or they were promptly sent back home. Yet the advantages were by no means all on the side of the younger brothers. Their outlook was made narrower, they could not develop tastes that were encouraged by the more varied society of Cambridge, where a certain desultoriness of reading was allowed to fellow-commoners. Edward had been able to feast himself on poetry. He had also become a gentleman of fashion, accustomed to fine clothes and lordly airs: his brothers at Douai led a monastic life, in which they were taught to see holiness as the principal virtue and obedience as almost the only other. Not allowed out unaccompanied, they might not speak English when they *were* out. They appeared always in cassocks. They lived with the sons of the gentry, but their fare was frugal, and they spent long hours kneeling in the chapel on a floor so damp that there was danger of lameness and swellings at the knees. [3] And for such privileges they risked arrest and imprisonment every time they crossed the Channel.

Yet Edward's mother and all his relatives were soon having reason to regret that they had not chosen for him also this austere, ascetic training. What were the graces of a gentleman, to set against the changes they saw taking place in him? When Edward had pondered his faith at Cambridge he had found the truth less certain than he had supposed. While William was being strengthened in the Catholic

---

[1] *Ibid.*, I, 238, 240, 252.
[2] *Ibid.*, I, 251-252, 274, 282, 286.
[3] *Ibid.*, I, 412.

faith, Edward was asking awkward questions of himself and reading
heretical books.

It is not possible to discover exactly what led Benlowes to change
his religion, but it seems reasonable to gather a hint at the way
his mind was tending during the 1620's from the kind of books
he gave to his Cambridge college in 1631. If these books[1] in any
way reflected his own reading, he took special interest in the relations between the temporal monarch and the spiritual father,
followed the celebrated controversy on the oath of allegiance, and
dipped well into other anti-Catholic literature. He went through
John Gordon's rejoinder to Bellarmine's attack on the oath; he
perused William Bedell's remonstrances against a Roman convert;
and when Richard Bernard's *Rhemes against Rome* came out in 1626
he could see a series of Catholic beliefs taken in turn and confuted
by an author who claimed that the English version of the scriptures
had removed the gag which the Romanists had placed upon the
word of God and planted it in their own mouths. This is singularly
interesting, because it illustrates one of the principal objections
that Benlowes himself came to have against the Catholics—that they
denied the right of Christians to read the scriptures in their own language
and to interpret them for themselves without priestly interference.

It is possible, though unlikely, that Benlowes had abandoned
the Catholic faith as early as 1623. For in that year there occurred
a Catholic disaster which was to be made the subject of one
of his anti-Catholic poems. In the afternoon of October 26th a
crowd of over three hundred people gathered in a second-floor
room in Blackfriars for evensong and a sermon by the Jesuit
Robert Drury; and in the middle of the sermon the summer
beam supporting the floor collapsed under the weight of people.
Most of them fell, many were buried under débris, and about
ninety-five, including Father Drury, were killed. Catholics accused
Protestants of having procured the calamity, while Protestants
saw in it the miraculous vengeance of God. It did not go unob-
served that October 26th in the old style was November 5th by
the Gregorian calendar. Benlowes accordingly began his poem
with a gibe about the day which Catholics had made notorious
in British annals. In the course of twenty lines of Latin verse
he told how while Drury was spreading the false phantoms of
his brain, his false brains were themselves spread about the
platform; and those who worshipped wooden idols were fittingly

[1] See below, pp. 59-60.

destroyed through a wooden beam. The poem has been preserved
for us by Thomas Fuller, who quoted it in his *Church-History
of Britain* in 1655. [1] But Fuller gives no clue to the date of
its composition. The disaster created a great sensation, which
was long remembered, and there is no need to suppose that
the poem must have followed immediately. Indeed Benlowes may
have written it any time during the next thirty years, and perhaps the most likely date would be during or just after the
Civil War, when Fuller was making collections for his *Church-
History* and Benlowes' wealth was assisting Fuller's literary work.
He probably passed the verses to Fuller and perhaps even wrote
them for him then. The grim analogies I have quoted will come
to be recognized as characteristic both of Benlowes' verbal ingenuity and of his sectarian bitterness, but the other evidence does
not suggest that he had by 1623 developed that confirmed hostility
to the Catholics which the present discussion may usefully anticipate.

However that may be, Benlowes' inquiry into the tenets of
Catholics and Anglicans can hardly have failed to fill his family
with alarm. The oath of allegiance, which William had learnt at
Douai to hold in special abomination, [2] Edward had not only taken
from expediency at Cambridge, but was now prepared to justify.
The son of the man who had died cursing King James was prepared
to obey the King rather than the Pope, whose authority over the
individual conscience Edward was beginning to dispute. Eventually,
by 1627, he had become a heretic. [3] One can imagine the grief of
his mother, who all her life had suffered persecution for her religion
and who in her old age was to get hold of her daughter's son and
have him sent to Douai in the hope of undoing a Protestant upbringing. [4] One can conceive the shock to William, studying Catholic
theology at Douai, and to Henry, just out of his Jesuit school.
Edward was the first Benlowes ever openly to leave the Catholic
church. If he had a sympathizer in his family, it must have been
his sister Clare, who, though still a Catholic herself, had recently
had Edward's consent to her marriage with a Protestant. [5]

---

[1] Book x, pp. 103-104.

[2] *Cf. The Douay College Diaries*, I, 365-367.

[3] *The Douay College Diaries* (I, 260) speak of William's *frater haereticus*, and
although this heretical brother is not named, there can be no doubt that Edward is referred to.

[4] *Ibid.*, II, 440.

[5] I do not know the date of this marriage. *The Douay College Diaries* (II, 440)
show her eldest son to have been aged 17 or thereabouts on May 28, 1643.

CHAPTER FOUR

TRAVEL

There was one thing necessary to complete the education of the perfect seventeenth-century gentleman. Benlowes had not yet made the grand tour. For the proper cultivation of the English masculine mind at this date it was held to be indispensable to spend two or three years rambling over the Continent. James Howell held "that one year well employ'd abroad by one of mature judgment.... advantageth more in point of useful and solid Knowledge than three in any of our *Universities*." [1] Howell seems to have expected the Englishman to go abroad before settling for a time in one of the Inns of Court; [2] but this was certainly to reverse the usual order. It was not customary for the expedition to the Continent to be made in extreme youth: the early twenties were the favourite age. In Benlowes' case, family responsibilities and the management of his lands may have combined with his own partiality for a quiet country life to cause a brief postponement: he spent four years at home after he had left Cambridge and Lincoln's Inn. But fashion was strong, and Benlowes did not wish to deny himself any educational opportunities that his station offered. And so, as he put it himself, for his better improvement and knowledge of tongues and affairs of the world, [3] he decided to go abroad. Though not well fitted by temperament for the ardours of foreign travel, in the summer of 1627 he made up his mind to try them. For a month or two he was very busy with preparations, for much had to be done. His affairs at home must be left in perfect order—in view of what might happen. At the beginning of July he made new deeds re-establishing his hereditary benefactions and bringing them up to date. [4] There were credits to be negotiated and letters of introduction to be procured. A royal permit to travel had also to be sought. On August

---

[1] *Familiar Letters*, p. 88.
[2] *Forreine Travell*, pp. 75-76.
[3] Chancery Proceedings, Collins 28/11.
[4] See below, p. 84.

10th the Privy Council granted "a passe for Edward Bendelosse, of the countie of Essex, gentleman, with one servant to travaile in forraigne partes and there to remaine for the space of three yeares next following." [1]

Benlowes has left us only some general references to his travels in his poems, with a few isolated particulars in legal documents; but the picture of him on his tour can be filled out a little by accounts of travels such as those of James Howell, roughly ten years earlier, and John Evelyn, a little over ten years later. [2]

The dangers of Continental travel were great and numerous. They varied from precipices and shipwrecks to the Inquisition, which was to be dreaded in all the territories under Spanish rule. In Milan it was said to be worse than in Spain itself, [3] and anyone who was not a firmly convinced Catholic kept a close watch upon his conversation all the time he was in Italy. [4] For Benlowes, a recent apostate from Catholicism, and still, it would seem, not fixed in his religious beliefs, the danger would be specially great. Less subtle, but not less real, was the danger of wild beasts: the Alps had bears, and large parts of France were infested with wolves. The human marauders were worse. Lonely roads were the regular haunt of armed

[1] *Acts of the Privy Council*, 1627, Jan.-Aug., p. 482.

[2] Evelyn's *Diary* is the most valuable record of the seventeenth-century gentleman's grand tour; the references are to H. B. Wheatley's edition. For Milton's works the Columbia University Press edition is used, and unless otherwise stated the reference will be to the *Defensio Secunda*, which gives an important, if brief, account of a Continental journey in the 1630's. There are several other important narratives of travels on the Continent in the seventeenth century. In the early part of the century James Cleland's *The Institution of a Young Nobleman* (1607), pp. 251ff., offered representative advice to one about to undertake the grand tour; and Coryat's *Crudities* and Fynes Moryson's *Itinerary* made the best guidebooks for the ordinary traveller. Moryson is specially interesting on prices and conditions of journeying. But though his *Itinerary* was first published in 1617, it was based on travels of twenty years earlier. For later on there are Lassels, Reresby, and Edward Browne. But I have preferred to cite specially those whose travels were nearest to Benlowes' in date. The others frequently offer corroborative evidence and Reresby is interesting as nearest to Benlowes in station.

[3] For instances of Englishmen arrested by the Inquisition there, see Pearsall Smith, *Life and Letters of Sir Henry Wotton*, I, 327, 399n.

[4] Milton, who made a point of not doing so, found himself treated with less warmth than he might otherwise have been, and some English Jesuits in Rome even laid a plot for him (*Works*, VIII, 125). Masson refers to *Horæ Subsecivæ* (1620), which says of the English traveller in Rome that if he "conuerse with *Italians*, and disclose, or dispute his *Religion*, he is sure, vnlesse hee fly, to be complained on, and brought within the Inquisition" (p. 412). The whole passage is interesting on the need for tactful behaviour in Rome.

brigands, [1] and the risk of being captured by pirates may in itself have been enough to keep Benlowes off the Mediterranean. In the towns there were frequent assaults by night. While one does not always rely on Howell for accuracy in detail, his account of an attack in Paris, when his companion was wounded and he himself had two sword-thrusts pierce his cloak before help came, may fairly be taken as a representative instance. [2] Padua was no better, [3] and in Venice you were liable to get your throat cut in the time of carnival or to be shot at by a noble Venetian if you were so unlucky as to disturb him when he was having an amour in his gondola. [4] It was sometimes very easy for a foreigner unwittingly to offend national sentiment. To wear, for instance, a red French cloak in the Spanish dominion of Naples would be to invite hostility. [5]

Yet, with all this, the seventeenth-century gentleman, well trained in weapons of defence and spirited in using them, feared violence less than disease. A battle in the Low Countries was much less noxious than a summer in Rome. The plague was bad enough in London, but very much worse in southern Europe. No traveller could expect to avoid at least the inconveniences of its recurrent proximity. There were irksome restrictions of quarantine at the numerous Italian frontiers, and during bad epidemics your bill of health had to be inspected at every town and village. [6] The dread of smallpox was almost as great, and obviously not without reason, for Evelyn had it in Geneva and Benlowes himself at Venice. The traditional disease to bring back from the Continent, of course, was syphilis, called the French disease for that reason, and many were the warnings, jocular and other, against it.

But this takes us into a different category. The graver threat was

---

[1] Even in England, which was *comparatively* safe, there were numerous instances of students being robbed as they rode or walked to the university after a vacation. An Elizabethan statute had sought to put down highway robbery by forbidding travellers to carry with them more than £20 to serve for the expenses of the journey.

[2] *Familiar Letters*, p. 45.

[3] Fynes Moryson said that "strangers live there in great jealousie of treason to be practised against their lives" (*Itinerary*, I, 156), and half a century later Evelyn found the situation unchanged. When the soldiery also gave trouble at Padua in 1645 there was housebreaking and murder, and Evelyn's party guarded their doors with pistols (*Diary*, I, 258).

[4] See Evelyn, *Diary*, I, 260; Thomas Raymond, *Autobiography*, pp. 55, 58.

[5] See Evelyn, *Diary*, I, 193.

[6] Evelyn, *Diary*, I, 93; Reresby, *Memoirs*, pp. 12, 15; Moryson, *Itinerary*, I, 145.

not to a man's health but to his morals. In many English circles Italy was regarded as the home of wickedness as well as culture. [1] The courtesans of Naples and Venice were celebrated; they would fling eggs of sweet water into the coach "and by a thousand studied devices seeke to inveigle foolish young men." [2] Milton, whose character and habits did not easily expose him to temptation, thanked God on his departure from Italy that he had "lived free and untouched of all defilement and profligate behaviour" in places "where so much licence is given." [3]

The grand tour, then, confronted Benlowes with a formidable as well as an exhilarating prospect. Warned against the mysterious uncertainties of the journey, but genuinely eager to undertake an enterprise becoming to a gentleman, to know something of foreign learning and to see the artistic treasures of the Continent, he could not but feel both joy and trepidation as he rode away from Finching-field for a long, momentous absence. The usual way was by post-horses [4] to Dover, and then across to Calais. The short sea-route had the same advantages then as now, and Benlowes seems to have taken it. But he resisted the obvious lure of Paris. John Evelyn was to advise a tour of the Low Countries first, since the traveller might best see there an epitome of what awaited him further afield; and this was evidently the choice that Benlowes made, for by September 20, 1627, within six weeks of getting his passport, he was to be found in Brussels. [5] Having come through

---

[1] "Tho' *Italy* give milk to *Virtue* with one dug, she often suffers *Vice* to suck at the other" (Howell, *Familiar Letters*, p. 146).

[2] Evelyn, *Diary*, I, 181.

[3] *Works*, VIII, 127.

[4] Horseback was the normal mode of travel for the young gentleman, horses being hired *en route* at the various posting-inns. Lord Herbert, however, took his own horses, and in 1615 rode them all the way from the Low Countries to Italy (*Autobiography*, pp. 84-85). He went post when there was need for greater "expedition" (p. 87). English travellers looked askance at the mules of Italy and the south of France. In the Alps they might even have to make do with donkeys. For variety the traveller might do a stage or two by coach, though seventeenth-century roads, especially in winter, were not kind to wheeled traffic. In Holland, where the towns were close together, many people went by waggon. Between coastal towns small sailing-vessels offered a more comfortable journey than going over land. There were also the natural waterways of the Continent, which Benlowes, who took pride in famous rivers (*Theophila*, p. 267), evidently used. And in the Low Countries and northern Italy there were what Evelyn called "artificial rivers," with horse-drawn barges. For a description of various modes of travelling at the end of the sixteenth century, see Fynes Moryson's *Itinerary*, III, 468ff.

[5] *Douay College Diaries*, I, 260. The precision with which Brussels can be dated

Artois, he must have passed quite close to Douai, where his brothers William and Henry were in college. But he did not go to see them. The place could have little attraction for one who was no longer a Catholic, and the poor and crowded condition of the college did not permit visitors to be welcomed. Yet Edward was in touch with his brothers, and they knew when he had arrived in Brussels. It was there that a meeting took place with William, who had gone over from Douai to see him. Permission for such a journey was not easily given to a Douai student, but the circumstances were unusual. A heretic brother was at hand, and attempts should be made to bring him back to the true religion. So William, by this time a senior student being trained in theology, left Douai with the fullest encouragement to do everything he could by exhortation to win his brother over. Exactly what happened no one can tell, but this much is clear: Edward was not yet unassailably Protestant, and William's training at Douai must have made him a learned and skilful advocate. Edward wavered, then or later, and two years afterwards at Venice he is said to have been a Catholic.[1]

Brussels would be the first important Continental city that Benlowes saw. It was the capital of Brabant, which, with Flanders, was then the Spanish Netherlands, over which the Infanta Isabella was at that time reigning. Her court at Brussels was probably one of those which Benlowes afterwards boasted of having visited. Outside the palace he would see stately gardens with cunning grottoes and fountains, and inside incomparable tapestries and celebrated paintings, especially by Rubens, the greatest living painter, whose fame was such that he had just been awarded an honorary degree at Benlowes' own university. Benlowes would feel to be in an artistic capital at once. And if the city was small, it had a distinguished society, and the gentleman visitor might meet many people of fashion. But

---

in relation to Benlowes' setting out helps to fix his route. The itinerary sketched in the following pages is admittedly conjectural in parts, but seems the only satisfactory way of fitting in all the places for which there is documentary evidence. A list of the countries Benlowes passed through is given in the "Peroratio Eucharistica" to *Theophila*, where it is probably significant that the Low Countries are mentioned first and France last: "Summas Tibi agit Grates...Servus tuus humillimus, quem post tot varias mundanarum Sollicitudinum Procellas, vastosq; Curarum Fluctus, cum olim *Hollandiam, Brabantiam, Artesiam, Germaniam, Austriam, Hungariam, Styriam, Carinthiam*, partem *Italiæ*, nec non *Galliæ* incolumem in *Patriam* reduxisti." (Saintsbury has pointed out that something is missing after "*Galliæ*," but that would not affect the itinerary.) Additional evidence for particular towns and rivers will be cited at the appropriate points.

[1] See below, p. 52.

Benlowes' most important encounter in Brussels was not with those, nor even with the brother who had come over to convert him. It occurred when somehow or other he came across a man called John Schoren, a Dutchman who had been born and brought up in Brussels.

Schoren was a printer, and it may be that Benlowes had to do with him through his own interest in the art of printing, in which at that time the Low Countries led the world. One does not know; but Schoren's trade was certainly a fascinating one, and the man himself, a knowledgeable fellow with ingratiating manners, soon won Benlowes' favour. He felt restless in Brussels, and in his eagerness to see more of the world he fancied entering Benlowes' service. One of his principal recommendations was his skill in languages: he claimed to know French, Spanish, and Italian, as well as Dutch and English. Benlowes himself does not seem to have taken quite the pains with languages that travellers like Fynes Moryson and James Howell advised, and there is no evidence that he ever attained mastery or even ease in the modern tongues. But the advantage of a foreign servant for foreign travel was well recognized; [1] and perhaps, at the beginning of his tour, Benlowes was on the lookout for just such a man as Schoren seemed to be. It later suited Schoren to say that Benlowes by fair promises "did inveigle" him from his trade. In any case, Schoren's accomplishments were found attractive, Benlowes engaged to pay him twenty marks a year, and sent back home the English servant with whom he had set out. [2]

Benlowes could not neglect any famous university that happened to be within reach, and before he left this region he spent some time at Louvain.[3] His references to the river Scheldt (in *Theophila* and *Oxonii Encomium*) suggest that he then went on to Antwerp, which indeed every tourist in the Netherlands made a point of seeing. One pictures Benlowes gazing perhaps at more of Rubens' pictures or buying books at Plantin's, doing the round of the churches, walking beneath the shady trees, and, no doubt, as every well-trained gentleman should, taking proper interest in the fortifications.

Going down the Scheldt, he saw the river branching into its delta, [4] and so presumably passed by sea to Holland. Dutch printing

---

[1] *Cf.* Cleland, *The Institution of a Young Nobleman*, p. 253.
[2] Chancery Proceedings, Reynardson 31/14 (answer), Collins 28/11.
[3] See p. 46, note 2.
[4] *Theophila*, p. 267: "Quà sese bifido *Scaldis* discriminat Alveo/Vidi."

and engraving must have been a revelation to one who was to develop a great interest in those arts. And pictures were everywhere: even the common farmers used to invest thousands of pounds in them. But Benlowes' studious disposition would take him quickly to the university of Leyden, where he settled for a time. It was possible, after taking an oath of obedience and a short catechism in Latin, to be matriculated as a temporary student, [1] and Benlowes was proud to attend lectures there, [2] especially, one presumes, those of the great scholar Heinsius, whom men from many countries came to see. There was a famous anatomy school at Leyden, which must have done something to stimulate the interest in medical studies which Benlowes shared with every proper seventeenth-century gentleman; and, to appeal to his taste for curiosities of every kind, there was the matchless array of "skeletons from the whale and eliphant to the fly and spider." [3] Poetry was much cultivated; and for the book-lover there was always Elzevir's.

Benlowes tells us that he saw the marshy lands of the Rhine delta and the place where the main stream divided. [4] This would be as he was leaving Holland and making for Germany, into which the Rhine was for centuries the traveller's main road. Most Englishmen would have gone from the Netherlands into France, and that way into Italy. They were assured that the rest of the world held little "but plaine and prodigious barbarisme." [5] Even Germans "did," as we say, France and Italy while knowing nothing of Germany itself. For most people, so long as they spent time enough in Italy, that would do for their grand tour. Benlowes had other ideas, and though late in setting out on his travels, proved in the end an energetic and even an enterprising traveller. Trusting in the resourcefulness of Schoren and ignoring the Thirty Years' War, he turned towards the centre of Europe. Looting armies had for years been overrunning northern Germany, but one could pass unmolested up the Rhine, past Cologne; and, since Benlowes sailed up the Neckar, [6] it is clear that he added Heidelberg to his list of famous universities.

---

[1] The process is described by Evelyn (*Diary*, I, 24).

[2] *Oxonii Encomium*, "On Oxford, the Muses Paradise": "We *have faire* Padua, Lovain, Leyden *seen*;/*At* Theirs, *as* OXFORD, *at* Your LECTURES, *been*."

[3] Evelyn, *Diary*, I, 24.

[4] *Theophila*, p. 267; his reference to the division of the Scheldt, quoted above, continues: "Teq; tuâ, *Rhene* palustris, Aqua."

[5] Evelyn, *Diary*, I, 193.

[6] "*Flexivagosque* NICRI, *ac* BRENTAE *sulcavimus* amnes" (*Oxonii Encomium*, "In Florentissimum Bellositum," stanza 7).

Then, through the cities of southern Germany he went on into
Austria and beheld the Danube, wondering at its might and volume. [1]
This implies a visit to Vienna, with its numerous baroque churches,
and there his mind, which, whatever its present views, had been
trained to Catholic worship, could hardly escape the influence of
the Counter-Reformation. In this part of Europe he would meet
few of his own countrymen, and east of the Rhine he might have
to "learne to feed on homely meat, and to lie in a poore bed,"
without necessarily agreeing with Fynes Moryson that this was
good for an English gentleman. [2] But in spite of difficulties, he went
on into Hungary. At length, half-way across Europe, he turned
back to make for Italy through the Austrian provinces of Styria
and Carinthia. The way lay through a lonely, mountainous region,
and a traveller by this route found that he could have quite a new
experience of what travel meant as he went through the eastern
Alps and over the Semmering Pass. [3] Alpine travellers had to get
used to ill-made tracks skirting precipices and crossing chasms by
narrow bridges, "in some places made onely by felling huge fir
trees...over cataracts of stupendious depth." [4] Benlowes followed a
snowy road amid lofty peaks which lost themselves in cloud; and
years later he was to recall it all when he thought of the mighty works
of nature he had seen. [5]

This way led into Italy through the Venetian Republic, and
Benlowes could take his first glimpse of Venice itself. But since
Venice seems to have been the last city in which he spent any length
of time before returning home, [6] he may have paid a second visit
there after going farther south. The urge to make haste would be

---

[1] *Theophila*, p. 267: "Vidimus inn[u]meras quas vehit *Ister* Aquas." See also
Oxonii Encomium, "In Florentissimum Bellositum," stanza 7.

[2] Moryson, *Itinerary*, III, 383.

[3] For a brief account of a journey through this part of the world, see *Ibid.*,
I, 143-145.

[4] Evelyn, *Diary*, I, 280. Once a horse with Evelyn's party fell down a precipice near the Simplon, and the travellers were so afraid that they trudged
on foot (I, 282-283). Lord Herbert, travelling at night, was carried down a
precipice in a chair, and his guide made fires of straw to light the way (*Autobiography*, p. 88). It is not surprising that at this date mountains inspired more
dread than delight.

[5] *Theophila*, p. 267: "Non iter excelsæ remoratæ Nubibus *Alpes,*/Quæ nec in
aeriis Nix sedet alta Jugis."

[6] Schoren said that after recovering from smallpox in Venice Benlowes "then
trauiled for England" (Chancery Proceedings, Reynardson 31/14, answer).

strong upon the art-lover who had, after many months, at length
arrived in Italy and had before him Florence and Rome.

For his journeyings up to this point Benlowes has mentioned
enough landmarks to leave no doubt that his tour followed roughly
the pattern I have sketched. His Italian itinerary is more difficult
to reconstruct, and I take the reader on with diffidence. There is
certain evidence for Venice and Padua, but no specific reference
to places further south. But cumulatively the circumstantial evidence is convincing. Benlowes' artistic tastes show abundant Florentine influence, and that he took back to England with him some
"tables" of *pietra commessa* [1] is almost a certificate in itself for his
having gone as far as Florence. It is significant also that the *pietre
commesse* that Benlowes later gave to St. John's College included
one representing a street in Rome. References to the Vatican in
Theophila (p. 268) and to St. Peter's in Benlowes' Latin verses on
St. Paul's Cathedral also suggest, without actually saying so, that
he had seen them. It is impossible to suppose that even illness could
have turned Benlowes home without a visit to these famous cities,
the climax of the Englishman's grand tour, when he had come so near.

From Venice, then, he would go by way of Ferrara and Bologna
and then over the Apennines to behold in Florence, the centre of
Renaissance art, a city of splendid palaces with statues of marble
and porphyry, ornate churches with richly jewelled altars, and a
wealth of pictures, vases, carvings, and mosaics. Literature also
flourished and Florence was full of poetical dilettanti from
whose pens streamed sonnets, canzoni, panegyrics, and epigrams
full of those elaborate conceits with which the influence of Marini
had but recently flooded Italy. The effect of all this upon Benlowes'
own taste in poetry was enormous. He must have met many of
these amateurs of the arts, who were always delighted to invite into
their academies and literary clubs foreigners of taste and distinction.
Semi-private academies, which Milton praised "as calculated to
preserve at once polite letters and friendly intercourse," [2] flourished
all over Italy, but nowhere more than at Florence. The most famous
of them all was the *Accademia della Crusca*, the Academy of the
Bran, which aroused widespread admiration and curiosity. Here one

---

[1] This peculiarly Florentine art may be described in Evelyn's words: "a
kind of mosaiq or inlaying of various colour'd marble, and other more precious
stones," "representing flowers, trees, beasts, birds, and landskips" (*Diary*, I,
227, 107).

[2] *Works*, VIII, 123.

could see the famous hall "hung about with impresses and devices painted, all of them relating to corne sifted from the brann," and the seats "made like bread baskets and other rustic instruments us'd about wheate, and the cushions of satin, like sacks." [1] This sort of enigmatic pictorial design greatly encouraged Benlowes' own instinct for decoration and influenced the methods by which he later ornamented his own books. He developed a love of emblems of all kinds, and he was not to be long back home before having impresas designed upon his own name to adorn the copies of *The Purple Island* that he presented to his friends. [2]

It is also significant that in the academies of Florence it was customary for members to avoid using their own names and employ instead some anagram or pseudonym wrought out of them. One did not, of course, have to go abroad to meet with this mannerism. It was common in literary circles almost everywhere, and, like so many of the literary fashions that we tend to associate with the seventeenth century, it had been discussed years before by Puttenham. Moreover, Edward Benlowes came of a family which had adopted as its motto, "Tende Solve" (Bend Loose), a pun on its own name. [3] Still, this sort of thing was particularly cultivated in Italy, and the evidence certainly points to Benlowes' having adopted during his travels the anagram by which he was afterwards celebrated. It was shortly after his return home that he taught his literary friends to refer to him not as Benlowes, but Benevolus. [4]

A normal excursion from Florence for a fashionable English tourist would be that along the Arno thirty miles to Pisa, with its famous leaning tower. And if, in a moment or two of fancy, we chose to follow a typical English gentleman, we should probably find him going on to Leghorn, a rising commercial port with a number of English merchants, through whom he would get credits or other favours. From Leghorn he might also ship to England specimens of *pietra commessa* or other treasures that he had bought in Florence before passing on to Rome. He would ride down through the olive-groves, feeling quite the Italian, wearing a fine embroidered

[1] Evelyn, *Diary*, I, 226.

[2] See below, pp. 71-73.

[3] See this motto, for example, along with the Benlowes crest (a centaur with *bent* bow about to *loose* an arrow) carved on the corbel of a beam in Great Bardfield church.

[4] I suspect that the anagram had something to do with his persistent preference for the spelling "Benlowes" instead of the "Bendlowes" which had been more normal with his forbears.

stomacher and holding an umbrella to protect him from the sun.
In Rome, if he did as Evelyn was to do, the English gentleman
would quickly be in touch with English residents to whom he would
have introductions, and they would advise him how to behave and
direct him what "masters and bookes to take in search of the antiquities, churches, collections, &c." Then, led round by a "Sights-
man," he would start being "very pragmatical," to use Evelyn's
favourite word. [1] He would visit the noble classic ruins and the
sumptuous Renaissance palaces; he would stroll through gardens
with many cypress walks positively "beset" with statues; he would
marvel at the opulence everywhere apparent—in the coaches in
the streets, or in such furniture as a bedstead "inlaid with all sorts
of precious stones and antiq heads, onyxs, achates, and cornelians." [2]
Perhaps he would hire a painter to copy pictures and bas-reliefs
that he particularly admired [3] among the multitude which Howell
thought to exceed the number of living people. [4] He would cross
the vast piazza, marvelling at the fountain, before the magnificent
St. Peter's, which would astonish him with its array of pinnacles,
cupolas, and turrets. He would of course go to the Vatican, and
if our typical English gentleman were Benlowes, his heart would
throb as he looked at the books in their wainscot presses, for he
would know (what indeed Benlowes said at the end of his *Theophila*)
that the Vatican library was the finest in the world. He might be
taken up by Cardinal Francesco Barberini, nephew of the Pope,
who was always courteous to Englishmen and took them under
his patronage at the papal court. An English Catholic, even if an
erring son, would have a special claim upon the Cardinal's favour,
and it could not be surprising if Barberini welcomed Benlowes—
he was to do as much for Milton [5]—at one of the musical entertain-
ments which delighted music-loving visitors to Rome. Through
his means, Benlowes might perhaps be admitted to the presence
of the Pope and kiss the papal toe. Was Benlowes able at this time
to do such a thing with reverent homage? If not, could he go through
with it as a curious experience, as others of the English did, to be
mockingly commented on later? There must have been for him many
moments of the greatest mental turmoil in this capital of the religion
which was still more than any other his, though he had been led

---

[1] *Diary*, I, 118.
[2] *Ibid.*, I, 128.
[3] *Ibid.*, I, 122, 134.
[4] *Familiar Letters*, p. 84.
[5] Letter to Holstenius, March 30, 1639, in *Works*, XII, 41.

to doubt its truth. Wherever he went, the power of the church would be demonstrated in the numerous priests among the crowds that thronged the streets. Sometimes one might see the Pope himself *in pontificalibus*, his tiara on his head, being "carried on men's shoulders in an open arm-chaire, blessing the people as he pass'd." [1] If he were in Rome over Christmas or during Holy Week, Benlowes would see such spectacles of religious pageantry as he had never seen before, and there would be tableaux of the Nativity or the Holy Sepulchre to fascinate one who, though always suspicious of worldly shows, loved ritual and display. There were many attractions in Rome to lure Benlowes back to Catholicism, and he must often have wanted to kneel in humble adoration. Yet in Rome he cannot have been entirely easy in his mind, and perhaps he felt even now what he afterwards maintained, that this was all vanity and the truth obscured by it.

It was usual to go on—with an armed guard to protect you from the bandits in the corkwoods [2]—by the Appian Way to Naples. But there is nothing to indicate whether Benlowes went so far. In any case, he would find less of artistic interest in Naples to overcome his distaste for gaiety and frivolity. It would be much more to his liking to go back north to the university city of Padua, where he certainly stayed for a while. Here it seems to have been usual for Englishmen to join together in groups of four or so and set up house together. [3] It was almost traditional to spend a lot of time at music, and if Benlowes was not already tolerably proficient on the lute and the theorbo, he would be likely to become so now. Men like Vesalius and Galileo had made Padua the leading scientific centre of the world, and when Benlowes attended lectures there [4] it still had the most distinguished professors to be found anywhere. If he were there at the right season, he would certainly be present in the excellently constructed theatre to watch the annual anatomy demonstration, which lasted "almost a whole moneth," perhaps to see, like Evelyn a dozen years later, "a woman, a child, and a man dissected with all the manual operations of ye chirurgeon on the humane body." [5]

One pictures Benlowes in Padua walking among its shady arches, thinking about Petrarch, hovering around the university, or gazing

[1] Evelyn, *Diary*, I, 205.
[2] See Moryson, *Itinerary*, I, 226; Evelyn, *Diary*, I, 173.
[3] Reresby, *Memoirs*, p. 13; Evelyn, *Diary*, I, 259.
[4] See p. 46, note 2.
[5] *Diary*, I, 260-261.

out towards the Euganean hills and the smiling landscape that he
loved. As much as forty years afterwards he was to remember with
joy those green and sunny meadows and fill them in his mind with
birds and flowers. [1] But eventually he betook himself to Venice,
to glide up and down the Grand Canal and to admire St. Mark's
and the Rialto—perhaps to go to the opera and, like all the other
tourists, to see how the Venetians made glass or treacle. This was
the strangest and most spectacular city of them all, with an oriental
splendour and piazzas full of "Jews, Turks, Armenians, Persians,
Moores, Greekes, Sclavonians, some with their targets and boucklers,
and all in their native fashions." [2] It was noted for its "dainty smooth
neat Streets, whereon you may walk most days in the year in a
Silk Stockin and Sattin-Slippers, without soiling them." [3] Along
the line of shops in the Merceria one saw damasks, silks, and cloth
of gold hanging from the first floor, one was beguiled by rich per-
fumes and the sound of nightingales. [4] Benlowes was a man to feast
his senses on such gorgeousness, yet also a man to think of vanity
at the spectacle of the grand ladies in their exotic jewellery, their
crownless hats, and dyed parti-coloured hair, with waists right up
to their arm-pits, crawling in and out of their gondolas on their
stilt-like chopines, and supporting themselves with their hands
on the heads of aged women servants incongruously mumbling their
beads. [5]

In Venice Benlowes was unlucky enough to catch the smallpox
and became dangerously ill. John Schoren, who had travelled the
Continent with him for two years since being engaged in Brussels,
now proved invaluable to the sick man in a foreign city. He waited
on his master assiduously. Afterwards he was able to say that he
knew Benlowes had been a Catholic up till the time of his sickness,
so it would look as if Benlowes in his extremity received a Catholic
confessor. Old beliefs die hard. In fear of death the apostate returns
to the faith; and the smallpox may have done more than all William's
exhortations. But Benlowes got better; and later on Schoren claimed
that the recovery was due to his care and industry. [6]

[1] *Oxonii Encomium*, "On Oxford, the Muses Paradise," stanza 3.
[2] Evelyn, *Diary*, I, 245; see also Coryat, *Crudities* (1905 reprint), I, 318. And
for a picturesque account of the more adventurous incidents of Venetian life,
see Raymond, *Autobiography*, pp. 47-59.
[3] Howell, *Familiar Letters*, p. 69.
[4] Evelyn, *Diary*, I, 237.
[5] *Ibid.*, I, 244.
[6] Chancery Proceedings, Reynardson 31/14 (answer); Collins 28/11.

CHAPTER FIVE

RETURN HOME

When Benlowes at length got better and was able to leave Venice he seems to have had enough of travel and decided to make for home. Schoren would already have despatched by sea the books and curios that Benlowes had inevitably collected in Italy. [1] The usual land route would take them through Milan, over the Simplon to Geneva, and then through France by way of Lyons and Paris. It was possible to do the journey in three weeks. [2] It would have been natural for Schoren to have left Benlowes at the Channel, but the attendant of a gentleman traveller did not fancy going back to printing again. He knew when he had been well treated, and if his accomplishments were something beyond the usual, his wages had also been high. Yet he felt that his services—and especially his nursing his master in Venice—demanded some recompense beyond his wages. Benlowes, whose liberality was matched only by his unbusiness-like methods, listened to his hints and made vague promises to requite him if he continued in his service. For during all these months Benlowes had come to depend on him. Schoren probably needed little encouragement to continue with him to England. [3]

Cutting short his tour after the smallpox, Benlowes had not stayed abroad the full term of three years permitted by his passport. He had left home about August 1627 and everything points to his being back early in 1630. When he referred to his travels later on he spoke of having been on the Continent two years. [4] On January 8, 1630, he was granted letters of administration in regard to the estate of his unmarried sister Mary, [5] whose death may have been an added reason urging him to hurry home. And on May 5, 1630, he was taking part in a transaction with his brother William, by

[1] *Cf.* Milton, *Works*, VIII, 127; Evelyn, *Diary*, I, 262.
[2] Howell, *Familiar Letters*, p. 75.
[3] Chancery Proceedings, Reynardson 31/14 (answer); Collins 28/11.
[4] Chancery Proceedings, Collins 28/11.
[5] P.C.C., Administration Act Book, 1630, fol. 144.

now back home from Douai. Edward gave William a recognizance
in the sum of one thousand pounds. [1] This was of course a form
of security—what for one cannot know, though I suspect that it
had to do with some provision that the head of the family was
guaranteeing to his younger brother at the time of William's approaching marriage.

Benlowes had returned a very polished gentleman, of fine address
and easy in discourse, as those who knew him bore witness. [2] He
had seen the world and broadened his mind. He had mixed with
men of many nations and could speak airily of the fickleness of
Frenchmen, the deceitfulness of Italians, and the drunkenness of
Germans. [3] He had been at six European courts. [4] He had worn
fine foreign clothes and eaten strange foods. He must have cut a
splendid dash in rural England. He had become an excellent horseman, as his friends were to discover. If he had got what most gentlemen travellers acquired, he was competent too in fencing, music,
and dancing—unless, of course, like Lord Herbert, he could never
find leisure to learn dancing through always employing his mind
on "some art or science more useful." [5] Certainly in the pleasure
of seeing famous sights and amid the gaiety of Continental cities
he had never neglected the earnest pursuit of knowledge.

But that did not exclude from his attention the superficial graces.
He was fond of labouring at trifles. His mind was never well equipped
to distinguish big knowledge from small, and travelling, running up and down in pursuit of the strange, the unique, did not
necessarily make for a good sense of proportion. In Italy he had
not only learnt courtly manners and acquired a cultivated taste,
but had been encouraged in a natural dilettantism. Perhaps he was

[1] P.R.O., Recognizance Entry Book, L.C.4/200, fol. 470. This recognizance
was cancelled two years later, on May 4, 1632, and a new series of recognizances
entered into (Recognizance Entry Book, L.C.4/201, fol. 119).

[2] Wood, *Fasti Oxonienses*, II, 358.

[3] *Theophila*, p. 268, lines 3-4. Reresby, who was not fussy, complains a quarter
of a century later of "the too great plenty of liquor which is too much imposed
upon strangers" in Germany (*Memoirs*, p. 18). Fynes Moryson had found drinking
the only German vice (*Itinerary*, IV, 34ff.).

[4] *Theophila*, "To My Fancie," stanza 10. Fuller (*History of the University of
Cambridge*, ed. Prickett and Wright, p. 179) and Wood (*Fasti Oxonienses*, II,
358) credited him with seven.

[5] *Autobiography*, p. 37. Herbert had, however, spent a whole summer practising riding the great horse (pp. 53-55). If Benlowes was, as there seems good
reason to suppose, much more in Italy than in France, it would have been easier
to cut out dancing, which was "not in much reputation amongst the sober
Italians" (Evelyn, *Diary*, I, 295).

not free from the Italianate poses which many returning Englishmen were mocked at for affecting. [1] The love of the ornate which
was already present in the boy who wrote the Latin exercises now
in the Bodleian had been developing during his grand tour into
an interest in exotic decoration, in curiosities and unusual forms of
art. It was not to be expected that he would anticipate the eighteenth-
century taste of Gray, who cried out for "grand and simple works
of Art" when he first came upon the Italian palaces with their "inlaid floors, carved pannels, and painting, wherever they could stick
a brush." [2] One of Benlowes' chief desires now was to practise
for himself some of the precious arts that he had seen. He was a
good Latin scholar and he had it in his mind to compose epigrams
and mottoes. He would turn his hand to emblems and devices. He
had learnt to love pictures, and, even more perhaps, engraving, in
which Italy and Holland were far ahead of England. He would like
to dabble a little in book-decoration himself. No doubt one of the
reasons why he wanted to bring Schoren back with him to Brent
Hall was that Schoren was a trained printer, and a Netherlands
one at that. He would be extremely useful in the artistic hobbies
that his master was eager to pursue. Already I see Benlowes toying
with the idea of setting up a rolling-press at Brent Hall and getting
Schoren to help him with the prints.

So Schoren, continuing in Benlowes' employ at Brent Hall down
in Essex, was to become one of the most important persons in his
life. He could smooth out all the unpleasantnesses with which life
confronted an unpractical man, and Benlowes, finding the control
of his large estates a somewhat irksome responsibility, allowed
much of it to fall into Schoren's hands—appointed him his bailiff,
left him to collect the rents, gave him charge of all buying and
selling. [3] He could then settle down himself to a quiet country life
with little to deflect him from his books and arts.

Howell recommended the gentleman, sometime after his return
home, to pay a second visit to the Continent and in a single summer
make a flying review of what he had already seen. [4] But Benlowes,
no more than Evelyn, [5] wished to become an *individuum vagum*. If

---

[1] The saying that the Italianate Englishman was a devil incarnate was a
stick often used to beat them with.
[2] *Correspondence*, ed. Toynbee and Whibley, I, 128.
[3] Chancery Proceedings, Collins 28/11; Whittington 71/87 (answer).
[4] *Forreine Travell*, p. 80.
[5] *Diary*, I, 193.

it was good to travel, it was better to be home again. A knowledge
of other countries was better in the possession than the gaining,
and he liked feeling a man of the world without any more having
to be one.

Very much a man of the world he must have seemed to his two
brothers, after their years shut up at Douai. Since the time about
ten years before, when he left home for Cambridge and they sought
an education in Flanders, he had seen very little of them. Now one
imagines him eagerly initiating them into all that he had learned,
especially William, who was nearer to him in age and whose dia-
lectical and theological training had not left him without a taste
for literature. There would be a certain poignancy for Edward in
renewing acquaintanceship with this brother whom he had last seen
in Brussels, when William had arrived an earnest missionary
with his elder brother as his object. Since then Edward had been
near death and had had (I have suggested) a Catholic confessor;
but he was far from being a Catholic at heart, and was gradually
coming to the stage when he not only troubled his family in their
secret prayers but openly avowed his enmity to their religion. He
could tantalize his brothers' minds with tales of Rome and the Pope;
but for them, all this would be poisoned by the thought that the
privileged eldest son, who had seen the holy city, was not convinced
of its holiness. Benlowes had no doubt fallen in with fellow-travellers
with a sturdy English scepticism—like Fynes Moryson, who, when
he "beheld the mimicall gestures and cerimoniall shew of holinesse
of the Roman Priests" and observed at the same time "their corrupt
manners," "could not refraine from laughter." [1] Henceforth his
own attitude was to be something like that—though he was usually
moved to anger more than laughter. The mood of many of his
writings was that of one who had been surfeited with pomp, who
had seen splendid processions—and thought of whited sepulchres.
The effect of Benlowes' contact with the Catholic religion at its
very centre seems to have been to confirm him in the doubts that
he had already entertained. It is, at any rate, certain that he had
abandoned Catholicism for ever very shortly after his return home. [2]

This was exactly what James Howell affected to believe would
be likely to happen in such a situation. He recognized the lures of
the Roman church as one of the traveller's principal dangers, but

[1] *Itinerary*, III, 362.
[2] See below, p. 63.

for this insular seventeenth-century Englishman, who, the more he saw of foreigners, grew more glad that he was English, one of the principal advantages of travel in Catholic countries was that a man was likely to come back with a new respect for the national religion. This was to ignore the large number of Catholic converts in the second quarter of the century; but Howell actually knew of some, he said, with a leaning towards Romish beliefs who were put off when they got to Rome by the fantastic ceremonies they saw. [1] Possibly he numbered Benlowes among them.

In Howell's view—though he was a moralist who did not observe his own lessons—it was useless for a man to visit all the famous places of Europe *"unlesse by seeing and perusing the volume of the* Great World, *one learne to know the* Little, *which is himselfe....But principally, unlesse by surveying and admiring his works abroad, one improve himself in the knowledge of his* Creator....and this indeed....should be the center to which *Travell should tend."*[2] Not perhaps in high ambition but in sincere piety, this Benlowes sought to do.

He could look back on his travels not without pride. He recorded his acquaintance with the wider world in the "Peroratio Eucharistica" of his principal poem, *Theophila,* and again in the course of his *Oxonii Encomium.* He could never resist the pleasure of posing as a man of fashion. That was the weaker side of his nature, which made him so easily the victim of flatterers. But there was another side, which found fashionable fripperies irksome. Benlowes must often have been tempted to agree with his contemporary, the Earl of Derby, that in going abroad to study men and manners he had wasted good years of his life. [3] He disliked the turmoils of the world and thanked God for having brought him safely back to enjoy a life of seclusion. He looked for nothing better than that. Fuller, who dedicated to him the sixth part of his *History of the University of Cambridge,* [4] was confident that he preferred the life of the scholar to that of the courtier, the court of the muses to that of princes. He held up Benlowes as one who had seen the splendid clothes, the banquets, and the vast retinues of foreign courts, who had experienced the magnificent entertainment of kings, but who had perceived the emptiness of decked-out miseries and would willingly

[1] *Forreine Travell,* p. 16.

[2] *Ibid.,* pp. 71-72.

[3] *History of the Isle of Man* (in the *Stanley Papers,* Part 3, Chetham Soc.), p. 33.

[4] Ed. Prickett and Wright, p. 179.

forgo these excitements for simple dress and frugal dishes and a life without display, for a peaceful repose allied to a fuller understanding of life's more real things.

Benlowes soon began to manifest the generous use of his wealth which made him renowned for benevolence among a wide circle of friends. One of his most esteemed benefactions was the gift of fifty pounds' worth of books to the library of St. John's College, for which he always had a warm affection. College benefactions were almost a family tradition, and Benlowes' father had similarly made gifts to the library of his own college, King's. It was a lordly gesture carried out by numbers of the fine gentlemen of the time, especially those who combined a care for serious things with a lively sense of their own importance. The youthful John Evelyn had hardly enrolled at Balliol in 1637 before he was presenting the college with seven or eight volumes of divinity. [1] But gifts like those of Edward Benlowes were not common. He had come back from the Continent with large ideas, and his munificence was great, though in perfect accordance with his worldly position. Naturally it did not seek to compete with that of the noble Earl of Southampton, who had left the same college four hundred books and manuscripts, worth £360. Southampton's books were delivered to St. John's in two instalments in 1626 and 1635. [2] Sandwiched in between these, Benlowes' gifts might almost have passed unnoticed had they been less distinguished in themselves. But on the contrary, they were afterwards acclaimed by numerous admirers, blowing trumpets Benlowes evidently loved to hear. A St. John's man made much of them in commendatory verses on Benlowes' *Sphinx Theologica*. And so did John Davies, the poet who translated Sorel's anti-romance *The Extravagant Shepherd*, who was also of this college. In dedicating to Benlowes his translation of a religious tract called *Apocalypsis; Or, The Revelation of certain notorious Advancers of Heresie* he could not pass over, he said, Benlowes' "excessive Benefactorship" to the college library. In his words, it "will stand upon the file of memory, as long as learning shall find professors or children." Benlowes' generosity to his college was also celebrated by Fuller, [3] and the *Liber Memorialis* of the college itself acknowledges in glowing terms its appreciation of one who, after he had done felicitous work

---

[1] Evelyn, *Diary*, I, 9.
[2] Stopes, *Life of Henry, Third Earl of Southampton*, pp. 376, 478-479.
[3] *History of the University of Cambridge*, ed. Prickett and Wright, p. 179.

in literary studies, in testimony of his grateful spirit, wonderfully furnished the library with books and other things. [1] Benlowes' portrait still has an honourable place in St. John's library.

All of the presentation books which survive have a book-plate speaking of the donor in terms almost identical with those used in the *Liber Memorialis* and recording the date of the gift as 1631. Although the presentation was therefore under way in 1631, it was not completed until the following year, for the gift of books included the third edition of Florio's Montaigne, which, though it has the same book-plate as the others, was only issued in 1632. Entering into the project with zest, Benlowes was busy buying some of the newest books. They included John Weever's *Ancient Funerall Monuments* and the *Praelectiones De Duobus in Theologia Controversis Capitibus*, by John Davenant, Bishop of Salisbury, who had been professor of divinity at Cambridge when Benlowes first went up to the university. Davenant's book, whether it reflected the taste of Benlowes himself or of St. John's library, would offset the complete works of the Jesuit theologian Martin Becan, in two large folio volumes. These had been published at Mainz the year before and may, but of course need not, have been one of Benlowes' Continental purchases. There was also the *Theologia Moralis* of Pedro de Ledesma, published at Douai in 1630. But none of these shows a particularly individual choice. Theological controversy was so much in the air that almost any up-to-date librarian might have chosen works like these. Some smaller argumentative writings and some slender volumes of Latin poems more certainly represent Benlowes' own reading. *Joannis Valacrii Scoto-Britanni Spectacula Veneta* was published at Venice in 1627, a five-page poem called *Nicrina ad Heroas Anglos* at Heidelberg in 1620. With their obvious English interest, these would naturally percolate to those English circles which took delight in Latin poetry, but they would equally catch Benlowes' eye in a foreign bookshop, and I cannot help feeling that he came across them while he was abroad. The same may be true of some other Latin verse: the *Liber de Triumphata Barbarie*, by "Matthias Leius," and the *Querelae Saravictonis et Biomeae*. There was a collection of Latin celebratory poems on the marriage of Charles I which the Cambridge University "muses" had got together six years before. But, significantly enough, among the Benlowes presentation books there is no record of anything in

---

[1] Baker, *History of the College of St. John*, I, 340.

any modern foreign language. In English poetry, Giles Fletcher's *Christs Victorie and Triumph*—a poem over twenty years old—undoubtedly reflected Benlowes' own taste as it had been in his university days. And even though his own poetry was to be more packed and crabbed in style than Fletcher's more Spenserian verse, Benlowes' great enthusiasm for the poetry of Fletcher's brother Phineas, with its combination of sweetness and piety and intricate comparisons, shows that this youthful taste was one that he had not outgrown. Who indeed in the 1630's had?

Most of the other books, showing clearly the direction in which Benlowes' mind had travelled, were controversial writings of a strongly anti-Catholic bias. *The Copies of Certaine Letters which have passed between Spaine and England in Matter of Religion* contains in particular the argument by which William Bedell, a distinguished English clergyman who was by this time Bishop of Kilmore, had sought to influence his friend, James Wadsworth, who became a Catholic during residence in Spain. [1] In *Rhemes against Rome* Richard Bernard attempts a confutation of a long list of Catholic heresies; *The Anatomie of Popish Tyrannie*, dedicated by Thomas Bell to the Bishop of Durham, is a fierce attack on the writings of the Jesuits; and *Antitortobellarminus*, by John Gordon, the late Dean of Salisbury, is an abusive reply—much fortified by puns and anagrams upon the offender's name [2]—to Bellarmine's attack on the oath of allegiance imposed by James I after the Gunpowder Plot. The presence of this last book would serve as another counterblast to the works of Martin Becan, who had warmly supported Bellarmine, and is no doubt due to the special interest that Benlowes' own Catholic upbringing had led him to take in this famous Jacobean controversy.

Benlowes not only presented St. John's College with books worth fifty pounds; according to the *Liber Memorialis* his gift included also two globes and some "tables" and other exquisite ornaments. [3] Thus he gently demonstrated how up-to-date he was in all the arts and sciences. The "tables" were evidently the "marbles" (*marmora*) which the panegyrist of Benlowes' *Sphinx Theologica* preciously

---

[1] And was of sufficient distinction at the Spanish court to be one of two instructors appointed to teach the Infanta English at the time of her projected marriage to the English Prince in 1623.

[2] Robertus Bellarminus = *Errorum tabens bullis*. And the attack begins: "*Bellarmine*, minas, bella...."

[3] Baker, *College of St. John*, I, 340.

compared to the elegant songs of Benlowes' muse. They were in fact *pietre commesse* which he had bought while he was abroad. No doubt he prided himself on being a leader of taste, and the manner in which the marbles were received at Cambridge must have given him immense satisfaction. They were the only things of their kind that the college possessed, and were so prized by refined seventeenth-century judgment that Evelyn, who visited Cambridge in 1654, singled them out for comment in describing the library which seemed to him the fairest in all the university. Evelyn was a connoisseur in these things, yet he pronounced "a table and one piece of perspective" to be "very fine." [1] One of these ornaments, though badly cracked, still hangs in its wooden frame (on which is painted the Benlowes shield) over the door of the librarian's room.

All this was characteristic of one who all his life used his means to encourage learning and the arts. A man of quiet habits who deplored ostentation, Benlowes sought for himself a life of devotion. But his temperament was not that of the ascetic. His taste in art, as is apparent throughout all his work, ran to the precious and to a certain fastidious elegance, often highly mannered; and his benefactions themselves were really an expression of an instinctive love of display which his gravity of mind forbade to manifest itself in more usual ways. He had not been long after coming from abroad in getting himself an arms-block made, and under Schoren's experienced supervision his family gentility was stamped in gold on the books he made haste to send to Cambridge.

The lavish scale of his gifts to St. John's provided a good example of his extravagant generosity. He gave also to the church and to the poor, treated the members of his family with a quite unfraternal liberality, and above all surrounded himself with poets, artists, and musicians, to whom he was in some sort a patron. His naturally unsuspicious mind laid him open to ingratitude, and some of those who benefited by his wealth took advantage of his unworldliness. More frequently, however, the genuineness of his affection was reciprocated, and the fulsomeness of the flattery he received was a mark rather of the manner of the age than of any lack of sincerity on the part of his many friends. For his part, he took pride in his name Benlowes, which he had learned in Italy could slip so readily into the anagram Benevolus. His friends delighted to call him by this name, and he did his best to live up to it.

[1] *Diary*, II, 70.

CHAPTER SIX

PROTESTANT

Most of Benlowes' friends shared his own serious cast of mind. Among them, for example, was Ralph Winterton, who, about the time of Benlowes' return from abroad, was engaged in translating some works of religion with a strong Protestant bias. Benlowes had been with him at Cambridge, though Winterton was three years senior. He became a fellow of King's at about the time that Benlowes was entering the neighbouring college of St. John's. A fine Greek scholar, he was also a physician, and ended up as Regius Professor of Medicine. He was also profoundly interested in religious controversy, and when he fell foul of the college authorities, to the extent of being refused the M.D. degree, it is thought to have been because of his conduct in hall, on two separate occasions, when he seems to have indulged in some acrid theological discussion. This happened in 1631 and 1633. Whether or not Winterton had had any influence on Benlowes in his younger days, they were certainly in contact round about this time.

The circumstances of Benlowes' life—the staunchness of his family in maintaining a persecuted religion, his long struggle to decide for himself between two warring creeds—as well as his natural disposition, led him to be specially ardent in matters of belief, even for that age of great religious passion. When he had once accepted the Protestant creed he pursued it with all the zeal of a convert and with a convert's characteristic intolerance for his former faith. Anthony à Wood, that mine of interesting and inaccurate gossip, who knew Benlowes in later years, was struck by the bitter hostility to Catholicism of one who in his earlier days had been "popishly affected." Wood thought that Benlowes came back from the Continent "tinged with romanism," [1] as though he had been brought up a Protestant and then fallen under some

---

[1] *Fasti Oxonienses*, II, 358-359.

Catholic influence while abroad. That an acquaintance of Benlowes in later life could even have formed this impression shows how reticent—not to say secretive—Benlowes was about those Catholic antecedents of which in the end he became ashamed. In all his writings he never sought to remind a reader that he had ever held any beliefs other than those of the Church of England.

Shortly after his return from abroad Benlowes had become finally, fiercely, and openly a Protestant. In 1632 his friend Winterton was rejoicing greatly, not only about his having been by divine Providence brought safely home, but because he had now become a member of the Church of England. And in that year Benlowes wrote some verses to be prefixed to Winterton's translation of the aphorisms of Johann Gerhard, the eminent Lutheran divine, whose skill in disputation made him reputed the foremost Protestant theologian in Germany. The nature of this book that Benlowes now sponsored showed that his conversion was very complete. He welcomed a publication which denied that the Roman Church was a true and pure church at all and which derided the power of the Pope: "For what markes soever the Scripture hath given to know *Antichrist* by, they all meete together in the *Pope* of Rome, as Histories do witnesse, and experience teacheth." [1] Benlowes was now in the company of those who boasted of having "gone out of the Romish Babylon according to Gods command," taking forth with them in the process "the precious from the vile." [2] By such zealots the papal claim to excommunicate atheists and other notorious offenders against religion was felt to proceed from motives of "private hatred, levitie, ambition, and desire of domineering." [3] Benlowes joined with them in their enthusiasm for getting the writings of the holy prophets and apostles without any admixture of mere human tradition. The appeal of Protestantism for him was its abandoning of authority to return to the fount of inspiration. He denied the need of any intermediary between earthly creature and heavenly Creator —and this was but an extreme example of his impatience with anything which tended to restrict his individual liberty. His later attacks on Catholics were always bitterest in their hostility to the priests; and he was fiercest of all against the Pope himself, arch-priest and arch-interferer between man and God. The Latin language, though

[1] *A Golden Chaine of Divine Aphorismes*, p. 342.
[2] *Ibid.*, p. 319.
[3] *Ibid.*, p. 343.

he himself delighted in it, was seen to be an infringement of the
right of the individual when it was used as the medium of Christian
worship in the presence of those who were unable to understand
it. Whatever stood between man and the word of God itself was
denounced with a scornful vigour which was an appropriate introduction to the work of Ralph Winterton and Johann Gerhard:

> Let the Antichristian Clergy keep
> Their Owl-ey'd Laitie pris'ners in the deep
> And horrid shades of everlasting night,
> Whil'st thy cleare beams, & more illustrious light
> Disperse these clouds of Language.

Winterton was also busy with a translation of *The Considerations
of Drexelius upon Eternitie*, and on June 1, 1632, he dedicated this
work to Benlowes. This dedication, written from King's College,
was the kind of honour that Benlowes was subsequently to receive
quite often, being specially marked out for it by his interest in scholarship and poetry and his patronage of their devotees. In receiving
it from Winterton he was in the company of no less a person than
Archbishop Laud, with whom Winterton stood well and whose
intervention ultimately removed the obstacles to Winterton's much
coveted medical degree.

Winterton's dedication addressed Benlowes as "The Right Wor-
shipfull and truly Religious Esquire" in a lengthy epistle which
reflected upon eternity in an edifying strain for two pages and a
half. One saw life to be but a meditation upon death and time a
prelude to eternity. In life it was good to remind oneself of this so
that thoughts of eternity might banish sin and provide consolation
for temporal afflictions. Winterton found in Drexelius a constant
remembrancer of eternity in whom he could take great delight,
and he explained that this author had first been commended to
him by a man who was in every respect as like as could be to Mr.
Benlowes himself. He had been bred in the Romish religion and
sent beyond seas to be confirmed in it, yet had been converted to
the Church of England and singled out among all his kindred to
be a most zealous Protestant. He was a man of good fortune but
little given to worldly pleasures. Instead he was wedded to his
books and devotions, spending what some call idle time in the
best company for the edifying himself or others, taking no pride
in his possessions but a good deal of care in using his money for
the good of others. His discourse was on things above and his
thoughts upon eternity.

To this paragon Ralph Winterton thought that Edward Benlowes was exactly comparable. The reflections of Drexelius seemed therefore suited to his taste, though, to be sure, as Winterton admitted, he could hardly be said to be in need of them. The excellence of Benlowes was of an order almost embarrassing to Winterton, who disliked praising a man to his face. He found it unnecessary, however, to run over the catalogue of Benlowes' Christian virtues; for his piety and temperance were apparent to all who daily conversed with him, while his charity and bounty, however much Benlowes might wish to hide them, were conspicuous wherever he went. Winterton particularly applauded his generosity to many poor scholars and godly and devout ministers at Cambridge and elsewhere, and he added his tribute to his "rare" gifts to the library of St. John's College. Altogether he left eloquent, if partial, testimony to the saintly character of Benlowes at the time when he was just approaching the age of thirty.

Benlowes' departure from the Catholic faith occurred at a time when it was actually receiving greater tolerance in official quarters. It was the religion of Charles I's queen, and by the terms of her marriage-settlement she was allowed twenty-eight Catholic clergy to help her practise it. Not surprisingly, therefore, it became quite fashionable at court, there being many conversions in the upper ranks of society. When Benlowes himself was becoming almost vitriolic against Catholics and generating a fury which until the end of his days he was never to exhaust, the High Anglican party, to which affinities of temperament led him, was concerning itself with Catholics much less than with Puritans, whom Laud was persecuting with vigour. The Catholics, in the words of Clarendon, "were grown only a part of the revenue, without any probable danger of being made a sacrifice to the law. They were looked upon as good subjects at Court, and as good neighbours in the country, all the restraints and reproaches of former times being forgotten." [1]

Benlowes carried on some energetic correspondence with other devotees of his new religion, and his enthusiasm, as frequently happens, also manifested itself in a proselytizing fervour. It grieved him especially that his servant, John Schoren, continued to adhere to the old faith and—to use his own phrase—he "did earnestly sollicite and much importune" him to follow his own example and abandon it. They often talked about it, and Benlowes took

[1] *History of the Rebellion*, ed. Macray, I, 194.

great pains in instructing Schoren in Protestant doctrine. Schoren, though less skilled in controversy, was more bound by tradition, and proved a stubborn subject for Benlowes' essay in evangelism. Benlowes, with mingled enthusiasm and naïveté, at length sought to bribe him, making him several useful gifts of money. These Schoren readily accepted. He had always been promised rewards for his faithful service in attending his master through the smallpox, and he considered that he had so far had nothing beyond mere necessities.

Yet Schoren fancied Benlowes as a master, and had been only too pleased to follow him to England. By all the means in his power he sought to make himself indispensable to Benlowes. More than anything he wished for Benlowes to put the relationship between them on a permanent basis and to settle upon him an annuity which would guarantee to him the amount of his wages—twenty marks— every year for life. Always harping upon the care and devotion he had shown Benlowes on his travels, Schoren became very pressing. Benlowes, with perhaps unwonted caution, did not readily respond to Schoren's blandishments, though he never seriously doubted his good faith. Eventually, however, in his eagerness to get a convert, he made Schoren a promise of the annuity if he would become a Protestant. Thus he thought to buy Schoren's soul for the true salvation. What he actually bought, of course, was only Schoren's outward observance of Protestant worship, though his optimistic view of human nature did not lead him to suspect it. At the same time, it was curious that a man as deeply religious as Benlowes was, and one moreover who had seen the behaviour of "church papists" in his youth, should have been so easily satisfied when Schoren allowed himself to be "outwardly" convinced. For a time Schoren regularly attended the English church, and this gave Benlowes, as he admitted, great joy. But in later years, with the annuity safely in his pocket and Benlowes his pledged benefactor for life, Schoren reverted to his former Catholicism. [1]

[1] Chancery Proceedings, Reynardson 31/14; Collins 28/11.

CHAPTER SEVEN

PHINEAS FLETCHER AND FRANCIS QUARLES

Meanwhile, Benlowes' association with Winterton continued. In 1633 he was one of a distinguished band of scholars and physicians who together filled forty-five pages with epigrams to swell the bulk and the prestige of Winterton's edition of the aphorisms of Hippocrates. This display of classical virtuosity was very characteristic of the highly academic, though quite sterile, productions which learned men at that time delighted to indulge in. In Winterton's volume Hippocrates appeared in his original Greek, in Latin translations in prose and verse by two different scholars, and, crowning glory, in a new form in Greek verse which was by Winterton himself. Benlowes' own epigram was a conventional compliment in conventional Latin verse, making what it could of the pretended paradox that Winterton, though a learned physician, was yet a virtuous man; which was as much as to say that he did not share the atheism usually attributed to his profession. [1]

If Benlowes, something of a pedant himself, lent himself to this sort of vain erudition, he also had a great interest in what the seventeenth-century might have called, had they been a little more self-conscious about it than they were, "new writing." When he had settled at Brent Hall again on his return from the Continent, it had not taken him long to get into the swim. He read Donne, of course —everyone with any poetical pretensions did. But there were other poets who were much more widely read among the ordinary educated public in the seventeenth century, and with one or two of these Benlowes was in closest touch. He had thoughts of using his wealth to promote the interests of literature. In a more modern age he would perhaps have been running and financing some new liter-

---

[1] Any more than did Sir Thomas Browne. It is interesting, however, that the line of the Doctor of Physic, whose "studie was but litel on the Bible" was not extinct. Colonel Hutchinson had a friend, "a young physician, who was a good scholar....but withal a professed atheist" (Lucy Hutchinson, *Memoirs of Colonel Hutchinson*, ed. Firth, p. 44).

ary review. As it was, within five years of coming home from abroad, he was associated with two of the most popular poetical works of the century. These were the compositions of close friends of his—*The Purple Island*, by Phineas Fletcher, which suited to perfection the taste for allegorical fancy, and the *Emblemes* of Quarles, which took advantage of the fashion for pictured poetry and, in its pious meditations, reflected exactly the spirit of an age to which religion and the soul were vital interests and economics and the living wage were not. Each of these two books was on its first appearance dedicated to Benlowes himself. The first was published and the second written at his instigation.

Phineas Fletcher was twenty years older than Benlowes. He had preceded Benlowes at Cambridge, where he had been a fellow of King's College. He had enjoyed a considerable reputation as a poet in university circles, and had distinguished himself also by writing university plays. His *Sicelides* was written to be presented before King James I when he visited the university in 1615, and it would have been if the King had only stayed in Cambridge another night. Fletcher left Cambridge some years before Benlowes went up, but his name still survived and his poetry brought honour to the university for a number of years. Most of his writing was done during his Cambridge days, but a lot of it was not published till much later. His *Locustae*, for example, was printed by the university printers, Thomas and John Buck, in 1627. This was a longish Latin poem attacking Roman Catholics, and one therefore which Benlowes would appreciate much more *after* his conversion.

Fletcher was rector of Hilgay in Norfolk, and led a somewhat secluded life there. Though it is not impossible that Benlowes visited him in his parsonage, their friendship must have been pursued largely by letter. [1] It arose out of their common interest in poetry. Benlowes knew some of Fletcher's work in manuscript, including *The Purple Island*, a good deal of which had been written at Cambridge years before and which was already familiar to a growing number of the elect. In view of his enthusiasm for this poem, it is as well, if one is to appreciate Benlowes' taste, to remember for a moment what sort of poem it was.

---

[1] A. B. Langdale (*Phineas Fletcher*, p. 90) suggests that Benlowes may have been taken by Quarles on a literary pilgrimage to Hilgay. But although he writes at some length on the friendship of Fletcher and Benlowes, his account is largely conjectural, not to say fanciful, and I certainly prefer to think that Benlowes introduced Quarles to Fletcher rather than the other way about (*cf.* below, p. 76).

The Purple Island was a poem wrought out of that traditional allegorical conceit which represented the body of man as a castle (or in later variants an island), with inhabitants who strove to defend it in a fierce struggle against attackers from without. First appearing clearly worked out in the thirteenth century in Robert Grosseteste's *Le Chasteau d'Amour* and in the homily *Sawles Warde*, this allegory developed through things like *Piers Plowman* and *The Castle of Perseverance*, and later took on an altogether more fantastic character in the hands of Renaissance poets, who delighted to pursue it through long series of ingenious physical correspondences. The most notable instances before Fletcher were in Sylvester's translation of the *Devine Weekes* of Du Bartas and the description of the castle of Alma in Spenser's *Faerie Queene*. [1] In these much admired authors Fletcher read how the mouth was a porch with a vine growing over it, a portcullis hung above, and twice sixteen warders sitting all armed within; or he came upon the stomach described as "that readie Cooke, concocting euerie Messe." So it was exactly in their vein that he himself pictured the teeth as "twice sixteen Porters" standing at the mouth of a cave, within which a groom, the tongue, despatched "the customarie rent" of victuals to be "shipt at fittest tide" to the port of Koilia, or the stomach. [2] His originality lay in numerous novel applications and in the degree of their elaboration; and also in the scientific knowledge which allowed him, within his framework of a traditional sunshiny pastoral, to develop his description of man as an island in the most thorough physiological detail. Sylvester had had much on nerves and veins and blood, and Spenser gives us the digestive tracts, with a conduit bearing off foul liquors, but in Fletcher there was a whole island seen as a maze of streams amid a veritable wilderness of muscles, intestines, and what not. There followed a description of the vices and virtues, presented in a series of allegorical portraits somewhat after the manner of Spenser, but verging also upon that of the seventeenth-century "character"-writers. This was a kind of writing which Benlowes enjoyed and himself exploited in a very small way in the later cantos of *Theophila*, but he never showed anything of the narrative skill with which Fletcher recounted, in the most Spenserian part of the poem, the death-fight between good and evil of which the isle of man was the venue. What particularly attracted Benlowes

---

[1] *Devine Weekes*, 1st week, 6th day; *Faerie Queene*, book II, cantos ix and xi.
[2] See canto ii, stanzas 30-31.

to the poem was, I suppose, the astonishing ingenuity and minuteness
with which the analogy of man and island was worked out and
the didactic purpose which underlay the whole. He admired the
kind of vision which could see the nose as a tower with a double-
door open at its foot; equally he approved the kind of morality
which upheld goodness in its struggle for the possession of man's
island and which ultimately brought the struggle to a successful
conclusion through divine intervention against a dragon. [1]

Benlowes pressed Fletcher to publish *The Purple Island*, and eventually it appeared along with a collection of piscatory eclogues
and other miscellaneous poems in 1633, put forth by the Cambridge
University printers. This did not happen without some demurrer
from the author, who, now in the autumn of his life, felt a little
modest about "these raw *Essayes*" of his "very unripe yeares."
Writing from Hilgay on May 1, 1633, he dedicated the volume to
Benlowes and protested that, in allowing it to appear, he was preferring Benlowes' wishes to his own. He was afraid that his poems
were unworthy of Benlowes' patronage, yet hoped, as he flatteringly
said, that by it they would be provided with some protection against
a censorious age. His dedicatory epistle, though written of course
with a mild flourish that came from thoughts of its public appearance,
was still a sincere avowal of friendship. Fletcher, indeed, took pride
in claiming Benlowes for his friend, wished to contend with him
in nothing but to "*out-love*" him, said that he owed more to him
than to anyone else, and praised him for the possession of an eye
that looked on things only with affection—"It doubles any good,
and extenuates what is amisse."

---

[1] For an indication of some of the items in the pre-Spenserian part of the
tradition see C. L. Powell, "The Castle of the Body," *Studies in Philology*, vol.
XVI (1919) and a paragraph in B. E. C. Davis's *Edmund Spenser*, p. 115. Among
the productions of Fletcher's contemporaries may be mentioned *Roome for a
Messe of Knaves* ("A narration of a strange but true battel fought in the little
Isle....of Man"), 1610; the play of *Lingua*, 1607; and *The Isle of Man* (or "The
Legall Proceeding in Man-shire against Sinne"), 1626, by Richard Bernard.
Bernard's book — with its account of the arraignment of Sin in a place called
"*Soules-towne*," where he is caught at a disreputable inn kept by a harlot called
Mistress Heart — was extremely popular. It had its fourth edition in under
two years. And I expect Benlowes, who knew Bernard's *Rhemes against Rome*,
was also acquainted with the more famous work. He was certainly a great admirer of
Lingua (see below, pp. 120-121). But conceits about the castle of the body and the isle
of man can be found throughout seventeenth-century didactic writing. They figured
especially in the sermons—Jeremy Taylor is in the line of Du Bartas and Spenser
when he makes the stomach the castle kitchen complete with ovens and cooks—,
and the whole tradition reached its final culmination in Bunyan's *Holy War*.

Part of the debt Fletcher acknowledged to Benlowes lay, I think, in Benlowes' private generosity. The poem appeared under his *"Patronage,"* and it was beautifully and expensively printed. A few copies were printed on large paper, no doubt as a compliment to their intended recipients. Some also contained engravings. All this provides a further reason, beyond his love of poetry, why Benlowes should have urged Fletcher to publish. He had come back from the Continent with a taste for fine books and engravings and, with Schoren as a tame printer at Brent Hall, he was anxious to try his hand at book-production. Fletcher's poem provided an excellent opportunity. Although the book was printed at Cambridge, I suspect that the engravings were commissioned by Benlowes and printed from the plates by him privately and then inserted in the copies intended for presentation to his friends. [1] That would explain why although three engravings were specially prepared as decorations for the volume, the possession of all three was a special privilege which few copies had. The ordinary undistinguished copy for public sale seems to have had none. This discriminatory practice was followed by Benlowes himself when he came to publish *Theophila*. It had a special subtlety in marking copies of the same book either for presentation within one's own circle of friends or for general appearance before a wider public. The three engravings belonging to *The Purple Island* [2] were all of a very personal nature and were clearly intended for the friends of Fletcher and Benlowes only. The first appeared on the verso of the title-page, a design amalgamating the arms of the two poets and enscrolled within it a flattering motto celebrating this conjunction: "Benevoli Coniunctio Animi maxima est Cognatio." The second and third engravings were both to the honour of Benlowes: they used anagrams of his name as a text for a poem. The second, at the end of "The Purple Island" and before the "Piscatorie Eclogs," consisted largely of some engraved verses by Fletcher. A scroll at the left had a Latin anagram of Benlowes' name, extending the usual "Benevolus" (= Benlowes) to "Durus, a Deo benevolus" (= Edovardus Benlowes); and this was matched on the right by a scroll with an English anagram, "Sun-ward[e] Beloved" (= Edward Benlowes). The scrolls were entwined one

---

[1] On his doing this with his own *Theophila*, see below, Ch. 20. And on his possession of a rolling-press for such a purpose, see below, p. 102. Of course it cannot be proved that he actually had his rolling-press as early as 1633.

[2] All three are reproduced in volume II of the *Poetical Works* of Giles and Phineas Fletcher, ed. Boas.

with a sunflower [1] the other with a pansy, at the top of the plate
an emblematic sun appropriately shone, and "Sun-warde beloved"
was used as the title of the verses, in which Fletcher, according to
the curious fashion of the time, compared the pansy upon whose
purple petals the sun prints its golden image to his own soul receiving upon it the image of the spiritual sun, that is, of God. I
give the poem in full, printing in italic the words which are writ
large in the original engraving:

> While *Panses sun-ward* look; that glorious *Light*
> With gentle *Beames* entring their purple *Bowers*
> Shedds there his *Love*, & heat, and fair to sight
> Prints his bright forme within their golden flowers.
> Look in their *Leaves*, and see begotten there
> The *Sūnes* lesse *Sōne* glittring in azure sphere.
>
> So when from *Shades* of superstitious night
> Mine eye turn'd to the *Sun*, his heavnly powers
> Stampt on my new-born spirit his Image bright
> And *Love*, *Light*, *Life*, into my bosome Showers
>   This difference; They in themselues haue moving,
>   But his sweet *Love* mee dead, and Sensles proving,
> First *Loves*, and drawes to *Love*,
> Then *Loves* my Soule for *Loving*.

To have based all this on the anagram of Benlowes' name was a
pretty compliment. [2]

The third engraving, when it appeared, was inserted between
the "Piscatorie Eclogs" and the "Poeticall Miscellanies." It was
a design of a ship on a river with, on the river-bank, a tree spotted
with fruit, everything being lavishly shone on by the sun. Some
Latin verses below, again from Fletcher to his most dear *(charissimo)*
E.B., repeated the theme: the power of the sun to ripen the fruit
and thaw the frost. "Durus" is turned into "benevolus" by God

---

[1] To compare oneself to a sunflower, which turns always towards the sun,
was a traditional conceit in love emblems (see Praz, *Studies in Seventeenth-Century
Imagery*, I, 99).

[2] That it is an elaborate compliment is clear. But there are different views
on what exactly the compliment is. In my view, it lies in the extraction from
Benlowes' name of an anagram which suggests the love of God for those who
turn towards him; and further, in the building of a poem upon such a suggestion.
The poem is a sacred one, and the sun which gives to Fletcher "*Love, Light,
Life*" when he turns to it from "superstitious night" is God. To interpret it
as Benlowes would be such blasphemy as Fletcher could not have intended.
Nor does Fletcher call Benlowes the sun in the line "The *Sūnes* lesse *Sōne* glitt-
ring in azure sphere" (as is maintained by G. S. Haight in *The Library*, 4th
series, XVI, 193). The lesser sun is surely the image of the sun in the centre
of the pansy's purple petals. In the 5th of the "Piscatorie Eclogs" (stanza 2),
Fletcher pays the same compliment in similar terms to the primrose.

and the anagram—this time the Latin one, "*Durus, à Deo Benevolus*" —was again triumphant.

These engravings, expressing in pictorial symbols a motto derived from the anagram of a man's name, were specimens of the Italian art of the impresa,[1] which enjoyed a certain vogue in England. Impresas, or *imprese*, if you prefer the Italian plural, had long been familiar in England in the form of devices on the ornamental shields borne by the pages of horsemen taking part in jousts. Shakespeare himself designed one for the Duke of Rutland, which Richard Burbage painted. They had already made an indelible mark on the imagery of English poetry and on the tableaux and pageantry of English drama.[2] Their literary vogue in the seventeenth century was encouraged by the popularity of the kindred art of the emblem. In both, the relation between picture and words was felt to be like the relation between the body and soul, and this explains part of the fascination which these arts had for the seventeenth-century imagination. Their pictorial design, their elaborate and graceful artificiality, together with the touch of vanity about the exclusiveness of an impresa, were exactly what one would expect to appeal to Benlowes. Attracted to impresas while in Italy, he could not resist, after he had got back home, devising some of his own and interesting his friends, including Fletcher, in this fantastic art.

Some of the copies of *The Purple Island* which contained the engravings had Benlowes' arms stamped on the covers back and front. Librarians and others have liked wrongly to suppose that some particular one of these was Benlowes' private copy presented to him by his friend;[3] but Benlowes did not follow the practice of making his arms on the cover of a book the sign that it belonged

---

[1] In that the motto not only explained the pictorial device but was itself the anagram of a name, these were refinements—or at least elaborations—on the strict impresa, in which an allusive motto and a symbolic picture met together in mutual explanation. The refinement itself Benlowes had no doubt learnt in Italy, where it was already common. The best succinct account of impresas, together with evidence of their classical origin, is given by G. F. Barwick in an article in *The Library*, 2d series, VII, 140-148. The most expert knowledge of the subject is that of Mario Praz, displayed for English readers in his *Studies in Seventeenth-Century Imagery*, vol. I, ch. 2. The Elizabethan conception of impresas can be seen from Puttenham, *The Arte of English Poesie*, bk. ii, ch. 12. See also Chambers, *The Elizabethan Stage*, I, 143, and Lee, *Life of Shakespeare*, 14th ed., pp. 455-456. The easiest place to find examples is in *Pericles*, II, ii.

[2] See, for a brilliant survey, Praz, *Studies in Seventeenth-Century Imagery*, I, 193ff.

[3] This claim has been made at different times for one of the copies in the British Museum, the copy at St. John's College, Cambridge, and for yet a third

to his own library. He used his arms-block for decorating books that he gave away. He had done this when he presented books to St. John's College on his return from abroad, and he was to do it again with the numerous gift copies of *Theophila*. His arms emblazoned on the leather provided a handsome ornamental binding which his friends prized, and it innocently expressed his mild vanity and a certain love of display.

The luxurious production of *The Purple Island*, then, and particularly of those copies intended as special gifts, either from the author or from his patron, was the result of Benlowes' taste and money. No wonder Fletcher spoke of his friend's generosity. Benlowes was so much responsible for the design of the book, at any rate in the presentation copies, that the whole was almost a joint production. Benlowes treated it as such and presented copies partly in recommendation of his friend's poetry, but partly with the air one employs in offering a token of one's own achievement. The copy of *The Purple Island* at St. John's College, Cambridge, has the inscription, complete with ornamental flourishes:

> Benlowes
> Esse suj voluit monumentum,
> et pignus Amoris.
> 1633.

Another copy is described by Dr. F. S. Boas [1] as having the same inscription, though with the punning form of the name, "Benevolus." It is necessary to repeat that these copies, and others like them, were not, as has always been assumed, presented *to* Benlowes, but *by* him. It was he who wished the gift to be a token of *his* love, as indeed the nominative form "Benevolus" should have suggested. [2]

---

copy, described by Dr. Boas in the *Poetical Works* of Giles and Phineas Fletcher, II, vi-vii.

[1] *Ibid.*

[2] I regret that the error of crediting Fletcher and not Benlowes with the gift of copies of *The Purple Island* containing such inscriptions has been made in the standard edition of Fletcher's works and perpetuated in the latest and fullest biography of Fletcher (Giles and Phineas Fletcher, *Poetical Works*, ed. Boas; Langdale, *Phineas Fletcher*, p. 89). One such inscription has been found by Dr. Boas to be "unmistakeably in Fletcher's characteristic hand," but it is not always easy for a seventeenth-century hand, above all in a formal inscription, to be unmistakable to a twentieth-century eye. With this admission I add that after considering all the external evidence, I have compared the *Purple Island* inscription which Dr. Boas reproduces with the inscriptions in the various presentation copies of Benlowes' *Theophila*, and I have myself no doubt that it is in Benlowes' hand.

The same or a similar Latin inscription was used by Benlowes a number of

The decoration was not the whole extent of Benlowes' contribution to the book. Naturally, he wrote prefatory verses in praise of the poem he admired. They consisted of two nine-line stanzas, in form an adaptation of the seven-line stanza used by Fletcher himself, and in style as near as Benlowes ever came to Fletcher's easily running lines. What Benlowes wrote, however, was not so much a straightforward panegyric as a moral reflection which *The Purple Island* had inspired. The island of the poem, this "isle of man," it was important that man himself should control. In his youth Benlowes, like the rest of "this vain world," had esteemed the power that lay in ruling countries that existed in the outer world of geography. He had admired those who were conversant with "the mysteries of state" and "who of learned arts could wisely prate." But now he was taught by Fletcher to see the emptiness of that sort of sovereignty and resolved to "dwell in *th'Isle of Man*, ne're travell forrain part." All this was, of course, partly the desire of the serious-minded man of the seventeenth century to preach a little sermon on every occasion. Fletcher's poem had not only suggested the occasion, but in its first canto had provided also the text. Benlowes made a personal application to himself, but his moralizing utterance did not mean that he was likely to forsake the "learned arts" which he for the moment scorned. Yet it had more than a momentary sincerity, and the principal sentiment was but the echo of what Benlowes repeatedly expressed elsewhere, a distaste for the vanities of courts and a reluctance, once he had made the grand tour, ever again to travel. He preferred to dedicate himself to a life of quiet piety. *The Purple Island* did little to influence his outlook on life, but it fitted in admirably with it.

In the same year as *The Purple Island* appeared, Phineas Fletcher had another collection of poems put forth at Cambridge by the university printers. This was a series of eclogues and other odd poems in Latin which formed a joint volume with a Latin poem by his father, Giles Fletcher the elder. Phineas's portion of the volume was entitled *Sylva Poetica* and it was again dedicated to his most dear and much vaunted friend, Edward Benlowes. These quite unremarkable pastorals had been among the first things Fletcher

---

times in presentation copies of his own poem, *Theophila*. But it may be as well to observe that this Latin tag was not peculiar to Benlowes; it seems to have been more or less a commonplace, at least in Benlowes' own circle. It would not prove anything if unaccompanied by the donor's name or arms.

wrote beneath the Cambridge willows, as he explained in the dedicatory poem, which was also in Latin. They made much appropriate talk of groves and streams and flocks of sheep, among which,
before he discovered a more original style, the poet thought he
loved to dwell. Benlowes looked kindly even on these youthful
Latinizings, and Fletcher was grateful for his favour. He again
spoke of him not simply as a friend, but also as a patron who gave
assistance to the labours of his muse.

The firm literary friendship which existed between Fletcher and
Benlowes was shared also by Benlowes' younger brother William,
though William was overshadowed by his elder brother, as was
no doubt both proper and to be expected. Quite as well educated in
the narrow sense, he had not enjoyed the same advantages of travel
and society. Nor had he the same glamour of wealth, status, or prestige.
But, perhaps encouraged by Edward, he had something of the same
literary tastes, and he was not lacking in the gentlemanly accomplishment of turning pretty compliments in verse. He also wrote a prefatory poem for *The Purple Island*. Prompted by the epistle in which
Fletcher disparaged this work of his youth, William exhorted the
poet not to be ashamed of it, and made that the excuse to praise
both the wit and art of Fletcher's poetry and the grave and modest
character of the poet who would now disown it.

Another member of the Benlowes circle also celebrated Fletcher's
muse in a complimentary poem. This was Francis Quarles, who
admired Fletcher well enough to call him the Spenser of the age.
The Purple Island was so much to his taste that he only regretted
that Fletcher had got the start of him and done with superior art
what he desired to do himself. He expressed the same taste in a
further page of verses, working out in detail the far from original
comparison of man's body to a house, where the ribs are laths
plastered with flesh and blood, the heart is the great chamber, and
the stomach is the kitchen. Quarles addressed Fletcher as "sweet
stranger," [1] and since he did not know him personally, he had presumably been shown the manuscript of Fletcher's poem by Benlowes.
The legend that Benlowes was the means of introducing to one another these two highly thought-of poets is therefore probably true.

[1] I do not see why Langdale (*Phineas Fletcher*, p. 46) chooses to regard Quarles's
use of the word "stranger" as a pretence. In yet another poem written for the
end of the volume Quarles addressed Fletcher as his "deare friend", "no more
a *Stranger* now," because by this time he had enjoyed his hospitality—in other
words, had read his poem.

The firm friendship which came to unite all three was acknowledged in a curious way in one of the engravings that illustrated Quarles's *Emblemes.* [1] It showed the Soul seated on a globe, a traditional item in religious emblems, and on the globe were marked four places: London, Roxwell, Finch[ing]field, and Hilgay. The last three were the villages where the three friends dwelt. Another engraving with the Soul seated on a globe [2] marked only Roxwell and Finchingfield, and thus linked Quarles especially with Benlowes. [3]

Quarles, though younger than Fletcher, was still ten years older than Benlowes. Like Benlowes he belonged to an Essex family and had been at Cambridge and at Lincoln's Inn. He had also travelled abroad, though in rather different circumstances, for he had spent some years in Germany as a member of the suite of the Princess Elizabeth after her marriage in 1613 to the Elector Palatine. He had more knowledge of courts and the world of affairs than Benlowes, but seemed nevertheless a match for him in quiet sobriety of character. He was, according to John Aubrey, "a very good man." [4] As Benlowes and Quarles lived just within reach of one another in the country, where Quarles, by his wife's account, devoted himself to study "late and early, usually by three a clock in the morning," [5] it was not surprising that a warm friendship grew up between them. To their similarity of background and character they added certain common tastes, of which a delight in poetry in general and an admiration for *The Purple Island* in particular were but examples. They both esteemed, as a matter of course, meditation on religious themes. Like all accomplished gentlemen of the day, they were also great lovers of music. It was told of Quarles that he once, while at Lincoln's Inn, bartered his law-student's gown for a lute-case. [6]

---

[1] Bk. v, no. 6.

[2] Facing the Invocation to Bk. i.

[3] A fantastic interpretation of this engraving is given by G. S. Haight (*The Library*, 4th series, XVI, 193). He takes the motto, "*Dum Cælum aspicio, Solum despicio*" to refer to Benlowes on the grounds that Benlowes' friends called him Sol, or the Sun. Even if this were true—the two arguments on which it rests are confuted in the notes on pp. 72, 184-5—I still do not see how *solum* (the earth) could refer to Benlowes as though it were the same as *solem*, nor why it should be a compliment to Benlowes for Quarles to say that he despised him.

[4] *Brief Lives*, ed. Clark, I, 240.

[5] Quarles, *Solomons Recantation*, sig. A3; *Works*, ed. Grosart, I, xxii.

[6] The anecdote was told by Sir Nicholas Lestrange, who was distantly connected with Quarles by marriage, he and Quarles's brother having married into the same family. "Francis Quarles had bespoken a lute case, and upon leaving

During the 1620's Quarles had written a number of poems on such Biblical subjects as Jonah, Esther, Samson, Job; and these had made him well known among serious-minded people in the higher ranks of society. He made a seventeenth-century reader like Fuller see Job's very sores as well as the anguish of his soul. [1] A volume of devotional meditations called *Divine Fancies* was very well received in 1632, and by 1633 there had appeared two collected editions of his Biblical narrative poems, with sundry other oddments added, which, under the title of *Divine Poems*, had been dedicated to the King. By the time, therefore, that he was praising *The Purple Island*, although he chose to affect some envy of its author and to speak of his own "lazie quill," he was himself already a moderately prolific and an extremely reputable poet, a man in whose friendship Benlowes could well take pride. The *Emblemes*, which were to swell repute into celebrity, followed in 1635.

The *Emblemes* themselves were the result of another grand artistic project that Benlowes had formed shortly after coming home from his travels. In dedicating the volume to Benlowes, Quarles addressed him in the warmest terms and signed himself Benlowes' "most affectionate Friend." He honoured him especially as the man who had encouraged him to play on this particular instrument: "*My deare Friend, You have put the* Theorboe *into my hand; and I have playd: You gave the Musitian the first encouragement; the Musicke returnes to you for Patronage.*" It was Benlowes, then, who had prompted Quarles to work in the emblem form, and one of the most famous seventeenth-century books owed its origin to Benlowes' stimulus and Benlowes' taste. No doubt also to his wealth. Since Quarles afterwards said that the plates for illustrating the *Emblemes*, together with those for the *Hieroglyphikes*, cost over a hundred and twenty pounds, [2] one naturally suspects that Benlowes helped to pay for them. [3]

------

the Inns of Court, and going into the country, call'd for it, and ask't what he must pay? 20*s*. sayes the workman. 'Faith', sayes he, 'I have not so much mony about me, and I am now going away; but if thou wilt take my case for thy case (meaning his Inn-of-Court gowne that he had then on), 'tis a match.' And so they agreed upon the bargaine" (W. J. Thoms, ed., *Anecdotes and Traditions*, p. 48).

[1] Fuller, *Worthies*, ed. Nichols, I, 355.

[2] *The Library*, 4th series, XV, 101.

[3] This is particularly interesting in view of G. S. Haight's statement (*ibid.*, p. 108) that Quarles "printed books at his own expense." Haight's article shows that the copy for the *Emblemes* was not made over to John Marriot, the publisher, but remained with the plates in Quarles's ownership; so that when the *Emblemes* was republished in 1639, together with the *Hieroglyphikes*, the edition of over

These plates were commissioned from the engravers William Marshall and William Simpson, and the designs were largely copied or adapted from two of the Jesuit emblem-books, the *Pia Desideria* by Hermann Hugo, published at Antwerp in 1624, and the *Typus Mundi*, published, also at Antwerp, in 1627. [1] Evidently Benlowes had admired these emblem-books, and probably he had brought copies of them from the Continent. He was in Antwerp just after the *Typus Mundi* came out. On his return he offered them to Quarles as models, and, one imagines, had something to do with the choice and adaptation of the designs that Quarles used for the pictures in his book. Such plagiarism was comparable to the manner in which Benlowes would frequently make use of other men's poems as the basis of his own. The touch of ingenuity which marked the dwelling-places of the two friends on the globes may quite easily have been his. There is a strong local tradition that Quarles actually composed the *Emblemes* at Brent Hall, where a path beside an old wall in the garden is still pointed out as his favourite walk while doing so.

Although the *Emblemes* came out only in 1635, they were being prepared for publication in the previous year. They had been entered in the Stationers' Register on May 2, 1634, and sometime during that year Benlowes had busied himself with writing a long Latin address to Quarles, which was intended to herald the new book with great flourishing of trumpets. This poem, "Quarlëis," [2] was dated from Cressing Temple, [3] which was the home of his kinsfolk the Nevills, with whom he was evidently staying at the time. Benlowes also wrote a more orthodox commendatory poem upon the *Emblemes* on the theme that Quarles was as profuse of flowers as Paradise itself; and this was written at home at Brent Hall, also in 1634. No doubt the bringing out of Quarles's book was for Benlowes one of the big interests of the year, just as the publication of Fletcher's book had been the year before.

"Quarlëis" was in print in 1634, ready to appear as an appendix to the *Emblemes*. [4] Benlowes had procured for it a handsome title-

---

two thousand copies did not belong to Marriot but to Quarles. This again throws light on what probably happened with the publication of Fletcher's *Purple Island* and Benlowes' own *Theophila*.

[1] See Praz, *Studies in Seventeenth-Century Imagery*, I, 145-146; and Haight in *The Library*, 4th series, vol. XVI.

[2] An English translation may be found in Quarles, *Works*, ed. Grosart, I, lxxxv ff.

[3] In some copies, however (for example, the Bodleian copy of the *Emblemes*), the words "Cressing-Temple. 1634" do not occur.

[4] That it was printed simply as an appendix to the *Emblemes* is clear both from

page, engraved by Marshall, which connoisseurs have always praised.[1] But the poem originally intended as a complimentary poem for Quarles's book had swollen into something big enough to appear in a pamphlet by itself. And Benlowes, it seems, could not resist the chance to appear in his own right. So he prefaced "Quarlëis" with a shorter Latin poem addressed to King Charles I, and gave the whole a new title-page calling it *Lusus Poëticus Poëtis*. In this guise his poem was available separately as well as with Quarles's *Emblemes*, where it properly belonged, when that book at length appeared in 1635.

If one may believe a remark at the end of "Quarlëis," Benlowes' volubility kept the press waiting. He apologized to the world in general for this, but excused his excessive length on the grounds of his great love. The sincerity of his regard for Quarles could be discerned throughout the poem, though there was a rather thick hedge of flattering epithets for it to come through. Benlowes was as lavish to his friends with praise as he was with money. In this instance he seems to have been anxious to persuade other people to be lavish too. Having no doubt of Quarles's great merit, he could but lament that his fortune lagged far behind it. Could Quarles be a pauper, he rhetorically asked, when the country owed him so much? Such a thing could not have happened in Augustan Rome, nor indeed in England under Elizabeth, who had been a liberal patron of poets. Yet Benlowes was tactful enough not to reproach the reigning monarch. Indeed, that was the paradox that absorbed him. Charles *was* known as a friend of poets and one, too, who valued piety. This was a daring hint that Quarles was deserving of royal reward.

The value that Benlowes placed upon Quarles went beyond the mere claims of friendship; it sprang from a strong moral sense of his goodness. In begging favour for Quarles, he was writing a didactic poem to show the age its duty. He ventured, then, to make his hint yet more pointed. In Venice the poet Sannazaro had once been given two thousand zechins. [2] Yet—to continue the paradox— Benlowes observed that London, a city renowned for its liberality

---

the colophon and from the fact that the signatures of its leaves are continuous with those of the *Emblemes*.

[1] In the Bodleian copy of *Lusus Poëticus Poëtis* this engraving does not appear, X2 being blank.

[2] For verses in honour of the city. They are quoted in Howell's *Familiar Letters*, p. 79, where this same contrast—apparently a byword among Englishmen—is made between the liberality of Venice and the "cold Reward" of London.

and justice as well as for its wealth and prosperity, had done nothing to recognize Quarles.

If Quarles had received very little in the way of court patronage,
it had not been for want of asking. He had inscribed two books
to the King, and had honoured various noblemen with the sort
of fashionable dedication which etiquette demanded should be
graciously received and a writer hoped would be handsomely acknowledged. Nor had he been altogether without profitable employment. He had been appointed secretary to Ussher, the
Archbishop of Armagh, and had therefore lived for a time with
his family in Ireland. In 1631 he had petitioned for and got "a lease
in reversion of the impositions on Tobacco and Tobacco pipes to
be imported into the kingdom of Ireland." [1] A reversion might
encourage hopes, but it could not satisfy present need. It was not
handsome enough for Quarles's admirers. In the prefatory poem
addressed to Charles himself, Benlowes added to his statement of
the King's paradoxical neglect of Quarles a more direct request
for Quarles's advancement. The King was urged to rescue seed
from the ditch and to see it planted in good soil. Benlowes was
very respectful. All things were easy for the King. And upon the
well-being of the King the well-being of his subjects was admitted
to depend. These were the sentiments of a sincere royalist. But if
Benlowes was respectful, he was also extremely outspoken. I do
not know whether the King responded. [2] The City of London did,
some years later, acknowledge Quarles's merit by making him its
official chronologer. But this was on the recommendation of the
Earl of Dorset, after Quarles had dedicated a couple of volumes
to the Countess. That the influence of the nobility should achieve
more than the entreaty of a brother poet must surely have stirred
the pious mind of Quarles to a series of rather melancholy reflections.

In "Quarlëis" Benlowes was in a positively fanatical mood. He
held Quarles to be the most renowned poet of his age, and he himself seemed to glow with the reflected glory of his association with
him. They were both men of Essex, and the very county that they
came from had to be praised for being so well stocked with the
good things of the earth. But even judged by the standard of the times, [3]

[1] Historical MSS. Commission, 4th Report, p. 369.
[2] G. S. Haight (*The Library*, 4th series, XV, 100), showing that a daughter
of Quarles was said to be of Catford in 1636, suggests that Quarles was at Catford
because it was near the royal palace of Greenwich and that he was occupied
therefore with some court duties. Does this seem a little thin?
[3] Literal sincerity was not expected of a panegyric. Milton in 1638 at Rome

his flattery became ridiculous when he held Quarles to excel Virgil, Horace, Martial, and Ovid together. He adjured Fame to commend Quarles to posterity beyond all others. His critical judgment, unfortunately, was always at the mercy of his feelings, which here had unrestrained expression. But at the core of his enthusiasm there was undoubtedly a genuine admiration for Quarles's work. In a volume of such uniform excellence, he found it hard to single out anything for special praise. So the problem was solved by eulogizing everything. The greatness of the theme was matched by the art of the poet, and the poet's skill in verse by the goodness of his life. Perhaps the most significant item was his praise of Quarles's curious wit.

Benlowes' exuberance could equally be expressed in contempt. He made a very savage attack on some odious man—perhaps rather fortunately nameless—a brainless, loose-living creature who had been harsh to Quarles and generous to another whom Benlowes despised. Quarles could hardly have found a more energetic champion. Benlowes not only tried to storm the Court and the City, but he also sought to sway the reading public by evoking the sort of aura which he thought the name of Quarles on any title-page must certainly create. And, as has been seen, Quarles had, like Fletcher, the grace to dedicate his book to Benlowes, his best if not his wisest friend, and perhaps the most generous of all his patrons.

The friendship between Quarles and Benlowes continued. When three years later Quarles brought out his *Hieroglyphikes of the Life of Man*, continuing the fashion of the *Emblemes* in what was almost a sixth book appended to the principal work, again with engravings by Marshall, Benlowes felt that the banquet offered to the reader was enhanced by the wisdom that went with it. His name was again associated with Quarles's book, for at the end of Quarles's address to the reader came a Latin epigram of his. This was not, however, a new one. According to Benlowes' habit when he was pleased with phrases he had fashioned, he here repeated from the address to Charles I which had been prefixed to "Quarlëis" the following ingenious word-puzzle:

> Rem, Regem, Regimen, Regionem, Relligionem,
> Exornat, celebrat, laudat, honorat, amat. [1]

---

received the tribute of an epigram which made him the equal of Homer and Virgil together. A second epigram threw in Tasso as well (Masson, *Life of Milton*, I, 753-754).

[1] It is odd, in view of their friendship and Benlowes' known munificence, that Quarles did not apply to him when short of money in 1640 but raised a loan through his bookseller and got himself entangled over it (see *The Library*, 4th series, XV, 101ff.).

CHAPTER EIGHT

MAN OF PROPERTY

The county of Essex, in which both Benlowes and Quarles lived, was one of the most flourishing in England at that time. It was excellent corn-growing country, and there was plenty of good pasture for the rearing of sheep and cattle. Essex calves especially were famous as "the *fattest, fairest,* and *finest flesh* in England." [1] In Benlowes' neighbourhood a number of small towns were engaged in cloth-making, which meant an unruly mob now and then when trade was bad and many workers were unemployed. But on the whole an active and relatively populous commercial community meant good markets for the produce of the farms round about. Local distress among the poorer cloth-workers did not prevent an English gentleman during the 1630's from thinking of his country as enjoying "the greatest calm and the fullest measure of felicity that any people in any age for so long time together have been blessed with; to the wonder and envy of all the parts of Christendom." [2] The Privy Council might find it necessary to appoint numerous commissions to inquire into the wages of spinners and weavers; but the poor, it was felt, were always with us, and the prosperity of the landowning classes was not seriously affected by the difficulties of textiles.

Edward Benlowes' total income was estimated at one thousand and fifty pounds a year. [3] Such wealth inevitably entailed numerous responsibilities, for the life of a man of property in the seventeenth century was a complicated existence. One regrets on Benlowes' behalf that it was not possible for the country gentleman to add to his mild education in the law the training of a professional accountant. The habit of his ancestors, and especially of his great-grand-father, Serjeant William Benlowes, of making charitable benefactions

[1] Fuller, *Worthies*, ed. Nichols, I, 340.
[2] Clarendon, *History of the Rebellion*, ed. Macray, I, 93.
[3] In a survey of his estate made in 1655 (Essex County Record Office, D/DAc 110).

meant that the property came to Edward heavily encumbered, since every benefaction was tied to some specified piece of land and had to be maintained by the land's successive owners. Without special reference to Serjeant William's will, one did not know exactly what all the charities were that had to be kept up. But this did not unduly worry Edward. When one's domain is large, one cannot know everything that goes on in it. He took it all for granted and did the best he could in a somewhat easy-going and muddled administration.

That does not mean that he took his obligations other than seriously. Before he left England in 1627 to confront the risk of travel abroad, he had a new deed drawn up to confirm his great-grandfather's gifts to the village of Finchingfield and "creatinge newe feoffees all the old ones beinge dead." The alms promised in this deed included "2 lodes of wood yearely twenty fower Red herringe and twenty fower white herrings yearly in Lent tyme." [1] Perhaps only Finchingfield recorded this in a "town book," but it seems likely that other villages had new pledges too.

For as long as Edward Benlowes was a landed gentleman he was responsible for the upkeep of innumerable alms-houses in all the neighbouring villages and for regular gifts to the poor of petty sums of money as well as firewood and food. The minute-book of Finchingfield town meetings enables us now and then to trace him fulfilling his obligations in his home village. The accounts of the churchwardens for the two years 1638-1639 show "40ˢ wch they recᵈ of Mʳ Bendlowes," while a further item of £3. 10s. was made up of "receits from Mʳ Bendlowes Mʳ Lumley & Edward Chote." The same three names were again listed in 1640 as contributors towards the "repayringe of the church," and from Benlowes there was "20ˢ more" to come for distribution amongst the poor. [2]

Charities of this kind cost Edward altogether twenty-one pounds a year. [3] He ought to have kept up the school in Great Bardfield and paid the schoolmaster his salary, but it was difficult to find a man with suitable qualifications who would carry out the schoolmaster's duties for ten pounds a year; for the seventeenth century had its own cost-of-living troubles and prices had risen since Serjeant Benlowes fixed the master's income. So eventually it became impossible to keep the school going.

[1] Finchingfield "Town Book," p. 71.
[2] Ibid., pp. 48-49.
[3] Serjeant Benlowes' will, P.C.C., Brudenell 10. Essex County Record Office, D/DAc 110.

The school was a duty that lapsed; but there was always the church in Great Bardfield village, as well as the chapel at Bardfield Saling, which Edward's great-grandfather had endowed. Edward Benlowes inherited the obligation to keep the parsonage of Great Bardfield in good repair. When he finally sold his estates in 1657, the sum of five pounds for a new parsonage barn was one of the deductions that he had to allow the purchaser. [1] For over forty years he paid the rector of Great Bardfield eight pounds a year and the priest of Bardfield Saling three pounds. It was both his duty and his privilege to select a clergyman for the Great Bardfield living, and though events conspired with long-lived incumbents to give him few opportunities to do this, he was concerned with the nomination of a rector even when in the middle of selling his estates for ever. When Great Bardfield church was in need of repair, it was to the head of the Benlowes family that the parishioners looked. In 1618, while Edward was still a boy, the chancel roof had been restored and embellished in his name, just as in 1635 the chancel of Finchingfield church was re-roofed by Robert Kempe, the patron of the living there. According to the Jacobean love of surface decoration, Edward Benlowes' roof at Great Bardfield had the two tie-beams painted and carved, in a somewhat gaudy style, with circles and crosses and a crown of thorns. These still provide their witness to the taste in which the boy was trained. On the corbels of one beam are his initials, the family crest of a centaur with bow and arrow, and the Benlowes motto, "Tende solve." This display of family pomp was a natural part of the pride with which the family fulfilled its proper obligations to God and the community. Even when a Benlowes refrained from worshipping in his parish church, he thought it right for him to care for the fabric and ornament the building. Edward had been accustomed to maintain the state religion in Great Bardfield long before it became his own.

All these responsibilities were an accepted part of the life of a gracious English squire, who took pride in the virtuous well-being of his poorer neighbours. With a man of Benlowes' pious character, the philanthropic habits bred in him were strongly reinforced by his sense of Christian duty, as repeated allusions in his poem *Theophila* make clear. A man was but the steward of God, and he should look upon his poor or homeless neighbours as his co-heirs in Christ. The difference between rich and poor was a natural part of the order

[1] Chancery Proceedings, Collins 140/147.

of things, but all shared in the love of Heaven and it was the divine will that the more fortunate should provide succour for those who lay "gasping in stiff'ning *Frosts*" with "no Cov'ring but the Skie" and those whose "wither'd *Skins*" stuck to their bones "for want of *food*." [1] This description aims rather at achieving poetic effect than at recording exact observation, but Benlowes cannot have been unfamiliar with the spectacle of rural poverty. In 1631, when falling trade was aggravated by famine, many of the Essex cloth-workers were "constrained to sell their beds, wheels and working tools for want of bread," and the Justices of the county put the number in distress at over thirty thousand. [2] Benlowes always spoke with great pity for the destitute and with fierce anger against those misers who, as he said in a characteristic phrase, were flintier to them than the street which was their bed. [3] Dives he held to have been very properly sent to Hell. Indeed he felt only satisfaction in thinking that the excesses of Dives' life hastened his death and with it the day of audit. [4] He loathed drunkards and gluttons and all who lived in luxury, because they squandered what others were in need of. His toper is scarce recovered from a bout of sickness before he is swilling again, while the starving have only their tears to moisten what crumbs they might be able to beg. [5] Echoing the poet Randolph, he had a word for those landlords who wasted what their tenants' sweat provided; [6] their own indulgence spread poverty around them, yet they protested loudly when the poor rate went up, making that an excuse for grinding down the poor still more. [7] He was angry at the enclosures by which the wealthy landowners appropriated the people's common-land, like spiders squeezing small flies, to use his own comparison. [8] Benlowes was never more savage than in denouncing rural oppressors.

He himself, sometimes at least, practised what he preached. Accustomed to wealth, he was accustomed also to giving it generously.

[1] *Theophila*, viii, 63-64 (references to *Theophila* are always to canto and *stanza*, not to lines).

[2] Bland, Brown, and Tawney, *English Economic History—Select Documents*, p. 358; Lipson, *Economic History of England*, III, 311.

[3] *Theophila*, x, 83.

[4] *The Summary of Wisedome*, stanza 49.

[5] *Ibid.*, stanza 48.

[6] *Theophila*, xi, 19; *cf.* Randolph, "On the Inestimable Content he Injoyes in the Muses," line 66.

[7] *Theophila*, xi, 20.

[8] *Ibid.*, i, 38.

His man, Schoren, even granting his versatility, was handsomely paid. His twenty marks a year (£13.6s.8d.) seem trifling out of Benlowes' own income; but four or five pounds was a normal wage for a bailiff or upper servant in the 1630's, [1] and Schoren's was a lordly existence compared with that of the workers in the villages round. In 1651, when wages were rapidly going up, the Essex magistrates fixed rates of pay which would enable the ordinary farm labourer to earn up to £18 a year and the artisan a little over £20; but the food for an artisan's family would cost over £16, and it would take him forty-three weeks out of the fifty-two to earn it, [2] whereas Schoren's income, guaranteed by a deed of annuity, was in addition to board and lodging. It will be relevant to remember Benlowes' lavishness to his servant when one finds disputes breaking out between them.

Benlowes' large-mindedness about money was also shown in that several of his farms were leased to tenants at rentals lower than a lawyer's estimate of their value. A man called John Harvey had a small farm which was worth about £7 a year leased to him for life at the nominal rent of 1s. a year and a few fowls. A blacksmith's forge in Finchingfield, with house adjoining, was valued at £4 a year but leased for only £2. [3] It was only when he got heavily into debt himself that Benlowes troubled to raise rents that he knew to be inadequate. [4]

As for collecting the rents, irksome business as it was, it mainly fell to Schoren, and we shall find that Benlowes lost something in the process. With equal indifference he saw the charges upon his estates accumulate. He had a fine faith in the power of a large landed estate to support every call that the individual, the family, or the community might make upon it. Schoren's wages could be secured to him by an annuity charged upon the Great Bardfield property.

[1] For one or two tables, see Campbell, *The English Yeoman*, p. 398. In 1659, after prices and wages had risen considerably, Sir John Reresby was still paying his bailiff ten pounds a year (*Memoirs*, p. 26).
[2] These estimates are taken from Thorold Rogers (*Six Centuries of Work and Wages*, pp. 392-393), the only authoritative economic historian I can find to give anything like precise information on this interesting point. But for wages, consult also Lipson, *Economic History*, II, 387-388; III, 248ff. Tradesmen like carpenters, masons, and bricklayers got about £18 a year up to the time of the Civil War and as much as £23 after.
[3] Apparently, for what purpose I know not, to Stephen Marshall, the vicar, and afterwards to his son-in-law Wale. (Chancery Proceedings, Collins 140/147 answer).
[4] Chancery Proceedings, Bridges 444/123.

A certain Mrs. Pate, whoever she was, was guaranteed £14 a year for life. [1] There were a few new minor charities. And there were also the numerous provisions that Benlowes, as the head of the family, had to make for many of the others.

Formerly Brent Hall had been populous with the Benlowes clan. When Edward had become lord of the Benlowes manors he was head of a household which included his grandmother, his mother, four brothers, and at least two sisters. For many years Francis Benlowes, his father's brother, also lived in Finchingfield with his wife and children, of whom there were altogether not less than eight. [2] They too are spoken of as being at Brent Hall. [3] So, even though *all* may not have been there, or even in existence, simultaneously, the family mansion must at one time have housed considerably more than a dozen of the Benlowes family, apart from servants. But Francis had considerable property of his own in Finchingfield [4] and he was not dependent upon Edward's bounty.

Almost from the time Edward came back from his travels and finally settled as a landed gentleman at Brent Hall, with Schoren as his bailiff and confidential servant, he had made up his mind that he would never marry. This was a very unusual decision for a seventeenth-century gentleman. More usually parents arranged eligible matches for their sons at quite an early age. Perhaps Edward escaped through his father's early death; but more probably an appropriate marriage was in store for him when plans were frustrated by the lady's death. A curious parenthesis in *Theophila* points to a lover's bereavement, which may or may not have caused him serious grief:

> T'have been affected by a *Virgin Heir*,
>   Rich, young, and chast, wise, good, and fair,
> Was once his first Delight, but HEAV'N restrain'd that Care!
>
> Thou, *Providence*, di[d]st both their Wills restrain;
>   Thou mad'st their Losses turn to Gain;
> For Thou gav'st *Heav'n* to *her*, on *him* dost *Blessings* rain!
>   (xiii, 28-29).

---

[1] Chancery Proceedings, Collins 140/147 (answer).

[2] Apart from John and Clare, for whom see above, pp. 21-22, there were, according to Francis' will (P.C.C., Fines 81), a son Richard and daughters Alice, Elizabeth, Mary, and Anna. Finchingfield parish register records also Frances. I ignore an unnamed daughter buried in infancy.

[3] S. P., Dom., Interregnum, G158/315.

[4] See, for example, an assessment for ship-money, S.P., Dom., Chas. I, vol. 358. Later on, from about 1641, one finds Francis settled at Norwich (S.P., Dom., Interregnum, G95/437), where (as the probate of his will shows) he died in 1647.

Whether such a bereavement was responsible for fixing Edward's thoughts so firmly upon Heaven, certain it is that he was wedded to piety and sought no other marriage. He prayed to be only "ambitious" of God and to have strength to prize him above the love of women. [1] It was Theophila, the soul, the lover of God, that henceforth he adored.

For a man in Benlowes' position, this decision to remain unmarried was a very serious thing. And making it, he had to take what steps he could to ensure that the family estates should not pass from the Benlowes name and blood. He could look to William, the eldest of his brothers, as his heir, and accordingly he made a settlement upon him. William married and Edward provided the jointure for his wife. [2] There was soon a daughter, but in August 1633 William died [3] without having produced a son. His interest in the property therefore reverted to Edward. William's widow Elizabeth went to live in London, but her jointure of £66.13s. 4d. a year came regularly from the Benlowes estates. [4]

Edward's two youngest brothers, Andrew and Philip, were also dead by this time, and his sister Clare long married to "a farre Countrey gentleman." [5] For his surviving brother, Henry, he made modest provision, granting him forty pounds a year out of his estates. [6] In February 1635 a business transaction took place between them, when Henry bought for five hundred pounds a wood called Oldfrith (or Holdfrith) Wood in the parishes of Great Bardfield and Thaxted. [7] Subsequently Henry also died, apparently unmarried, and this property came back to Edward. By that time his mother was living in London on what Edward's liberality allowed her, and with the large family one by one removed by death or circumstance, Edward was left the only Benlowes still living at Brent Hall.

A confirmed celibate, he had at length to resign himself to being without an heir. He was to be the last to bear the family name. The

[1] *Theophila*, The Author's Prayer.

[2] It seems possible that the recognizances of May 5, 1630, and May 4, 1632, have to do with this. See above, p. 54, and see Recognizance Entry Books L.C. 4/200, fol. 470 and L.C. 4/201, fol. 119.

[3] See his will at Somerset House, Russell 111.

[4] Chancery Proceedings, Collins 140/147. Only one third went to Elizabeth, the rest to the state because she was a recusant.

[5] S.P., Dom., Interregnum, G95/432.

[6] Chancery Proceedings, Collins 140/147.

[7] Close Rolls, 11 Chas. I, pt. 1, no. 17.

only descendant of all his brothers was William's child, Philippa. She was looked on by Edward as his special responsibility, and it was she who was to enjoy the biggest gift of his unfailing generosity and receive at his hands all that was left of the Benlowes' wealth.

The deaths of all his brothers certainly did not absolve Benlowes from family duties. With all his repugnance to financial dealings, he could not hope to keep free of them. Some years later, in 1646, he had to act as trustee on behalf of his second cousin, William Nevill of Cressing Temple, [1] and in 1649 he was drawn into the affairs of his sister's family. The "farre Countrey gentleman" she had married was, in fact, Thomas Peirce, of Alveston in Warwickshire, and he had now died. The eldest son, another Thomas Peirce, inherited, but had to make dispositions for his brothers and sisters. So he granted to them certain lands in Alveston as a security for their patrimony, and poor Edward Benlowes, his respected uncle, who found his own estates something of a burden, was again called upon to carry out the duties of trustee in connection with other people's property. [2]

Trusts, deeds, indentures, all the paraphernalia of legal settlements —these were the insignia of the duties that the status of landed gentleman entailed. It is so easy to get a picture of spacious and untroubled affluence that I have thought it just to stress these things a little here. And it would be a pity to close this chapter without a reference to one of the most interesting charges which Benlowes allowed to be imposed upon his estates.

It bears witness to his interest in educational projects, and it arose from the assistance he gave to Mrs. Ellen Goulston in establishing an annual lectureship in anatomy at the Royal College of Physicians. Dr. Theodore Goulston had in 1632 bequeathed two hundred pounds to the College of Physicians, which they were to lay out in the purchase of some land to provide an annual income for the payment of a lecturer. The lecturer was to be one of the four youngest doctors of the college, and he was to treat of two or more diseases and to illustrate his discourse by the dissection of a dead body, if by any possible means such a body could be procured. His lecturing was to occupy the morning and afternoon of three successive days sometime between Michaelmas and Easter. Like so many testamentary endowments, this bequest was easier to make than

[1] Close Rolls, 22 Chas. I, pt. 8, no. 41.
[2] Close Rolls, 1649, pt. 46, no. 23.

execute, and the doctor's widow found herself in considerable difficulty. She repeatedly offered to put down the necessary two hundred pounds if the College of Physicians would find a suitable piece of land. Their endeavours to do so came to nothing, and they then asked the widow herself to buy lands or a rent-charge. The doctor had been dead just over three years when the matter was finally settled by Benlowes coming to Mrs. Goulston's aid. This he did the more gladly for having seen the great respect paid to anatomical studies at such universities as Padua and Leyden, where some lectures of the sort that Goulston desired were possibly among those that he attended. And he cannot have been uninfluenced by the general esteem in which anatomy was held among both the cultured and the pious—Lord Herbert commended the study of it among gentlemen and thought no one who considered it could ever be an atheist. [1] Mrs. Goulston paid Benlowes the two hundred pounds of the bequest, and in return he granted her twelve pounds per annum to be paid out of his manor of Fennes_in the parish of Bocking. Indentures to that effect were signed on June 30, 1635. It only remained for Mrs. Goulston to make over her interest to the president of the college for the lectureship to be established; and this she immediately did. [2] Thus was the man of property able to advance the course of learning, to add a small service to medicine to what he had already done for poetry. And an interesting link was established between Benlowes and a poet of the next century, for the lectures on the Goulston Foundation were given in 1755 by Akenside, who had become a Fellow of the College of Physicians the year before.

[1] *Autobiography*, p. 31.
[2] *Catalogue of the Legal and Other Documents in the Archives of the Royal College of Physicians*, pp. 82, 247ff.

CHAPTER NINE

OCCUPATIONS OF A GENTLEMAN

However much he valued quiet and retirement, a man who owned a large slice of the English countryside could not be a recluse. Nor, indeed, in the opinion of the pious George Herbert, should he try to be. He should exert himself in "the improvement of his grounds, by drowning, or draining, or stocking, or fencing, and ordering his land to the best advantage both of himself, and his neighbours." And he should take his part in managing village affairs for the public good. [1] This was certainly the manner of the Benlowes tradition. In Edward's younger days his uncle Francis had not disdained to take office in the village: in 1624 he was overseer of the poor and in 1628 surveyor of the highways. [2] On the second occasion the "Town Book" simply records the appointment of "Mr. Bendlowes," and this has wrongly been taken for Edward, [3] who in 1628 was abroad. But with Edward's return home, as he gathered the reins into his own hands, probably he soon supplanted Francis as the "Mr. Bendlowes" referred to in the townspeople's appointments. It may have been he who acted as surveyor four times between 1634 and 1641; it was certainly he in 1650. [4] Neither his interest in the production of Quarles's *Emblemes* nor the composition of his own sacred poem *Theophila* kept him aloof from Finchingfield roads and bridges. Of course the surveyor's duties were hardly onerous: as his horse carried him about the parish, he would easily notice if a bridge was falling down and give an eye to the state of the roads. This was the office in village affairs that the gentry mostly took. They lent prestige and showed goodwill with not too great an effort. But more important, they were the people who could put things right without troubling rates or village meetings. Sir Robert Kempe or Edward Benlowes could easily provide timber

[1] From *The Countrey Parson. Works*, ed. Hutchinson, pp. 275-276.
[2] "Town Book," pp. 27, 33.
[3] Vaughan, *Stephen Marshall*, p. 75.
[4] "Town Book," pp. 41, 42, 45, 50, 60.

and a man to repair a bridge; their labourers could be sent to scatter stones or gravel on a bad patch of road.

These figureheads among the local folk were not among the most zealous in attending parish meetings. Too much concern with village affairs might not have become their station: their lives had a larger circumference. But they were pleased to put in an appearance now and then, to lend their ear to constables' reports and their signature to the year's accounts. On these occasions Sir Robert Kempe, as lord of the manor, invariably signed first. Edward Benlowes' signature, if he were present, tended to come next. He joined in threatening the law upon the inhabitants of some new cottages for unstated nuisances, and in deciding what was to be done about five Bocking labourers whom Finchingfield was to find employment for by order of the Justices of the Peace. [1]

George Herbert's ideal English gentleman, untiring in public service, would seek to be a Justice of the Peace himself. [2] But lists of Justices show that appointments to such offices went very much by tradition and tended to become the preserve of certain families. A Catholic family could not be one of them, [3] and Edward Benlowes, though he broke from the family religion, did not break into the ring where his Protestant kinsmen, the Nevills of Cressing Temple, quite naturally had their place. [4] But a Justice of the Peace was not everything. Indeed he might be merely a rustic landowner, and Edward Benlowes was much more. Wealthy, elegant, accomplished, it was only to be expected that in his early manhood, when he reigned at Brent Hall in the years before the Civil War, he would cut quite a graceful figure in his county. And this was not, of course, for a man of varied parts, in any way inconsistent with scholarly and artistic pursuits or with a devout habit of life.

One of his accomplishments was horsemanship, and a fine horseman was in the seventeenth century immensely admired. Horsemanship, like the science of fortification, was of the greatest importance in war; and war was an affair for gentlemen. Peacham, for example, whose manual *The Compleat Gentleman* was widely read and much thought of in the decades before the Civil War, put riding first among the exercises of a gentleman; for by it "you are ennabled

---

[1] "Town Book," pp. 53, 58, 62, 63.

[2] *Works*, pp. 276-277.

[3] Recusants themselves were debarred by statute, and there was pronounced official reluctance to appointing Protestants who had recusants in their family.

[4] Historical MSS. Commission, 10th Report, Appendix, part 4, pp. 502-510.

for command, and the service of your Countrey." [1] It was the ideal, even of a moralist, that all gentlemen should "know the use of their Arms: and as the Husbandman labours for them, so must they fight for, and defend them, when occasion calls." The words are George Herbert's, and he, though a cleric and not expected to do this himself, thought it proper for a gentleman every morning to "ride the Great Horse, or exercise some of his Military gestures." [2] Herbert's brother Edward did, in fact, spend his time after returning from France partly in study and partly in "riding the great horse," keeping a well-furnished stable for the purpose. He too put this first among all the "exercises" of a gentleman. [3] The "great horse" was one used exclusively for war and martial exploits. It was an animal of size and power to support the weight of armour it had to carry, and it had to be proficient in all the recognized leaps and "turns" and "manages." Hence there was a special technique for training and handling it, [4] which needed a good deal of practice. The best performers learned their skill on the Continent; and Benlowes, who had done the gentleman's round of European training, acquired some celebrity for his prowess. As a skilled performer, he was not merely an ornament, but a prop of his society, and was made captain of a troop of horse in the Essex militia.

The militia was a citizen army raised by the various counties. Essex at this time contributed four thousand foot soldiers as well as fifty heavy and two hundred light horse, divided into two troops. The captains were nominated by the Lord Lieutenant of the county and were expected to be prominent men of means resident in the area from which the company was drawn. It was an appointment thought fitting for the best knights and gentlemen in the county, and a command of horse carried greater prestige than one of foot. [5] Finchingfield was proud of "Captayne Bendlowes," as the villagers liked to call him, with a touch of that snobbery which is almost universal. [6]

[1] Clarendon Press reprint, p. 213. *Cf.* Cleland, *Institution of a Young Nobleman,* pp. 217-218.
[2] *Works,* p. 277.
[3] *Autobiography,* pp. 37-42.
[4] Described by Lord Herbert (*ibid.*, p. 39), and in detail in various treatises by Gervase Markham, especially *Countrey Contentments,* I, ch. 2. For Markham "there can be no g[r]eater or better recreation either for health, profit, or renowning of their owne vertues, then the riding of great *Horses,* which in the verie action it selfe speaketh Gentleman to all that are performers or doers of the same."
[5] *Essex Review,* XVII, 103-105.
[6] Finchingfield "Town Book," p. 49.

Benlowes, too, was vain enough to boast of his captaincy, and was much admired by his friends for his military and equestrian exploits. When he wrote a poem to append to a panegyric written by John Sictor to celebrate the inauguration of Richard Fenn as Lord Mayor of London in 1637 and it therefore seemed appropriate for him to boast his own official status, he took pleasure in signing himself "Edvardus Benlowes *Armiger, Turmæ Equestris in Comitatu Essexiæ Præfectus.*" In the previous year, when his own volume, *Sphinx Theologica*, was published, one of the commendatory poems addressed him in similar terms as captain of a troop of horse in Essex. The writer of the verses felt this to be a special distinction, praised Benlowes for his ability to control fierce horses, and applauded him for his combination of military and poetic achievement. This was not, in the reign of Charles I, at all the paradox that, from such flattery, might be inferred. Yet Benlowes did indeed seek to link poetry and arms more intimately than most. His fantastical nature, which always revelled in anagrams, chronograms, emblems, and all sorts of verbal devices, together with the old-fashioned habit of allegory which sought a pious text in everything, led him to work out parallels between the items of his harness and an array of moral virtues. For this pretty absurdity he was especially mocked at by Samuel Butler, who wrote of him:

When he was a Captain, he made all the Furniture of his Horse, from the Bit to the Crupper, in beaten Poetry, every Verse being fitted to the Proportion of the Thing, with a moral Allusion of the Sense to the Thing; as the *Bridle of Moderation, the Saddle of Content*, and *the Crupper of Constancy*; so that the same Thing was both Epigram and Emblem, even as a Mule is both Horse and Ass. [1]

Most of the English gentry were on horseback every day. They spent their time in the national sport of hunting, the "most healthful" of exercises in Peacham's view. [2] Many country families did very little else. The Guises of Gloucestershire perhaps were typical. Their young heir Christopher, when he had been through Oxford and the Middle Temple, was left to his own devices with no example from his father but that of "a country gentleman and a good huntsman." The two things were apparently more or less synonymous. The young man grumbled that hunting "must be follow'd like a trade." [3] In a way that was its advantage, for so many of the country

[1] *Characters*, ed. Waller, p. 53.
[2] *Compleat Gentleman*, p. 218. *Cf.* Cleland, *Institution of a Young Nobleman*, pp. 222-223.
[3] *Memoirs of the Family of Guise*, pp. 118, 120.

squires, brought up, as Peacham complained, to know nothing beyond pride in their birth and large estates, had no other resource. Beyond hunting, this sort of family could only play cards on rainy days and move backwards and forwards from one country-house to another, growing fretful and bad-tempered, scraping round for money—borrowing it or selling land—trying to effect advantageous marriages for their often too numerous children. The Civil War, when it came, gave them almost a *raison d'être*. Hitherto, to sum up in the words of a modern historian, they had "recognised no other function in life save the daily hunt, followed by the nightly carouse at the ale-house whither they repaired after dinner with the ladies of the family; a scheme varied by little else than the statutory church service on Sunday." [1] Even the church service often meant little enough, for the gentry would "somtimes make it a piece of state not to come at the beginning of service with their poor neighbours, but at mid-prayers, both to their own loss, and of theirs also who gaze upon them when they come in." [2]

Benlowes was too reverent a worshipper to have behaved like this. Much as he loved to nurse his prestige, it was not his way to seek such petty distinction. The renown he sought was to be gained by one's own efforts through a range of courtly accomplishments, by showing the bounty of an appointed lord to his less fortunate subjects, by genuine piety, and by that further desideratum of the gentleman, "the knowledge of good Learning." [3] Although the hunting squire was well represented in his part of the country, Benlowes had little in common with him. He was capable of twitting a neighbouring gentleman for devoting all his energies to the frivolities of the chase: when he gave Sir Martin Lumley a copy of his long divine poem, he regretted that he could expect nothing better than a stag in return. [4] In the poem itself he made a savage attack upon Sir Martin's like. It was the hunting gentry that he

---

[1] Trevelyan, *England under the Stuarts*, p. 8.
[2] Herbert, *Works*, p. 232.
[3] Peacham, *Compleat Gentleman*, Epistle Dedicatory.
[4] Inscribing a copy of *Theophila* to Sir Martin Lumley, he wrote half-seriously:

> Mitto Equiti Servum, Cervumq[ue] remitte Poëtae;
> Munus ita alterius Muneri esca venit.
> Sit Mens larga Tibi, fuge ludicra: Judice Coelo,
> Nobilius Cervi Munere Munus habes.

A variant form of this "epigramma serio-jocosum" appears in the Dyce copy inscription (see below, p. 232 n.).

accused of enclosing the lands of the poor. Nimrod—"a mighty hunter," we remember—stands for them all in the stanza:

> When *Nimrods* Vulture-Talons par'd shall be,
> Their Houses *Name* soon chang'd you'l see;
> For their *Bethsaida* shall be turn'd to *Bethanie*. [1]

The last line is still threatening the hunter in Benlowes' typically cryptic style. But lest this should be too enigmatic for some of his readers, he added in some copies—I have seen it in two—a marginal note in ink explaining Bethsaida as the house of hunting and Bethany as the house of mourning. Benlowes' nature was more satisfied with the quieter and more peaceful country pursuits, in which the country-side was not molested and in which the fatigue of the body did not hamper the meditation of the mind. The only sport he spoke of in his poetry was fishing. It was a recreation that Peacham commended for the "honest and patient" man, [2] and it hardly needs enthusiasts like Gervase Markham and Isaak Walton to let us know the esteem in which the seventeenth century held it. Benlowes could think affectionately of the brook running through the valley, the "bright-scal'd gliding *Fish*," and the angler's "trembling Line." [3] Sometimes he went round the village calling on tenants and acquaintances with his devoted spaniel in attendance. [4] On such occasions he would watch the mower and the shepherd, the sheep with their lambs or the cattle at the plough. [5]

These delights meant just about as much to him—or as little—as the similar country scenes described in "L'Allegro" meant to Milton, whose rural description Benlowes was to imitate closely. For Benlowes too, in his different way, was a man of the study rather than the fields. If in their "sloath and idlenes" [6] many of the gentry seemed to George Herbert to have gone to grass like sheep, while their sons spent their days "in dressing, Complementing, visiting, and sporting," [7] Herbert himself admitted to exceptions; and at no other period in English history has the ideal of the gentleman, for the elect who strove to achieve it, embraced so much of

---

[1] *Theophila*, i, 39. I adopt Benlowes' pen-and-ink correction "*Bethsaida*" for the printed "*Bethesda*." See Appendix III.

[2] *Compleat Gentleman*, p. 257.

[3] *Theophila*, xiii, 3-4.

[4] Letter of Clement Paman to Edward Benlowes, Bodleian MS. Rawl. D. 945.

[5] *Theophila*, xiii, 2, 5, 9-10.

[6] Peacham, *Compleat Gentleman*, p. 16.

[7] "The Church-Porch," stanza 16; *The Countrey Parson* (*Works*, p. 277).

scholarship and culture. Intensely serious-minded aristocrats combined elegance with sobriety, industry with leisure. Not a few could have agreed with the Earl of Derby, who preferred retirement in the country to the amusements of the court, that they were never less idle than when they took their ease. [1]

Benlowes shared this preference for a life of quiet activity, and in the life that he led at Brent Hall he came much nearer than most of his contemporaries to their conception of what a gentleman should be. This ideal, attained by few and not approached by many, was "to be equally versed in the arts of war and of peace, to enjoy sports, to be skilled in music, to know literature, to speak several languages, to be a courtier but withal civil to all classes of men, to have been to Oxford or Cambridge, and to have travelled." [2] The man whom Aubrey called "a gentleman absolute in all numbers" was Sir James Long, who, having been educated at Westminster and Oxford, was a colonel of horse in the Civil Wars. He was a good horseman and swordsman and a "great falkoner"; but he was also a "great historian and romanceer," with a notable memory, and an "admirable extempore orator pro harangue." He was a great man "for insects" and "exceeding curious....in naturall things." [3] Benlowes perhaps did not altogether share this exceeding curiosity, but he admitted its propriety. In his ideal life, as described in *Theophila*, he found time to watch and marvel at ants, moths, gnats, and bees. [4]

In the gentlemanly combination of physical and mental prowess, Benlowes undoubtedly laid the greater emphasis on the attainments of the mind. And with his studious disposition he did not affect the "apparently effortless and rather disdainful grace and ease" [5] that the true Cavalier pretended to in his accomplishments. Yet a seriousness of mind was in no way inconsistent with an elegant way of living and a gallant show before the world. A solemnity of outlook upon life was natural and commendable. A long series of family bereavements and other reminders of the proximity of death visited most men in those times and made it seemly to give thought to one's soul and its eternity.

[1] *Stanley Papers* (Chetham Soc.), pt. 3, I, xxii.
[2] Davies, *The Early Stuarts*, p. 267. See also Lovelace, *Poems*, ed. Wilkinson, I, lxi-lxii. *Cf.* Mrs. Lucy Hutchinson's character of her husband (*Memoirs of Colonel Hutchinson*, ed. Firth, pp. 20ff.) and Clarendon's portrait of Falkland (*History of the Rebellion*, ed. Macray, III, 179ff.).
[3] *Brief Lives*, II, 36-37.
[4] xii, 72ff.
[5] To adopt Wilkinson's translation of the Italian *sprezzatura*.

Benlowes saw his own family gradually dwindle, and this intensified his devotional cast of mind. It also meant that he became more and more isolated at Brent Hall. It was not that he sought solitude: the circumstances of time and place forced him, in pursuing his ideal, into a position of aloofness. The cultivated classes were not congregated in a central metropolis, but widely scattered in large houses through a sparsely populated countryside. A seventeenth-century gentleman might be "civil to all classes of men," but decorum forbade him to mix too freely with his inferiors in rank, and most of what society was left to him might well, as has been seen, be uncongenial. Well known as Benlowes was among the Essex gentry, his real friends were mostly at a distance. Communication with them was principally by letter and at longish intervals. He was on good terms with Sir Robert Kempe, [1] who lived in Finchingfield over at Spains Hall, and when Sir Robert's kinsman, Clement Paman, came to visit there, he found a man after his own heart. [2] Among the country occupations listed in *Theophila* is making "a Visit to a Grave *Divine*," [3] and of course Benlowes could easily enough ride over to Bocking, eight or nine miles away, when John Gauden, a college contemporary of his, was dean there, especially as he had estates in that parish to give an eye to now and then. But to visit his friend Quarles at Roxwell, some twenty miles away, would be practically a day's journey. No doubt he did it a few times in 1634 when the *Emblemes* were being prepared for publication, and sometimes Quarles must have been over at Brent Hall. I have referred to a local tradition that the *Emblemes* were actually composed there. Various other friends among the many who wrote poems to Benlowes or received poems from him would, I suppose, know the hospitality of his house. He liked to gather round him men of cultivated tastes, and some may have paid him extended visits. Occasionally he himself went on a visit to his cousins the Nevills at Cressing. He was there, for example, when he wrote his panegyric on Quarles's *Emblemes*, and again in January 1636. [4] Now and then he went up to London. But when all this has been said, visits of friends and absences from home were mainly interludes which hardly interrupted the easy monotony of his life.

---

[1] Letter of Clement Paman to Edward Benlowes, Bodleian MS. Rawl. D. 945.
[2] See below, pp. 156 ff.
[3] xiii, 4.
[4] See his complimentary poem on *The Soules Conflict* by Richard Sibbs.

The country gentleman who was more than a huntsman had need
to develop a good deal of self-reliance. Driven much upon his own
resources, he was obviously going to be happiest if he enjoyed
the advantages of a well-stocked mind. Segregation severely cir-
cumscribed the energies of any mind not of the first order. The
man of learning easily tended to pedantry, and a delight in elaborate
trifles was fostered. A great deal of the preciosity of many of the
minor figures of seventeenth-century literature was undoubtedly
due to this cause. With few outstanding experiences to stir his
creative impulse, Benlowes could spend long hours on frigid Latin
poems. He could perfect a beautiful ornate handwriting, toy with
acrostics and shaped verses, worry over the position of a comma,
and laboriously correct in pen-and-ink the punctuation and mis-
spellings of the printer of his poems. One is constantly amazed at
the littleness of the ends upon which so much effort was bestowed,
when perhaps one ought rather to admire the untiring resource
which made leisure a delight and not a burden, and which made for
the attainment of a highly civilized existence.

Benlowes spent much time in reading, and as the years went
by more and more time on his own composition. His literary activities were probably the centre of his life and must be described
in subsequent chapters. But a seventeenth-century gentleman, even
within doors, could not be a man of letters and nothing else. Benlowes,
who had seen the multitudinous statues and palaces of Italy, who
had come back from the Continent with *pietre commesse* in his baggage
and a printer in his service, was interested in all the visual arts.
And the times demanded of him some sign of manual dexterity as
well as mental ingenuity.

The pen, for example, was not simply a means to record the inventions of his brain. It was an artist's tool in itself. "Whatsoever
is done with the Pen or Pencill," Peacham decreed, was "a quality
most commendable, and so many wayes usefull to a Gentleman." [1]
The care for pretty writing which Benlowes had been taught in
his youth had now developed into a delight in elaborate flourishes
and fantastic arabesques. A few samples of his handwriting can be
seen in the exercise-book in which as a boy he had written his Latin
themes. [2] There were blank pages at the beginning, and these at
one time in his later life served Benlowes as a scrapbook for phrases,

[1] *Compleat Gentleman*, p. 124.
[2] Bodleian MS. Rawl. D. 278. See above, p. 25.

and—I suppose in an idle moment when he had the book open in front of him—for the exhibition of his most decorative handwriting. In boyhood he had been taught more than one mode of handwriting, and it was his habit still to write in two or three different styles, sometimes just capriciously, but sometimes deliberately choosing an ornate style to serve a particular purpose. A quick jotting down of an odd phrase might be in a careless and somewhat angular hand, but some of the inscriptions that he wrote in presentation copies of his books were quite beautiful, in the elaborate style of a period which raised penmanship to a place among the minor arts. A signature was often not just a signature but something to be wrought into a design occupying a whole page. A capital letter was not a mere orthographic convention but a golden opportunity. On one occasion Benlowes went through the last poem in the exercise-book drawing out the capitals at the beginnings of the lines to exaggerate their flourish. He also decorated the tails of a couple of p's. Probably at the same time he added two lines to the poem—again in a beautifully ornate italic of a skill obviously beyond the range of his boyhood. The two blank pages at the beginning of the book offered a positive invitation that did not fail of acceptance when the quill was in the hand. The first page was almost filled with exercises of the pen, exploiting in different styles of handwriting the Latin text, "Morere Mundo ut vivas Deo," as well as the writer's own name. The instinctive choice of a theme when the mind cast about for something to write showed quite a representative sentiment. The words that formed the motif for a design of the pen on the verso of the second leaf, however, are a little surprising. They are "Johannes Schoren," the name of the servant whom Benlowes had brought back with him from abroad and who was making himself invaluable to Benlowes in various ways at Brent Hall. The man may have been in the room at the moment when Benlowes wanted something, anything, to write; but even so, the choice of Schoren's name after his own, rather than that of a friend or relative, suggests a degree of attachment beyond the ordinary relation of master and man. This, I think, is supported by Benlowes' unnatural anxiety to convert his servant to his own religion and by the curious hold that Schoren had upon his master even after his trustworthiness as a servant was open to grave doubt.

Benlowes certainly depended on Schoren a great deal and found him exceedingly useful in helping with his artistic hobbies. A trained

printer was an extremely useful servant to a master who was passionately fond of all the arts of book-production. Benlowes bought
a rolling-press and had it installed at Brent Hall, and Schoren used
to work it. [1] The rolling-press, a large, upright wooden frame
supplied with a wheel and a couple of rollers which made prints
from engraved plates of brass or copper, was specially used in preparing illustrations for books. It would seem to have been a rare
piece of furniture in the house of an English gentleman, for, although the Ferrars had one at Little Gidding, John Evelyn read
a paper on the construction and use of the rolling-press to the Royal
Society in 1662 for the benefit of those who were "remote from
the places where this convenience is to be found." [2]

Engraving itself was a fairly expensive art either to practise or
encourage. Francis Quarles said that the copper-plates used for
illustrating his *Emblemes* and *Hieroglyphikes* originally cost over
a hundred and twenty pounds, [3] and Thomas Fuller in his *Worthies
of England* excused himself for not providing maps and illustrations
of coats-of-arms by referring to his "dear" experience of what cuts
cost. [4] This was an economy that Benlowes was most unlikely to
practise, and he gave commissions for engravings somewhat freely.
Once an engraving had been executed, the plate of course passed
out of the possession of the artist. Quarles, we know, owned the
plates for his *Emblemes*, and Benlowes presumably owned those
which he had had made for decorating *The Purple Island*. With
his rolling-press he could himself take from the plates such
copies as he wanted. This was also a costly process, "the working
them off at the *rowling presse* being," according to Fuller, "as expensive as the *graving* them."

It is not possible to tell whether Benlowes ever tried his own
hand at engraving, though I feel it would be surprising if he did
not. He must surely have designed plates, if he did not execute
them, and in so doing would again have won Peacham's full approval; for it was an admirable thing for a gentleman if he could
"furnish [his] conceipts & devices of *Emblems*, *Anagrams*, and the
like with bodies at [his] pleasure, without being beholden to some

---

[1] Chancery Proceedings, Reynardson 31/14 (answer).
[2] This paper was largely translated from a French work by Abraham Bosse.
It is printed, together with illustrations of the rolling-press, in C. F. Bell's edition
of Evelyn's *Sculptura*.
[3] *The Library*, 4th series, XV, 101.
[4] ed. Nichols, I, 73.

deare and nice professed Artist." [1] Benlowes certainly used to paint, and practised also the expensive and complicated art of gilding. [2] This again suggests the decoration of books, and again Schoren came in handy. Probably he imprinted Benlowes' arms in gilt on presentation volumes. Evidently Benlowes saw to it that his house was well enough equipped for the indulgent pursuit of all the arts and crafts he delighted in. And all this ultimately led up to the splendid production of the folio of *Theophila* when Benlowes' long poem was at length ready to be given to the world in 1652.

Benlowes was very fond of music—like the perfectly accomplished gentleman he was, for whatever one's knowledge of the other arts, without some skill in music claims to gentility were hardly possible. Benlowes would have learnt to play the viol at Cambridge, if not before, and taken it up again at Padua. Music graced the fashionable Cavalier and lit up the life of the unworldly scholar. George Herbert in his parsonage at Bemerton was said to be a good hand on the lute, and his brother Edward taught himself to play it so that he might entertain himself at home and refresh himself after his studies. It removed him from dependence on the society of the high-spirited gentle youths whose tastes were for debauchery. [3] The two things hardly went together, and a man's attitude to music might be an index not only of his culture but also of his virtue. "There is no one Science in the world," Peacham wrote, "that so affecteth the free and generous Spirit, with a more delightfull and in-offensive recreation, or better disposeth the minde to what is commendable and vertuous." "It is an immediate gift of heaven, bestowed on man, whereby to praise and magnifie his Creator." Peacham cited Scripture to confute the sectaries who said that the service of God was "nothing advanced by singing and instruments," [4] and Benlowes too was scornful of the Puritan dislike of music in church. When the Puritans were having organs removed from churches and destroyed, he whimsically reflected on their sad fate if they should have to endure the ceaseless hymns of heaven. [5] No doubt he thought of them when he said that a dislike of music went with a propensity for making *discord* among men. And the adjective for discord was "barb'rous." It was by the fitness of things, he felt, that "SAINTS

---

[1] *Compleat Gentleman*, p. 129.
[2] Chancery Proceedings, Reynardson 31/14 (answer).
[3] *Autobiography*, p. 23.
[4] *Compleat Gentleman*, pp. 103, 96, 97.
[5] *Theophila*, Address to the Ladies.

sing, the *damned* howl." [1] One of the supreme delights of heaven, as repeatedly described in *Theophila*, was its perpetuity of music; and Theophila herself was always pouring forth heart-ravishing strains. A certain "M.G." who wrote in praise of *Theophila* called Benlowes *"Philomusicus,"* [2] and this passion was a bond between Benlowes and Quarles. Benlowes was a patron of musicians as well as poets, and there was an obscure musician called William Collins who seems to have received from him at one time a regular income. [3] It would also appear that so distinguished a musician as John Jenkins, whom Benlowes showed a good deal of favour, [4] actually resided for a time at Brent Hall. [5] He was a composer who was much patronized by the country gentry and also something of a figure at the court of Charles I. Anthony à Wood called him "the mirrour and wonder of his age for musick." [6] His stay at Brent Hall would no doubt have been at the time when he was writing airs for parts of *Theophila*. Did Benlowes' house then know musical evenings like the one celebrated in *A Poetick Descant upon a Private Musick-Meeting*?

What with his mind on literature and the arts and his eye on his ancestral estates, one gets a picture of Benlowes leading a life which, if quiet and retired, according to his expressed preference, was far from being empty. The ordinary pleasures of the world, however, he, like his friend Quarles, disdained. He filled his verse with aspersions upon the world's vanities and with exhortations to attach no value to wealth and luxury. Wealthy himself, he saw a danger in the "Opulency of an indulgent Fortune," which might easily lead to "Dissoluteness of Manners" and from there to the "dreadful Destruction" of hell. [7] He was not uninfluenced by such an idea as that expressed by Richard Brathwait, that gentility lay rather in *"goodnesse* of *Person*, than *greatnesse* of *Place*." [8] He wrote scornfully of ambition, and passionately against misers and the love of gold. It seemed to him a pretty piece of irony to paint the miser's

[1] *Ibid.*, vi, 99.
[2] *Ibid.*, p. 122.
[3] This is the natural inference from the fact that there was some dispute later, when Benlowes was selling his lands, about whether he had actually settled an annuity upon Collins (Chancery Proceedings, Collins 140/147).
[4] Wood, *Fasti Oxonienses*, II, 359.
[5] *Life and Times of Anthony Wood*, II, 335.
[6] *Ibid.*, I, 209.
[7] Preface to *Theophila*.
[8] *The English Gentleman*, Epistle dedicatory.

son as a spendthrift. Peacham, as well as Brathwait, prescribed temperance and frugality, and Benlowes, true to type, loathed gluttony and drunkenness. These, however, were among the prevalent vices of the age. At the court of James I it was not a novel sight to see ladies as well as gentlemen rolling about intoxicated. Mrs. Hutchinson described the court as "a nursery of lust and intemperance." [1] Things improved under Charles I, whom even his political foes admitted to be "temperate, chaste, and serious." [2] Yet Clarendon, a Royalist, stigmatized Charles's court as "full of excess, idleness and luxury." [3] And the ways of the court spread to the country. When all allowance has been made for picturesque rhetoric about great country-houses being sties of uncleanness, [4] there is still plenty of evidence for hard drinking, at any rate among the hunting gentry, who swore water was the drink of frogs. Squire Western, in fact, was not born in the eighteenth century. The typical squire, Samuel Butler said, had "but one Way of making all Men welcome, that come to his House, and that is, by making himself and them drunk; while his Servants take the same Course with theirs, which he approves of as good and faithful Service." [5] Before the Civil War drunkenness was so common among all classes that Parliament introduced a bill in 1641 for the suppression of alehouses and tippling-houses. Small wonder that Benlowes, within fifty lines of the opening of *Theophila*, was protesting against the "*jovial Sin*" and thinking "*Cheeks dy'd in* Claret *seem o'th' Quorum*" (i, 20).

Much drinking led to quarrelling, and every high-spirited gentle-

---

[1] *Memoirs of Colonel Hutchinson*, ed. Firth, p. 64.

[2] *Ibid.*, p. 69. It was accorded Charles for righteousness that he encouraged "men of learning and ingenuity in all arts" and was himself "a most excellent judge and a great lover of paintings, carvings, gravings, and many other ingenuities." It is a mark of the civility of an age when interest in the arts is thus approved of as an indication of a good standard of values and so of a superior morality. Amid the intolerance of Puritans and the licence of courtiers and squires, one should always remember judgments such as this.

[3] *History of the Rebellion*, ed. Macray, I, 96.

[4] Mrs. Hutchinson again, p. 64.

[5] *Characters*, ed. Waller, p. 41. As a particular example one might cite Sir Edward Baynton, one of the deputy-lieutenants of Wiltshire, who was very active in relieving the poor in his county, but who was none the less a gallant adulterer and drinker. It was his habit to make the servants of all his guests so drunk that they could not drive their masters home (Nethercot, *Sir William D'avenant*, pp. 154-155). Evelyn, who suffered at Baynton's house in 1654, thought the custom "barbarous, and much unbecoming a Knight, still lesse a Christian" (*Diary*, II, 59). It happened to Evelyn again in 1669 at Sir William Ducie's; the coachmen fell off their boxes and had to be left behind (*ibid.*, II, 236).

man was quick to draw a sword. The memoirs of Lord Herbert and Sir John Reresby are full of challenges and duels. Yet although the gentleman must not and did not submit to public insult, the ideal of the seventeenth-century conduct-books [1] and the sentiment of the more religious gentlemen like Benlowes were equally in favour of forbearance.

A form of excess that Benlowes was fond of declaiming against was extravagance in dress. The *Theophila* folio was to satirize the rakish Cavalier by reproducing a pair of engravings which excellently show the more irresponsible fashions of the reign of Charles I. The hair, for example, may well illustrate what offended Prynne when, in a pamphlet on *The Unlovelinesse of Love-Lockes* (1628), he inveighed against the wearing of "Supposititious, Poudred, Frizled, or extraordinary long Haire." The bulk of it is combed out loose upon the shoulders, but on either side a single long beribboned lock hangs forward half-way down the breast. The most striking of the clothes are the wide-brimmed hat with its gigantic feather, the breeches much betagged at the knees, and the boots, with their enormous tops, which, half-way up the calves, surround the legs with trays of foaming lace. There is more lace at the cuffs, the doublet is open and frilled at the edges, a sword swings behind the thighs, slung on a sash from the shoulder, and there are a pair of ostentatious spurs. [2] "Thy Cloaths outworth Thee," Benlowes said. With his habitual regard for the less fortunate of mankind, he thought how the poor might live for a year on what a fashionable young man, coaching through Hyde Park on May Day, spent in a single day. He mocked at the gallant's dependence on a tribe of servants—they were needed even to open his eyes. He disapproved of being pounced and perfumed—though the wearers justified their pomander-chains as preventives against plague—and of the effeminateness of wearing patches on the chin. He satirized feminine affectations—"Her glancing Eye, her lisping Lip, her mincing Pace"—and wenching, like all other sensuality, he abhorred. [3]

---

[1] For example, Brathwait, *The English Gentleman* (1630), pp. 206ff.

[2] This sort of costume was a subject for general ridicule at the time of the Civil War. Among the Thomason tracts at the British Museum (669 f. 10/99) is a very similar engraving, with satirical comment, called "The Picture of an English Antick, with a List of his ridiculous Habits, and apish Gestures." (It is reprinted in Traill and Mann, *Social England*, IV, 440). Another broadsheet (669 f. 10/106) puts similar clothes on a wolf when it wants to present a caricature of a bloodthirsty Royalist.

[3] *Theophila*, xi, 27; xiii, 21; xi, 8, 29-30, 56.

The one indulgence Benlowes allowed was tobacco. Celebrating its supposed medicinal properties and the stimulus it gave to the fancy, he contributed three stanzas [1] to the large tobacco literature of the seventeenth century. Tobacco, after all, was natural, one of the gifts which Nature had bestowed on man. From Nature came all that man should require in its best and simplest form. Water from the next fountain, food from the uddered cattle, cloth from the sheep, and wood from the hedgerows—that was an ideal to be expressed in verse. [2]

But for all its earnestness, one may question whether Benlowes sought to live up to this ideal. It was an ideal in the mind which had little root in experience. Even the words which gave it shape had already been chosen for it by Randolph [3] and were not Benlowes' own. Benlowes was temperate of habit, but not ascetic. Yet there were ascetics among seventeenth-century poets: Crashaw was noted for "his rare moderation in diet" and for spending whole nights in prayer. [4] The community at Little Gidding practised nightly vigils and ate its meals in silence. But it was more characteristic

[1] *Ibid.*, xii, 116-118. "Divine tobacco" was repeatedly celebrated in English poetry, beginning with *The Faerie Queene* (book iii, canto v, stanzas 32-33). But it is interesting to find Benlowes, severe as he was upon excesses of all kinds, on the side of tobacco against his admired Sylvester, who had written about 1616 a diatribe in which tobacco was "battered" and "the pipes shattered... by a volley of holy shot." Benlowes' poetical acquaintance Thomas Pestell had also written an attack upon the "damned weed" in 1618. The objection to tobacco was principally Puritan, but the most famous "counterblaste" was that of James I (1604), which denounced smoking as "a custome lothsome to the eye, hatefull to the Nose, harmefull to the braine, dangerous to the Lungs, and in the blacke stinking fume thereof, neerest resembling the horrible Stigian smoke of the pit that is bottomelesse" (Arber reprint, p. 112). Against this was the widespread belief in the medicinal properties of tobacco (*herba panacea*), given currency in England by, among other works, Gerard's *Herball* (1597). The kind of virtues popularly claimed for it in the seventeenth century may be seen from James Howell (*Familiar Letters*, pp. 521-522): not only did it clear the brain when stupefied with study, but a leaf or two steeped in white wine made, it is not perhaps surprising to learn, an infallible emetic, and the smoke, "let in round about the Balls of the Eyes once a-week," was a prevention against blindness. If this sounds at first like an Anglo-Saxon charm, it is of course the same superstitious seventeenth century as is reflected in the *Vulgar Errors* of Sir Thomas Browne.

A famous collection of tobacco literature, made by George Arents, Jr., is now in the New York Public Library, and the big four-volume catalogue of this by J. E. Brooks gives the fullest, though still not an exhaustive, survey of the subject.

[2] *Theophila*, xii, 114-115.

[3] Translation of Horace's second epode, lines 57-58.

[4] See the anonymous preface to *Steps to the Temple*.

of Benlowes that when his house was burnt down, he found no other in the neighbourhood worthy of a man of his quality. He did not really affect the simple life. He loved the gaudy, and was a man led by wealth to extravagance, though this manifested itself in favourable forms like art, friendship, and philanthropy. Nor did his disdain of sartorial vanities prevent him from dressing the part of the elegant gentleman he was. He would well have understood and approved the distinction made by one of the St. John's College tutors in describing one of his young charges as "well enough cloathed for a poore scholler in St. Joh: Coll: but short of a Kentish gentleman." [1] If Benlowes' dress was not ostentatious, it was not very plain either. He was to wear black when he sat for his portrait in 1650, [2] but he liked a frill or two better than the plain cuffs and narrow band of the Puritan. When the illustrators of *Theophila* introduced the figure of the author into their allegorical designs, there was nothing monastic about him. He might be gazing rapt upon a heavenly image, but the artist tended to see him as a gentleman of fashion. His dress knew restraint—there were none of the absurdities ridiculed in the engravings of the rakish Cavalier described above; but, in the illustration to Canto i for instance, there was an unmistakable touch of opulence. An outstretched leg showed both a long garter of ribbon and a rose upon the shoe, which had the long square toe then in vogue. The engraving of the author which served as a frontispiece for *Theophila* suggests a man wellgroomed. His beautiful hair of a rather reddish tinge he wore—not in the most extravagant kind of lovelocks, it is true, but yet long and loose in the fashionable style.

The mingled regard and contempt for the world's opinion is quite typical of the seventeenth-century gentleman who is simultaneously conscious of the nothingness of this life and of his own importance in it.

---

[1] *Oxinden Letters 1607-1642*, p. 104.
[2] The one now in the Library of St. John's College, Cambridge.

CHAPTER TEN

READING

Something must be said in this chapter about the kind of books that Benlowes read, especially in poetry. But it may be illuminating first to approach the matter negatively and remark on something that he chose to ignore.

It may be said at once that he took little interest in the new science which was in the course of the century to revolutionize man's conception of the world he lived in. The Stationers' Register was showing an increase in books on astronomy, mechanics, physiology, and other sciences; [1] but the minds of poets, as Professor Whitehead complains, [2] soaked in classical and Renaissance literature, have not always been readily adaptable to scientific studies. Benlowes' preface to *Theophila* showed him curious about the size of the earth, but his celestial geography was as fantastic as that of the Middle Ages. Like Sir Thomas Browne and so many of his contemporaries, he was fascinated by "the secret Magick of numbers." [3] "From the Surface of the Earth to the Center," he announced, "is 3436 Miles, the whole Thickness 6872 Miles, the whole Comp[a]sse 21600 Miles; from its Center to the Moon is 3924912 Miles." [4] Such figures were more comfortable to a mind that readily settled into dogmatism than the uncertainties of inquiry.

That Benlowes seems never to have felt the impact of the Copernican theory may be taken as typical of his conservatism in thought, though in this he was no different from many others of his day. The new astronomy was indeed being emphatically rejected by many influential Englishmen a hundred years after it had first been put before the world in 1543, [5] as two or three examples will rapidly

---

[1] *Cf.* Marjorie Plant, *The English Book Trade*, pp. 51-52.
[2] *Science and the Modern World*, p. 95.
[3] *Religio Medici*, pt. i, sec. 12.
[4] *Cf.* also *Theophila*, v, 49.
[5] This of course is not true of English *scientific* writers, among whom the old Ptolemaic astronomy was quite discredited. See Johnson, *Astronomical Thought in Renaissance England*.

make clear. The five Puritan divines who collaborated under the name of Smectymnuus in 1641 jeered confidently at the strange notion that the earth moved and the heavens stood still;[1] Sir Thomas Browne believed that it was the nature of the sun to make a revolution every day, "because of that necessary course that God hath ordained it";[2] and Benlowes' close friend, Alexander Ross, who in 1634 had put forth scriptural arguments for a stationary earth in his *Commentum de Terræ Motu*, was in 1646 still denouncing the opinion of Copernicus "as erroneous, ridiculous, and impious" in a pamphlet called *The New Planet No Planet.*[3] But it must be emphasized that this attitude was that of men who cling to the established order. For on the other hand, by 1621 Robert Burton was anxious "to examine that maine controversie of the earths motion, now so much in question";[4] and in 1623 Drummond of Hawthornden was left "in a thousand Labyrinthes" with the admission that "the Earth is found to moue, and is no more the Center of the Vniverse."[5] By the 1640's sufficient progress had been made in what may perhaps be called the general mind for James Howell to await eagerly what one of his correspondents would say about "*Copernicus's* opinion touching the movement of the Earth, which hath so stirr'd all our modern wits."[6] Yet some wits, as we see, obstinately remained unstirred. Benlowes was one of those who continued to prefer a theological to a scientific exposition of the nature of the universe; and instead of that scientific investigation of facts which had been advocated by Bacon (who himself, however, decided against the Copernican theory) and was soon to be practised by Newton, he gave himself to metaphysical speculations upon the nature of infinity and the super-celestial beings. In fact, he illustrates

---

[1] *An Answer to An Humble Remonstrance*, p. 16.

[2] *Religio Medici*, pt. i, sec. 16.

[3] In reply to Wilkins' *Discourse Concerning a New Planet*, which had attacked Ross's earlier work. On "The Ross-Wilkins Controversy," see Grant McColley in the *Annals of Science*, III, 153ff. On Milton's use of Ross's arguments in *Paradise Lost* see McColley in *Publications of the Modern Language Association of America*, vol. 52. On Ross's hostility to the new science in general, interesting here in that Ross was a man who had Benlowes' warm approval, see Johnson, *Astronomical Thought in Renaissance England*, pp. 277ff.

[4] *Anatomy of Melancholy*, part. II, sec. ii, memb. 3.

[5] *A Cypresse Grove (Poetical Works*, ed. Kastner, II, 78). But these new labyrinths did not divert Drummond from the traditional paths of thought when at the same time he spoke of the Heavens' "euer-rolling Wheeles" (p. 71); and Burton gave his testimony that a fixed earth in the centre of the world with the heavens revolving round it was still "the most receaued opinion."

[6] *Familiar Letters*, p. 528.

the familiar seventeenth-century survival of mediaeval attitudes in the midst of a scientific revolution.

Benlowes had, of course, read some philosophy at Cambridge—Aristotle undoubtedly, and probably Duns Scotus. He had been put through the usual text-books of logic and rhetoric. Cicero and Quintilian and the great Roman poets of the Augustan age seem to have been familiar authors from his youth, and in his own writings he could borrow from them upon occasion. But in mature life, though he never forsook the classics, he seems to have given his liveliest interest to the work of his contemporaries both in English and Latin. His interest in Latin verse was that of any scholarly poet of his day, and he seems to have picked up some volumes of it during his travels and brought them back to England. [1]

He read studiously rather than desultorily. The private library of a country gentleman—even of a gentleman of bookish tastes and commanding wealth—was of necessity restricted. In consequence, every volume was read and re-read and intimately known. That in itself contributed to the pedantic interest in the minutiae of learning which characterized many seventeenth-century writers. In Benlowes himself one notices no power of allusion to a wide range of literature, but instead a very frequent borrowing from a limited number of favourite authors. Who some of these authors were it is luckily possible to discover from Benlowes' habit of incorporating in his own poetry phrases that struck him in his reading.

According to the convention of the poets of the time, an admired phrase could always be taken over into the admirer's own composition. Benlowes drew heavily in this way from many published works and from friends who lent him their manuscript verses. Some passages of *Theophila* were rather like a patchwork quilt in which one might recognize in new surroundings a long familiar fabric. The compliment was, of course, received with glad surprise, and no one

---

[1] See above, pp. 59, 79. Some clues to Benlowes' reading as a young man —that is, in the 1620's—will be found on pp. 38, 59-60. His enthusiasm for Phineas Fletcher has also been discussed. What indications there are of his reading in later years will also be dealt with in their chronological place. In this chapter I indicate a few of the authors Benlowes read in the period which was most significant for the work he produced—the years after his return from abroad and before the Civil War. Some of them he no doubt knew already, but he must certainly have gone over them again. If I confine myself largely to English works, the limitation is in me and not in him. I have little doubt that there would be similar (though possibly not such numerous) clues to his Latin reading for anyone informed enough to spot them.

thought of plagiarism. [1] Or if this was plagiarism, all poets of the period were plagiarists to some degree. But Benlowes borrowed from his fellow-poets infinitely more than most. He copied not only more frequently but more exactly. [2] Some of his poetry was therefore little more than pastiche, though he had a knack of imposing his own pattern on all the fragments that he borrowed. Even when word and thought, body and soul together, were taken over, they had at least to adapt themselves to his own highly individual rhythm. For the moment, however, I am less concerned with the method, important as a consideration of it is for any estimate of Benlowes' poetical ability, than with the evidence it affords of authors read. Obviously, one cannot attempt anything approaching a complete survey of what Benlowes read: what one can do is to list a few authors for whom there is particular evidence. And those for whom there is evidence are plainly those who were among the most influential in the formation of Benlowes' poetic style. They also provide significant pointers to the taste of his time.

Like all educated men of that age, Benlowes was of course well read in the Bible. In his mind, as in Milton's or in Browne's, all

[1] There were, of course, a number of favourite comparisons so much repeated by the metaphysical poets that it is not now possible to discover, and probably the poets themselves did not always know, who had actually invented a particular conceit. Images were common property, just as they had been among the Elizabethan dramatists. The comparison which Shakespeare's imagination gave perfect form to in "this my Hand will rather/The multitudinous Seas incarnadine" had been used by two or three dramatists before him and seems to have originated in Seneca. One such stock image among the seventeenth-century poets was that used by Benlowes at *Theophila*, iii, 39: "*Earth:* Shade shuts up soon/Her Shop of *Beams*." It is also found in Cleveland ("Upon Phillis Walking in a Morning before Sun-rising"), and is best known in Vaughan ("Faith"). But it is not to such stock conceits that I refer in the text. Benlowes would often use in his own work phrases and images that he had deliberately taken from a particular source. Perhaps one should add that it is naturally not always possible to distinguish between a direct borrowing and the repetition of a common image. What looks like a borrowing from a specific passage may be the use of a conceit that was commoner than we know; and on the other hand, a phrase may have been a stock one and yet derive in Benlowes from a particular original.

[2] A. B. Langdale, in his book on Phineas Fletcher, seems to suggest that Fletcher had a similar habit. He lists 103 passages borrowed from Spenser and others from other poets; but most of them are general echoes only. In Benlowes one may properly speak of copyings. There may be a variation in the thought, as there will certainly be in context; but a new-made compound epithet, a striking conceit, or a fanciful and highly unusual combination of words first found in another poet will reappear in his work in a quite unmistakable form. Examples will be given as the text proceeds.

the figures of Hebrew story could dwell side by side with those of Greek mythology or mediaeval legend. Naboth met with Heraclitus in his verse. Naturally he paraphrased a psalm [1] or alluded to Bezaleel's decoration of the tabernacle of the Israelites in the wilderness. [2] His favourite reading lay in that kind of poetry which clothed religious meditation in the figures and fancies of his own age. That meant inevitably the *Devine Weekes* of Du Bartas in the translation of Sylvester, which had begun to appear in 1592, achieved its first complete edition in 1605, and ran through four editions in the following decade. Everybody read it who had any pretensions to poetry at all, and Benlowes' friend Phineas Fletcher had already been deeply influenced by it. [3] Its continuing popularity brought further editions of Sylvester's works in 1633 and 1641. Sylvester's ornamental phrasing and extravagant images were among the most remarkable influences upon the style of the minor poets of the seventeenth century. Even Milton borrowed from Sylvester. Benlowes echoed him constantly, borrowing many of the most showy conceits for his own verse, to offer them to his friends as prized familiar jewels appearing in new settings. It was Sylvester who taught Benlowes to make dawns "Opal-colour'd" [4]; to address God as "LORD *of all grassie and all glassie Plains*"; [5] and to describe the "bald-pate Wood" in winter "periwig'd with *Snow*." [6] This last image was one of Sylvester's most famous, and it is worth citing the parallel passages to illustrate how far Benlowes follows and how far he departs from the original. Sylvester wrote:

> But, when the Winters keener breath began
> To christallize the *Baltike* Ocean,
> To glaze the Lakes, and bridle-vp the Floods,
> And Perriwig with wooll the bald-pate Woods.

And Benlowes:

> When periwig'd with *Snow*'s each bald-pate Wood,
> Bound in Ice-Chains each strugling Flood;
> When *North-Seas* bridled are, pris'ning their scaly *Brood*.

[1] *Theophila*, vi, 54-56; *cf.* Psalm 104.
[2] *Theophila*, i, 89; *cf.* Exodus xxxi : 3.
[3] See Langdale, *Phineas Fletcher*, pp. 115ff.
[4] *Theophila*, i, 66 (*cf.* "Opall *East*," *ibid.*, viii, 75); *cf.* Sylvester, *Devine Weekes*, II, 2, pt. 2 (1605, p. 418; 1641, p. 121).
[5] *Theophila*, xii, 109; *cf. Devine Weekes*, I, 3 (1605, p. 76; 1641, p. 21).
[6] *Theophila*, xiii, 54; *cf. Devine Weekes*, II, 1, pt. 4 (1605, p. 363; 1641, p. 105).

Benlowes' "*Snow*" for "wooll" derives from another passage where Sylvester uses a similar figure:

> Chill shiu'ring Winter dresses
> With Isicles her (selfe-bald) borrowed tresses:
> About her browes a Periwig of Snow. [1]

Benlowes, like Sylvester, used the image twice. On the other occasion, [2] he can hardly be said to have made an improvement in departing farther from his original and having the trees periwigged with "frosty *Cream*." [3] Benlowes was far from alone in his admiration for this striking image. Dryden "was rapt into an ecstasy" when he read it in his boyhood [4]—that is, sometime in the 1640's. And this description of the frost had often been imitated—as, for example, by William Browne, [5] whose *Britannia's Pastorals*, which began to appear in 1613 and went into a second edition in 1625, introduced a little of Sylvester's eccentric phrasing into their pleasant descriptions of English rural life.

Browne, with Giles and Phineas Fletcher, was among the popular authors at the time of Benlowes' youth. His easy-flowing verse showed the influence of Spenser and Drayton; it was somewhat less to Benlowes' taste than Sylvester, who was both pious and ornate, but was probably familiar to him. Benlowes had certainly read Sandys, the translator of Ovid's *Metamorphoses*, another poet who enjoyed a flattering vogue and who, himself influenced by Sylvester, was perhaps the biggest single influence on later seventeenth-century poetic diction. [6] Sandys, like Sylvester, had Milton in his debt, and he also gained the admiration of Dryden, who even at the end of his career, when he had come to think Sylvester fustian, still regarded "the ingenious and learned Sandys" as "the best versifier of the former age." [7] Towards the end of his life, in the 1630's, Sandys was writing a good deal of religious verse, and it was this,

---

[1] *Devine Weekes*, I, 4 (1605, p. 138; 1641, p. 37). This famous image illustrates well how Sylvester decorated Du Bartas, who merely said at this point: "L'Hyuer au lieu de fleurs se pare de glaçons."

[2] *Theophila*, iv, 68.

[3] It is impossible to examine or even to enumerate all of Benlowes' extremely frequent borrowings from Sylvester. I have merely pointed to one or two representative examples. The same will be done when I come to refer to borrowings from other authors; the reader should understand that the examples could easily be multiplied.

[4] *Essays*, ed. Ker, I, 247.

[5] *Britannia's Pastorals*, book I, song 4, lines 397-398.

[6] See Tillotson, *On the Poetry of Pope*, pp. 66ff.

[7] *Essays*, II, 247.

of course, rather than the Ovid, that appealed to Benlowes. He was acquainted with some at least of Sandys' metrical paraphrases of the Scriptures—the Psalms, the Lamentations of Jeremiah, the Book of Job, and so on. The sort of image he took from Sandys was the reference to camels as "*Arabias wandring Ships*," a commonplace perhaps now, but striking enough when thought of first. [1] It is abundantly clear that what Benlowes most looked for in poetry was ingenuity in metaphor. When this was used upon a devotional theme the combination was irresistible.

Inevitably therefore he went to the fount of metaphysical wit. It was in Donne's words that, turning his back upon the world, he prayed to God, "Seal Thou the *Bill* of my *Divorse*"; [2] and it was by two striking conceits of Donne's that he celebrated the holy martyrs—their blood was the oil which lit the lamps of the Church and the dew which watered its seed. [3] He does not seem to have been very interested in Donne's love poems or indeed in the love poems of Donne's numerous imitators, though it may have been in Habington's *Castara*, which first came out in 1634, that his keen eye for an epithet found "swift-heeld Death." [4] But if he was not, on the whole, attracted to erotic poetry, he did not eschew the secular. It is quite possible that his library included a copy of one of the Shakespeare folios. When he taunted the gallant lover with "Deaths *Serjeant* soon thy courted *Helens* must Attach," he may have had *Hamlet* directly in mind. [5] And there are numerous other possible echoes of Shakespeare. To mention only two: to represent pride crushed Benlowes uses the metaphor, "That flats the *Nose*"; [6] and the man who lives for sensuous pleasure is said, like Richard II, both to waste time and to be wasted by it. [7] Few of the echoes are unmistakable: if Benlowes frequently reminds us of Shakespeare,

---

[1] *Theophila*, xii, 110. The phrase "ship of the desert" goes back to the seventeenth century, and the Oxford Dictionary attributes it first to Sandys in 1615 in the form "ships of Arabia"; but Benlowes seems to have copied the metaphor exactly from Sandys' *Paraphrase Upon Job* (1638), line 12.

[2] *Theophila*, xiii, 116; *cf.* Donne, "A Hymne to Christ, at the Authors last going into Germany."

[3] *Theophila*, vi, 4; *cf.* Donne, *The Second Anniversarie*, lines 351-352.

[4] *Theophila*, xi, 88; *cf. Castara* (Arber reprint), p. 43 ("Upon Castara's Departure," line 2).

[5] *Theophila*, x, 14; *cf. Hamlet*, V, ii, 347-348: "this fell Sergeant death / Is strick'd in his Arrest" (I cite the first folio).

[6] *Theophila*, x, 70; *cf. Timon*, IV, iii, 157-158: "Downe with the Nose,/Downe with it flat."

[7] *Theophila*, xi, 26; *cf. Richard II*, V, v, 49.

it may be simply that Shakespeare has provided the most familiar expression of what became the commonplaces of seventeenth-century poets. Yet it can, I think, have been only with a clear recollection of the storm in *Othello* that Benlowes described

> *Storms*, when Eol's *Rave*
> Plough'd up the *Ocean*, whose each *Wave*
>Might waken *Death* with *Noise*, and make its *Paunch* a *Grave*...
>We seem'd to knock at *Hell*, and bounce the *Firmament*. [1]

It is quite characteristic that Benlowes should go farther than his model and use Shakespeare's description of a storm at sea as the basis of a gigantic metaphor, in which physical and spiritual are superbly blended in the best "metaphysical" manner.

In spite of his preference, then, for religious and didactic verse, Benlowes was attracted to a wider range of poetry, provided only that it were marked by bold conceits. When the poems of Randolph were published in 1638 he was delighted by their witty phrase-making, and later on he was to be a great admirer of Milton and Cleveland. [2] As a lover of country life Benlowes was particularly attracted to Randolph's pastorals, but throughout the volume he found conceits that he was glad to ponder over. Eagerly he followed Randolph's allegory of man as his own government, with Memory for his treasurer and the tongue as secretary to the heart; he saw through Randolph's eyes the fascination of the porcupine, which had on its own person the whole artillery of war; [3] he could not resist, when Randolph had once tempted him, seeing Theophila's breasts as snow-clad Alps. [4]

Benlowes could enjoy Randolph's poetic fancy and at the same time approve the sentiment of a poet who often wrote against the vanities of men. He would obviously be pleased also to come upon

---

[1] *Theophila*, x, 38-39; *cf. Othello*, II, i, 188-191:

>May the windes blow, till they haue waken'd death:
>And let the labouring Barke climbe hills of Seas
>*Olympus* high: and duck againe as low,
>As hell's from Heauen.

[2] See below, pp. 162 ff.

[3] This was not new in Randolph. The porcupine had been a favourite device with Louis XII (*cf.* Puttenham, *The Arte of English Poesie*, book ii, ch. 12, and Praz, *Studies in Seventeenth-Century Imagery*, I, 56).

[4] For these imitations of Randolph, see *Theophila*, xiii, 20; ii, 74; ix, 59. Randolph, "On the Inestimable Content he Injoyes in the Muses," lines 50-52; "De Histrice," lines 53-57; "A Pastorall Courtship," lines 65-68. For other borrowings from Randolph, see above, pp. 86, 107.

a poem in Randolph's volume in praise of Owen Feltham's *Resolves* and that "modest wit" and pithy style of Feltham's which he admired himself. The *Resolves* was a very popular book of meditation, which Feltham, who was Benlowes' exact contemporary, had published when he was eighteen. It was to go into its seventh edition before the middle of the century. But Benlowes knew more of Feltham than was printed, for he was able to quote an unpublished poem of his in the middle of his own *Theophila* volume.

Still more in Benlowes' vein were the pious meditations of his friend Quarles, and he had a good knowledge of Quarles's *Divine Fancies* and some of those verse paraphrases of Bible stories in which Quarles rivalled Sandys, as well as of the *Emblemes*, which he had done so much to engender and through which Quarles succeeded in appealing to the general reader of his day more than any other devotional poet. If he could not hope to rival Sylvester in the pure gymnastics of language, Quarles had a great appeal through his ability to present the commonplaces of pious meditation in exciting verbal forms. Benlowes was provided with many a daring epithet. He appropriated, for example, his friend's allusion to "Troy-bane *Hellen*" and his conceit of "queazie-stomack'd" graves vomiting forth their dead. He could also copy from Quarles such curious observations as that although Christ once wept, there is no record of his having laughed.[1]

There was much more than this, however, in the *Emblemes*, and a very brief digression, which is all that is in place here, may serve to suggest a little further the nature of Benlowes' literary predilection.[2] An emblem not only elaborated a conceit in order to present an accepted truth to the mental eye, but the physical eye was also served by an engraving which embodied the same thought in pictorial form. The appeal lay of course neither in the poem nor the picture but in the conjunction of the two. And this conjunction of a visual art with poetry was very much to the taste of the seventeenth century in general and of Benlowes in particular. It is certainly not surprising to find emblems fascinating one who brought back marble perspectives from Italy, who delighted in elegant bookbindings with coats-of-arms in gold, who loved anagrams and de-

[1] *Theophila*, i, 12; ii, 50; i, 29; *cf.* Quarles, *Emblemes*, II, vi (stanza 4); III, xiv; *Divine Fancies*, I, 48.

[2] For the history of the emblem cult, see Praz, *Studies in Seventeenth-Century Imagery*, vol. I, ch. 1, and Rosemary Freeman, *English Emblem Books*, in view of which the more extended digression that I originally intended would be redundant and presumptuous.

vices wrought upon his own name, and who encouraged Fletcher in *The Purple Island* to honour him with an impresa. Moreover, emblems had a particular appeal to one who was interested in the life of the soul because one of their motives was to provide a visible manifestation of man's spiritual aspirations and temptations. As Quarles himself put it in his address to the reader, they sought to present our Saviour "as well to the eye as to the eare." For such purposes they were especially cultivated by the Jesuits, under whose influence both Quarles and Benlowes fell. [1]

Although Benlowes had become a fierce anti-Roman in theology, he never shook off the effects of his Catholic education, which encouraged him to rely a good deal on symbols and rituals. Out of sympathy as he was with many of the tenets of the High Church party of Laud, he could not but be attracted to all their ceremonial, and he responded eagerly to the art of the Counter-Reformation, which was everywhere marked by the most vivid visual symbolism. It delighted in paintings and sculptures of Christ, the Virgin, cherubs and angels, bleeding St. Sebastians and weeping Magdalenes, as well as in the concrete symbolization of the soul, which, personified as Anima, often formed the centre of allegorical designs. The religious emblem-books were a great deal occupied with the pictorial celebration of Anima's adventures. It was in this tradition that Benlowes was to have his *Theophila* illustrated with engravings representing Theophila, the soul, as a woman with wings and surrounded by angels, beasts, cherubs, or spirits of the damned. These designs also incorporated the stock ornaments of baroque sculpture, and introduced plenty of globes and rings, which satisfied the Counter-Reformation mind by their symbolism of the world and unbroken eternity respectively. Other engravings which adorned the book showed the favourite figure of a woman weeping or at prayer. The elaborately printed and decorated books which were common throughout the period all bear witness to the close connection that existed in men's minds between poetry and the pictorial arts.

A variation of the vogue for *"visible Poetry,"* as Fuller wittily

---

[1] Not only did the plates of Quarles's *Emblemes* derive from two of the Jesuit emblem-books, the *Pia Desideria* and the *Typus Mundi* (see above, p. 79), but it has been shown that "Quarles' poems are frequently variations on the themes expounded in the verses of his sources" (Praz, I, 146; see also Haight, "The Sources of Quarles's *Emblems*," *The Library*, Sept. 1935).

called it, [1] is found in those verses which a number of seventeenth-century poets (including Benlowes) wrote in such metres as made them appear on the printed page in the shape of an altar, a pyramid, or a pair of wings. [2] Words had somehow to force a pattern on the retina. Many of the startling conceits of the time owed their origin to a desire to provide a visual sensation. [3]

The relation between the visible and the invisible, the body and the soul, is of course the great subject of seventeenth-century poetry. The whole of creation was regarded as one gigantic emblem, with God as the supreme emblematist, who had created all natural objects as the visible symbols of a higher spiritual life. To draw from them an analogy with spiritual experience or even a moral lesson was, therefore, not merely to exercise one's ingenuity, but to discover the divine purpose. [4] Quarles himself looked upon "the Heavens, the Earth, nay every Creature" as "*Hierogliphicks* and *Emblemes* of His Glory." [5] Sir Thomas Browne, whose *Religio Medici* Benlowes read soon after its publication, believed that "this visible World

---

[1] *Worthies*, ed. Nichols, I, 355.

[2] These fantastic devices, though most popular in the seventeenth century, had a literary tradition going back to ancient Greece. Specimens in the shape of wings, altars, and shepherd's pipes can be found in the Loeb edition of *The Greek Bucolic Poets* (ed. J. M. Edmonds). They also had their Latin imitations, as, for example, the "Phoenix" of Laevius about the beginning of the first century B.C. For their origin in England, see Margaret Church, "The First English Pattern Poems," *PMLA*, vol. LXI (Sept. 1946). Puttenham, who had been introduced to such things by a man he met in Italy, commended verses which yielded "an ocular representation, your meeters being by good symmetrie reduced into certaine Geometricall figures"; and he illustrated how poems might take the shape of a lozenge, triangle, spire, or pilaster (*The Arte of English Poesie*, book ii, ch. 12). A revulsion of taste was beginning when Hobbes described them as "unprofitable difficulties" (*Answer to D'Avenant*) and Addison, of course, found them an excellent example of false wit (*Spectator*, no. 58).

[3] See Praz, *Studies in Seventeenth-Century Imagery*, I, 11-12: "Emblems and conceits are fruits of the same tree.... In need as he was of certainties of the senses, the seventeenth-century man did not stop at the purely fantastic cherishing of the image: he wanted to externalise it, to transpose it into a hieroglyph, an emblem. He took delight in driving home the word by the addition of a plastic representation."

[4] Obvious examples are found in such poems as Vaughan's "The Tempest" and "The Water-fall." See also John Smith, *Select Discourses*, 1660, pp. 430-431: "God made the Universe and all the Creatures contained therein as so many Glasses wherein he might reflect his own Glory." Wherefore men may "easily find every Creature pointing out to that Being whose image and superscription it bears"; and "while they are thus conversing with this lower World, and are viewing *the invisible things of God in the things that are made*, in this visible and outward Creation, they find God many times secretly flowing into their Souls."

[5] *Emblemes*, "To the Reader."

is but a Picture of the invisible, wherein, as in a Pourtraict, things are not truely, but in equivocal shapes, and as they counterfeit some more real substance in that invisible Fabrick." Even the vulgar music in a tavern seemed to him, if only a man had ears to hear, a manifestation of a heavenly harmony. "There is something in it of Divinity," he said, "more than the ear discovers: it is an Hieroglyphical and shadowed lesson of the whole World, and creatures of God; such a melody to the ear, as the whole World, well understood, would afford the understanding." [1]

A man like Browne, then, hoped by studying the universe to come to some understanding of the nature of God and the principle of all being. And God's wisdom could most of all be discerned in the structure of man himself. Nature, as well as Scripture, told Browne that he was made in the divine image; and anatomy and physiology were thus but a way of revealing the glory of God. So no one need be surprised that many of Browne's contemporaries continued the mediaeval tradition of using the human body as the basis of moral allegory. Benlowes greatly admired *The Purple Island* for its elaborately geographical study of man's physical formation.

If an examination of man's body led inevitably to a moral lesson, conversely a moral lesson could often be expressed in a parable in which the body and its members were the principal actors. The personification of the various members and the faculties of the mind was a favourite ingenuity in seventeenth-century poetry. This was a great part of the appeal for Benlowes of his favourite poem by Randolph, "On the Inestimable Content he Injoyes in the Muses." And it is evident that he took special delight in the play called *Lingua*, of which the theme is adequately described by its alternative title, "The Combat of the *Tongue*, and the fiue Senses for *Superiority*." This had been written early in the century by Thomas Tomkis, of Trinity College, Cambridge; it was a product of the university which also nurtured *The Purple Island*, and it had enjoyed a considerable vogue. First published in 1607, it had gone through five editions. From these, it is clear that it was popular round about 1620, and although there is no evidence for a Cambridge revival, one may wonder whether this favourite piece was acted at the university in Benlowes' time. However that may be, his extremely detailed knowledge of the text must have come from a perusal of the play in print. It is reasonable to infer that a copy of it was among his books. It was

[1] *Religio Medici*, pt. i, sec. 12; pt. ii, sec. 9.

just the thing to delight him by its carefully wrought and often fantastic allegory, and he had also a great admiration for the wit of its expression. He made use of several of its images in his own work. If he borrowed from it less frequently than from Sylvester's translation of Du Bartas, that was partly because it offered fewer opportunities on account of its very much smaller scale. [1]

Some of the borrowings from *Lingua* are specially interesting as illustrating how Benlowes, while making use of an image, would vary the phrasing or adapt the image to a new purpose, perhaps by fitting it into a totally different context. For example, Tomkis made the tongue taunt the ear that

> a speech faire fetherd could not flie:
> But thy eares pit-fall caught it instantly.
>
> (*Lingua*, I, i)

Benlowes used identical phrasing to describe the eagerness of his own ears for the holy words that fell from Theophila's lips. [2] From a passage in *Lingua* on the ostentatious clothes of women he took three separate images which he flung together into a stanza; but whereas Tomkis' gentlewoman needed "seauen Pedlers shops" to "furnish her," Benlowes' courtesan had "nine Pedlars" to "lanch her forth." Yet his verb "lanch" was suggested by Tomkis' comparison, which he also copied, of a woman being dressed to a ship being rigged. [3]

Benlowes often borrowed from various authors descriptions of country landscapes which one would have expected a country gentleman to depict from his own observation. When he described the cottages of the poor, it was to hang them about with cobwebs, a "Spider-woven Arras," in the fashion of Sylvester. [4] But Sylvester's walls were merely hung "with Spiders caules" "insteed of Arras." It was left for Benlowes, with a farther reach of fancy which saw the cobwebs *as* arras, to compress Sylvester's description into a poetic image. He would usually risk introducing original touches of his own, and these were often very successful. Tomkis had described

> The sturdie Mower, that with brawnie armes,
> Wieldeth the crooked sithe
>
> (*Lingua*, V, xvi)

---

[1] On the other hand, I must point out that the imitation of *Lingua* is confined to the last three cantos of *Theophila*. Perhaps he read or reread *Lingua* shortly before composing those.

[2] *Theophila*, xii, 87.

[3] *Ibid.*, xi, 55; *cf. Lingua*, IV, vi.

[4] *Theophila*, xii, 23; *cf. Devine Weekes*, II, 1, pt. 4 (1605, p. 360; 1641, p. 104).

and Benlowes copied, but, by replacing "brawnie armes" with "big-swoln Veins," [1] produced the one valuable detail in the picture. To build up his poems by hints from a diversity of sources was a frequent method of composition. He had a good eye upon occasion and a daring turn of phrase, but he badly needed the initiative of another mind to stimulate activity in his own. He typified what Samuel Butler pungently said of a small poet: "Bar him the Imitation of something he has read, and he has no Image in his Thoughts." It would not, however, be fair to add, as Butler did of his hypothetical poet, "He believes it is Invention enough to find out other Men's Wit... Imitation is the whole Sum of him." Benlowes was not "but a Copier at best." [2] As a borrower he often tried that bettering of the borrowing which Milton allowed to be a justification. [3] Frequently heterogeneous scraps of other poets' phrases are welded into something new by Benlowes' own poetic fire. Nevertheless, Benlowes' work, even while showing marked individual preferences, is largely derivative and therefore of peculiar interest as the expression of one not uncommon type of seventeenth-century mind.

[1] *Theophila*, xiii, 2.

[2] Butler, *Characters*, ed. Waller, pp. 47-49. Butler's description of a Small Poet includes some satiric references to Benlowes, who served as one of the models for it. "There is no Feat of Activity, nor Gambol of Wit, that ever was performed by Man, from him that vaults on *Pegasus*, to him that tumbles through the Hoop of an Anagram, but *Benlows* has got the Mastery in it, whether it be high-rope Wit, or low-rope Wit. He has all Sorts of *Echoes*, *Rebus*'s, *Chronograms*, &c. besides *Carwitchets*, *Clenches*, and *Quibbles*—As for *Altars* and *Pyramids* in Poetry, he has out-done all Men that Way." But Butler's character of the Small Poet is, of course, a composite portrait. Some of the traits are clearly taken from others, and it is a mistake to suppose, as has sometimes been done, that Butler intended *all* of his description to be even a caricature of Benlowes.

[3] *Eikonoklastes*, ch. xxiii (*Works*, V, 259).

CHAPTER ELEVEN

WRITING

Since what Benlowes read is mostly to be discovered from what he wrote, an inquiry into his reading has led quite naturally to a consideration of his manner of writing.

It seems as though all the time he was reading his mind was on the alert for some flower of fancy that he might some day make his own. And there is evidence that images and phrases, whether borrowed from another or invented by himself, took root in his brain before he quite knew to what purpose he would put them. He was one of those secondary poets whose preoccupation was with words and figures rather than ideas. The excitement of language became a substitute for the excitement of experience. Once it had caught his fancy, a phrase would be cherished and used again and again. Whole stanzas would reappear in different poems with only minor alterations.

At one time Benlowes used the blank pages of one of his boyish exercise-books [1] to jot down odd, disconnected phrases and fragmentary lines of verse, which were to be stored against the convenient moment for fitting them into some poem. For example:

> Him need compels not, nor disasters sad
> Disturb nor joyfull things make glad
> Oblivion takes not nor to Him că Mem'ry adde.

This was a stanza ready formed in the peculiar metre which he was to use for eleven and a half of the thirteen cantos of his one big poem. Subsequently it got into the poem, not as it stood, but with the personal pronoun altered because this praise of the Almighty was to be incorporated into an invocation. A second thought had also by that time removed the tortured inversion of the opening, and in *Theophila* the stanza went:

> No *Need* compels THEE, no *Disasters* sad
> Disturb thy STATE, no *Mirth* makes glad;
> *Oblivion* takes not from THEE, nor can *Mem'ry* adde!
> (viii, 13)

---

[1] *Cf.* above, pp. 25, 100. The phrases I go on to quote occur on the verso the first leaf. For a transcript of this, see below, Appendix I.

Pains were also taken to try and improve the awkward ellipsis of the last line, though not with any success. The juggling with the words to try the effect of different orders was part of Benlowes' habit. His jottings in the exercise-book left a little record of his laboured methods of composition. He played with his treasured thoughts and phrases as with a jig-saw puzzle until he finally got them fitted in the pattern that pleased him best. One half-formed stanza went into the exercise-book thus:

> not Aristotles eye
> y^t Ipse of Philosophy
> who into Natures Mysteries did pry.

The third line is in a different ink, which points to a later addition, and even there "Mysteries" seems to have been a second thought, since the word has evidently been altered. At this stage the first and third lines were still fragmentary, but even so there was not room to express the idea, which was that in spite of his penetrating "eye," Aristotle could not attain to the higher wisdom. The poet wrote tentatively in the margin, "unbounded learning had," but this obviously did not help and he rejected it. He came to see that since the main emphasis should fall on the insufficiency of Aristotle, this should be mentioned last. His last line was therefore abandoned and its thought compressed to suffocation into the phrase "Natures Professor." The "Ipse of Philosophy," however, a phrase in Benlowes' odd but characteristic manner, pleased him from the first and could not be displaced. Eventually he wrote in *Theophila*:

> Abstruser Depths! here *Aristotles* Eye
> (That *Ipse* of Philosophie,
> Natures Professor) purblinde was, to search so high.
> (xii, 78)

Another thought, ready for one of his diatribes against the wicked, was this:

> They pillowe stone to vice & virtue quell
> Turn Moses into machivel
> Devious to peace & Truth they lead to war & Hell.

Again the second line showed a certain astuteness in compression, but the last lacked vividness and was displaced in the notebook itself by the more picturesque, if equally unoriginal, "To peace run counter, in ye braud high way to Hell." Another stanza in Benlowes' usual metre but not his usual sentiment, read:

> come let us glut o^{r}selves wth rampant wine
> & let sweet oyntm^{ts} on us shine
> & let us crown o^{r}selves wth Rosebuds ere they pine.

As the image clarified the roses were placed on "oʳ Heads," and "selves" was deleted. A brisk epigram produced the first two lines of another stanza,

> In amplitude penuriously scant
> The more they haue yᵉ more they want,

but no last line occurred to him, and so this came to nothing. Another fragment lacked a first line:

> The poysnous Dragons Thou dost slaue
> And makst Hyrcaniã hungry Tigers cease to raue.

All this was written on the back of the first leaf of the exercise-book, squeezed up into the top left-hand corner, jumbled together with even tinier scraps—a single line of twisted paradox with characteristic seventeenth-century play on words, "In tyme past time this Being may not be at all"; and such brief phrases as satisfied Benlowes' invariable taste for a conceit, "The sun beam prints yᵉ houre" and "couldst monarchize yᵉ Globe." The last of these scraps, at least, was almost a commonplace of expression in the twenties and thirties of that century, and all of them were exactly typical of one of the styles of the minor poetry of the time—the style which valued paradox, antithesis, compression, and conceit, in the hope always of expressing pregnantly a general truth, and which, to achieve a shock to the understanding, would consent to mangle metre or syntax and sometimes sense. Benlowes' method was to hammer out his lines with tireless patience. Once he wrote—again in the exercise-book [1]—a whole string of words to see which offered the best possibilities in his quest for a rhyme: "provide descry'd side imply'd spy'd defy'd ty'd ride."

Thus one gets a glimpse of Benlowes pursuing his principal hobby of poetry. All his reading, consciously or unconsciously, had been preparing for his big poem. But until middle life he was known rather as a friend of poets than as a poet in his own right. He had been energetic in publishing volumes by his friends, and if not much of his own had appeared, it must have been because not much had yet been written. In 1634, in "Quarlëis," he had spoken of his muse as an infant one. He had, however, turned out various occasional poems of a complimentary kind. There were those to Winterton, Fletcher, and Quarles. There was also one in praise of *The Soules Conflict*, by Richard Sibbs. Sibbs had been famed as a preacher when

---

[1] On the recto of the first leaf at the top.

he was a fellow of St. John's College, Cambridge, but he had been expelled for Puritanism some years before Benlowes' time. Later he became Master of St. Catherine's College, and he died in July 1635, four days after he had commended *The Soules Conflict* to "the Christian Reader." [1] Shortly afterwards two such readers were both perusing this devotional treatise; and Benlowes in Latin and Quarles in English wrote in celebration of it. Benlowes' poem was composed on January 1, 1636, when he was staying with his cousins, the Nevills, at Cressing. The two panegyrics appeared together prefixed to a second edition of *The Soules Conflict* in 1636.

For Benlowes to address an eminent divine as one worthy to be honoured by many titles was characteristic. It is a little more surprising to find this lover of rural life a year or two later writing a Latin poem in praise of the illustrious and most flourishing city of London ("De celeberrima & florentissima Trinobantiados Augustæ Civitate"). This poem was appended to a panegyric written by John Sictor to celebrate the mayoralty of Richard Fenn in 1637; it occupied the last two leaves of an eight-leaved quarto. Benlowes' name turns up again along with Sictor's many years later: they both had complimentary verse prefixed to Payne Fisher's *Marston-Moor* in 1650. So evidently Sictor continued to hover round the circumference of Benlowes' circle.

The purpose of Sictor's *Panegyricon Inaugurale* in honour of the Lord Mayor was not far to seek. Sictor was a Bohemian exile who arrived in London shortly before 1629, having fled from his own country with few assets beyond his Protestantism and a reputation for Latin verses, both of which he sought to turn to account by appealing to the "charitie of well affected and disposed men." His university career was impressive—not only had he graduated at Prague, but in exile he had been at Heidelberg, Groningen, and Leyden; his Latin was beyond cavil; and he had a talent for presenting himself as "a looking glasse and example of common miserie."[2] So he was bound to be an object of Benlowes' compassion. Benlowes was already becoming celebrated for his bounty to impecunious poets and scholars, and no one need doubt that he gave Sictor money. In a gesture of characteristic kindness, he also gave him the use of one of his Latin compositions to recommend him to the Lord Mayor.

---

[1] It had, however, been entered on the Stationers' Register as early as May 16, 1632 (Arber, IV, 243).

[2] See a short monograph on Sictor by R. F. Young: *A Czech Humanist in London in the 17th Century.*

Benlowes' generosity was not, however, incompatible with one sort of economy—that curious literary economy which he shared with his friend Phineas Fletcher, which refused to waste the inventions of the muse but used them a second time over in slightly different guises. He did not write Sictor a new poem; he only refashioned an old one. Though there are many variations in order and phrase, one recognizes the passage in praise of London which he had included in the "Quarlëis" three years before in the hope of flattering the City dignitaries into giving Quarles some remunerative office. Apparently Benlowes still had hopes that something would come of it. And since Sictor followed up his poem on Richard Fenn with several further panegyrics upon City magnates, one would judge that the publication Benlowes now sponsored was thoroughly successful in its purpose.

Benlowes' new-old eulogy of London also exhibited incidentally another odd trait. Even for an age remarkable for a love of anagrams and similar verbal toys, Benlowes' delight in these things was excessive. He could not resist making anagrams of the names of the cities to which he compared London in his poem. He planted asterisks to guide the reader to the margin, where he would find Mediolanum (Milan) turned into "En odi Malum," Lovanium (Louvain) into "Vinum alo," Vienna into "En vina." The correspondency was quite a fictitious one and it could not be relevant to the poem to associate Milan with the hatred of evil (or of the apple either, for that matter) or Louvain with the growing of grapes. But this sort of parlour-game with letters—which had previously been played by the much-admired Sylvester—was greatly enjoyed by a mind more restless than inspired.

The mind, however, was essentially a serious one. The biggest work that it had so far undertaken was a book of piety. This was called *Sphinx Theologica*, and, like so many of the more scholarly and pedantic of her contemporary muses, this theological sphinx, disdaining all vulgar popularity along with the vernacular, chose to present her sacred riddles, or her temple music, as she called her devotions, in Latin. Benlowes did not at the same time disdain to copy the example of his friend Quarles in making use of scriptural paraphrase and in mingling prose and verse. The first part of what was intended to be a work in three books was published in 1636 [1]

---

[1] Benlowes gave the date, with an ingenuity quite typical, in a chronostich on the title-page: — "TrIn-VnVs DeVs Mea LVX & saLVs." Anthony à

at Cambridge, and it boasted of coming from the university printing-house. Its title-page announced the book as divided into three parts, and the contents of three books were listed; so the second and third were presumably written though never printed. Evidently something caused a change of mind in the author when the book was actually in the press. The volume as it appeared was made up of a series of ten devotional meditations—on faith, the blessed Trinity, God the Father, the Old Testament miracles, Our Lord Jesus Christ, the Blessed Virgin Mary, the Nativity, the boyhood of Christ, the New Testament miracles, and the Eucharist. Each was headed with a collection of scriptural texts and consisted of verses closely following the thought suggested by the Biblical extracts together with a meditation in prose. The volume was dedicated in some introductory verses to Benlowes' young kinsman, William Nevill, with Benlowes' habitual wordplay ("Nevili, NE VILE VELIS, Emblema verendi. . . ."). Nevill was about to go up to Cambridge, and it may have been with a view to the young man's spiritual welfare that Benlowes put the book together. He prefaced it with a guide to poetical piety, in which he specially praised *The Purple Island*, Quarles's *Emblemes*, and the skill with which Winterton had imposed the rules of metre upon the aphorisms of Hippocrates. There were also complimentary poems at the beginning and end by unidentifiable admirers, coupling Benlowes' horsemanship with his poetry and his poetry with his piety, or matching his generosity to his college with the generosity of Apollo to him. This last compliment was from a member of St. John's College, and Benlowes responded to it by again remembering the college and presenting it with a copy of the book.

In that age, when a man's religion so often meant more to him than his life and when the devout were wont to look on earthly

---

Wood, with an inaccuracy also typical, miscalculated this and made it 1626, thereby creating an amusing instance of a ghost-book. The Bodleian originally catalogued the volume 1626, and though it has now corrected the mistake, all the bibliographers, down to and including Pollard and Redgrave, have been misled. It has been regularly stated that there are two editions, dated 1626 and 1636, and that the Bodleian has a unique copy of the first. And since the volume contained a prefatory poem addressing Benlowes as a captain of horse in the county of Essex, it was assumed that Benlowes was a captain in the militia in 1626 (Andrew Clark in *Essex Review*, XVIII, 14), which would be before he went abroad, as well as later on. This "fact" was repeated by Dr. Carl Niemeyer in "New Light on Edward Benlowes" (*Review of English Studies*, XII, 34). This is the sort of thing that makes every biographer tremble.

existence as a mere preparation for the life after death, such works of spiritual meditation could always find readers. A not uncharacteristic production of the very minor writers of the time was an octavo volume of verse, published in 1640, called *A Buckler against the Fear of Death*. It claimed to consist of "Pious and Profitable Observations, Meditations, and Consolations" on "Man's Mortallity," it was written by someone with the initials E.B., and it was said to have been perused by Quarles on his deathbed. It has in the past usually been attributed to Benlowes, and it has therefore to be mentioned here, but since there is no good reason for the ascription, further reference can cheerfully be consigned to a footnote. [1]

[1] The ascription appears in, among other places, the *Short-Title Catalogue* and the *Dictionary of National Biography*. The objections to it are the statement on the engraved title-page that the writer was a "minister in G.B." (which must outweigh the identity of his initials with Benlowes' own and the association with Quarles); a highly unlikely dedication to two society ladies, granddaughters of the Marchioness of Northampton; and the style of the work itself.

In recent years a good case has been established for the authorship of Edward Buckler. See C. A. Moore, in *Modern Language Notes*, XLI, 220ff; W. H. Buckler, in *The Library*, 4th. ser., XVII, 349ff; H. R. Mead, in *The Library*, 4th. ser., XXI, 199ff. (The British Museum cataloguers accepted this attribution in the course of working through B, so that their current catalogue as printed gives the book to both Benlowes and Buckler.)

Quarles's reputation was such that a chance to state on the title-page that Quarles had perused the book on his deathbed was held sufficient advertisement to warrant a new edition. This duly appeared in 1646 with a new title, *Midnights Meditations of Death*. A hasty bibliographer mistook the puff about Quarles for a statement of Quarles's authorship and was followed in this by such reputable authorities as Lowndes and Hazlitt. The bibliographical puzzle is complicated still further by a third edition in 1649 under yet another title, *Death Dissected*, claiming to be the work of Thomas Jordan. According to one bibliographer, "The plagiarisms of this writer are certainly to be numbered amongst the phenomena of the literature of the seventeenth century" (Corser, *Collectanea Anglo-Poetica*, VIII, 310). They are of a piece with his practice of printing a book with a blank at the head of the dedication so that he could insert the names of different patrons in different copies. Apparently he had a small press of his own to do the insertions with. This all throws light on the world of books at the time.

CHAPTER TWELVE

CIVIL WAR

Benlowes was achieving, at Brent Hall in the reign of Charles I, an existence of sober tranquillity. But while he was in his own person and surroundings trying to perfect a model of cultured ease and profitable leisure, big events were in train which were soon to destroy it.

It was because the age encouraged artistic preciousness and literary dilettantism and engendered a fierce religious passion that a life like that of Benlowes succeeded in becoming anything at all. It was because the age brought also civil strife and social upheaval that a life like that of Benlowes was bound to fail of ultimate happiness and destined to end in sudden catastrophe or protracted disappointment.

Yet the first thing to disturb the peace for Benlowes was of a domestic character. This was the departure from Brent Hall amid mutual unpleasantness of Benlowes' much loved and trusted servant John Schoren, upon whom Benlowes depended in his daily life to help him with his artistic hobbies and to relieve him of many of the irksome details of administering his estates. Unfortunately, Schoren had always an eye to his own advantage and proved hardly worthy of the confidence placed in him.

About 1641 there began a dispute about money which was never to be properly settled. Benlowes, on his side, although he had established an annuity on Schoren guaranteeing the amount of his wages, was not keeping up the payments. Schoren, on his side, since he as steward collected Benlowes' rents, had no difficulty in helping himself to his master's money. Whether he was led to do this by Benlowes' neglect to pay him, or whether Benlowes refused to pay him because he had started to do it, is not clear. Neither master nor man had the mind of an accountant. What seems probable is that Schoren was given too free a hand and was left to pay himself his own wages. Honestly or dishonestly he got the accounts into a muddle, and rightly or wrongly was suspected of fraud.

Schoren asserted that Benlowes was in his debt for a considerable sum for wages and for money laid out on his master's behalf. On one occasion he put this debt as high as £120, though this was certainly an exaggeration. For his part, Benlowes had no doubt that Schoren had had plenty of opportunities to pay himself his wages and recover his other disbursements and had in fact done so. Eventually, in January 1642, the parties came to terms and Benlowes signed a bond in promise to pay Schoren £44.18s. It was drawn up by William Tym, a gentleman of Lincoln's Inn, who was one of Benlowes' tenants; [1] and Tym and Benlowes' brother Henry witnessed it. But Schoren was not satisfied, and soon after this he justified suspicions of his honesty by absconding. [2] Thus was broken —though only temporarily—an association which had lasted fifteen years and one which, as between master and man, was unusually intimate.

This personal quarrel was trifling in comparison with the grave events which followed. When the Civil War broke in 1642, Benlowes strove to keep aloof. He had never sought to take part in the political *mêlée*. Indeed, between the factions in church and state he held a somewhat equivocal position. He disliked the plainness of Puritan worship, which offended his taste; his natural instincts were all in favour of the increasingly elaborate ceremonial of Laud. On the other hand, like many good churchmen who opposed the Puritans, he had only abhorrence for the Arminian tenets of the High Church party. As his poem "Quarlëis" had shown, he was instinctively respectful towards the reigning monarch; yet he was bitter against the Catholics, whom the King and the bishops were coming more and more to tolerate. Paradoxically enough, it was his Catholic connections quite as much as his Royalist sympathies that were to bring him into difficulties during the early part of the Civil War.

Royalists in Essex were few, and Benlowes found himself shut in amid a society of Parliamentarians. The county had eight members in the Long Parliament, and when the war broke out all of these were found siding against the King. [3] One of these, Sir Martin Lumley, who lived at Great Lodge in Great Bardfield, whose estates converged with Benlowes' own, and who was an influential figure

---

[1] Subsequently a very unsatisfactory tenant, who mortgaged his leasehold and then forfeited it to his creditors.

[2] Chancery Proceedings, Whittington 71/87; Collins, 28/11. Depositions, C24/835/92.

[3] Masson, *Life of Milton*, II, 435.

at Great Bardfield church, [1] where the living was in Benlowes' gift, allowed his ardour shortly to cause bad blood between Benlowes and himself. Not all of these leaders, however, showed any great hostility to Benlowes so long as his sympathy for the unpopular party did not express itself in action. With one of them, Sir Thomas Barrington, he was on very good terms. There was also Harbottle Grimston, the recorder of Colchester, who, though a leader of the Puritans in the Commons, shared Benlowes' love of peace and, when hostilities opened, kept himself well in the background. [2] Benlowes had known Grimston since their Cambridge days, if not before, and had come to share his zeal against papists. Disapproving of the Romanist tendencies of Laud, he might well have enjoyed Grimston's fierce attack upon the Archbishop when the motion for Laud's impeachment was debated in Parliament. Yet they were bound to differ on fundamentals, for Grimston spoke also in favour of curbing the power of the bishops, which was one of the chief causes of contention at the beginning of the war. Grimston also rejected the notion of divine right. And his were the tenets which met with applause down in Essex.

In a war which was as much religious as political, the greatest influence on public opinion was wielded by the clergy, and in that part of England the clergy too were largely on the Parliament side. In Finchingfield itself, under the patronage of Sir Robert Kempe, the minister was none other than Stephen Marshall, destined to become the most eloquent, passionate, and influential of all the Puritan preachers. He had already for some years been a force for Puritanism in Benlowes' neighbourhood. He was accused of neglecting some of the prescribed ceremonies of the church, in particular of omitting the name of Jesus when he spoke the blessing; but Archbishop Laud's investigator, Sir Nathaniel Brent, had not been able to prove anything against him in 1636. Even so, his conformity was thought to be only superficial and Brent pronounced him "a dangerous person but exceeding cuning." [3] Benlowes, who raged

---

[1] Under the Presbyterian régime he was an elder there (Shaw, *History of the English Church, 1640-1660*, II, 384).

[2] Grimston's Puritanism was largely inspired by his concern for the defence of the rights of Parliament, which the followers of Laud were careless of. "The very embodiment of a constitutional Conservative" (Shaw, I, 10), he was not the man to follow either party to a revolutionary extreme. He did not wish "to set up a new form of government" which Englishmen had no experience of.

[3] S.P., Dom., Chas. I, 339/53; 351/100.

against those who renounced catechisms, communions, and creeds, [1] certainly cannot have approved of him.

No one could have been a more striking contrast to Edward Benlowes of Brent Hall than this vicar of the parish. Easy and humorous in social intercourse, Marshall was a master of homely phrase and piquant illustration—which was "very taking with a Country Auditory" [2]—but he had little point of contact with one who gave himself to the fastidious cult of learning and the arts. He was swarthy and thick-shouldered. To his foes his deportment seemed "clownish, like his Breeding; his Garb slovenly....his Gate shackling." [3] To Benlowes he must have represented much of what a gentleman despised, and as his influence spread in a time of growing faction he came to stand for what Benlowes abominated in the national life. He took a leading part in the agitation against the bishops, sponsored the petition for the reform of the episcopacy which over seven hundred of the moderate clergy presented to Parliament in 1641, and then in the same year was one of the foremost advocates of the Root-and-Branch Bill for abolishing the bishops altogether. By this time he had become a national figure, and Clarendon reckoned that in 1641 Marshall, together with Cornelius Burges, had a greater influence upon the Houses of Parliament than the Archbishop of Canterbury had upon the court. [4]

[1] *Theophila*, iii, 77.

[2] *The Life of Mr. Stephen Marshal* (Anon., 1680), pp. 7-8. This, in spite of its scurrility, is the most vivid account of Marshall and his preaching, much more effective than "A Brief Vindication of Mr. Stephen Marshal" (1681), in which Giles Firmin sought to answer it. Most of the contemporary gossip is gathered up in Brook's *Lives of the Puritans*, but Marshall is surely one of the most significant figures in English history still without a full-length biography—and that although, or perhaps because, "to trace the whole of his career, would be in great part to write the history of the entire [Civil War]" (Davids, *Evangelical Nonconformity in Essex*, p. 392). E. Vaughan's *Stephen Marshall*, though slight and not always accurate, is useful for its local knowledge, but makes no attempt to place him before a national background.

[3] *The Life of Mr. Stephen Marshal*, pp. 29-30.

[4] *History of the Rebellion*, ed. Macray, I, 401. Here is one instance of Marshall's influence. When the Root-and-Branch Bill was hanging fire, a plan to get it brought before the Commons in Committee was hatched one evening at a secret meeting at which Marshall was present with Hampden and Pym and a few others. The next day D'Ewes, who had no idea that the bill would be sprung upon the House, left the chamber "to walk in Westminster Hall behind the shops, near the Court of Common Pleas, when Mr. Stephen Marshall, minister of Finchingfield, came to me and asked me how chance I was not in the House, and desired me to make haste thither, because they were in agitation about this great business for abolishing bishops. I told him I thought it was not possible, because I was but a little before come out of the House. He answered me that

One of Marshall's activities during the events that led up to the war was to take part in the Smectymnuus controversy. After Bishop Hall had published a couple of pamphlets maintaining the divine right of the bishops, five of episcopacy's principal assailants collaborated in a rejoinder, which set forth their demands for a reform both of the bishops and their liturgy. The combined initials of the five authors made up the rather fearsome nom-de-plume Smectymnuus, towards which Stephen Marshall contributed the first two letters. The authorship nevertheless was no secret, and much abuse was directed at this five-headed monster, familiarly called Smect by the High-Church party and the Royalists in general. [1] In this abuse Benlowes joined with passionate fury when he came to write *Theophila*, and nothing could better illustrate the bitterness he felt towards the minister of his parish than his attack upon the "dissembling Pulpeteers" who played "*fast and loose, beneath* Smects *Hood*." [2]

Even so, things were outwardly quiet in Finchingfield at the beginning of 1642. Trained from his Catholic childhood in quietly maintaining without openly proclaiming unpopular views, Benlowes kept his opinions for his meditations and his poetry. He and Marshall could be together at parish meetings and their signatures still jostle one another in the Finchingfield "Town Book." On April 11th they were both present for a discussion about a broken village bridge. [3] A few months later Marshall was with the Parliamentary army, praying in their camps and exhorting the soldiers at Edge Hill. Benlowes, who found Edge Hill "a Theam for Tears in unborn Eyes to be still shed," [4] must have agreed with Marshall's enemies that "he had better have been in his Pulpit at *Finchingfield*." [5] Yet at Finchingfield the vicar had already done harm enough to the cause Benlowes cherished. If in the eastern counties the principles of Root-and-Branch were "distinctly predominant among the farmers

---

it was undoubtedly so, and that some of the House had determined to call for it today." So D'Ewes went off rather out of temper and delivered a long, if hastily prepared, speech in favour of the bill (D'Ewes, Journal, as cited by Shaw, *History of the English Church*, I, 81-82).

[1] The Smectymnuus pamphlet war went on throughout 1641. One of the principal reasons for interest in it nowadays is the contribution made by Milton to the side of the reformers. The most satisfactory account of the controversy as a whole will be found in the second volume of Masson's *Life of Milton*, book ii, chapters 3, 4, and 5.

[2] *Theophila*, iii, 76.

[3] "Town Book," p. 53.

[4] *Theophila*, xii, 59.

[5] *Life of Mr. Stephen Marshal*, p. 23.

and tenantry," [1] Marshall had more to do with it than anyone. It was said that he governed "the consciences of all the rich Puritans in those parts." [2]

Even if one looked beyond the clergy and the landed gentry, the Parliamentary influence was still strong throughout Essex. In Benlowes' immediate neighbourhood, the town of Bardfield was full of cloth-workers, who, in one Cavalier view, "being poore and populous," were "naturally mutinous and bolde." Their masters, being but tradesmen, were "sordid men," and of course supported the Parliament, "whose constant stile was tenderness of commerce." [3] Altogether, Benlowes' position in the county cannot have been other than difficult. But at the same time his very isolation would have prevented him from lending any active support to the King, even had he wished it. The few attempts that were made in the King's behalf in that Parliamentary stronghold met a swift disaster. A man from Benlowes' neighbourhood, it is true, Sir Charles Lucas of Colchester, went off to the King and became a prominent Royalist leader; but when Lucas' brother, Sir John, collected arms and horses and was about to ride out to join the King, the Colchester mob— the place was full of poor weavers—broke in upon his house. There were disturbances in the town and a good deal of plundering, es pecially at the expense of the Catholics. Lady Rivers, for example, lost property valued at forty thousand pounds, [4] and had to be rescued from the mob by her friends among the Parliament's supporters. [5] But order was soon restored. December 1642 saw the formation of the Eastern Association, which was to become a principal agent of the Parliament's power. Essex of course was part of it—and, according to Fuller, not a mere limb, but the very heart. [6] It was through the Eastern Association that Cromwell himself came to wield authority, and by April 1643 Royalism in this region had been effectively extinguished. [7]

Wars unfortunately have to be paid for, and the financial burden in the eastern counties seems to have fallen most heavily on those unsympathetic to the Parliament. Active support of the King was

[1] Masson, *Life of Milton*, II, 200.
[2] S.P., Dom., Chas. I, 351/100.
[3] Historical MSS. Commission, 12th Report, Appendix, part 9, p. 23.
[4] Gardiner, *Civil War*, I, 12.
[5] Arthur Wilson, *The Tract of My Life* (in Peck, *Desiderata Curiosa*, 1779, II, 474-475).
[6] *Worthies*, ed. Nichols, I, 371.
[7] Gardiner, *Civil War*, I, 142.

called delinquency and was punished by the sequestration of the delinquent's estates, out of which the loyal supporters of the Parliament proposed to reimburse themselves for all charges they had incurred in the fight. [1] Even passive support was likely to be expensive. Under a series of ordinances beginning with that of February 24, 1643, a weekly payment was imposed upon every county, and the money was collected by committees appointed for the purpose, who were given a free hand in assessing the owners of property. [2] Not unnaturally, King's men and papists fared ill in the assessments.

Lenience towards the Catholics had been one of Charles's offences, and as soon as Parliament got power it set to work to remedy this. In 1643 a much severer oath was introduced, demanding the renunciation of the doctrines of transubstantiation and purgatory and other cherished beliefs of the Catholic religion. [3] And in the meantime recusants were being denounced all over the country. All laxity in enforcing fines for absence from State worship now ceased, and the estates of Catholics fell under sequestration. The Benlowes family suffered, and Edward himself was suspect.

Francis in Norwich had to provide a certificate for church attendance, and Francis' daughter Clare lost her jointure. The last glimpse one gets of this branch of the family is of Clare in 1650 petitioning for the restoration of her property and claiming to be a Protestant. [4] A Mrs. Mary Benlowes, widow, of Little Bardfield, whose exact connection with Edward is obscure, was "sequestred for Popish recusancy" on April 29, 1643. She owned lands also in Finchingfield, which Edward rented from her, and, according to the usual procedure in such cases, he was called on to pay £29. 12s.6d., being two-thirds of the annual rent, to the government instead of to his kinswoman. [5] Edward himself was looked on with suspicion when Richard Pulley, acting for the Essex Sequestrations Committee, prepared a survey of amounts due from sequestrations; for under Little Bardfield the clerk tentatively mentioned Benlowes in his list, though he did not know his Christian name nor whether

---

[1] *Ibid.*, I, 17; Firth and Rait, *Acts and Ordinances of the Interregnum*, I, 106ff.

[2] Firth and Rait, I, 85, etc. The Essex Committee included, of the people mentioned in this biography, Sir Thomas Barrington, Sir Martin Lumley, and Harbottle Grimston.

[3] Firth and Rait, I, 254-260.

[4] S.P., Dom., Interregnum, G95/422-445; G158/307-18.

[5] *Ibid.*, G252/136; G261, p. 29.

to call him a delinquent or a recusant. He therefore left a blank. [1] Since he never filled in, either, the value of the property or the amount due to the sequestrators, presumably his doubts about Benlowes could never be substantiated. The survey for Finchingfield, better informed from the start, vouched for the respectability of one of the principal landowners in the parish by ignoring Edward Benlowes and Brent Hall altogether.

Nevertheless, Benlowes' position was certainly precarious, and there was a big strain on his finances. He paid the weekly dues levied by the Parliament, but his own rents were not always forthcoming. Sometimes the commissioners descended upon him for extra money. An ordinance of August 12, 1643, demanded that a thousand dragoons should speedily be raised in the county of Essex and further charged the county with the sum of £13,500 for the payment of the Parliamentary army. [2] A fortnight later, to meet this demand, certain landowners had been assessed for the payment of one twentieth of their estate over and above the weekly tax, and Benlowes was one of the sufferers. On top of this, his mother's recusancy was made the excuse for persecuting him. Some of his tenants were commanded to withhold their rents from him. If Benlowes had held the lands "in trust for" or "to the use or uses of" a papist and not for himself, the sequestration would have been legal, [3] and evidently someone was trying to pretend that he held them for his mother. He suspected his close neighbour, Sir Martin Lumley, with whom he was on bad terms. Sir Martin Lumley was by this time, inevitably, a very powerful man in the district as a member both of the Committee of Sequestrators and of the committee responsible for the assessments. On both those bodies, however, Benlowes had, as well as an enemy, an important friend; and he decided to make an appeal to him to use his influence on his behalf. So on October 11th, two days after his tenants had been forbidden to pay their rents, he sat down and wrote the following letter to "his most honoured friend" Sir Thomas Barrington, of Barrington Hall in the parish of Hatfield Broad Oak. [4]

[1] British Museum, MS. Addit. 5505, fol. 17^v. Although Benlowes' Christian name is left blank, the lands were said to be in the occupation of one Mason, and a later Chancery suit shows that Benlowes had a tenant called Mason, so that there can be no doubt about the identification.

[2] Firth and Rait, I, 245-246.

[3] Ordinance of March 27, 1643 (Firth and Rait, I, 107).

[4] Although Sir Martin Lumley had been made High Sheriff of Essex in 1639, a knight of the shire in 1640, and a baronet in 1641, among the landed gentry

Noble S^r

Were I confident of y^r being at Hatfield, I would haue personally waited
there on y^u, to haue ye favour frō y^u, to know when & where y^r self
& ye cōmission^rs next meete, for I am enformed by my Bardfield Tenants,
y^t they were last munday forbidden at Dunmow to pay me their due rents,
because it is conceived (though unprooved) y^t my Moth^r is a Papist, who
never being legally convicted, & living in London, paying all Parliamentary rates & taxes, & contributing nothing to ye oth^r side, I hope, my
Moth^r comes not wthin ye compasse of ye Ordinance. S^r, no Tenants
lease is made to her, shee hath no visible estate nor can they sweare shee
hath oth^r ioynture then my Liberality. Half my rents thus sequestred
for not my fault, & ye oth^r rents scarce to be had disable me (who haue
payed all things for ye whole estate heth^rto) to discharge ye remainder
of ye 20 part wherein I was rated beyond ye ordinance. But (I feare) these
things arise frō some personall differences between Sr M. Lumley and my
self, wherein passion may overact. I beseech y^u, y^t at y^r next publike
meeting I may reioyce in ye fruition of y^r iust favour,

for wch I rest
y^r most obliged serv^t
Benlowes

Brenthall
Oct: 11 1643.

Benlowes was obviously the victim of injustice on account of his
unpopular views. Yet his letter contained at least one unwise e-
quivocation. It may have been "unprooved," but no one had any
doubt that his mother was still the ardent papist she had always
been. Edward himself cannot have been ignorant of what she was
doing in this very year, though it was just as well that her activities
were not generally known. Somehow or other she had got hold
of her daughter's son, Thomas Peirce, who, then about seventeen
years old, had been brought up so far as a Protestant. And she sent him
over to Douai, as she had done two of her own sons twenty years
before, to be instructed in the Catholic faith. He was admitted on
May 28, 1643. [1] Unfortunately for her, Thomas Peirce's education
had been sadly neglected and the boy had none of the Benlowes
aptitude for learning. He got weary of studying and found the Douai
discipline irksome. Towards the end of 1645 he left the college in
search of a freer life, spent some time in Brussels, and then, with

the Lumleys were relatively upstarts, and Edward Benlowes could remember
before they ever came to Great Bardfield at all. Sir Martin's father, an eminent
London merchant, had bought the manor of Great Bardfield from the Wrothe
family about 1621. The Barringtons were an older family and Sir Thomas was
cousin to Oliver Cromwell himself. The repute that he enjoyed among the
Puritans in the House of Commons is indicated by their appointing him one
of the twenty members to sit with the divines in the Westminster Assembly
(Firth and Rait, I, 181).

[1] *Douay College Diaries—Third, Fourth and Fifth*, II, 440.

his grandmother's permission, returned to England. [1] But for two years and a half his grandmother paid three hundred florins a year for him at Douai, and if it is true that she had no means beyond what Edward Benlowes allowed her, this is a very strange fact. It means that Benlowes, militantly anti-papist himself, was indirectly providing money for the Catholic education of his nephew. But it is only one instance of the way in which his strong family loyalty influenced some of the most important acts of his life. At a time when political and religious allegiance often broke the most intimate personal ties, Edward's affection for his mother triumphed over everything else. But what a case his enemies among the local gentry could have brought against him if they had only suspected! It could easily have been made to appear that he was conniving at what his mother did.

Still, there were no just grounds for Edward's persecution, and he had reason to hope that Sir Thomas Barrington would be able to secure him some relief from the confiscation of his rents. What result his letter had is unknown, but it was duly received at Barrington Hall and endorsed as being "ffrom Capt Bendlowes." The military title was in itself an act of courtesy indicative of goodwill; Benlowes had with the outbreak of war relinquished his command in the Essex militia, [2] but it was as captain that Sir Thomas Barrington still thought of him.

It seems as though for the next year or two Benlowes was let live at Brent Hall without undue molestation beyond the Parliament's ever-increasing demands for money to meet the cost of war. But even without the molestation of person or property, the Civil War was bound to be profoundly shocking to all those of Benlowes' temperament. One of his former *protégés*, John Sictor, already exiled from his own country by religious strife, could capitalize their emotion in 1644 in a compendium of the Christian religion in Latin verse especially compiled for "these turbulent times." Benlowes' own agitation was to colour several pages of his *Theophila*. In spite of his captaincy in the militia, he came to have a fierce hatred of war. To him Alexander was not the Great, but "*Philips* hot-brain'd *Son*," a "prosp'rous *Thief*," despised and loathed as one who "tore the *Nations* all asunder." He was slain by a "Just *Fate*," and Benlowes

---

[1] *Ibid.*, II, 449.

[2] The Essex troops had given their allegiance to the Earl of Warwick, the Lord Lieutenant of the County and one of the Parliamentary leaders.

did not doubt that he was now suffering appropriate torments in hell. [1] Civil war was even more abhorrent, and especially when taken part in by churchmen. In attacking the clergy who promoted war Benlowes had Stephen Marshall, the vicar of Finchingfield, particularly in mind. Marshall not only justified those who took up arms against the King; he preached against those who did not. "The Lord acknowledges no *Neuters*," he said in his most famous sermon, which was delivered upon the text: "Curse ye Meroz (said the Angell of the Lord) curse ye bitterly the inhabitants thereof, because they came not to the helpe of the Lord....against the mighty." Marshall is said to have delivered this sermon sixty times. [2] He reminded his audiences that they might "be called, as souldiers, to spend [their] blood in the Churches cause"; he cited God's curse upon Moab, "Cursed is every one that withholds his hand from shedding of blood"; and he argued with a logic that was irrefragable once the divine inspiration of the Old Testament had been accepted, that God's work might conceivably be "to spill and *powre* out the *bloud* of *women* and *children*, *like water* in every street." To Benlowes these were terrible sentiments. He knew that "*uncivil* Pray'r" and "*civil* Blood" were alike hateful to God, and could not see how "Presters, *rudely fierce*," could proclaim it good "*To wade through* Seas *of native* Blood." He was filled with grief to see the common people diverted from their fruitful occupations. There was something monstrous, against nature, when the peasant's hand turned to bearing arms instead of sowing the earth. [3]

Benlowes, then, did not so much weigh up the political issues involved as passionately sympathize with those who desired peace. And these were not few. Some mild rioting had broken out in London in December 1642 in protest against the war, and at the beginning of 1643 the Parliament, influenced by a strong peace party in the Lords, opened negotiations with the King at Oxford. Proposals went backwards and forwards between the parties, but even preliminaries could not be agreed and hopes of a truce were dashed. [4] A year later overtures for peace came from the King's side, [5] and although there was even less likelihood of success now, hopes and longings were again stimulated—in Benlowes as in others.

---

[1] *Theophila*, viii, 60-61.
[2] *Life of Mr. Stephen Marshal*, p. 26.
[3] *Theophila*, iii, 75-76; ix, 34.
[4] Gardiner, *Civil War*, I, 74-109.
[5] *Ibid.*, I, 300, 307.

It was now that Benlowes made his only direct contribution to the literature of the war, in a pamphlet discussing an honourable cessation of the fighting and the restoration of peace with faith. [1] Unfortunately, there was no faith and there could be no peace. Each party called the other traitor, claimed itself as the legal government, and wanted peace on its own terms.

There was no fighting in Benlowes' own vicinity, where village life indeed was on the surface barely interrupted, though the vicar was now a perpetual absentee. Sir Robert Kempe had presented a petition to the Commons asking that the village might be allowed to retain its pastor, but the Finchingfield residents had been disappointed. He was much in demand elsewhere—and not only among the forces in the field. He was the favourite preacher for Parliament itself on special occasions and at solemn fasts; he was one of the regular lecturers at St. Margaret's, Westminster; and when the Westminster Assembly of divines was formed in 1643 for the purpose of advising Parliament upon church matters, Marshall at once assumed a leading role. [2] In the same year he was one of the two clergymen who accompanied six Parliamentary representatives on the mission to Scotland which resulted in the famous Solemn League and Covenant. The Covenant upheld the Puritan faith in religion and accepted the Presbyterian form of church government. It was the declaration of those who found the Book of Common Prayer offensive and swore to abolish the episcopacy. On February 5, 1644, it was decreed by Parliament that allegiance to the Covenant should be sworn by every Englishman over eighteen. [3] Mild in

---

[1] *Honorifica Armorum Cessatio, sive Pacis et Fidei Associatio Feb. 11. An. 1643* (that is, 1644, new style). I have not traced a copy of this. The authority for it is Anthony à Wood (*Fasti Oxonienses*, II, 359), who calls it an octavo. He has been followed by Lowndes, Hazlitt, and Bullen *(D.N.B.)*; but none of these gives one the slightest reason to suppose that he ever saw it.

[2] According to Fuller (*Worthies*, ed. Nichols, I, 473), "In the late *long lasting Parliament*, no man was more gracious with the principal Members thereof. He was their *Trumpet*, by whom they *sounded* their solemn *Fasts*, preaching more *publick Sermons* on that occasion, than any *foure* of his Function. In their *Sickness* he was their *Confessor*; in their *Assembly* their *Councellour*; in their *Treaties* their *Chaplain*; in their *Disputations* their *Champion*." In view of Marshall's zealous Presbyterianism and his consistent opposition to the King, Fuller's gibe at him as being "of so *supple* a *soul*, that he *brake not a joynt*, yea, *sprained not a sinew*, in all the alteration of times" is difficult to excuse. There was a streak of tolerance in Marshall which sometimes made him disliked among his own party (by Baillie and the Scots, for example) but which Fuller might have been expected to approve. It was certainly not due to a lack of strong conviction.

[3] Firth and Rait, I, 376-378.

politics, Benlowes was passionate in religion. He might refrain from active support of the King; he could not subscribe to this hated Covenant. In *Theophila* he cried

Avant
*With your six-hundred-sixtie-six-word-*Covenant.

(iii, 78)

To appreciate the exact degree of his abomination one must remember that six hundred and sixty-six is the number of the Beast in the Book of the Revelation. In Benlowes' view the Presbyterian, as a "corrupted" churchman, was worse than an atheist. The clergy who refused the Covenant were ejected from their livings, but the penalty to be imposed upon laymen was left vague. Benlowes was left in possession of his house and lands, but he became more suspect than before.

Benlowes' spiritual distress at all these events was shared by his friend and fellow-poet, Francis Quarles, but Quarles's life did not retain the same outward tranquillity. Much more ardently than Benlowes he was a supporter of the King. When Benlowes' views on the Covenant found expression, they were embedded in a poem unpublished until after the war; he confined his political writings to hopes of peace and his controversial writings to attacks upon the Catholics. These were safe enough. But Quarles entered vigorously into the vexed political and religious disputes of the day. As a result he suffered persecution, which hastened his death.

Quarles was a man of peace, and, according to his widow, "he used his pen and powred out his continuall prayers and tears to quench this miserable fire of dissention." [1] He could see good and evil on both sides, as when, with the Civil War at its height, he wrote a pamphlet called *The Whipper Whipt* in defence of Dr. Cornelius Burges, the man whom Clarendon linked with Stephen Marshall as a divine of great prestige and influence among the Parliamentary party. Yet it seemed to him that peace could only come through the faithful allegiance of all the people to the King and to the established church. And his belief in the sacrilege of attacking a king, whose divine right he regularly justified by scriptural quotation, had led him inevitably to the Royalist side. He is said to have been with the King at Oxford, and in 1644 he published a pamphlet, *The Loyall Convert*, in which he defended the King's position and

---

[1] Quarles, *Solomons Recantation*, sig. A3; *Works*, ed. Grosart, I, xxii.

attacked his enemies with some vehemence. The recent successes of the Royalist armies he held to be a mark of God's displeasure with the rebels, and the deaths of Hampden and Brooke a just punishment for their sins. Cromwell was attacked as a "defacer of Churches", and Quarles had heard that his "prophane Troopers. . . .watered their Horses at the *Font*." [1] For this degree of partisanship some sort of reprisals could only be expected. A petition was preferred against Quarles, with many aspersions on his character, and according to his wife "the first news of it struck him so to the heart" that he said "*it would be his death*." Mrs. Quarles said that he never recovered from the shock, but that his last illness was brought on by it. [2] His death from grief was also said to have been hastened by the destruction of his books and manuscripts. There can be little doubt that he was the victim of plundering, and he died in great poverty, leaving his widow with nine children and little means to support them beyond her hopes of income from his surviving manuscripts, the possession of which she proceeded to dispute with a couple of his publishers. [3]

The Civil War brought Quarles a hasty death, but he fared better than some who survived, as he himself realized when he thanked God for "*taking him into his own hands to chastise, while others were exposed to the fury of their enemies, the power of pistols, and the trampling of horses*." [4] The troubles of Benlowes had hardly yet begun. But although he did not think of stopping his habits of benevolence or his indulgence in costly artistic pursuits, his letter to Barrington shows that he had already had difficulties about money. The Parliament's extortionate assessments continued to fall heavily upon him, and on May 9, 1645, he mortgaged to his own tenant, Matthew Reeve, a farm called Pitfield Barnes in the parish of Hatfield Peverel. The mortgage was for £300, and Benlowes paid Reeve interest at 8 per cent. [5] Even so, what Benlowes most suffered at present was fear and alarm. It was partly in order to have protection against the danger which he feared from the forces of the Parliament—that "vsurped power," as he called it—that he allowed John Schoren

[1] *Ibid.*, I, 144. There is a full discussion of Quarles's pamphlets during the Civil War in an article by G. S. Haight, "Francis Quarles in the Civil War," *Review of English Studies*, XII, 147ff.

[2] Quarles, *Solomons Recantation*, sig. A3^{v}; *Works*, I, xxiii.

[3] Haight, in *RES*, XII, 161.

[4] Quarles, *Solomons Recantation*, sig. A3^{v}; *Works*, I, xxii.

[5] Close Rolls, 21 Chas. I, pt. 1, no. 31.

to re-enter his service about 1645. [1] Where Schoren had been since he parted from Benlowes and what he had done, beyond getting married, is unknown. But he had not been very successful, and according to Benlowes he was very poor when he reappeared at Brent Hall, having decided to try and get employment again with the master who had been so generous to him. In spite of what had happened two or three years before, when Schoren had deserted his employment and been suspected of embezzlement, Benlowes listened to Schoren's earnest entreaties, had hopes of his amendment, and renewed his trust in him. Schoren was capable and versatile; Benlowes liked to be relieved of responsibility, and was also grateful for the security afforded by his old servant's presence in those troubled times. Moreover, Schoren said that his wife had a good knowledge of housekeeping, and as Benlowes listened to her praises he thought of the comfort that "a frugall Gou[er]nesse in the house" might bring to his bachelor existence. So John Schoren became bailiff again and Sarah was housekeeper. For the time being life was more comfortable with them; yet in his old age Benlowes bitterly regretted ever having the pair of them in his house. When Sarah Schoren took to pursuing him with writs he must have thought much of vipers in the bosom. But that was much later. For the present he felt safer and more easy in his mind. Schoren worked the rolling-press again and made himself generally useful both inside and outside the house. Very soon they were on their old footing, and Benlowes reaffirmed the annuity guaranteeing Schoren's wages, which of course had lapsed while Schoren was away.

The fear Benlowes had of suffering from the depredations of the Roundheads was not just capricious. Plenty of peaceful households were descended on by Parliamentary troops, who confiscated all weapons and demanded corn and hay for their horses. It was wisest to comply with their demands, for a hostile reception was likely to be followed by looting, and later on a passive resister might find his property sequestrated just as much as if he had been openly on the King's side. Among Benlowes' own friends Quarles was certainly not the only one who had been pillaged for his political allegiance. There was Thomas Pestell, for example, a clergyman over at Packington in Leicestershire, sixty years of age, who com-

---

[1] The Chancery suits from which this information derives are sometimes self-contradictory and often inaccurate as to dates. The incident is variously dated about 1644 and about 1646 (Chancery Proceedings, Reynardson 31/14; Collins 28/11).

plained that by 1646 he had been robbed of his cattle, corn, and household goods "at eleuen sundrie plundring[es]," so that ultimately he had "not a bed leaft. . . .nor a bitt of Bread or cupp of Drinke." [1] Benlowes himself was "threatned" that he would be plundered for his loyalty to the King. On one occasion he took the threat seriously enough to give thirty pounds over to Schoren in the belief that it would be safe in his hands. That unfortunately was just where it would not be safe. A faithful servant in other ways, Schoren was still not to be trusted with money, and Benlowes could never get it back. Seventeen pounds of it Schoren tried to account for by saying that it had been stolen out of his chamber window by a carpenter who was in the house at the time. Benlowes believed him, and only long after, when his eyes were opened, did he realize that the story was false. [2]

[1] *Poems*, ed. Buchan, p. xliii.
[2] Chancery Proceedings, Collins 28/11.

CHAPTER THIRTEEN

THE LITERARY GENTLEMAN DURING
THE CIVIL WAR

So far Benlowes was able to preserve the continuity of the country gentleman's life, no matter what the difficulties. One feared one's neighbour, paid the heavy taxes, refrained from flaunting sympathies with an unpopular party, and hoped for the best and the return of quiet times. Of course an opposite temperament would soon lead into the thickest of the fray a poet like Milton, with his burning sense of political justice and his demand for liberty not only for an isolated individual but in the constitutional framework of the state. "What safe retirement for literary leisure could you suppose given one," he wrote to his Italian friend Dati in 1647, "among so many battles of a civil war, slaughters, flights, seizures of goods?" Soon after his return from Italy the "most turbulent state of our Britain" had obliged him to divert his mind from study "to the defence anyhow of life and fortune." [1] Yet in contrast the Civil War was Benlowes' time of greatest literary activity. Many indeed managed, however precariously, to hold themselves aloof while disturbances went on around.

Even those who were not aloof could sometimes, by taking an ambiguous line, come to an accommodation with the times. An interesting case is that of Benlowes' friend John Gauden, who exhibited considerable skill in not allowing his political or religious views to interfere with his ambitions for preferment. He had been chaplain to the Earl of Warwick, who got the Parliament to nominate him Dean of Bocking in or about 1641, and he nearly got into the Westminster Assembly. [2] His real sympathies, however, gave rise to "Certaine Scruples and Doubts of Conscience about taking the *Solemn League and Covenant*," which he published in anonymity. In spite of his scruples he seems to have taken the Covenant: his foes

---

[1] *Works*, XII, 51.
[2] For his own account of this, see *Anti Baal-Berith*, pp. 88-89.

accused him of it and his own denial is sufficiently tinged with casuistry to leave more than a little suspicion. [1] Nevertheless, he continued to use the prayer-book after the Parliament had banned it longer than any other clergyman in his neighbourhood. Eventually he had to desist, but, then conforming to Presbyterian dictates, he retained his office, though he busily used his pen in arguments favouring the episcopalian church. During the Interregnum he was to come out more strongly on the King's side, and after the Restoration more strongly still, with the reward of a couple of bishoprics. He owes his fame, of course, to his reputed authorship of the *Eikon Basilike*, the celebrated pamphlet presenting the "pourtraicture of His sacred Majestie in his solitudes and sufferings." Benlowes must have known Gauden years before at Cambridge; even if their difference in status would prevent anything like intimacy, yet they had been together at the same college. Now, with Gauden eight miles away at Bocking, he was able to renew the acquaintance, and the two must have seen a good deal of one another during these early years of the Civil War. They must at times have been in violent disagreement, and Benlowes certainly did not follow Gauden's various shifts of creed. But they had a respect for one another, and a neighbourly friendship continued for some years. When Gauden prefixed a Latin poem to Benlowes' *Theophila*, it was to celebrate in Benlowes one of those paradoxical conjunctions that the seventeenth-century panegyrist delighted to discover. Benlowes, he said, combined piety with poetry; in his numbers Zion united with Parnassus. A certain admiration for the religious fervour of Benlowes' life breaks through the conventional superlatives. On a later occasion Benlowes was to turn to Gauden for friendly assistance when he was about selling his estates and had need of the name of a man of standing. Benlowes' prospective purchaser entered into a bond of six thousand pounds with John Gauden as a guarantee that the purchase money would be forthcoming. [2]

Gauden was the sort of man who was "content to....go along hand in hand with the rest of his company; *dissenting privately*, but consenting publickly." These words were said, however, not of Gauden, but of another distinguished friend of Benlowes—Thomas Fuller, the author of *The Worthies of England*. [3] Even the judicial

[1] *Ibid.*, pp. 275-276.
[2] Chancery Proceedings, Bridges 444/123.
[3] By Peter Heylyn, who attacked Fuller's *Church-History of Britain* with his *Examen Historicum* (1659), in which see p. 234.

estimate of the *Dictionary of National Biography* finds that Fuller "steered rather too skilful a course, perhaps, through a revolutionary time." But this is the sort of accusation that can always be made against men of moderate views, and the trouble with Fuller was that, like Quarles, he saw good and bad on both sides. [1] He refused to accept the Parliamentary Covenant without reservations, was deprived of his income, and joined the King at Oxford. But he was too mild and reasonable for the King's ardent supporters. He astonished his contemporaries by refusing to allow his political sympathies to mar his private friendships. Who else, in that age, after being a chaplain in tow with one of the Royalist armies, would have been glad to be a guest in the house of Sir John Danvers, one of the men who signed King Charles's death warrant? Fuller had friends who were not only influential but wealthy, and while many of the ejected clergy were in pecuniary distress, he enjoyed a liberal patronage for the copious literary work he was all the time engaged on. He rewarded his patrons later on by dedicating to them a certain portion of one or other of his works. Among them was Edward Benlowes, who in 1650 was honoured with one of the double-page engravings which adorned *A Pisgah-Sight of Palestine* and then as a "benevolent Maecenas" received the dedication of the sixth section of Fuller's *History of the University of Cambridge*, when this work was eventually published, along with *The Church-History of Britain*, in 1655.

Fuller was only one of the men of letters whom Benlowes was coming into contact with during the period of the Civil War. A more intimate associate was "old Alexander Rosse," as Evelyn was wont to call him, "the divine, historian, and poet." [3] Ross had been a chaplain to King Charles and had made a name for himself as a preacher in the city of Southampton. A prolific author of prose and verse, he was much given to controversy, and although now principally remembered through Samuel Butler's jest about the

> ancient sage *Philosopher*,
> That had read *Alexander Ross* over, [4]

his pronouncements carried considerable weight in his own day— which fact, indeed, gives point to Butler's line. "The general Trumpet

---

[1] For a very generous estimate of Fuller's character, see Gardiner, *Civil War*, I, 277.

[2] Ed. Prickett and Wright, p. 179.

[3] Evelyn, *Diary*, II, 6, 47.

[4] *Hudibras*, part i, canto 2, lines 1-2.

of Fame," asserted the poet John Davies, blazed him abroad for a great "advancer of Vertue and Learning." [1] This sort of reputation gave him an exaggerated confidence in correcting what seemed to him to be the errors of men like Bacon, Harvey, and Hobbes—not to speak again of Copernicus. His very title-pages exhibit his eagerness to have "the ancient opinions vindicated" against the encroachments of the new science. Benlowes perhaps was less sensible of the scientific danger to long-received opinions. But it was Benlowes himself, admired by his friends for the extent of his intercourse and influence with Ross, [2] who prompted Ross to assail Sir Thomas Browne.

Benlowes read Browne's *Religio Medici* very soon after its appearance in 1642. And he thoroughly disapproved of it. He detested the tolerance which the Roman Catholics were receiving at the hands of the King's party and the Anglican church; and he perceived the same dangerous tolerance in Browne. For Browne showed himself a humane and moderate man who ventured to dislike the usual animosities of seventeenth-century religious controversy. While choosing the middle way of the Church of England and holding himself orthodox because, as he said, in matters of religion he loved "to keep the Road," [3] he was not prepared to say that there might not be something good in Catholics and Puritans. For Benlowes and his circle, not to be violently partisan was to be Laodicean. Benlowes would be horrified, too, to find Browne saying: "I was never afraid of Hell, nor never grew pale at the description of that place." [4] He himself, for all his kindness to his Catholic relations, liked, when he thought theologically, to picture heretics and sinners "frying" in agony.

Browne's book had not, of course, gained in the eyes of Ross and Benlowes by the enthusiasm of the distinguished Catholic, Sir Kenelm Digby, who read it with great excitement and then dashed off some *Observations* upon it, all within the space, he would have one believe, of a mere twenty-four hours. But Browne's own heresies were enough in themselves to explain why Benlowes "so earnestly desired" Ross to attack them. Benlowes seems to have had a way of suggesting books for his friends to write—one remembers Quarles and the *Emblemes*—and he easily prevailed on Ross to launch an attack on the *Religio Medici*. Although at the moment short of books

[1] *Apocalypsis*, Epistle Dedicatory.
[2] *Ibid.*
[3] *Religio Medici*, pt. i, sec. 6.
[4] *Ibid.*, pt. i, sec. 52.

and leisure, Ross took up his pen to "satisfie" Benlowes' "desire" and wrote his *Medicus Medicatus* as a refutation of Browne and Digby together, seeking to cure "the Physicians Religion. . . .by a *Lenitive* or *Gentle* Potion." In a shocked pedagogical way the book rebuked Browne for his errors one by one. He had thought Anglicans and papists shared something of the same faith; he had not always been indignant at the sight of a crucifix; he saw no objection to praying in Roman churches; he did not find it obvious that the Pope was antichrist, "the man of sin, and childè of perdition." In Ross's view Browne had doubts which showed him to be a "bad *Christian*," and his book was aptly named *Religio Medici*, for—with one of the puns perpetual in seventeenth-century controversy—it was "the religion of the House of *Medicis*, not of the Church of *England*." Ross's attitude throughout—indeed in all his controversial pamphlets —is that of scandalized orthodoxy confronted with a man who lets his pen "run too much at randome"—in short, dares to think for himself. And this was the attitude that had Benlowes' full approval. Ross dedicated *Medicus Medicatus* to him "as a testimony of his service and love." It was entered on the Stationers' Register on March 7, 1645, [1] and came out shortly after.

Medicus Medicatus was naturally despised by those who had acclaimed the *Religio Medici*: Ross was alone, said one of them, in having *"the face to appeare against it,"* sarcastically adding that this demonstrated the fact that "Bookes have their fates from the Capacity of the Reader." [2] But *Medicus Medicatus* also had its public and in Ross's own circle was said to be "generally applauded." [3]

The opponents of the *Religio Medici* sought to counteract its dangerous influence with all the greater zeal because they were alive to its great artistic merits. Ross had to admit that there was "much worth and good language" in the book. [4] And his perception of this may also have been due to Benlowes' suggestion. For Benlowes, delighting in Browne's picturesque imagery, paid him the compliment he usually gave to authors he admired by copying some of his phrases. Browne, for example, with his delight in mathematical similitudes, had seen man's life as running "not upon an Helix that still enlargeth," but on a circle, which brought man, after he had attained his meridian,

[1] Eyre, I, 153.

[2] Thomas Keck, in the *Annotations* appended to the 1656 edition of the *Religio Medici*.

[3] *The Oxinden and Peyton Letters 1642-1670*, p. 76.

[4] Page 80.

back below the horizon again. [1] Benlowes, characteristically enough, borrowed the image while contradicting its application. Man's higher nature could not be compared to a circle, he thought, a thing complete in itself. But

> Mans *spirit'ual State*, enlarg'd, still widening flowes,
>   As th'*Helix* doth: A Circle showes
> Mans *nat'ral Life*, which *Death* soon from its *Zenith* throwes. [2]

Ross's attempt to cure the physician's religious distemper was not enough to abate Benlowes' fervour. He planned to attack the Catholics on his own account as well. And the result was *Papa Perstrictus*. This Latin poem should, then, be viewed as a retaliation for Sir Thomas Browne's reluctance to see the Pope as the incarnation of evil. It is full of the same sectarian bitterness as had marked Benlowes and Winterton when Winterton translated Gerhard's aphorisms over a dozen years before. Otherwise it was chiefly remarkable for its illustration of Benlowes' fancifulness in juggling with words. The date was given by chronogram in the motto, "tV, CHrIste, tV sIs sVpreMVs DVX In VIIs," and the poem was headed by a verse dedication to "Petrus Beauvisus," whose name fell as readily as Benlowes' own into a complimentary anagram. Petrus Beauvisus was "verus, pius, beatus," and when that had been perceived, his truth, piety, and blessedness naturally became the theme of the dedicatory lines. This was elementary compared with the principal poem, the whole method of which was the exploitation of echoes. This device had been used before, [3] but never, surely, with greater thoroughness. It began in the title itself. The Pope was not only "Perstrictus," censured, but the censure was reinforced by the echo, which made him also "Ictus," smitten. In the body of the poem the Pope is continually tormented by the echo, which ingeniously contradicts what he is made to utter. This is the sort of thing: the Pope contends that the papal bull is "pretiosa Gregi," precious to the people; the echo insists that it is "Osa Gregi," hated by the people. The Pope is walking by the Tiber, hoping to speak to himself alone, when the voice sounds from the hollow caverns, and an elaborate dialogue ensues. The Pope holds that he is the head of the Church, but is

---

[1] *Religio Medici*, pt. i, sec. 17.

[2] *Theophila*, iii, 20.

[3] Perhaps the best known example is George Herbert's poem, "Heaven." For other contemporary specimens, see Herbert of Cherbury, *Poems*, ed. Moore Smith, pp. 46-47. For a list of instances from Euripides to Hardy, see F. L. Lucas' note on the echo scene in *The Dutchesse of Malfy* in his edition of Webster, II, 195-196.

told that the head of the Church is Christ. The echo attacks the
Roman clergy, accusing them of lustful living. The Pope protests
at this rage against the priests' bald heads *(calvos)*; the echo rejoins
that it is against their bellies *(alvos)*. The Pope entertains them
(invito), the echo shuns them *(vito)*. They are not beggars *(men-
dicantes)*, but devourers *(manducantes)*. The Jesuits are attacked and
Huss defended. Benlowes could never forgo a pun on a name, so
the Pope reminds us that Huss, in the Bohemian vernacular, means
a goose. But the echo transforms him into a swan. Eventually the
Pope accepts the echo's view of affairs, and when he repents, the
echo supports instead of contradicting him, so that the poem ends
with the two voices in unison.

The phonetic cleverness of all this was accompanied by an appeal
to the eye such as Benlowes, with his love of ornament, frequently
made in his poems. The speech of the echo was "rendered visible"
by being printed throughout in red. Later on, when the vogue for
echoes and emblems had passed, Samuel Butler laughed at Benlowes
for his pains. What Butler thought of a production like *Papa Perstrictus* is clear. He pretended to have heard of "a *Tobacco-Man*,
that wrapped *Spanish* Tobacco in a Paper of Verses, which *Benlows*
had written against the *Pope*, which by a natural Antipathy, that
his Wit has to any Thing that's Catholic, spoiled the Tobacco." [1]
Benlowes' own circle, however, viewed *Papa Perstrictus* very differently. Alexander Ross quite naturally saw it before publication,
and quite as naturally applauded it. He wrote eight lines of Latin
verse to congratulate Benlowes on having made plain and visible
the goddess who was wont to hide in waves and hollow stones.
And presumably he was unaware of any inconsistency in praising
this jeering and abusive echo-poem immediately after he had found
fault with the *Religio Medici* for replacing logical argument with
rhetorical phraseology. If you agreed with the echo, no doubt it
seemed to have logic on its side. Benlowes' own attitude can be
seen in the sixteen-line poem which he appended to *Papa Perstrictus*,
insisting that the echo was not a jest or a fabrication, but a voice
of conscience which was constantly making itself heard in the minds
of those who, being in error, were sufficiently blest to have a conscience or an echo to reprove them.

The *Papa Perstrictus* was being printed in London—and by the

---

[1] *Characters*, ed. Waller, p. 54. Ridicule of echo-poems in general occurs also
in Butler's *Hudibras*, part i, canto 3, lines 189ff.

same printer, James Young—not so many months after the *Medicus Medicatus*. It was entered on the Stationers' Register on July 8, 1645. [1] The chronogram shows that it was in fact composed in 1645, and it was issued with a 1645 imprint. But if we are to accept Thomason's correction of the imprint in his copy and his date August 20, 1646, as that of publication, then there was a quite unaccountable delay before it finally appeared. It was a single folio, intended to be mounted on a board; and in this form it was distributed among Benlowes' friends. One of its first recipients was James Howell, shut up in the Fleet prison, from where he acknowledged it [2] in a letter written on August 25th [3]—a letter which gives testimony to that generosity which Benlowes always showed to writers and artists in misfortune. It was while Howell was in prison during the war years that Benlowes chose to befriend him.

Howell had not, of course, always been as humble a figure as he was now. He had, indeed, had considerable success as a hanger-on of great men, and there is some mystery about how he came to be in prison. According to his own account, his only offence was his loyalty to the King; [4] but probably Anthony à Wood had some justification for his assertion that Howell was "seized on" for his

---

[1] Eyre, I, 180.

[2] Jacobs, in his edition of the *Familiar Letters* (p. 782), suggests that the "*Table of exquisite* Latin *Poems*" was probably *Lusus Poëticus Poëtis*, without considering why Benlowes should send a book ten years old when he had a new poem just published. And Howell's praise of the "*Echo*" is only intelligible with reference to *Papa Perstrictus*.

[3] Howell adds the year, 1645, and I have sometimes thought that this apparent corroboration of chronogram and imprint suggests that Thomason for once may have been in error. Yet this seems unlikely in view of his punctilio in these matters and of his clear intention in this instance to overrule the printer's date. Howell's dates are notoriously unreliable and do not occur at all in his first edition. Yet his August 25th, when set beside Thomason's August 20th, does not look like a fabrication. I therefore suppose that Howell correctly dated his letter August 25th but without giving the year, which he afterwards supplied from the imprint of *Papa Perstrictus* when he was adding the dates to the letters for their second edition.

[4] *Familiar Letters*, p. 355. He tells how five armed men rushed into his chamber and seized all his books and manuscripts, how he was brought up for examination and his papers perused. Nothing incriminating was discovered, and his own story therefore does not make clear how he came to be imprisoned. It reads as though he had written it just after his arrest, but obviously he had not; for he dated it November 20, 1643, and in a letter dated December 1644 he said that he had already been in prison 31 months (*ibid.*, p. 370). To share a little in Anthony à Wood's malice, one might say that as time went on Howell got through the months more quickly, for in February 1646 he claimed to have been in prison 55 months (*ibid.*, p. 434).

debts. In the Fleet, "having nothing to trust to but his wits, and" (said Wood, somewhat unkindly adapting a phrase of Howell's own) [1] "the purchase of a small spot of ground upon Parnassus....he solely dedicated himself to write and translate books; which, tho' several of them are meer scribbles, yet they brought him in a comfortable subsistence, during his long stay there." [2] He seems indeed, in spite of his frequent reference to fits of melancholy, to have been tolerably happy in the Fleet. In the early part of 1645, possibly while Benlowes was elaborating the echoes of *Papa Perstrictus*, Howell was busy preparing for the press the first collection of those *Familiar Letters* which are now his principal title to fame. He also had a varied throng of visitors, and held almost a sort of salon in what he called "this little *Fleet-Cabin* of mine." [3] And there at least he was, as his friend Endymion Porter reminded him, "free from plundering" and such other current "Barbarisms" [4] as one like Benlowes lived in constant dread of in those years of civil war. Benlowes several times came to see Howell in his "cabin," and perhaps allowed Howell some benefit of his purse. He was, no doubt, one of those who helped Howell to the reflection that "among other effects of affliction, one is, to try a Friend; for those proofs that were made in the fawnings, and dazzling Sunshine of prosperity, are not so clear as those which break out and transpire thro' the dark clouds of adversity." [5] Sometimes Benlowes sent Howell presents, including—a gift which satisfied his own vanity as well as Howell's taste for literature—a copy of Fletcher's *The Purple Island*, which Benlowes, of course, had had printed and decorated and of which copies were evidently still on hand at Brent Hall. Howell added his gratitude for this and "other fair respects" when he wrote to thank Benlowes for *Papa Perstrictus*.

Papa Perstrictus delighted him; or, at least, he delighted to say so. The "slender board" which held those "rich and elaborate Poems" seemed quite inadequate for them. They deserved "a far more lasting monument to preserve them from the injury of Time." Unlike Butler, Howell admired the skill which had contrived the echo, and decided: "Your '*Echo*' deserves to dwell in some marble porphyry Grot, cut about *Parnassus* Mount near the source of *Helicon*,

---

[1] *Ibid.*, p. 373.
[2] Wood, *Athenae Oxonienses*, III, 745.
[3] *Familiar Letters*, p. 528.
[4] *Ibid.*, p. 431.
[5] *Ibid.*, p. 366.

rather than upon such a slight superficies." The pleasure was not entirely unreciprocated; for Benlowes read the *Familiar Letters* and his liking for them is, as usual, attested by his borrowings.

Perhaps Howell spoke truer than he knew when he praised this sheet of poems as the table of Benlowes' soul. At least it gave a good illustration of Benlowes' attitude of mind. He who desired above all else a quiet life was accustomed to violent passion in matters of religion. He made no attempt at rational controversy, but exposed his opponents to elaborate ridicule. After joining the English church, he always seemed to approach theological issues with a sealed mind. He took those who differed from him in religion to be wickedly perverse—an attitude characteristic of his age, though, on the surface of things at least, odd in one who was himself a convert. Benlowes was not proud of being a convert: he never advertised his own Catholic connections. Yet it was no doubt because of them that the Catholic-Protestant controversy loomed unduly large in his mind. As the main feature of the English religious struggle, it had been long superseded by the antagonism of Anglican and Puritan; but this was an antagonism of which Benlowes showed awareness only occasionally, when he permitted himself some sudden scornful outburst against the Covenant, the Presbyterian system of church government, or the Puritan distrust of music. He loathed the Puritans in so far as he blamed them for the war: when he was engaged on strictly theological disputes he hardly thought of them. His feelings had hardly kept pace with the times. But that in itself was an index of their sincerity. He was quite happy to be attacking the Catholics at a time when the Catholic support was invaluable to King Charles and when more tactful men on the King's side kept silent. [1] He was like many of his age in being swayed more by his religious than his political opinions; but he was highly exceptional in keeping the two almost entirely separate.

---

[1] Howell was more characteristic among Royalists in preferring Catholics to Puritans. Later, when he contemplated the "*Babel* of all Opinions" into which England had fallen when she "thought to run away so eagerly from *Babylon*," he remembered all that he had "noted to be praise-worthy and imitable" when he "had eaten [his] Bread often in those Countries where that Religion is profess'd." He praised its "admirable" system of government and the Catholics' "frequent long fastings" and "comely prostrations of the body" (*Familiar Letters*, pp. 618-623). I cannot help suspecting that *one* reason why Benlowes sent Howell *Papa Perstrictus* was that he could not approve of the degree of sympathy which Howell showed for Catholic practices. It could have been no recommendation of Howell that he was a friend of Sir Kenelm Digby.

Most who hated the Catholics as Benlowes did naturally went over to the Parliamentary side. But Benlowes, with his predilection for the ornate in art, despised the bare churches of the Puritans and their somewhat graceless services. Yet he was a little of a Puritan himself, if he had only known it. In a passage of Latin prose which filled the bottom of the *Papa Perstrictus* broadsheet he, in art a lover of the emblem, inveighed against the worship of images and prayers to the saints. For too many years, he thought, the individual will had been ruled by the priest, and he abominated the priestly tradition, for it had bred superstition and had drowned the words of Christ, to which alone Benlowes appealed in defence of his own creed.

Papa Perstrictus was only a by-product of Benlowes' literary activity at this time. He had in fact begun to write *Theophila*. And before very long parts of it were being shown round in the circle of friends with whom he was in the habit of exchanging compositions. Alexander Ross saw it, of course: by the time it came to be printed he had translated its first canto into Latin.

Among those who knew that Benlowes was working on his long poem during those years of civil war and who took great interest in its progress was a clergyman called Clement Paman, to whom Benlowes wrote on one occasion, about 1646, [1] that the poem was yet only in the bud. He was so much in the throes of composition, however, as to be fettered to the poem, or, as he put it, in danger of shipwrecking his liberty. To this the earnest Paman, who was breathless with admiration of one who was poetically tracing the history of the soul and its translation into Heaven, replied in gentle reproof: "W^t speake y^u y^n of ship-wracking yor liberty here? Was

---

[1] The exact date is obscure. The letter is not extant, but its nature is clear from Paman's reply, a fair copy of which is to be found in a manuscript volume in the Bodleian (MS. Rawl. D. 945, fols.29-32), along with eight other items, of which five are letters by Paman to various people. Unfortunately, the letter to Benlowes, written from Spains Hall in Finchingfield, is undated. The dates of the other letters vary from before January 1641 (the date of the death of Paman's brother Robert, to whom two of the letters are addressed) to January 7, 1657. The letters are not in chronological order, but that to Benlowes is followed by one to William Sancroft, written, also from Finchingfield, on Sept. 29, 1646, and it probably belongs to the earlier part of the same year. Internal evidence makes it clear that it was written sometime while fighting was still going on, and so, since it is before Paman became vicar of Thatcham (Berks.) in 1648, it cannot be later than 1646. On the other hand, it seems to have been written while Benlowes was at work on the third canto of *Theophila* (see below, p. 160), which was later than the publication of Milton's *Poems* in January 1646 (see below, p. 163). For fuller argument, see my article, "Benlowes and Milton," *Modern Language Review*, XLIII, 193.

euer any man afraid of being wrackt vpon yᵉ coast of Paradise, wⁿ he might be sure to come safe to land? And for yoʳ liberty; you gaine more. For wᵗ fredome can be greater yⁿ to goe to yᵉ whole magazine of Excellencyes when yᵘ please?" And as for Benlowes' modesty in talking of buds, buds like Theophila (or Sacrata, the holy one, to give her her alternative title) "weare their sweetnes wrapt vp in Modesty, & haue theire beauties cover'd by Nature wᵗʰ a veile: But wⁿ she shall be full blown, I doubt not but she will make good yᵉ vertues she is descended of, both by Father & Mother: wᵗʰ both whose goodnes I am so well acquainted yᵗ I haue wisht Sacrata perfect enough wⁿ I haue wished her like yᵐ."

Like many of the seventeenth-century gentry and clergy who had studious and artistic interests, Paman was something of a poet himself. He had a pleasant lyrical faculty, and although he never published, his poems were known to a number of seventeenth-century poetry-lovers, as is clear from their not infrequent occurrence in the private manuscript anthologies which that period plentifully produced. [1] Benlowes must naturally have seen some of Paman's compositions in verse as well as prose.

Paman showed himself no whit inferior to Benlowes' other poetical friends in his command of fantastic flattery. In his letter to Benlowes he called Theophila the South Indies, a "Kingdome of jewells vndiscouered," but destined soon to be discovered and inhabited as well. For though her virtues lay now sealed up, yet Time and Fame would "break ope yᵉ volume, & reade yᵐ out aloud unto yᵉ world." Heaven itself was reflected in Sacrata like the sun shining in the water. This maiden whom Benlowes' muse "Courted in an high & orderly passion" deserved "a morning rapture" before the author's thoughts had "convers'd with any thinge yᵗ is mortall."

Paman had evidently perused the first two cantos or so of *Theophila*, which was as far as it had got. Benlowes had formed the habit of sending him copies of his compositions. The last poem Paman had received he promised to keep a copy of, since it was certainly not the sort of poem that was "borne to dye as soone as it spoke." Yet keeping a copy was hardly necessary, for he avowed that he could not forget it and that even if it were lost everywhere else it would be found in his memory. [2]

[1] On this, see Ault in *Seventeenth Century Lyrics*, where one of Paman's poems is for the first time printed.

[2] If the poem was *Papa Perstrictus*, the praise is peculiarly extravagant. But perhaps Paman is simply referring to the latest instalment of *Theophila*.

Poems, however, were not the principal topic of discussion in the correspondence that Benlowes carried on with Paman. They were in the habit of writing to one another on topics of devotion, each of them suggesting a theme for the other's pen. Thus Paman's extant letter, obeying a request from Benlowes, is largely given over to an essay on the "deuout soule," which must have followed a great deal of pious meditation on his part and was no doubt the occasion of as much more on the part of the recipient.

One of the peculiarities of this sort of epistolary correspondence is that it was more easily carried on when the two writers were within easy reach of one another than when they were at a distance. Like so many of Benlowes' friends, Paman belonged to the eastern counties and had been up at Cambridge.[1] Though not a contemporary and not of the same college, he must have known, at least by repute, the distinguished gentleman-scholar, who, about the time that Paman was taking his degree, was celebrated for his benefactions to St. John's. He got to know Benlowes well through visiting in Finchingfield, where he used occasionally to stay with his relative Sir Robert Kempe [2] at Spains Hall. He was there, for example, in September 1646. [3] Being ten years younger than Benlowes, he tended to look on him as a mentor, and by his own account—he had "but newly learn'd to speake"—was less practised in writing on devotional subjects. This was a lack that he was doing his best to remedy, for he was carrying on a correspondence of similar fervour with at least one other of his friends, William Sancroft, [4] who also replied in kind. On one occasion Paman received from Sancroft an extremely long dissertation in Latin on chapter ii, verse 16, of the Second Epistle to the Corinthians, which was subsequently copied into the volume where such treasures were preserved. From Benlowes he received every encouragement, which was natural enough; for in proposing the devout soul as a theme, Benlowes was asking Paman

[1] Venn, *Alumni Cantabrigienses*, III, 302.

[2] An earlier Clement Paman had married Bridget Kempe, the aunt of the Robert Kempe who held Spains Hall at this time.

[3] As appears from the address he appends to the letter to his friend Sancroft.

[4] Sancroft was of the same school and university as Paman, and, spending the war period at Cambridge and part of the Commonwealth period at Fressingfield in Suffolk (where he busied himself with literary work and an attack upon the Calvinists), he was probably also in the orbit of Benlowes' acquaintance. He was, of course, a man of much greater renown. He obtained high preferment in the church after the Restoration, and eventually, two years after Benlowes' death, was to become Archbishop of Canterbury.

to reflect on the subject with which he was himself most occupied as he worked at *Theophila*. Paman at Spains Hall settled to his task with alacrity, but could not reply at once because of a journey which Benlowes made to London. Then, one evening, he heard that Benlowes was back at Brent Hall. With some tact he did not send his letter over at once, not wanting it to descend on Benlowes just as he got home, already tired. He waited till next day, when the letter might take its recipient "at yᵉ best advantage," and then dispatched it along with the kind messages of Sir Robert and Lady Kempe. And if Benlowes was not already tired of the correspondence, then the subject of his next "recreation" was to be "The holy Poett." For, added Paman, "I long to see him drawn by one yᵗ's soe: And indeed none else can doe it, as nothing can shew us yᵉ Sun but itselfe."

Paman's own exercise had this in common with Benlowes' *Theophila*, that the writer's mind saw the soul "lifted up aboue oʳ earth" and pursued her as she left the revels of worldly courts to be "drown'd in euerlasting hymns & Anthems." Only then could she begin "to know wᵗ she is, & for wᵗ she was made." Part of what Paman wrote, however, was in the nature of a character-study of the kind the seventeenth century made famous. The devout soul was to be shown in all her characteristic attitudes and habits. Paman told how she behaved at prayer and during the sermon, how she gave alms and was charitable "euen to yᵉ loose & impious," how when she fasted, she did it earnestly, "neither couzening God in a corner with a full belly, nor men in yᵉ Church with a soure face." Various false devotions were also distinguished—hypocritical devotion, as practised by those who, so long as their coach was seen at a lecture-door in the morning, were willing for it to stand all afternoon at a tavern; devotion falsely austere which, with insupportable fastings and whippings, scared men from God. In Paman's view, devotion should be cheerful and service a delight. He scorned that "hott & angry piety" which offered up "its deuocōns in blood & smoke as if it hoped to please God by offering him yᵉ mangled world for a Sacrifice."

This last was exactly what the furious religionists of the day were doing, and there was much sincerity in Paman's lament over the Civil War. He admired how Benlowes retained his composure of spirit. He saw his fine soul "stand vnmou'd on its pillars in yᵉ midst of earthquakes." Benlowes, singing of "Loue & Sacrata" in a storm, was "in Tune" when three kingdoms were "miserably out." "The

Muses," said Paman, "were wont to dwell on yᵉ tops of hills, secure, & quiett, aboue yᵉ disorders of clouds & tempests, where their laurells stood assur'd not only from yᵉ *stroke of thunder*, but yᵉ *noyse*." But Benlowes had given them "security in yᵉ plaine, & taught them priuacy in yᵉ midst of drums, & canons." Another of Benlowes' friends, Thomas Pestell, praising later on the completed *Theophila*, found his thought arrested by wonder that Benlowes alone "could warble Thus" in "such *Combustions*, wherein *Thousands* grone." [1]

But Benlowes could not fail, as I have shown, to be deeply stirred by the violence around him. In *Papa Perstrictus* he deplored an age which studied wars instead of books; he made the Pope and the Echo unite in denunciation of an angry, bloodthirsty world. If so far he had ignored the Civil War in *Theophila*, it was because in his poetical ecstasy his soul soared into the "Suburbs of PARADISE" [2] and could view the wicked world in grand perspective, seeing the strife of mortals as a "childish broil," an affair of "shot-bruis'd *Mud-walls*." [3] It was because he regarded the world of men as thus small and insignificant that he could keep calm, with a temper, as Paman himself said, beyond the strength of Paman's courage. So that, as Paman saw, Benlowes stood as if he "bestrid Parnassus," with "all yᵉ tumults of yᵉ world" under his feet.

Yet Paman's letter had a remarkable effect on Benlowes. It made him ask if he was right to turn his back on the distresses of mankind and give himself up to religious ecstasy. In the third canto of *Theophila*, which he must have been already at work on when Paman's letter came, he put the question: Could Theophila still "use her *Lyre*" in time of war? And confidently the answer came in terms which Paman's talk of storms and earthquakes had itself suggested:

> Yes. She's unmov'd in *Earth-quakes*, tun'd in *Jars*;
>   (Fear argues Guilt) She stands in *Wars*,
> And *Storms* of thund'ring *Brass*, bright as coruscant *Stars*. [4]

Nevertheless, the war now pressing in upon Benlowes' consciousness, Theophila had to pour out

>   a Flood
>   Of *Tears*....for *Albions* Blood,
>   Shed in a *Mist*. [5]

---

[1] See *Theophila*, 1652 folio, sig. Cᵛ.
[2] *Theophila*, iii, 8.
[3] *Ibid.*, iii, 14.
[4] *Ibid.*, iii, 63-64; *cf.* quotations from Paman above.
[5] *Theophila*, iii, Argument.

And as she cried on God for help, she feared that she might *"sink as deep in* Bloud, *as* Tears." [1] Benlowes' passionate outburst upon civil war followed, largely provoked, one therefore sees, by Paman's having marvelled at his being able to give himself to devotional poetry at such a time. As he went on writing his sacred poem Benlowes more than once lamented that *"Unthrifty* Death *has spread where thriving* Peace *did range."* [2] Even wild beasts did not make war upon their own kind; but man was his own Apollyon and in fighting himself did *"CHRISTS mystick* Body *tear."* [3] Benlowes cried out against those whose sectarian quarrels led them to shed Christian blood:

> *Ye* Sons *of* Thunder, *if You'l needs fight on,*
>   *Lead your fierce* Troops *'gainst Turkish Moon,*
> *Out of the* Line *of* FAITHS Communication. [4]

But if Benlowes desired peace, he had no spirit of compromise and he never doubted where heresy lay. He went on at once to the passage I have already cited in which he denounced the Covenant. He was savage, as only the devout can be, against those "Proteustants" who denied even the incarnation of the Son and thus disowned what was *"The* Grand Day *of the Year,"* the dearest of the Church's prerogatives, and the joy of the archangels themselves. [5] He knew only that seventeenth-century tolerance which might forgive an opponent who had confessed himself in the wrong, but expected that confession from him. So, he was ready to pass an act of oblivion and pardon what had happened if the Puritans would *"smite Hand on Thigh, and say,* What have we done!" [6] His hope that Theophila's love-song would make converts among those suffering from "misguided *Zeal"* was inevitably vain. [7] But no one can doubt the sincerity with which he implored God to renew his gift of peace to men *"worn out with* Wars *Distress";* [8] and in making his own picture of Theophila, the aspiring soul, he created his own lode-star to guide him to the love of God.

Benlowes was appalled by schism in God's church. More than once he echoed Milton's line about the hungry flock who were

[1] *Ibid.*, iii, 68.
[2] *Ibid.*, iii, 67.
[3] *Ibid.*, iii, 71.
[4] *Ibid.*, iii, 72.
[5] *Ibid.*, iii, 79-80.
[6] *Ibid.*, iii, 85.
[7] *Ibid.*, iii, 97.
[8] *Ibid.*, iii, 91.

not fed, though no doubt his "Scramblers at the Shearing Feasts," [1]
the corrupt clergy, had not quite the same identity as Milton's.
The world seemed a fit object for God's and his own rage and he
achieved happiness by shutting himself away from it. In the twelfth
canto of *Theophila*, writing of "the Happinesse of a Private Life,"
he told how, seated secure "in safe *Repose*," it was possible to "manage Mirth," even when the country round about suffered by
"Rage of War, and Dearth." [2] He sang an idyllic landscape, with
violets and strawberries, and tulips opal-coloured in the gray light
of dawn; rustic contentment in a thatched, elm-raftered cottage.
And there, where trees instead of troops, and fields of corn instead
of combat were, happiness could be his. At least, in theory that
was so; though it seems never to have been more than a dream.
Even here he could not forget how "thirsty *Spears* were drunk with
Blood." He wept for the massacre at Edge Hill. And beyond the
number of the dead, he thought of the sufferings of those in prison:

> How many bound with Iron, who did scape
> The Steel! and Death commits a Rape
> On them in Jayls, who Her defy'd in warlike Shape! [3]

A great deal of the landscape of Benlowes' rustic retreat is copied
straight from Milton. However troubled by the uneasy state of
England, he found plenty of time and thought not only for his own
writing but also to indulge his reading tastes. In prose he had read
the *Religio Medici*, and, very naturally, the *Familiar Letters* of Howell
soon after they came out. In the way of poetry not very much was
printed in the first three years of the Civil War, [4] for as the publisher
Humphrey Moseley said, "the slightest Pamphlet" was in those
days "more vendible then the Works of learnedest men." [5] Moseley,
however, was one of those high-minded publishers who are determined to offer good literature to the public, and he brought out
Milton's *Poems* in English and Latin on or just before January 2,
1646. [6] For the interruption of literary leisure which the Civil War
made inevitable for Milton had not prevented his preparing his poems

---

[1] *Ibid.*, xii, 12; borrowed, of course, from "Lycidas", line 117.
[2] *Theophila*, xii, 34.
[3] *Ibid.*, xii, 58-60.
[4] *Cf.* Masson, *Life of Milton*, III, 446.
[5] Milton's *Poems* (1645), The Stationer to the Reader.
[6] Thomason's dating. *Comus* and "Lycidas", which had of course appeared
before and which Benlowes may have known already, now reappeared with
all of Milton's verse composition to date.

for the press. Benlowes, fairly knowledgeable about what was going on in the literary world, was soon perusing them; and with no suspicion of how closely Milton was to become identified with a cause that he abhorred, he could not restrain his admiration. Before long he knew these poems very intimately indeed, and as he wrote *Theophila* he punctuated it all through with echoes of Milton's phrases. *Theophila* had almost certainly been begun before 1646, and it is notable that the first two cantos show little of Milton beyond some epithets which were taken from the already published *Comus* and which in any case might have been introduced in revision. But the Miltonic influence gets greater in the third canto, which I suppose Benlowes to have been writing in 1646. [1] By the time he came to the twelfth canto—where *Theophila* was developing a pastoral theme—*Comus* and "L'Allegro" were drawn on to an extent that suggests that he had his Milton almost off by heart. Prone as Benlowes was to take to his own use whatever he admired in the verse of others, only from Sylvester did he borrow more than from Milton. And Sylvester was, of course, a much more bulky author. In Milton's relatively slender volume almost every page provided Benlowes with treasure trove.

Especially Benlowes admired Milton's felicity in epithet. His miser's hoard, like Milton's, was "unsunn'd." His angels, too, were "bright-harnessed." He copied Milton's "rocking Winds" and "Golden-tressed Sun." All those happy compounds which seemed to occur so easily to Milton were too good not to become part of his own poetic vocabulary. *Comus* provided "night-founder'd," "vermeil-tinctur'd," as well as a "rushy-fringed bank." The genius of the stream which Milton conjured up stayed behind to do duty for Benlowes too. Borrowing often went beyond single words. Benlowes' gnats, like Milton's grayfly, were wont to "winde their Horn"; his oxen had already stepped out of the ode "On the Morning of Christs Nativity," following Osiris and "trampling Grass with Lowings loud," before, like those in *Comus*, they went "in loose Trace home." He remembered from the Nativity ode "the wakefull trump of doom," and from Milton's ode "On Time" the "individual kiss" with which Eternity will "greet" souls entering into "bliss." Milton also showed him God "at Heav'ns high Councel-Table" in the "midst of Trinal Unity." The profound admiration

---

[1] He was writing it while corresponding with Paman not later than 1646 (see above, pp. 156, 160), and the Miltonic influence seems to prevent its being earlier.

which Benlowes obviously felt for Milton's style shows that Milton's poems, if they made no great stir immediately, [1] did not everywhere fail of recognition. And—even if his method of showing it reveals a lack of originality in his own imagination—it is of course a lasting tribute to the excellence of Benlowes' taste. [2]

It is perhaps curious to find Benlowes reading Milton even more closely than he read Cleveland, a poet who did make a big stir in the world at that time. A wide circle of men with a taste for poetry were already familiar with some of his work in manuscript, and when his poems were published in 1647 their success was so startling that they had at least five editions in a single year. [3] A few other of his poems as yet unpublished were also circulating among his admirers; and Benlowes himself almost certainly knew "Fuscara" and perhaps *News from Newcastle* before they got into print. [4] Whether there was any direct contact between the two poets I cannot say; they must at least have had some common friends. A Cambridge man, Cleveland had been a fellow at St. John's when Benlowes' repute stood high there; Benlowes, on his side, would hold in esteem the man whose poetry, wit, and oratory had brought renown upon their college. With this would go a great deal of passionate sympathy when Cleveland refused to take the Covenant and when the Parliamentary party, having quartered their soldiers in the Cambridge colleges, having robbed the scholars of their books and stoned them in the streets, ejected Cleveland from his fellowship. [5]

[1] A second edition of the shorter poems suggests that they *were* read later in the century. But this edition came only in 1673, when Milton's longer poems had attracted a little attention. In his time Benlowes seems to have been quite exceptional in not neglecting Milton's lyrics. When Norman Ault went through seventeenth-century manuscript collections he could find several poems by Clement Paman; yet "Milton makes but one appearance in these collections, late in the century and in an insignificant volume, with a song from 'Comus.' " This does not mean that Milton had *no* admirers. Sir Henry Wotton's praise of *Comus*, quoted by Milton in his "1645" volume, is well known. For further references on this point see *Modern Language Review*, XLIII, 195 note.

[2] For a completer list of Benlowes' borrowings from Milton, with references, see Appendix II.

[3] *Poems*, ed. Berdan, p. 249; Saintsbury, *Minor Poets of the Caroline Period*, III, 13. *Cf.* Wing, *Short-Title Catalogue, 1641-1700*.

[4] "Fuscara" first appeared among Cleveland's poems in the second of the two 1651 editions; *News from Newcastle* in a quarto pamphlet in the same year. Benlowes had by then been engaged on *Theophila* many years, and his imitation of "Fuscara" in the first canto cannot, I think, have been as late as 1651. For a borrowing from *News from Newcastle* in Canto xii, see below, p. 210.

[5] On Cleveland's life, see introduction to his *Poems*, ed. Berdan, and S.V. Gapp, "Notes on John Cleveland," *PMLA*, XLVI (1931), 1075ff.

In a witty satire Cleveland had voiced some of the contempt they both felt for Smectymnuus; he had produced a stinging character-sketch of the typical member of the county committees under whose semi-legalized extortion Benlowes had suffered. Yet the skill in pungent topical satire which made Cleveland acclaimed as the poet of the Court party during the Civil War was not what Benlowes princip-ally admired in his poems. He liked them most for that special develop-ment of "metaphysical" wit which soon came to be known as Clevelandising—for epithets, that is to say, "pregnant with *Metaphors*, carrying in them a *difficult plainness*, *difficult* at the *hearing*, *plain* at the *considering* thereof" [1]—in fact, for that very yoking together of heterogeneous ideas which Dr. Johnson and most later critics have disapproved of. Benlowes learned from Cleveland to see the bee as the confectioner of Nature and an alchemist turning the garden into gold. [2] Cleveland, smitten "dumb" with love, fancied he had "pratling eyes," and Benlowes seized on this as a fine conceit to describe the oglings of a courtesan. [3] This is a good example of Benlowes' borrowing someone else's idea and "re-thinking" it, using the same words with a different application. So is his copying Cleveland in a characteristic pun to speak of verse with "*badger Feet*": Cleveland thought of iambic verse, alternating syllables of unequal length, like the badger's legs; Benlowes' badger limped, and its feet belonged to verse that was halting. [4]

Benlowes was, then, reading, among the new poets of the 1640's, the two who became most celebrated—the one by his own and the other by later generations. Other poetry of the period which one might expect to have found its way easily into Benlowes' hands includes Crashaw's *Steps to the Temple* and *The Delights of the Muses*, which had come together from Moseley's in 1646. No one can miss the similarities in vocabulary between Crashaw's "Musicks Duell" and Benlowes' *Poetick Descant upon a Private Musick-Meeting*. But the identity of a whole phrase as big as "the Spheres of *Musick*'s Heav'n" [5] is exceptional, and I suppose little significance attaches to the occurrence in both poets of such an epithet as "grumbling"

---

[1] Fuller, *Worthies*, ed. Nichols, I, 572. For Dryden, a "Clevelandism" was the same as a "catachresis," "wresting and torturing a word into another mean-ing" (*An Essay of Dramatick Poesie*, in *Essays*, ed. Ker, I, 31).

[2] *Theophila*, i, 67; *cf*. "Fuscara," lines 1-4.

[3] Cleveland, "To Mrs. K.T.," line 40; *Theophila*, xi, 44.

[4] Cleveland, "The Rebell Scot," line 27; *Theophila*, i, 58.

[5] *A Poetick Descant*, stanza 18; "Musicks Duell," lines 148-149.

for a musical bass. [1] So, in spite of the great affinities of temperament between the two poets, the signs of direct borrowing are less clear than is usual with Benlowes; and likenesses are explicable without it when one remembers that both Benlowes and Crashaw had been deeply influenced by the *Pia Desideria* and other emblem-books. It seems difficult to establish, then, for certain whether Benlowes did read Crashaw.

But in any case Milton and Cleveland were by no means the only contemporary poets he was paying attention to. At the other end of the scale was a verse translation of Aesop's *Fables* by John Ogilby [2] in which Benlowes found things to like, remember, and of course adapt to his own use—as, for instance, the line, "Such Trumpeters would blood turnd Ice unfreeze." [3] Ogilby's Aesop was published in 1651; but some of it at least was written several years before in Ireland, where Ogilby went as a dancing-master in the household suite of the Earl of Strafford. "He was," in the words of Aubrey, "undon at the Irish rebellion; returning to England, was wreckt at sea, and came to London very poor and went on foot to Cambridge." [4] In his distress he was befriended by several scholars and men of means, and, being of "an excellent inventive and prudentiall witt....when he was undon....he would make such rationall proposalls that would be embraced by rich and great men," [5] so that he was very soon out of his difficulties. If Benlowes did indeed cast a kind eye on the as yet unpublished Aesop, none would be more likely than he, an ever-generous patron of writers, to help Ogilby to "gaine a good estate again."

Quite a different sort of man from Ogilby was Joseph Beaumont, who also suffered hardship during the Civil War. He had been a fellow of Peterhouse, but was ejected as a Royalist in 1644, along with his more famous friend, Richard Crashaw. Thereupon he calmly retired to Hadleigh in Suffolk and wrote his gigantic poem called *Psyche*, said to be the longest poem in the English language. In this

[1] The contexts, though, are worth comparing. *Theophila*, iii, 51; "Musicks Duell," line 49.

[2] Whom Dryden thought fit to be the uncle of his King of Dulness in *Mac Flecknoe*. Pope followed with a similar gibe in the *Dunciad*.

[3] Fable VI, line 16; *cf. Theophila*, xi, 65. The nature of the two passages certainly suggests that Benlowes was the borrower, but again he quite changed the application of the image, associating—or rather, refusing to associate —this feat of "unfreezing" with a courtesan.

[4] *Brief Lives*, II, 102.

[5] *Ibid.*, II, 103.

he set out, as the title-page explained, to display "the Intercourse betwixt Christ, and the Soule." In spite of his lament that Crashaw was not at his elbow to revise the poem, he made such good progress that the twenty cantos of it were ready for publication in 1648. He was writing *Psyche* less than thirty miles away from where Benlowes was writing *Theophila*, and, with its narrative of the soul passing through the tribulations of life into an eternal felicity, *Psyche* had obvious resemblances to Benlowes' own poem. I certainly think Benlowes knew of *Psyche*'s existence before it came out in print. He must have liked the intense religious zeal with which its very solemn subject was handled, though Beaumont varied this much more than he himself was wont to do with passages of luxuriant description. The whole poem had more of narrative and allegory in it, belonging more to the tradition of Spenser and Phineas Fletcher than Benlowes' own work did. And he found nothing in its prolix style nearly as stimulating as the novel felicities of Milton. Yet he was echoing Beaumont in his own first canto when he called the Nile "Spermatick," [1] and he may have had *Psyche* in mind when he went on to taunt humanity as "our *Wormships*." [2]

Another sacred poet from Cambridge whose work Benlowes knew was Mildmay Fane, Earl of Westmorland. He was another, too, who had suffered as a Royalist. Having taken the King's side in 1642, he had been for some months imprisoned in the Tower and had suffered the sequestration of his estates, though afterwards he got them back again when he made his peace with the Parliament and took the Covenant. He retired to his Northamptonshire seat and was given to writing plays for his family to perform in private, as well as making use of the leisure which God had given him—"Deus nobis haec Otia fecit," he said on his title-page—to compose suitable poems. His *Otia Sacra* came out (for private circulation) in 1648. Again, however, Benlowes may not have had to wait for publication before getting to know some of Westmorland's poems; for already in the third canto of *Theophila*, which he had been writing about 1646, Benlowes had repeated Westmorland's line about the well-spring of life

where
Crystal is lymbect all the *Year*. [3]

---

[1] *Theophila*, i, 26; cf. *Psyche* (1648), ix, 30 (2d ed., ix, 34).

[2] *Theophila*, ii, 18. Cf. *Psyche* (1648), v, 149 (2d ed., v, 172): "Vain *Son of Dust* pull down thy foolish Crest, / And in this Glasse thy feeble *Wormship* see."

[3] *Theophila*, iii, 96; cf. *Otia Sacra* (ed. Grosart), p. 137. The relevant poem of

Westmorland's praise of a quiet country life, not itself without a debt to the admired "L'Allegro," very naturally appealed to Benlowes, and he made other minor borrowings. Here was another fine gentleman and dilettante who took his dilettantism fairly seriously; who wrote pious verse and shared to a high degree the fashionable taste for making epigrams, anagrams, and especially acrostics in English and Latin. There are plenty of these in *Otia Sacra*, and others are extant among the Westmorland manuscripts. [1] How well Benlowes knew Westmorland I cannot say; a poem could pass from friend to friend and Benlowes need not have had direct contact with its author. Yet it is possible that they corresponded and exchanged compositions. When *Theophila* was published a few years later Benlowes sent Westmorland a presentation copy.

Westmorland's may be found in Marshall, *Rare Poems of the Seventeenth Century*. As with Beaumont, it is of course *possible* that the borrowing was the other way. But this sort of thing was so much a habit of Benlowes in composition that the debt seems more likely to have been his.

[1] See Historical MSS. Commission, 10th Report, Appendix, part 4, Earl of Westmorland MSS. (1885), pp. 44ff.

CHAPTER FOURTEEN

IN ACTION FOR THE KING

While Benlowes was giving himself to literary pursuits and religious musings, interrupted as little as he could manage to be by the
threat of the times to his worldly estate, many things happened
to change the political aspect of England. In 1645, about the time
Benlowes was busy with *Papa Perstrictus*, the King's infantry surrendered at Naseby and the Royalists could never again put a powerful army into the field. During the next year, while Benlowes was
working on *Theophila*, reading Milton, corresponding with Paman,
sporadic fighting still went on. But in June 1646 the King's headquarters at Oxford surrendered. [1]

During the war all landowners had suffered from taxation, from
bad harvests, and from the serious decline in rents, which, even
when they could be got in, were down by at least a seventh. [2] Those
who had fought for the King had their property sequestrated and
were now busily arranging to compound for their estates with the
committee at Goldsmiths' Hall which had been set up for that purpose; and although they got them back—if they took the Covenant
and swore allegiance to the Parliament—to pay the fine imposed
they might have to sell or mortgage land or cut down much-prized
woods. [3] The fine might be anything from a sixth to a half of the
whole value of the estates. And as one historian dramatically puts it,
"months and years after the last shot had been fired, Royalist gentry
were still....sending up their wives to soften the Roundhead
Committee-men in London, with meed of bribes and tears for the
lords of the hour." [4] Nor was this hardship reserved only for those
who had borne arms. Sir Ralph Verney, for example, who had never
even spoken in the King's behalf, suffered sequestration because he
absented himself from the Parliament of which he was a member

---

[1] Gardiner, *Civil War*, III, 109.
[2] *Ibid.*, III, 196.
[3] *Ibid.*, III, 199.
[4] Trevelyan, *England under the Stuarts*, p. 274.

and refused to take the Covenant. [1] So Benlowes, who identified the Covenant with the number of the Beast—though not as yet in public—was perhaps lucky to escape. It was difficult to sustain this attitude to the Covenant in view of the success of Parliamentary and Presbyterian arms, but Benlowes, who had been brought up to belong to a persecuted religion, stayed faithful.

Not far away from where Benlowes lived, Fairfax, the victorious general, had his headquarters at Saffron Walden, and this town became the centre of very great interest when a breach occurred between the Presbyterians, who held a majority in Parliament, and the New Model Army, which had just won Parliament's war. On the one hand were petitions from the people that the army which oppressed them should be disbanded; on the other were petitions from the army that it should first be paid. It looked like a war between Parliament and army, when each party began intriguing with the defeated King, with whom each still hoped to come to some profitable arrangement. This dissension among the victors gave the Royalists a chance which they were quick to take. In the summer of 1648 the Scottish Royalists descended upon the north of England, and there were risings in Kent and Essex and in the west.

The eastern counties, which had always been Cromwell's stronghold, were prepared to support the Parliament, but were determined against military rule. And so from Essex, "the first borne of the Parliament," as one writer called it, [2] came a vast petition demanding that the soldiers should be dispersed and the King in some way satisfied. This petition, brought to Westminster by two thousand men, was said to have the support of thirty thousand of the men of Essex. [3] And although men like Sir Martin Lumley and the Parliamentary Committee for the county tried to suppress it, a strong Royalist movement had the support of many leading gentlemen in the county, who found inspiration in the fiery zeal of Sir Charles Lucas of Colchester, a passionate supporter of the King with a distinguished record in the earlier Civil War. It was now that Edward Benlowes, who had formerly been a captain of horse in the Essex train-bands but who at the age of forty-six had seen no service in the field, at length went into action. [4]

---

[1] Gardiner, *Civil War*, III, 211.
[2] Historical MSS. Commission, 12th Report, Appendix, part 9, p. 20.
[3] Gardiner, *Civil War*, IV, 125.
[4] That he went into action *sometime* is proved by Chancery Proceedings, Reynardson 31/14; that he was in action *now* is proved from his being fined

The new alignment between the King's supporters and some former Parliamentarians who saw themselves fighting for liberty against an oppressive soldiery rather than as opposing the country's rulers perhaps explains why Benlowes could now be described as serving "King and Parliament." But whatever inner compulsion took him into the field, he was swept up into Lucas' army and found himself with a commission. At the same time his servant John Schoren entered the Royalist ranks as a common soldier. [1] The regular soldiers, of course, were almost all on the other side, and the men of Essex were mostly undisciplined and frequently unarmed. Nor was their army more orderly for being supplemented with many riotous apprentice-boys from London. His repute as a horseman presumably gave Benlowes command of a troop of cavalry, but the horse he led can have been no less a rabble than the foot. They were quite untrained, and one member of this army has left it on record that they had less than a hundred horse "in any forme" that they "could trust." [2]

There is no means of telling how much of the campaign Benlowes saw; but to have had a commission he must have been present at Chelmsford in the confused days of early June, when Lucas' insurrection started. The Parliamentary Committee for Essex was sitting, and was not being very amenable about the Essex petition or about an indemnity demanded for the refugees who had just crossed from Kent after Fairfax had crushed a rising there. The Royalists forced their way into the committee-room and took the committee-men prisoner, while their followers raged round Chelmsford in a fury. There was much passion and little discipline among them as the leaders contended about their course of action. The uproar continued for some days while Lucas' men stayed in the town gathering together supplies for their ill-fated campaign. And Benlowes must have been one of those high-spirited country gentlemen upon whom Lucas was depending and of whom a disgruntled military man wrote that although their relations with the people made them indispensable, they lacked the skill to conduct the followers they enlisted; and were yet "soe zealous of the esteeme of theire courage and judgements" that they would not "endure the assistance of

---

for "delinquency" in the Essex insurrection (see below, pp. 178-9). The evidence that he had not been in action *before*, in what has come to be called the First Civil War, is cumulative and convincing and is given above in Chapters 12 and 13.

[1] Chancery Proceedings, Reynardson 31/14 (answer).
[2] Historical MSS. Commission, 12th Report, Appendix, part 9, p. 22.

experienc'd souldiers." [1] The Royalists eventually moved off towards Braintree, pausing on the way to remedy their lack of weapons by pillaging the armoury at the house of Warwick, the Parliamentary leader, which was conveniently near at hand. There they were resisted by Warwick's steward, Arthur Wilson, and Benlowes therefore found himself fighting on the opposite side to one who much admired *Theophila* for its spiritual quality and was later to write a poem in praise of it. Wilson recognized several of the local gentry among the civil and fair-spoken Cavaliers who came into the house to parley. One of them was Benlowes' young kinsman William Nevill, of Cressing Temple, and it is not of course impossible that Benlowes was of the party too. These visitors took what arms they could as graciously as possible; but they did not get away without trouble —from their own disorderly followers, who were bent on looting the house, so that the officers had to draw their swords in the courtyard to keep them back. Then, through Braintree, they went on to Colchester, but if Benlowes went on with them right through the siege of Colchester, it is strange that no record of the fact has survived. Perhaps he took an earlier opportunity to slip back home to Brent Hall. One of the constant difficulties of the Royalists on campaign was that the Cavalier horsemen tended to vanish as quickly as they gathered; and Benlowes, who in his more solemn moments looked on warfare as a sort of treason against the state of bliss intended by God for man, must have had difficulty in sustaining his martial zeal.

Although surrounded in Colchester by Fairfax's forces, the Royalists put up such stout resistance that they could only be starved into submission. The siege began on June 14th. Exactly a month later, after various ineffective skirmishes in the suburbs, the defenders were forced to evacuate the Lucas family mansion, which was just outside the city walls, and the besiegers, elated at this success after their long frustration, ran amok. They broke open the tombs in the family burial-vault, where Lucas' mother and sister "were so lately buried, that their sinues and haire were unconsumed." Scattering the bones with profane jesting, they cut off the hair and wore it in their hats. A month later, the defending army had eaten the horses of their cavalry and the supply of dogs for meat was giving out. Some of the townspeople were eating soap and candles. Starving women and children who went out from the city

[1] *Ibid.*, p. 21.

to appeal to Fairfax were shot at and sent back terrified. The final agonies of hunger compelled surrender on August 27th. Next day Sir Charles Lucas and Sir George Lisle were condemned and shot in the castle-yard. The rest of the Royalist officers were imprisoned or held to ransom, and if Benlowes had not in fact retired to Brent Hall before these desperate days, no doubt he quickly bought his liberty and did so now. [1]

The fate of the common soldiers was worse. They were shut up in the churches, pillaged by the victors and mostly stripped to their shirts—though, since they were allowed to keep their skins whole, this was called having "faire quarter." [2] Yet Schoren, who in his most whining mood supported his claims upon Benlowes by pleading how he had followed his master into the King's army, never made mention of hardship such as this. He, at least, cannot have been at Colchester or he would surely have made much of his sufferings there. It is further clear that he did not share the ultimate ignominy of those of the Colchester prisoners who were neither starved nor shot, which was to be sold into servitude in the Venetian army or to be shipped for forced labour in the West Indies. [3]

I think, then, that Benlowes' part in the rising was small and his experience of battle slight, though it was quite enough for him afterwards to be listed for complicity and mulcted of several hundred pounds. Whatever it was, he did not look back on it with pride. It was Schoren, not he, who afterwards boasted of having borne arms for the King. [4] Benlowes was naturally contemptuous of formal

[1] The foregoing account of the siege of Colchester and the events leading up to it is principally based on the contemporary record of one who took part in the siege, as printed in Historical MSS. Commission, 12th Report, Appendix, part 9, pp. 19ff., together with Gardiner, *Civil War*, chs. 63 and 65, and Morant, *History of Colchester*, I, 57ff. The affair at Warwick's house at Leighs is described in Arthur Wilson's autobiography (in Peck, *Desiderata Curiosa*, 1779, II, 479-481).

[2] For this, see Ellis, *Original Letters*, 3d series, IV, 270.

[3] A letter dated September 6, 1649, from Fairfax to Colonel John Moore, the chairman of the Parliamentary committee that disposed of prisoners-of-war, told how Fairfax had engaged immediately after the siege of Colchester to deliver to Lt.-Col. Rushee a regiment of 1050 men "to transport beyond the seas for the service of the states of Venice" (Historical MSS. Commission, 10th Report, Appendix, part 4, pp. 93-94). The other fate of transportation to the West Indian plantations evidently befell some of the Colchester men, as it did some of the Scottish prisoners taken at Preston (Gardiner, *Civil War*, IV, 193), for there is the testimony of a certain William Friend that at the surrender of Colchester "he was sold for Barbadoes, but escaped" (Historical MSS. Commission, 9th Report, part 2, p. 126).

[4] Chancery Proceedings, Reynardson 31/14.

edicts when they went against his conscience, and it can have meant nothing to him that the Parliament had declared all who took part in the second civil war guilty of high treason. But to have been remotely connected with an episode so rich in human suffering—possibly the most painful in the whole of the civil wars—cannot have been easy for a sensitive mind to reflect upon. It was not Benlowes' habit to speak of it, but a curious passage in a late canto of *Theophila* suggests that this man of pacific temper who loathed the bloodshed of the times cherished a sense of guilt for having had some part in it. Speaking of the number killed and imprisoned through the war, of swords devouring flesh and spears drunk with blood, he considered the woes of men, who were wont to spin out their own ruin through their own perversity of wickedness, their "Cross-biasnesse to *Grace*." [1] And in this context he who was accustomed to write of his soul's aspiration, to extol his chosen way of life, or to glorify his own convictions—in this context he used for once the language of remorse. So that it was, surely, something more than the ordinary self-reproach of the devout in the sight of God when he spoke of himself as "the *Chief* of Sinners, and the *Worst* of Men" and proceeded to lay his "Guilt" before the mercy-seat of God. [2]

The composition of poetry was for Benlowes not so much an overwhelming impulse as a practised diversion, even if a very serious one; and so further reference in his verse to what came to be looked on as a most regrettable incident in his life was not to be expected. It was not for him to do as one poet in his circle did. The Earl of Westmorland wrote a poem "Upon yᵉ petitionall rising in Kent, June 1648 & their defeat by Fairfax." Westmorland had already had his estates sequestered once—he had compounded for them early in 1644. His part of the country was now quieter and he was able to keep the parole he had given to the Parliament. Was he not even a little unsympathetic about the Royalist failure now when he wrote:

Is Kent o'recome? Their enterprize dispatcht?
Twas 'cause they'd count their chickens 'fore their hatch't? [3]

[1] *Theophila*, xii, 61.
[2] *Ibid.*, xii, 62-63.
[3] Historical MSS. Commission, 10th Report, Appendix, part 4, Westmorland MSS., p. 45.

CHAPTER FIFTEEN

AFTER THE WAR

Westmorland's verses were not printed, but others of Benlowes' friends sought to make financial as well as literary capital out of the sufferings of the King's party which they had shared. John Quarles, the son of Benlowes' great friend Francis, had borne arms for the King in the garrison at Oxford and had been banished for it for a time. Relinquishing now the sword for the pen, he was quick, after the siege of Colchester, to write an elegy upon that "Son of Valor, Sir Charles Lucas." In the following January Charles I was beheaded and a wave of utter horror passed over even the more moderate of the King's supporters. A great shock was sustained by all who looked to the monarchy as one of the essentials of that stable society upon which peace and happy living depended. Something of this was reflected by Evelyn when he wrote in his diary: "The villanie of the rebells proceeding now so far as to trie, condemne, and murder our excellent King on the 30th of this month, struck me with such horror that I kept the day of his martyrdom a fast, and would not be present at that execrable wickednesse." [1] Howell also was struck "with consternation and horror" and, writing nearly two months after the event, said, "The more I ruminate upon it the more it astonisheth my imagination and shaketh all the cells of my brain, so that sometimes I struggle with my faith and have much ado to believe it yet." Howell was not, however, so shaken that he could not enjoy a pun about England's being now cured of the king's evil. [2] Nor was any remarkable abnegation shown by those others who rushed to the printing-houses in order to weep in public. John Quarles followed up his elegy on Lucas by one upon the King's "Martyrdome." But such an attempt to exploit the King's execution was bound to be outdone by the *Eikon Basilike*, that brilliant piece of imposture which ministered to the heartbreak of

[1] *Diary*, II, 2.
[2] *Familiar Letters*, p. 552.

the King's followers and satisfied the curiosity of the general public by what purported to be the King's own meditations and self-portrait in his "solitudes and sufferings." The very audacity of this production probably deserved the stupendous success of its forty-seven editions within the year. If posterity is right in approving the claim of John Gauden to its authorship, then it also came from the Benlowes circle.

Another production for which Charles's execution gave opportunity was a single sheet called *Chronosticon Decollationis Caroli Regis.* The chronogram which this title implied was quite a trivial piece of ingenuity. The appropriate date (1648, old style) was proclaimed by the sum of the Roman numerals (printed in red) contained in a Latin verse motto, which recorded how on the 30th of January King Charles was deprived of his throne and sceptre by the executioner's axe. To this were appended some verses in English on Charles's "murther"—verses drenched with the "Blood" of Charles, defender of the faith, who had died "to re-Baptize" his country, leaving his triple kingdom like "Three Bleeding Bodies left without a Soule." The blood was symbolized by the red type which was used to pick out the emphatic words and which had a special sanguinary appropriateness when those were words like "Bleeding" and "Butcher'd." The verses were printed within a heavy framework of mourning black, and much play was also made with capitals. Perhaps it was Benlowes' known partiality for such typographical play as well as for chronograms that led one or two bibliographers [1] wrongly to assume that Benlowes was the author. The anonymity of the publication was dictated by tact, which likewise suggested a new edition [2] when the reasons for anonymity were past and Charles II was on the throne. The true author was then proclaimed as one "Major *P.F.*" and the initials stood for Payne Fisher, who belonged to a group of opportunist poetasters who were the hangers-

[1] For example, Hazlitt, *Hand-book*, p. 36; see also *D.N.B.*

[2] The *Chronosticon Decollationis* enjoyed in its day some little celebrity. It appeared in a collection of elegies on Charles I published in 1649 under the title *Monumentum Regale*, and then proceeded to masquerade as a composition of John Cleveland, who is bibliographically remarkable for having had foisted into his works a number of poems with which he had nothing to do. A collection in 1659 called *J. Cleaveland Revived* was very largely spurious, and Williamson, the editor, quite frankly admitted that he had included poems by other authors and trusted to his readers' penetration not to confuse those with the fruits of the genuine muse. In this way the *Chronosticon Decollationis* appeared five times between 1659 and 1669 and again with Cleveland's poems in 1687 and 1699.

on of Benlowes or any other man of means and influence who would give them any encouragement.

Fisher had been, like so many seventeenth-century poets both great and small, at Cambridge, and after that he was for a time a professional soldier. He led a troop of foot on the Royalist side at Marston Moor, but after the King's army had been routed in that battle he gave up soldiering, and being, as I have suggested, something of an opportunist and blest with a facility in Latin verse —"it being as 'twere natural to him" [1]—he took to writing about events instead of taking part in them. According to Anthony à Wood, whose tinge of malice seems for once to have been deserved, Fisher was "a true time-server" who did what he could for himself by "palpable flatteries" of the great. "His usual way when he had written and printed a book, was to write many dedication papers to be put before them as occasion served, or his necessities required relief." He had read Benlowes' *Theophila* and written a poem on it, a veritable paean of triumph, full of purple and jewels and comparisons with Sophocles and the phoenix. Reference to Benlowes' skill in echoes and enigmas deftly showed, too, that he was acquainted with the *Papa Perstrictus* and with Benlowes' long-published *Sphinx Theologica*. It could not have been difficult for Fisher to get a little help from Benlowes, whose benevolent impulses remained unchecked even by the Essex insurrection and his own misfortune. Fisher followed up his *Chronosticon Decollationis* by capitalizing the one historic event in which he himself had had a part. He wrote a Latin poem on *Marston-Moor*, and Benlowes financed its publication in 1650. The poem on *Theophila* was included in the volume and Benlowes was thus celebrated as "eruditissimus" and "ornatissimus"; also—with no doubt very genuine feeling—as a champion of letters and a most munificent Maecenas. Benlowes returned compliment for compliment and wrote some Latin verses to commend Fisher's poem, addressing Fisher as his most dear friend, as much celebrated by Mars [2] as by Mercury; distinguished, that is to say, in battle as in eloquence. Fisher seems generally to have known the people in Benlowes' circle, and further verse eulogy was forthcoming from Alexander Ross, James Howell, and John Sictor; and also from two

---

[1] This and the succeeding quotations are from Anthony à Wood, *Athenae Oxonienses*, IV, 377-378.

[2] "TAM ARTE" in 1650 is a misprint for "TAM MARTE" (*cf. Piscatoris Poemata*, 1656).

others who wrote in praise of Benlowes' *Theophila*—Peter de Cardonel
and Thomas Philipot.

In spite of his record in the Civil War and his having just called
the regicides "Fell Feinds" and "dire Hydra's of a Stiff-neck't-State," [1]
Fisher succeeded in finding favour with Cromwell. He *tried* to
find favour with Charles II, but he had written under the Commonwealth too many panegyrics on Cromwell and too many elegies
on the Parliamentary generals to dazzle the new ruler with red-and-
black chronograms and suchlike trifles. Like most men of that day
who sought to get a living by their wits, he alternated good fortune
with bad, enjoying a brief insecure renown before finding himself
in poverty and then in the Fleet prison for debt. Anthony à Wood,
still unrelenting, added that he "lived always poor, as not knowing
the true value of Money... and became the object of charity."
He was like a bit of flotsam on a troubled sea, bound to keep bobbing
up on the surface of the times until at length flung ashore by the
tide of events. It was a man of substance who was more likely to
go down.

Benlowes himself was not submerged just yet. He could go on
cultivating poetry and patronizing poets as before, but his share
in the Civil War was not, like Fisher's, very easily paid for. The
Parliament, continuing its habit of making the Royalist gentry bear
the expenses of the war, had on May 7, 1649, passed an act empow-
ering the Standing Committee for Essex to proceed against those
who had been concerned in the Essex insurrection. [2] The estates
of these "delinquents" were of course sequestered, but could be
redeemed on payment of heavy fines. About the collection of the
fines the Essex committee at once got busy. Only three days later
they complained that some of the delinquents had treated with the
Parliamentary committee which sat at Goldsmiths' Hall, with the
effect that money paid to get Essex estates out of sequestration was
going into the national exchequer and not into Essex funds. They
were depending on such money to cope with the expenses of the
army which had been active in suppressing the revolt, and they now
claimed for themselves sole right to treat with the delinquents.
They promised speedily to forward to the central committee an
account of what they had done in the way of assessing fines; [3] and

---

[1] In the *Chronosticon Decollationis*.
[2] See S.P., Dom., Interregnum, G248/12.
[3] *Ibid.*, G248/14.

they were as good as their word. Already by July 5th they were able to supply a list of those delinquents whose estates had been compounded for. [1] And in that list was the name of Edward Benlowes, whose property was valued at £322 a year. The composition for sequestered estates was put at one tenth of their value, and with the gross value reckoned generally at about eighteen times the annual value, the fine Benlowes had to pay worked out at £600. This was a large sum to fall into the committee's coffers—Benlowes was one of the wealthiest landowners they had to deal with. But since on all other occasions Benlowes' estates were admitted to be worth not £322 but £1000 a year, the penalty exacted was not as rigorous as it might have been. [2]

Six hundred pounds, however, was more than any landed gentleman could conveniently lay hands on at that time, and how Benlowes managed to pay is not known. He was already suffering from the fall in rents and the exorbitant taxation, and, as we have seen, had begun the fateful business of mortgaging property about four years before. As additional troubles came upon him, additional bits of land were pledged. [3] Many of the Cavalier gentlemen were again having to sell lands—at the bottom of a glutted market: Benlowes himself was for the present able to hold on to the bulk of his ancestral estates; but sale was only deferred for a few years, and the beginning of his financial entanglements is to be dated at this time.

From somewhere he got some ready money, and his position was sufficiently secure for him to have a spare £250, which he proceeded to invest in buying some copyhold property—four dwelling-houses and land adjoining—at Claines in Worcestershire. [4] This was to take advantage, for once, of the unsettled state of the times and, like so many of his contemporaries, to reap the benefit of someone else's misfortunes; for these houses had belonged to the estate of the Bishop of Worcester and came up for sale only as a result of Parliament's decision to sell all bishops' lands for the benefit of the Commonwealth.

---

[1] *Ibid.*, G248/31.

[2] No personal estate is recorded for him either, only the annual value of his real estate. The document, it is true, does state that some compositions are not yet finished, but it is implied, I think, that such cases are not included in the present list at all.

[3] For a list of four mortgages of unspecified date, see Chancery Proceedings, Collins 140/147 (answer).

[4] Close Rolls, 1649, pt. 10, no. 18.

In the midst of Benlowes' own difficulties, there were also the duties to his kinsfolk to make life more complicated. I have referred in Chapter 8 to some of the responsibilities which devolved upon him as the head of a family. More than one of them came at about this time. In the interests of William Nevill, his second cousin, in 1646 he had already become a trustee of some lands in Lincolnshire; and now, just as the question of his delinquency and the fine to be paid for it was occupying the Sequestration Committee, he had to undertake similar obligations on behalf of his sister's children in Warwickshire. Their father had died and had bequeathed £700 to the three younger children. According to a common practice, the eldest son, the heir, did not pay out in cash, but assigned a part of his estates to be farmed in their interests. The deeds which were signed on May 14, 1649, made Edward Benlowes and two of the Nevills administrators. [1]

About this time Benlowes was having further difficulty with his servant Schoren. While they had both been fighting for the King, Benlowes had not paid Schoren's wages, and since these were guaranteed by an annuity, Schoren was now able to claim arrears. [2] He said, however, that Benlowes owed him over £50, and if this were true, it would mean that Benlowes was in arrear by about four years—in fact, that he could have paid Schoren nothing since re-engaging him about 1645. [3] This seems preposterous on the face of it, and even on his own showing Schoren had not failed to receive some money during that time. It is clear, therefore, that what Schoren now claimed was not merely wages from 1645 onwards; he was trying to make Benlowes pay him for the two or three years' interval before 1645 when he had not been in Benlowes' service at all. Because, years before, Benlowes had foolishly settled an annuity upon him, £13.6s.8d. had to be paid to Schoren every year. And although this no doubt was not what Benlowes had originally intended, Schoren could claim it whether he was in Benlowes' employ or not. However, when Schoren absconded from Brent Hall, Benlowes considered that the annuity thereby ceased and that all Schoren's claims upon him were annulled. And when Schoren returned as Benlowes' servant on the old terms, although the annuity was renewed, it depended on a fresh deed. Benlowes must therefore have experienced a nasty shock when Schoren suddenly demanded pay-

[1] Close Rolls, 1649, pt. 46, no. 23. *Cf.* above, p. 90.
[2] Chancery Proceedings, Reynardson 31/14 (answer).
[3] See above, pp. 143-144.

ment under the old deed for the years he had been away and even
confronted his master with a bond given him as far back as 1642. [1]
Now, Benlowes was always kind in response to appeals; but he
could be extremely stubborn in resisting demands—especially when,
as in this case, he felt them to be unjust. The trouble, of course, was
that if Schoren produced the bond, it was difficult for it to be repudiated before the law. According to Schoren's story, Benlowes
was very high-handed about it, got possession of the bond by a
trick, and then refused to give it back. He "did desire to have a
sight of the bond," pretending that he would pay what was due
upon it, or, according to another version, promising to settle a house
and land on Schoren. Then, as soon as he got hold of it, he "did
withdraw privately" into another room and either burnt it or de-
faced it, or at any rate, refused to give it back, though he all the
time assured Schoren that he should not lose a farthing of what
was due to him. [2] Schoren was, it will be seen, a little vague about
the details of what took place, and he also contradicted himself in
his later statements about what bond exactly this was. His story is
therefore not above suspicion, and Benlowes roundly denied every
bit of it. [3] So one cannot know what happened, though it is certain
that Schoren got nothing for his pains and remained dissatisfied
to the end of his life. The bond may have been destroyed, but it
was far from being finished with. Years later it figured in the centre
of a dispute which led to prolonged litigation and perhaps did more
than any other thing to torment Benlowes' existence during his
declining years.

Benlowes was always liable to a certain dilatoriness in business
matters. One remembers that the Great Bardfield school had lapsed.
Most of the local charities got dutifully paid; but perhaps not quite
punctiliously, and they were sometimes in arrear. He seems to have
kept them going throughout the Civil War, but in 1650 the Finchingfield town meeting recorded that Benlowes had not paid either
his annual 13s.4d. towards church repairs or the same amount which
was due from him "for the poore." So the churchwarden was instructed to collect. [4] The tiresomeness of that may have been aggravated a little by the churchwarden's being none other than the
William Tym who had drawn up Schoren's bond.

[1] See above, p. 131.
[2] Chancery Proceedings, Whittington 71/87; Reynardson 31/14.
[3] Chancery Proceedings, Collins 28/11.
[4] "Town Book," p. 60.

These small defaults were evidently oversights. The meeting
that recorded them appointed Benlowes surveyor of the highways,
as he had been before the war. And he had clearly no wish to withdraw from village life. In the month of December 1650 he was present at two meetings of the townsmen; and on December 6th his
signature to a memorandum was followed, as it used to be years
before, by that of Stephen Marshall. The fervent Parliamentarian,
who had preached men into battle against the King, and the Royalist
gentleman-soldier were back in their own village (with what feelings
who shall guess?) and peacefully joined together to dispatch the
business of the village overseers. [1]

Benlowes' own affairs were beginning to get further embarrassed.
On February 21, 1651, he gave a recognizance of £800 as security
for a debt to Thomas Kempe of London. [2]

But there was always a part of Benlowes' mind which kept well
aloof from his personal troubles and which was never compromised
by whatever happened among his Essex neighbours. All the time
he was going calmly on with *Theophila*. That he could do so when
"some Sparkles of the *publick Flame*" had seized on his possessions
and "*scorcht* the same" was a cause of amazement to his friend Thomas
Pestell. [3] During 1650 he also found time to sit, solemnly and tran-
quilly if one may judge by results, to a little-known portrait-painter
called Walter. The pose adopted for it was striking and characteristic.
He held an open book in his left hand and pointed to it with his
right forefinger, but his eyes looked upwards. This portrait, along
with the one he caused to be engraved for the frontispiece of *Theophila*, shows him to have been fair-complexioned, with high cheek-
bones and a prominent, though weakish, chin. Apart from his
beautiful hair, his most striking feature was his earnest and penetrating
eyes. When the portrait was finished he presented it to his old college
along with a curious picture, in a carved ebony frame, of a kitchen
and larder with game and provisions. The college, which had long
honoured Benlowes for his generosity to it, was glad to hang these
pictures on its walls. [4]

All this time Benlowes was constantly in touch with the world

---

[1] "Town Book," p. 62.
[2] Recognizance Entry Book L.C. 4/203 fol. 137.
[3] *Theophila* (1652), sig. Cᵛ.
[4] Cole, "Athenae Cantabrigienses," Brit. Mus. MS. Addit. 5863, fol. 61ᵛ.
The portrait must have been given to St. John's College almost at once, or it
would have perished in the Brent Hall fire of 1653.

of books and especially with the literary activities of men in his own
circle. I have told of his recent association with Payne Fisher and
his complimentary poem on Fisher's *Marston-Moor*. But by no means
all the verses written by his friends in the years just after the war
were fastened on to topicalities. Benlowes continued to receive
dedications of works which, as more remote from current ills,
were more congenial to his taste. John Quarles, writing more in
his father's tradition than when he penned elegies on the great
departed, put out in 1651 a devotional poem called *Gods Love and
Mans Unworthiness* and continued tradition also in dedicating the
volume to Edward Benlowes, whom, like his father, he could call
his "much-honoured and Esteemed Friend" and "Patron." Benlowes
had also received in 1649 the dedication of the first of the two books
of a poem, called *Plantaganets Tragicall Story*, on the death of Edward
IV and the crimes of Richard III. It was a production of the more
lurid school of contemporary verse, as its titlepage sufficiently suggested in its reference to "the unnaturall Voyage of *Richard the
Third*, through the Red Sea of his *Nephews* innocent bloud, to his
usurped Crowne." The titlepage gave the author of this as
"T. W. Gent"; and the initials stood for Thomas Wincoll,[1] a wealthy
young Essex gentleman from Twinstead, near the Suffolk border
and scarcely more than a dozen miles from Benlowes' home. He
seems to have gone straight from Cambridge into the Royalist army,
but his friends, while celebrating him as "Captaine," thought of
him as one who preferred the Muses to Mars. This naturally commended him to the neighbouring poet at Brent Hall, and Wincoll was
privileged to join the growing band of those who made acquaintance with *Theophila* in manuscript. He extolled Benlowes for those
"*spritely Raptures*" in which he rose above the material world. He
admired Benlowes' "*soul-entrancing Calentures*" and the "*Blest measures
of the most accomplisht Man*." He would have all altars overturned at
which no incense was burnt in praise of Benlowes' muse.

Few poems can have been more highly eulogized than *Theophila*
by those among whom it circulated in manuscript. By this time it
had achieved considerable length and was gradually approaching
the stage when it might be committed to the press and seek a wider
audience. Meanwhile, in November 1649, [2] there appeared *A Poetick*

---

[1] The poem was often formerly ascribed to Thomas Weaver. The author's
name is given in full in the Stationers' Register (Eyre, I, 318).

[2] Date according to Thomason.

Descant upon a Private Musick-Meeting, which, though he had several
small works in Latin to his credit, was the longest poem in English
that Benlowes had so far published. It was on a single sheet, signed
E. BENEVOLUS, which was explained (in Greek) as an anagram of
the author's name. It consisted of twenty-five stanzas in the metre
which the composition of *Theophila* was making habitual to him;
and here and there it repeated, as was Benlowes' custom when he
was pleased with any poetic conceit, phrases of the major poem.
There were, also according to his custom, deliberate variations, often
for variation's sake. In *A Poetick Descant upon a Private Musick-
Meeting* "roaring" instead of "hoarse-thundring *Diapasons*" did "the
whole Room fill"; the catlings and basses took turns as to which
was grumbling and which tortured. [1] But other echoed comparisons
served to increase the hyperbole of the poem. It was not now the
eyes of Theophila herself that left the poet "*Planet*-struck"; it was
the mortal beauties of the drawing-room that were compared to
planets. [2] In *Theophila* the grace of God had been the philosopher's
stone and God's word "pure *Projection*"; now it was the music of
the violin which had this miraculous power. [3] The effect of such
imagery was to shed a divinity over the poem. And to bring into
the drawing-room the music of the spheres was what Benlowes
sought to do. A great lover of music, nowhere did he write of it
more passionately than here. He had been at a musical evening,
and enraptured with what he had heard, his fancy had by the morning
so wrought upon the experience that he thought of himself as having
been present among deities at play. His opening suggestion that
his muse was using no metaphors but merely rehearsing "last *Evening*'s
Sweets," was of course the biggest hyperbole in the poem; for the
gentlemen performers and the lady spectators were at once identified with the stars in their courses. The skill of the composition
lay in the way the image was sustained throughout: bows, strings,
and pedals were touched by sun, moon, and planets, and the poet
himself was "chair'd midst the Spheres of *Musick*'s Heav'n." [4] The

[1] *A Poetick Descant*, stanza 10; *Theophila*, iii, 51.
[2] *Theophila*, i, 9; *A Poetick Descant*, stanza 5.
[3] *Theophila*, i, 90; *A Poetick Descant*, stanza 17.
[4] The introduction into the poem of Sol, Luna, Jove, Mars, and Mercury
is all part of the expanded metaphor by which the music is described as though
it were the music of the spheres. I hardly think Benlowes intended individuals
among his friends to be recognized under those names, as is maintained by
G. S. Haight (*The Library*, 4th series, XVI, 193). In any case Benlowes is not,

extravagance was characteristic of the author and of his age; but something of his transport got into the poem.

---

as Haight assumes, Sol. He certainly did not identify himself with Sol and then go on to address Sol thus:

> *Patron* of Sweetness! *Soul* of Joies!
> How were wee ravisht with thy *Viol*'s warbling Voice!

> Thy Nectar-dropping Joints so plai'd their part,
>   They forc'd the *Fibers* of our heart
> To dance.

Actually, Benlowes writes throughout the poem as though he himself had been a spectator. To identify Sol in Benlowes' poetry with Benlowes himself would have some very queer results if it were extended to *Theophila*.

CHAPTER SIXTEEN

INTRODUCTION TO A MAGNUM OPUS

It is now time to say more about the big work on which Benlowes had been engaged for several years and which was eventually to be published in 1652. No attempt at describing Benlowes' life during the fifth decade of the century could be complete without *Theophila* running like a thread through the narrative. I do not know quite when Benlowes first conceived this work in his mind, but it was probably during the early years of the Civil War. He seems to have been well advanced on the third canto about 1646.[1] The poem went ahead fairly rapidly during the later war years and probably the bulk of it was written before Benlowes went to fight in 1648. At any rate, he had got as far as the twelfth canto while still able to contrast his "safe *Repose*" with the "Rage of War" which was upon the surrounding country. [2] Nevertheless, only twenty-five stanzas farther on, still in the twelfth canto, he put those stanzas which I have taken to allude to his own share in the war.[3] But there is some reason to think that passage an interpolation, for it is not integral to the thought. After the birds have sung in the branches in stanza 55, Benlowes strays from his country idyll to speak of war and his own war-guilt and only gets back to the dew upon the meadows in stanza 67. I think, then, that the twelfth canto was nearly finished when the war overtook its author and that he inserted a lament and a repentance when he came back from the fighting and read what he had written. That may have been the reason why for the first time a canto was allowed to extend itself beyond the hundred stanzas which had, up till then, been the limit rigidly imposed by the pattern of the poem.

By the time it appeared in 1652, *Theophila* had spread to thirteen cantos and had gathered round it various additional embellishments in prose and verse, English and Latin—all of which tended to obscure the original design. *Theophila* proper, or *Theophila's Love-Sacrifice* as the canto headings have it, is a poem in nine cantos describing the

---

[1] See above, pp. 156, 160.
[2] Stanza 34.
[3] See above, p. 174.

poet's rapture as he contemplates the infinite love of God and the ineffable joys of heaven. The soul is personified as a beautiful maiden-spirit, Theophila, the lover of God, who, going through the humiliation which comes from awareness of sin, achieves grace through the fervour of her devotion, and passes into an ecstasy in which she is received among the angels and enjoys a foretaste of heaven. [1] The four additional cantos really comprise two separate poems, companions to one another but only remotely connected with the main poem. Although they were numbered as if they were additional cantos of *Theophila* and sought to maintain the same form and style, their separateness was acknowledged in the printing. They did not use the word "Theophila" in their canto headings and the running titles. Instead, the first of these two appended poems (Cantos x and xi) was called "The Vanitie of the World" and the second either "The Sweetnesse of Retirement" (Canto xii) or "The Pleasure of Retirement" (Canto xiii). The initial intention had been to write not thirteen books, nor even nine, but only eight.[2] But with composition becoming both a habit and a joy, the design had got considerably swollen before publication was sought. Although prone to a good deal of repetition in his sentiments, Benlowes found himself as he went on quite prolific in language. Yet he well understood that "in a *Poem*, as in a *Prayer* 'tis Vigour not Length that crowns it," and was to say so in the course of his twelve-page preface to *Theophila*, where he laid out the purpose of his poem.

Like many men in the seventeenth century, Benlowes still held the mediaeval view of the world as old, running down like a clock, and rapidly deteriorating. [3] Its last days were its worst, and "in this *Dotage* of the *World* (where *Atheism* stands at the right hand of *Profaneness*)," he saw many men "most wretched" whose "undisciplin'd Education" prevented them from devoting themselves to anything above sensuality, drink, and duels. Something of this educational deficiency he hoped might be supplied by a poem which treated of Sub-celestials, Celestials, and Super-celestials. The nature of these three orders of beings and their exact location in the universe Benlowes went on in his preface to discuss. Men of his age could still take a very lively interest in scholastic speculations on

---

[1] See *Theophila*, p. 15, "The Summary of the Poem."
[2] See below, pp. 203-204.
[3] Henry Reynolds in *Mythomystes* (*c.* 1632) speaks of the world as decrepit, of its "age & doating estate" (Spingarn, *Critical Essays of the Seventeenth Century,* I, 144); cf. Donne, *The First Anniversary,* and see Leishman, *The Metaphysical Poets,* pp. 62ff.

such subjects as the physical nature of angels; and the seventeenth-
century mind, delighting to yoke the physical and the spiritual,
was fascinated by such an impossible blending of opposites as went
to make up the super-celestial beings. For, as Benlowes here said,
they were somehow substantial like man and incorporeal like God;
and although incorporeal, would yet starve if denied the contemplation of the "All-filling" God.

No doubt a vast number of the extravagances of the poetry of
this period were due simply to a delight in conceits—the agility of
the mind, as it leapt among incompatibles, was admired like the
performance of an acrobat. But much of the apparent extravagance in
imagery was also due to the subject that was being grappled with.
No comparison could be excessive when one sought to encompass
in words the nature of infinity itself and the sublime paradoxes of
God's creation. The habit of oxymoron and other daring figures
was something more than a desire for startling phrases. A "dazling
darkness" was Vaughan's conception of God;[1] Crashaw knew a

> louing strife
> Of liuing DEATH & dying LIFE.[2]

And here in the preface to *Theophila*, Benlowes sought to describe
the nature of "Incorporeal *Substances*." The most wondrous paradox
of all was of course God himself, "present without Place, ever-
lasting without Time," as Benlowes here expressed it. Admitting
his incapacity at definition, he finally rejoiced in God's very "*Incomprehensibility*."

To a nature like Donne's, which combined passion with an impulse to reason, this incomprehensibility gave many hours of torment.
A man like Vaughan, on the other hand, had no longing to argue
or to prove celestial truths. He sought to be flooded with a light
in which eternal mysteries would be revealed. In this Benlowes

---

[1] "The Night," l. 50.

[2] "A Song of Divine Love," ll. 13-14. Crashaw's poetry, especially, is full
of this figure. He is always having, for example, "delicious Wounds" ("A Hymn
to... Sainte Teresa," l. 108) from a "healing shaft" ("To the... Countesse
of Denbigh," l. 47). He knows "dear & diuine annihilations" ("Prayer," l.
78), and his St. Teresa is to experience "intolerable IOYES" in her "still-sur-
uiuing funerall" ("Hymn," ll. 99, 78). The masochistic delight in triumph
through surrender is particularly characteristic of Crashaw and occasions some
of his most passionate verses. It is less common in Benlowes, and less ecstatic
when it comes; but such lines as these are very much in Crashaw's vein: "Darts
of intolerable *Sweets* her *Soul* did wound" (*Theophila*, iv, 82); "The way to
gain more *Ground*, is to *retreat*" (*Ibid.*, x, 6).

resembled him. But even Vaughan, apart from a few trance-like visions of the radiance of eternity, knew his intensest experience in yearning rather than in exaltation. [1] Benlowes' adoration of God had more in common with that of the Catholic Crashaw. He could know an ecstasy of faith which did not need knowledge to sustain it. Content to accept God as a mystery, he gloried in a God who could not be known. His "very *Ignorance*" was valued as testifying to God's transcendency. [2] Contemplating the ineffable with none of Vaughan's anxiety, he ventured to ascend to "amazing *Heights*" and appeared in his preface confident in the power of man's mind to transcend in poetry all bodily limitations and to catch at a music more ravishing than mere earthly jubilation could aspire to.

The preface to *Theophila* also touched on the virtues of poetic style. These were not what would have been chosen by the critics of our day, nor perhaps by all of Benlowes' own. Any poet of the seventeenth century would have been likely to begin with "*Wit*"; yet it by no means follows that they would all have meant the same thing by it. [3] For Benlowes it existed in the combination of those

[1] For example, "The Night"; "The Retreate"; and even "They are all gone into the world of light." I cite some of his most famous poems.

[2] "The Authors Prayer," p. 20.

[3] This is responsible for a certain amount of confusion in the literary criticism of the period. I give here only a few pointers to a complex subject. It is more fully dealt with in R. L. Sharp, *From Donne to Dryden*, especially ch. 5. See also Spingarn, *Critical Essays of the Seventeenth Century*, I, xxixff. (1) Literary criticism at the beginning of the century tends to equate wit not with invention and judgment, but with the inventive faculty alone. It can be glossed with the Latin *ingenium* and distinguished from the "art" which is necessary to discipline it. At the end of the century the word is still capable of being used in this sense by Dryden (for example, "boistrous *English* Wit with Art indu'd," in the verses on Congreve's *The Double Dealer*. See also Locke's explicit opposition of wit and judgment, *Humane Understanding*, bk II, ch. xi, sec. 2). This use survives also among the bewilderingly fluctuating meanings given to the word by Pope ("supreme in judgment, as in wit," *Essay on Criticism*, l. 657). (2) Yet already by the middle of the seventeenth century wit was beginning to be regarded as the combination of both invention and judgment. For D'Avenant it comprised care as well as happiness, labour as well as luck *(Preface to Gondibert)*; for Hobbes "*Celerity of Imagining*... and *steddy direction* to some approved end" *(Leviathan*, pt. I, ch. viii). With a specialization of the meaning of "judgment," wit became the combination of dexterity of thought with neatness of expression. Following on this the definition of "wit" which most satisfied Dryden was "a propriety of thoughts and words" *(Essays*, ed. Ker, I, 190), and this, I think, became the commonest sense of the word in Pope. (3) Dryden of course also knew a "stricter sense" in which wit was a "sharpness of conceit" *(ibid.*, I, 172). And this was the usage which had been particularly encouraged by the poetic practice of the metaphysical poets.

The meaning of the word, then, was gradually changing through a shift in two other items which were the regular desiderata of seventeenth-century criticism, *"Judgement"* and *"Invention."* *"Judgement,"* he said, "begets the Strength, *Invention* the Ornaments of a Poem." This has all the air of being copied from Hobbes's "Answer" to D'Avenant, [1] which, together with D'Avenant's *Preface to Gondibert,* had been first published in Paris in 1650, and then in London, along with *Gondibert* itself, in 1651. Again Benlowes would seem to have been quite up to date in his poetical reading. But his echoing of Hobbes's critical theory does not mean that he assimilated it. While Hobbes put particular stress on judgment, Benlowes, not only in practice but in theory, preferred the other half of the conjunction. Though wit included both, he all but ignored judgment to expatiate on fancy. He mentioned perspicuity in passing, and the need for artful selection. But clinging to an older poetic tradition, he was unmoved by Hobbes's distrust of conceits and, as they were called, "strong lines." He desired "Vivacity of *Fancie* in a florid Style." And "florid," though the temper that began in Jonson and Hobbes has brought it in the end to be a term of disdain, was of course an epithet of esteem among Benlowes' contemporaries and in the poetic tradition in which he wrote. Of this one instance must suffice. Writing to Isaak Walton in 1664, Bishop King praised Sir Henry Wotton as "a Man of as Florid a Wit and as Elegant a Pen, as any former (or ours which in that kind is a most excellent) Age hath ever produced." [2]

Benlowes looked to the fancy, then, to give "Light and Life to a Poem," because it could provide — again in Hobbes's words [3] — "grateful Similies" and "apt Metaphors". Of these the sublime poet, aided by divine inspiration, had naturally a plentiful stock. He was, however, a little diffident about his own success in wit. The merit of his poem lay in its subject, which he expected—pathetically in the light of events—would be a *"Balsam"* to preserve it. Yet

---

poetic values, and a revolt against the values of the metaphysical poets led to the animadversions upon false wit by Dryden, Addison, and Pope. Addison himself was sufficiently influenced by the tradition coming through the metaphysicals, however, to demand that wit should surprise. If this was not a novel notion, it had not previously been thus explicitly formulated, and the meaning that we now attach to the word "wit" owes something therefore to this legacy of metaphysical poetry. (For Addison, see the *Spectator*, no. 62).

[1] "Judgment begets the strength and structure, and Fancy begets the ornaments of a Poem" (Spingarn, II, 59).

[2] The letter is prefixed to Walton's *Lives*.

[3] *Humane Nature*, ch. x, sec. 4.

he was not led to write by any "Titillation of *Fame*" but by "Instigation of *Conscience*." His sole aim was by presenting a vision of glory to lead his readers to it.

So, with all his delight in fancy, his confessed intention was didactic. His view, in line with the traditional defence of poetry throughout the Renaissance, was that poetry taught as well as pleased. He was also following a worthy tradition of Renaissance critics, who included, in England, Sidney and Jonson, when he heard the voice of Plutarch echoing down fifteen centuries and wrote that "*Poems* are speaking *Pictures*." [1] Poetry should teach the reader by offering him an "*Original*" which would serve as an "*Example*" of Life." [2]

These critical views on the nature of poetry recurred in the poet's address to his Fancy which followed. Fancy was to unite judgment with invention and profit with pleasure, deep truth for the wise with wit for the youth. Flying from earthly beauty and its "peach-bloom *Cheek*-Decoies," she was to be rebaptized in tears and espouse the joys of the New Jerusalem. There was also an exhortation to the Soul which developed at length one of those painstaking analogies in which such a chaser of anagrams, emblems, and mottoes

---

[1] Plutarch, of course, did not originate this. He refers to it in his *Moralia* as an oft-repeated saying. Nor did Benlowes first say it here. It occurs in *Sphinx Theologica*.

[2] The preface ends with an admonition to the reader which is of considerable interest, incidentally, as being obviously adapted from an inscription which was in the "great parlour" at Little Gidding, the home of the famous religious community established by Nicholas Ferrar. The community, with its quiet life of simple piety and its monastic ritual, had much about it that would have appealed to Benlowes, and he may, like Herbert and Crashaw, have visited the Ferrar family at Little Gidding. Yet his hatred of Arminianism would not have allowed him altogether to approve of a community that could be called by its detractors an "Arminian nunnery." And of course he need not have gone there in order to have known of the inscription. It was very much remarked on by visitors, and George Herbert advised that it should be engraved on brass and hung up so that everyone could see it. At least one visitor made a copy of it to take away with him (see Peckard, *Memoirs of the Life of Mr. Nicholas Ferrar*, pp. 233-234; Mayor, *Nicholas Ferrar*, pp. xxix-xxx). Benlowes' adapted version runs: "*He* who shall contribute to the Improvement of the *Author*, either by a pruden[t] Detection of an *Errour*, or a sober Communication of an irrefragable *Truth*, deserves the venerable Esteem and Welcome of a *good* ANGEL; And *He* who by a candid Adherence unto, and a fruitful Participation of what is *good* and *pious* confirms *Him* therein, merits the honourable Entertainment of a *faithful Friend*: But he who shall traduce him in *Absence*, for what in *Presence* he would seem to applaud, incurres the double Guilt of *Flattery* and *Slander*; and he who wounds Him with *ill Reading* and *Misprision*, does *Execution* on Him before *Judgement*." The reader might also be interested to compare Benlowes' poetic theories with those of the Ferrar circle as set out by Bernard Blackstone in an article in the *Times Literary Supplement*, March 21, 1936.

naturally delighted. Since the life of the true Christian was a continual conflict, the world was God's *pitched field*, his *colours* blood,
his *standard* the cross. The Soul was to *press* Zeal to battle, with
Prayer held as a force in *reserve*; to *cashier* Fear and distrust the *spy*,
Doubt. Raiding-*parties* of tears were to stand in readiness until a
recruit arrived from Heaven with free supplies of grace. [1] An address
to the lady readers which preceded the Preface used a very different
imagery. In urging the ladies to follow Theophila's example, it
besought them to walk in her *"Spring-Garden"* and "take fresh
Heav'nly Air."

Theophila was unusual in having no dedication, but the poet had
to begin his volume by laying out in Latin and English verse his
design to show Theophila "Off'ring *pure* SACRIFICE with *sacred*
MIND." He dared to name Jesus himself his patron, and prayed:

> Close up my Cracks by *Faith*, so shall I be
> A *Vessel* made of HONOUR unto THEE.

After this medley of introductions and invocations the reader of
the 1652 folio had still to go through twenty pages of eulogies by
many different hands, [2] a disclaimer by Benlowes at finding himself
too much praised, a poem on the function of divine poets, who
find in Heaven's sphere "a vast Librarie," and one further celebration
of Theophila's soaring flight. Only after such great pomp of preparation was the ceremony allowed to begin.

---

[1] Elaborate military conceits were very common in the poetry of the time.
One has only to think of such different poets as Crashaw and Marvell, in whose
work the military metaphors can be well seen in, for example, "To the Countesse
of Denbigh" and "Upon Appleton House." I cite these poems not as extravagant examples, but as being *characteristic* of their authors. For an attack on
military metaphors and similar conceits when they were ceasing to find favour
with the more discriminating but were still apparently prevalent in sermons,
see Eachard, *The Grounds and Occasions of the Contempt of the Clergy and Religion*
(1670).

[2] Not to interrupt here the description of the composition itself, these are
discussed below in Chapter 19.

CHAPTER SEVENTEEN

THEOPHILA

Not even yet did Benlowes' heroine make her entry. The first canto was but "The Prelibation to the Sacrifice." This was, however, at length the poem itself, and the reader met—though, if he had read *A Poetick Descant upon a Private Musick-Meeting*, not for the first time—Benlowes' unique stanza and the full blossom of his ingenious conceits.

It is not possible to attempt any sort of narrative synopsis of the poem. Benlowes moves from ecstasy to ecstasy without coherence of incident. Such order as the poem has is the artificial symmetry produced by cantos with matching titles and equal length. This, it is true, gives it the air of obeying the logical disciplines on which Renaissance education so much insisted and which some of the literary masterpieces of the seventeenth century achieved. The subject seems to be precisely divided into its natural categories. An early repentance or "humiliation" of the soul, which is marked out as the subject of Canto ii, is a pre-requisite of the eventual "contemplation" of the divine in Canto vii. But this hardly disguises the lack of a deeper order derived from the logical progression of thought. I shall seek, therefore, while following its outline, to indicate the general character of the poem rather than to suggest a continuity of argument which the poem itself does not possess.

The theme of the first canto—the attack on worldly pleasures and an exhortation towards a religious life—was a common one with Benlowes. The interest of the canto lies in its exhibition of his poetical eccentricities. He seeks less to win the reader by persuasion than to shock him into compliance by startling figures. When he denounces the world, his conceits have their place in making the subject seem the monstrous and perverted thing that Benlowes sees it as. Women, the enemies of spiritual life, have "Flame-darting *Eyes*" as their "Munition," and they lay traps for the unwary with their "Ambush-hair." Their kisses are but "*Lip-traffick*," which, along with "*Eye-dialogues*," is always to be shunned. Drunkards have "frothy" heads. To suggest the magnitude of their excesses, Benlowes sends them like a fleet to sea on an ocean of drink, to "sail by *Sugar-rocks*

through *Floods* of *Wine*." With an abrupt change of image they
become "intombed *Souls*," for in them man's spirit rots alive. The
salt of life is changed to dregs. The pleasures men pursue Benlowes
sees as illusions, and so he mocks, "Can *Fire* in *Pictures* warm?"
The thought, beneath its layers of figures, progresses only slowly,
but within the whirligig of metaphor there are many striking econo-
mies of phrase. For example, when Benlowes looks back to the
time when it was the sole ambition of university men to attain
preferment in the church, he flashes out his thought in four words:
"*Lambeth* was *Oxfords* Whetstone." He denounces those verses
which extol human love in the pretty fancy: "Quills, pluckt from
Venus Doves, impresse but shame."

While he shows little original observation of what life is like, he
can rapidly twist traditional views of it to offer some new image.
And the image is often hurled forth with a good deal of vigour.
He creates the figure of Sin in a fury:

> *Time*, strip the writhel'd *Witch*; Pluck the black Bags
> 　　From off *Sins* grizly Scalp; the *Hags*
> Plague-sores shew then more loathsom than her leprous Rags.

But then he abandons the rage "That acts the toilsome *World* on
its *tumultuous* Stage." The soul turns to religion and awakes from
its lethargy. So the mood changes, dawn breaks upon the poem, and
Sol "shoots delight through *Nature* with each arrow'd Ray." But
the "fancy" continues to display itself on the new subject. The
sun is regularly transformed into Sol in a manner which a "correct"
poet like Pope would only use in *mock*-heroic. Benlowes will turn
everything he sees into something else for the sheer delight he finds
in embroidering—like his own spiders, which of course do not
enter the poem as spiders but as

> Industrious *Spinsters*, who with fair
> Embroid'ries checker-work the Chambers of the *Air*.

An instance of the number of metaphors Benlowes can in a single
statement shake kaleidoscopically together is provided by the stanza
on the bee, which he imitated from Cleveland: [1]

> As *Natures* prime *Confectioner*, the *Bee*,
> 　　By her Flow'r-nibling *Chymistrie*,
> Turns *Vert* to *Or*: So, VERSE gross *Prose* does rarifie.

---

[1] *Cf.* "Fuscara," ll. 1-4:

> Nature's Confectioner, the *Bee*,
> Whose suckets are moyst *Alchimie*:
> The Still of his refining mould,
> Minting the Garden into Gold...

The bee making honey easily becomes a confectioner, but honey-making in the next line is a sort of chemistry, while at the same moment the eye remembers the actual process and sees the bee on the flower—not, however, like a bee, but with yet another metaphor, nibbling. The third line continues the magical transformations made by confectionery and chemistry, but, departing now from Cleveland, for no obvious reason and with no apparent gain, substitutes a heraldic metaphor. [1] And finally the bee, which seemed to have appeared just because of the sunshine, is revealed as in itself a symbol of another magic-maker, the poet who turns common prose into verse.

As the poem continues, the radiance of the dawn is compared to that of poetry, which, however, only achieves its full function if, as well as shedding brilliance around, it is productive of good works. Through them the soul approaches God,

> Steering by GRACES Pole-star, which is fast
> In th'APOSTOLLICK Zodiack plac't
> Whose *Course* at first four EVANGELICK Pilots trac't.

This I quote as another curious illustration of Benlowes' fancy, but it is unnecessary to go on multiplying examples. Instead, let Benlowes hurry on his voyage with "*Loves* full Sail," past the "*Wrack*" of Sin; let him stop struggling under his "sad Load of Clay" and end his canto, in faith, hope, and love, with a vow of self-dedication to God. The vow is itself turned into a picture by being expressed in a stanza in the shape of an altar.

Benlowes here inserted a further summary of the poem, and then a prayer in which, drawing strength from the rhythms of the Prayer-book, he revealed an unexpected power of impassioned prose. "Grant that my *Sorrow* for Sin may be unfeigned, my Desires of *Forgiveness fervent*, my purpose of *Amendment stedfast*," he prayed; and adapting his rhythm to the shape of a pilaster, ended by offering his "Mite" with "an *adoring Awfulness*, & *trembling Veneration*."

Canto ii, "The Humiliation," had to describe Theophila's repentance for sin, and Benlowes, with his unfailing delight in the Bible story, traced sin's ancestry from the beginning. So the poem celebrates the Creation and man's first innocence. "*Skin* was his Robe: *Clouds* washt, *Winds* swept his Floor." It is a good subject for

---

[1] One should notice, though, that Cleveland has a heraldic metaphor at line 35, describing Fuscara's *argent* skin streaming with *or*. So perhaps that *is* the reason. In Cleveland the bee *nibbles* at line 44.

Benlowes' wit, and he sees man "Chanc'lour install'd of *Edens Universitie.*" Then, with the eating of the forbidden fruit, with which our nature still is sick, doom of death is pronounced and the angel of vengeance can at once greet men as *"Wormships."* Sin leads to Hell, which the poet describes with vehemence. Repentance is urged before old age shall come and "round thy palsy'd *Heart* Ice be congealed quite." The decrepitude of age invites Benlowes to indulgence in conceit:

> E're in thy Pocket thou thine *Eyes* dost wear;
> E're thy *Bones* serve for Calender;
> E're in thy *Hand*'s thy Leg, or Silver in thy *Hair.*

The cleverness no doubt obtrudes, though less so to one accustomed to the seventeenth-century manner; and the fancifulness perhaps does justice to the theme. [1] Whether or not this style is equally in place in describing Theophila's repentance must be a matter of opinion. Saintsbury thought it "fantastic enough but not uncharming," [2] and if one accepts the metaphysical habit of describing religious experience in material terms, has one the right to object to the particular symbols used? Yet I suppose some symbols may be more naturally appropriate than others, and some modern readers may feel an incongruity which the poet does not succeed in resolving when Theophila's hands are described as "Breast-hammers." Benlowes shares with Crashaw an inability to describe passion without some physical insignia. His early Catholic training had developed what must have been a natural predilection, and his mind habitually worshipped with images and rituals. His objection to Catholicism now was to the papal authority rather than to the Roman mode of worship. It is very significant that at this stage in the poem he feels the need to pray to some saint or *"Angel-Intercessor"* (stanza 67), while admitting that he is forbidden to do so by the tenets of his present church. But of course, though

---

[1] Like so many of the most curious conceits in Benlowes, this again is not his own invention. He seems to have adapted it from James Howell. *Cf.* Howell, *Familiar Letters,* p. 458, where the aged are described as carrying *"their legs in their hands, their eyes upon their noses,* and an *Almanack in their bones."* And similar conceits about old age were not uncommon and may, if one wishes, be referred back to Ecclesiastes xii : 3-4: "The day when the keepers of the house shall tremble, and the strong men shall bow themselves, and the grinders cease, because they are few, and those that look out of the windows be darkened, and the doors shall be shut in the streets." This passage is directly imitated at *Theophila,* xiii, 52.

[2] *Minor Poets of the Caroline Period,* I, 312.

he can write no hymn to St. Teresa, his whole poem depends upon the literary convention by which the soul is personified as a spiritual maiden to whom he may address himself in adoration and who thus serves as a focus for his religious emotion. Theophila, therefore, though without his recognizing it, takes in his emotional life the place of the rejected Catholic saints.

The habit of worshipping in images is reflected here in the nature of the repentance. Tears make a lake in which sin is drowned, and the flames that rise from Theophila's breast are as visible as the holy water that drops from her eyes. The incense of sacrifice rises from the "bruis'd *Spiceries*" of Theophila's breast, which again reminds of Crashaw, only to outdo him. Some battle-imagery, of the kind that Crashaw also uses, though I think more effectively, follows. Theophila makes a breach in Sin's wall with "the loud Volleyes of her *Pray'rs.*" The physical violence of such imagery has been objected to but is not inappropriate to some kinds of religious experience nor out of line with the more sensational kind of Counter-Reformation art. The danger is rather that the poet, grasping after a startling comparison, may find himself clutching two incompatibles. The notion that one may by abasing oneself become triumphant leads to the conceit of Theophila scaling Heaven's wall on her knees. But this paradox in itself runs risks of absurdity by the emphasis it places on the physical action, and when her knees are made to "cry loud, as her *Tongue*," when her eyes at the same time speak, and then the eyes and tongue join the knees in scaling, incongruity is patent. [1]

Yet frequent lapses of this kind are sometimes triumphantly offset by an imagination which can lift itself above the earth and incorporate material things in a brilliant other-worldly vision. In the ambitious third canto, "The Restauration," the poet is transported into unearthly regions where

Saints ply
Their Sails through airy Waves, & anchor still on High.

When Benlowes is at his best one feels the rush of winds and a beating of angels' wings. He can be at home with vastness. One can hardly doubt that he had moments of rapture when Theophila, shimmering creature of his imagination, was more real to him than the men who walked about Finchingfield. In this canto he catches his first

---

[1] The contrast with *The Dutchesse of Malfy*, IV, ii, 239-241, where there is no incongruity, is instructive.

glimpse of the heavenly radiance, from which of course Theophila, the immortal soul, has sprung, and he is led on therefore to the portrait of his heroine. No hyperbole can be extravagant in the depiction of one who reflects Heaven's glory and must incomparably outshine all earthly beauties. But her fascination is of the same kind as theirs, only superlative in degree. The spiritual again expresses itself in concrete terms. Theophila's skin is whiter than snow or milk. She has a *"gold-thatcht"* head, a silver voice, and teeth of pearl; her lips are rubies and her veins "wrought Saphyrs." The metallic and bejewelled opulence of some passages in *Theophila* is no doubt encouraged by the traditional Christian heaven (if perhaps one ought not lightly to vie with St. John of the Revelation in his own sphere). But the clearer debt here is to the main Renaissance tradition of rich decoration in narrative poetry. An obvious comparison, for example, would be with Spenser's celebrated description of Belphoebe, who had legs "like two faire marble pillours," an "iuorie forhead," hair "like golden wyre"; and when she spoke

> twixt the perles and rubins softly brake
> A siluer sound. [1]

Benlowes' description is certainly not excessive or bizarre when judged by the taste of his own period. What makes it remarkable is the degree of solid brilliance it bestows upon the insubstantial soul. Yet in one passage Benlowes combines brilliance with the suggestion of a feminine warmth and softness which makes Theophila the worthy object of the passion which pulsates throughout this canto:

> Her *Hands* are soft, as swannie Down, and much
>   More white; whose temperate *Warmth* is such,
> As when ripe *Gold* and quickning *Sun-beams* inly touch.
>
> Ye *Syrens* of the Groves, who, pearcht on high,
>   Tune gutt'ral Sweets, *Air-Minstrels*, why
> From your Bough-Cradles, rockt with Windes, to HER d'ye flie?
>
> See, *Lilies*, gown'd in *Tissue*, simper by Her;
>   With *Marigolds* in *flaming* Tire;
> Green sattin'd *Bayes*, with *Primrose* fring'd, seem all on Fire.

However tangible he makes his spiritual heroine, Benlowes never forgets that hers is to be a skiey beauty. He keeps all the heavenly bodies in motion, and so long as he fuses, not confounds, the actual with the fanciful, he may make a beautiful myth. He sees the

---

[1] *The Faerie Queene*, book II, canto iii, stanzas 24-30.

> winged *Hours*
>   Dandle the *Infant-Morn.*

The moon becomes

> That *Lady-Prioress* of the cloyster'd *Skie*,
>   Coacht with her spangled *Vestalls* nigh.

The affinities with Milton and Crashaw are obvious. [1] In similar vein, but with a daring pun, which is just like Benlowes but which Milton at least would have avoided, Benlowes makes the moon president of the Star Chamber, "Rallying her starrie *Troop* to guard her glittering *Tent.*"

The dazzle of Theophila's appearance is equalled by her power of song, as befits her creator's passion for music. Her lyre is heard above the din of battle, and in the song she now sings is found Benlowes' horror of civil war, his scorn of Presbyterian theology, and his detestation of all who bring schism into the church. With a hymn to peace Theophila pauses.

She resumes in Canto iv—"The Inammoration"—with a soliloquy of self-exhortation and a song of love. Here, for the first time, the metre changes and Theophila speaks in couplets, with a resounding alexandrine at every sixth line. Benlowes' love of method, however, equates this canto with the others by counting a stanza for each three lines. It is a curious metre to have chosen for a passionate love-transport. Beside Crashaw, for example, Theophila seems to soar broken-winged. And the Soul celebrating the *"Heav'nly Comforts"* of which she is already "prepossest" cannot rid herself of her restless brain. When she is born again, there must be imagery of parturition and *"After-births* of Penitential Mones." Her marriage with Christ makes her long for children—virtuous deeds. His love is guaranteed by an indenture signed by a pen dipped in an inkwell of his blood. Yet some of the "metaphysical" imagery is as effective as it is inge-

---

[1] Though the last image is said to be based on Cleveland's "The Senses Festival," ll. 11-12: "the fair Abbess of the skies,/With all her Nunnery of eyes." (Williamson, *The Donne Tradition*, p. 176.) If it is, then no better example could be given of Benlowes' improving on what he borrowed. When I compare with Milton, I am thinking especially of the imagery of the ode "On the Morning of Christs Nativity," which shows how very seventeenth-century Milton can be. (Such an eighteenth-century imitator of Milton as Collins perpetuates what was in harmony with the seventeenth-century tradition as well as what went against it. I do not think this is sufficiently realized.) What Benlowes most admired in Milton was the pictorial character of his imagery, especially perhaps the use made of the splendour of the heavenly bodies. See below, Appendix II, and especially examples 8, 9, 22, 24, 27.

nious. Like most poets of this period, Benlowes is skilled in analogies for the relationship of body and soul.

> HE's thy bright *Sun*; 'twixt WHOM, and thy *Souls* Bliss,
> Thy earthie *Body* interposed is;
> Whereby such dread *Eclipses* caused are,
> As fam'd *Astronomers* can ne're declare.

And he experiences almost a sensuous thrill when his mind sees
opposites miraculously conjoined, as when Heaven's *altitude* bowed
low and Christ's death united man's supreme *grief* with supreme
joy. The contemplation of a love which "do's so strangly bound
ALMIGHTINES IT SELF" fills him with ecstasy, and in her love-song
Theophila quivers with passion as she approaches Christ, her spouse.
The song over and the poet returning to his accustomed metre,
the lyrical abandon increases. Theophila dreams of her future union
with "a comely PERSON, clad in white," who outshines the sun.
She swoons in excess of zeal and is wounded by "Darts of intolerable *Sweets*." In a trance she mounts to Heaven. Her flaming sacrifice of love is crowned with glory. Like the phoenix she is reborn
in her own holocaust and from it springs up in triumph to the sky,
where Heaven's choir greets her with Hosannas. [1]

Installed in Heaven, Theophila is now able to appear to the poet
in a vision of light; and this she does in Canto v, which is called
"The Representation." The poet seeks to suggest her gorgeousness
with stars upon her brow and "Amber-curling *Tresses*...like a
glittering Veil" about her "snowy *Shoulders*," but does not repeat
his previous endeavour to portray her physical splendour. To attempt the face would be presumption, and wisely he describes rather
the dazzling radiance in which it is enveloped. This too he approaches
with judgment, and, showing again the influence of Milton, [2] makes
the effect by a sudden wondrous light which burst upon the darkness
when

> theevish *Night* had *stole*, and *clos'd* up quite,
> In her dark *Lantern*, starrie *Light*.

The poet's mystical enthusiasm is at its height in this canto, when

---

[1] This whole passage, with its longing for the life that comes of being slain
with Love's sweet wounds, inevitably reminds one yet again of Crashaw (*cf.*
especially Crashaw's "Hymn to Sainte Teresa" and see above, p. 188 n.). The
similarity between these two poets is partly one of temperament, but partly also
rests, I have no doubt, on a common influence of the Catholic faith, though
one of them had eagerly embraced it as a convert and the other had rejected
it with scorn after being nurtured in it.

[2] *Cf. Comus*, ll. 195-197.

his soul ascends to his eye to peep upon "ANGELITIE" and is drawn into his ear by the unimaginable music of Theophila's voice. Here again he excels in suggesting the immensity of space through which Theophila travels in her heavenward flight, "*swift as a glancing* Meteor," past the sun to where the stars "*nail* HEAV'NS *Court*." The spheres suspend their music to listen to her "*psalming Tongue*" as she passes into the radiance beside which the sun itself seems shade. Benlowes' description of heaven again copies the jewelled structure of the Book of the Revelation, and prettily completes it with "*loose* Pearls, *instead of* Pebbles" on "*every* Angel-trodden Way." Heaven can only be described to sense, he says, in terms of courts and gems; but he has the insight to place the true heaven beyond the apprehension of the senses. He avoids, therefore, some of the bathos and lapses of taste that are always a danger to him when he seeks to achieve a description by listing concrete details. "*Ev'n* SPIRITS, *who have disrob'd their* Rags *of* Clay" are dazzled by what could not be told even if one had "*more* Tongues, *than* HEAV'N *has* Eyes." It is with comparisons of this sort that he now for the most part seeks to *suggest* Heaven's power; and some of his fancies are not unworthy of their purpose:

> *Had I a* Quill *sent from a* SERAPHS *Wing,*
> *And* Skill *to tune't! I could not sing*
> *The* Moity *of that* Wealth.

In Canto vi, "The Association," the rapturous account of heaven continues in a description of its inhabitants. These are of two kinds, those who were formerly "grosser and unpolish[t] Clay" and the angelic attendants upon God, who are described in their hierarchies according to Benlowes' literal-minded delight in a systematic theo logy. Those who have *ascended* into glory are the martyrs, saints, and apostles, and finally the Virgin herself, to whom Benlowes writes an ode. In it his literal-mindedness is again apparent in his elaboration of the paradoxes of the Virgin's nature. She is a "VIRGIN-SPOUSE," and she gave breath to him who made her breathe. In speaking of the birth itself, he is more fantastic. Since it did not result from sexual union, but from an angel's annunciation, he celebrates the Virgin's conception of Christ by the ear. The poet is happier in the song which follows, in which David, the psalmist, leads the praise of God. Here the inspiration of the Psalms [1] enables Benlowes to rise to his theme in a vast sweep of imagery. This

---

[1] *Cf.* especially Psalm 104, vv. 2ff.

is one of the grandest passages in the poem and the one that I would choose first, if asked to support a comparison between Benlowes and Milton on the grounds of their "profound sense of the immense space which surrounds human life." [1]

> *Whose Thunder-clasping* HAND *do's grasp the Shole*
> *Of total* Nature, *and unroul*
> The spangled Canopy *of* HEAV'N *from* Pole *to* Pole!
>
> *Who, on the* Clouds *and* Windes, *thy* Chariot, *rid'st*;
> *And, brideling wildest* Storms, *them guid'st*;
> *Who,* moveless, *All dost* move; *Who, changing All,* abid'st!
>
> *The* Ocean *Thou begirt'st with misty* Shrouds;
> *That* Monster *wrapt'st in swathing Clouds,*
> And, *with thy mighty* WORD *controul'st tempestuous* Flouds!

Perpetual song is the traditional characteristic of heaven; and for so great a lover of music as Benlowes was, that in itself meant perfect felicity. He ends this canto with a description of angelic harmonies.

In Canto vii, "The Contemplation," Benlowes has to suggest the nature of God himself, and this, the most difficult task of all, he is least qualified to fulfil. Approaching the purely spiritual, he is bereft of many of his usual picturesque aids. The reader is dazzled by "ETERNITIE," "IMMENSITY," "UBIQUITIE," which leap out at the eye in huge capital letters. If every star were a sun and all were rolled into one and then the brightness were increased a thousandfold, still their light would seem a mere flash beside the radiance of heaven—which is repeatedly described in similar superlatives. This light of heaven is eclipsed by the sight of God himself. A few vast metaphors seek to suggest God. Eternity is but his hourglass, and winds are "Van-Curriers, & Postilions" to his will. The rhythm swells and there is again a fine surge of majesty as the created universe is described responsive to God's power. But by now repetition is perhaps beginning to tell upon the reader and accumulated comparisons grow wearisome. Yet the sceptic should not object. To the devout man of the seventeenth century nothing could be more satisfying than to linger over God's infinity, goodness, and love; to return again and again to the joys of heaven; and to tell yet once more the central all-dominating episode of human history—Christ's life on earth and his resurrection. But when all this has been said, the lack of novelty in Benlowes' presentation

---

[1] Williamson, *The Donne Tradition*, p. 176, where, however, this passage is not cited.

here of the Christian faith makes this one of his least characteristic
cantos. The supreme wonder of the Trinity fails in his poem to
thrill. Perhaps it should be left only to intellects capable of grappling
with metaphysics. And dangerous as have been some of Benlowes'
acrobatics with concrete symbols, nothing could better show Benlowes' unphilosophic mind than the flagging of inspiration when
concrete symbols are denied. Never again, I think, does he rekindle
the passion which, though intermittent, burns through Cantos iii—vi.

The eighth canto, "The Admiration," seems indeed a somewhat
dutiful one. The poet fulfils his scheme, but without music or a
visible revelation to inspire it the ecstasy is gone. Theophila speaks
to him of God's hidden nature, and though she confesses the impossibility of containing the idea of God in mortal language, she yet
may interest the modern reader in giving an example of the theological and metaphysical ideas of seventeenth-century orthodoxy.
God has neither form nor matter, is everywhere at once. The only
comparable thing is air, which is "*Ubiquitie* unseen," and "*Inviolable*,
though it *pierced* be." But even the air is a created thing, and God
has "SELF-LIFE." There is a further attempt to explain the Trinity.
God has added to his own nature the function of the Son, and being
Infinity, has in the Son given all while yet retaining all within himself. No good Christian could shirk these ideas and Benlowes did
not try to, but he took the opportunity which offered of returning
to something less abstract with a reference to the incarnation. This
easily led to the nature of sin and hell, God's love, and the duty of
prayer. All these had been previously expatiated on and there is
no new experience to make this canto other than an academic commonplace. Only once does Benlowes seem to relate religion with
the lives of men—in his reference to the wretched of the earth,

> Whose wither'd *Skins*, sear as the saplesse Wood,
>   Cleave to their *Bones*, for want of *food*.

Only occasionally is there an effective figure, as in the picture of
"wry-mouth squint-ey'd *Scoff*," who cannot stay the saints in their
flight to heaven. Finally, Theophila bids farewell, leaving the poet
disdaining "Earths giddy Mirth" and with Joy running races in
his blood.

With Theophila's final description of God, Benlowes completed
his design. If this has not generally been realized, that is because
no heed has been given to the obvious clues provided. To each
canto the author appended a Latin quatrain in which he commented

upon the progress of his poem, and, using the common metaphor of a voyage, prayed God to guide his bark to its goal. After two cantos he thanked the stars for the light they had given but knew that the longer part of the journey remained. After four cantos, however, he was half-way through his course. After five, he promised, with God's help, a sixth, which would be the antepenultimate. When he had written it, the end of the journey, the *"optatam...* Terram,"* could be discerned afar off. At the end of the seventh canto, he could already see the haven. After the eighth his weary bark had arrived, and he looked back at the finished work ("Opus *exactum"*) with satisfaction.

So, too, did one whose initials were M.G., who praised the work in Latin prose. M.G. saw a wonderful harmony between the work and its author. A music-lover had produced a poem that was song itself; a celibate poet a virgin work. Nowhere had more been done to exhibit the power of love.

CHAPTER EIGHTEEN

ACCRETIONS TO THE WORK

The work, then, was finished; but Benlowes quickly decided on another journey. The British sea had been sufficiently explored, but he was now determined to sail the Ausonian main. [1] In other words, he proposed to treat the same theme in Latin. Accordingly he wrote "The Recapitulation." Having written it, he warned the "*English Reader*" not to stray on "*Latian Alps*," [2] and proceeded to "lead *Him* home" by translating it into English couplets. The two versions were ultimately printed face to face and called Canto ix. [3]

As the development of an argument was never Benlowes' prime purpose, his "recapitulation" was not a synopsis. He simply picked out some of the main themes of the poem for repetition here. Again he made a sacrifice of verses upon the flame of love, again he gave a groan for the evils of the world and its civil strife, again gibed at the "new Kirk." [4] The best, though characteristically extravagant,

[1] *Theophila*, 1652 folio, p. 122.

[2] *Ibid.*, p. 147.

[3] That the Latin was the original could also be established by internal evidence. The English is not always able to reproduce the word-play of the Latin, as, for example, in stanza 10:

Solus

S<small>OL</small> *meus es, meus es* S<small>AL</small>, *mea sola* S<small>ALUS</small>.

Thou alone

Art *Health* unto my Soul, my *Salt*, my *Sun*.

In stanza 65, "*Desuper extat* Amor; *Tibi* Mens *contermina* Coelo" becomes "*Love to thy Soul* deriv'd is from *Above*," the second half-line not being able to be rendered. Theophila gleams with flowers and "glitt'ring *Buds*" ("Gemmis *nitentibus*"), but the English, of course, cannot reproduce the play with jewels which is present in the Latin.

[4] I cite his pen-and-ink correction for the text's "our *Church*" (stanza 30). In the seventeenth century the word *kirk* as the ordinary word for church was gradually falling out of literary use in Scotland and was, in fact, replaced by *church* in the official designation of the Church of Scotland at the date of the Westminster Assembly. Nevertheless, *kirk* continued in occasional use for the Scottish church when it was desired to distinguish it from the Church of England. Benlowes' substitution of "new Kirk" for "our *Church*" must therefore be held to absolve the church as a whole from his criticism while pointing his attack directly at the Presbyterians.

passage is yet another description of Theophila, whose neck causes
the swan to pine and whose rosy cheeks make grapes hang their
heads, while the emerald grove envies her golden hair. Theophila
enraptures the man, but can only lead the poet into temptation.
When he compares her breasts to the Alps with a "*lasting* Snow"
upon them, his too picturesque touch makes him surpass an already
extravagant conceit of Randolph's. [1] Beholding God, he is changed
to "flaming *Spice*," an image forced on him by the need of a rhyme
—the Latin has only "Favillis," embers. But in spite of such awk-
wardnesses, Benlowes here recaptures some of the glow of his
earlier cantos, approaches God with tears and passion, and in a
sudden transport of love finally becomes one with his Maker.

The poem was now finished for the second time. Benlowes tacitly
recognized this when *Theophila* was printed by having inserted here,
as a sort of appendix, Latin translations of two of the early cantos.
It is even possible that the poem had started to be printed before
its author decided on a continuation. But continue he did. In a
Latin fill-up for page 161 he confessed that it might seem a crime
to attempt a heroic poem after Homer and Virgil; but although
he could not write as he would like to, he wished nevertheless to
write what he could. And desire not yet being satisfied, at the end
of the Latin translations he promised a quick return to British shores.

The subject of the new work was, according to Benlowes' custom,
much heralded before it began and was first announced by the ci-
tation of some verses by Owen Feltham "Upon the Vanitie of the
World," [2] and then again by fragments of Latin verse and prose,
and also in English, when, for what seems the only time in his
career, Benlowes tried his hand at blank verse. Theophila had made
almost her last appearance, but the new subject was of course
largely the old one again. Heaven had already been elaborately described, and so the emphasis now returned to that of the opening
canto of *Theophila*: it was upon "the base Licentiousness o' th'
Age," which the man who desired heaven must flee from. At the
end of his Latin verses Benlowes amused himself with a typical

---

[1] "A Pastorall Courtship," ll. 65-68.

[2] Curiously enough, this poem was printed here by Benlowes before it came
out with Feltham's own works. It was to do that in 1661, when, under the title
of "True Happiness," it appeared in *Lusoria*, a collection of occasional verses
included in the eighth edition of the *Resolves*. Benlowes' version has many
variant readings; but these are mostly of an insignificant kind and suggest that
Benlowes may have been quoting the poem from memory.

word-puzzle, summing up the whole subject of life on earth in one letter, R, which, if you say it in Latin, Greek, and Hebrew, gives you "eR-RO-RES_h."

In Canto x, then, "The Abnegation," Benlowes wielded "the Scourges of *Satyrick Vein.*" He set himself to "undisguize" such worldly "*Ware*" as "*Ermin'd* Mantles," "rich caparison'd champing *Coursers*," and "*Cupboards* with throng'd massy *Plate.*" He sought to hit off his horror of the world by a string of comparisons. Some of them are admirable, like the tremendous sustained metaphor which, making use of Shakespeare's storm in *Othello*, presents life as a storm at sea, with winds which "might waken *Death* with *Noise*," when you seem "to knock at *Hell*, and bounce the *Firmament.*" Then, influenced by the mode of the seventeenth-century character-writers, he described some specimen sinners. These are not, however, in Benlowes, types of humanity—he never seems to examine the manners of the world closely enough for that—so much as personifications in some vague allegory. They are quite literary in their inception. Benlowes chooses to write on the ambitious man, the miser, the dandy—the very stock figures which occur in most of the edifying literature of the period, ranging from Brathwait's *The English Gentleman* to Joseph Beaumont's *Psyche.* And, naturally enough, there is no attempt at character-analysis, but rather at vast, striking images which will suggest the absolute of vice and which are sometimes successful in bringing the whole universe within their scope. Aspiro, the ambitious man, kicks empires into the air, and

> Though *Prides* high *Head* doth brush the *Stars*, yet shall
> Its *Carkass* like a Sulphur Ball,
> Plunge into *Flames* Abyss. *Pride* concav'd *Satans* Hall.

Here, the use of "concave" as a verb is a typical piece of linguistic licence, and the unnatural compression it gives may seem to stunt the figure. I am not sure that it suggests the mighty thud intended. Yet this so briefly touched allusion to Satan's expulsion from Heaven adds something to an already immense conception. Benlowes' best writing has remarkable compactness and is strictly metaphysical in striving to bring *all* experience within *one* figure. At other times effects are obtained by Benlowes' quaint humour and eccentric word-play, not out of place in presenting the miser Avaro. He has a "pursie" conscience and, since irony delights to see a miser's wealth wasted by a spendthrift son, so his wealth is a dropsy which "breeds *Consumption*" in his heir. Gold is said to be "the Fautress of all civil Jarres," and here the spelling "fautress" brings out a characteristic pun on "fault," which an intrusive *l* in modern English has in part destroyed.

The description continues in Canto xi, "The Disincantation," with Avaro's son, Volupto. Here Benlowes' fantastic phraseology has one of its most fitting themes, and he is very satirical about patches, powdered hair, and extravagant dress. Onomatopoeia bids the gallant "sheath'd in rusling Silks, new Suits display"; ridicule creates a vivid picture of the roisterer; and anger shows the noble wastrel grinding down the poor. One hears of lascivious verses and tears of false love. Their object, the courtesan, is also described, and here Benlowes excels himself in bitter, mocking wit. This dame of pleasure, with her patches,

> does, to seem more bright,
> Lattice her Day with bars of Night.

Patches at this date were the mark of the prostitute—"like Tickets on the Door," they show that she is to let. With some help from the old play, *Lingua*, Benlowes describes her fabulous dress:

> Scarce is the *Toy* at Noon to th' Girdle drest;
> Nine Pedlars need each Morn be prest
> To lanch her forth: A ship as soon is rigg'd to th' West. [1]

With continued eccentricity of phrase, Benlowes warns all these rioters how Time, quickly passing, "shall one Day find its Præter-tense." The fiery hell of the earlier cantos shows no sign of dying down, and worldly gaiety ends, of course, in "Brimstone Torrents."

Benlowes had not yet exhausted his eloquence on these themes of vice. He had nothing new to say, but there were still possible variations in the way it could be said. His limited imagination, however, did not show him truth in new forms; the variations never went beyond the decorative details. But a mind which set out to invent "grateful Similies" and "apt Metaphors" could still approach a long-familiar subject with energy and vigour. And there was always the poet's second language to enlarge the variety of phrase. So a series of short Latin compositions were appended to continue the castigation of the drunkard and the courtesan.

In a fierce but witty satire the poet attacks the painted

---

[1] *Cf. Lingua*, IV, vi: "There is such doing with their looking-glasses, pinning, vnpinning, setting, vnseting...that yet shee is scarce drest to the girdle... seauen Pedlers shops, nay all Sturbridge Faire will scarce furnish her: a Ship is sooner rigd by farre, then a Gentle-woman made ready."

face and bold attire of the loose woman, [1] who buys her face and exposes her body for sale—how could even Ovid describe her metamorphosis when she has a new shape every day? Then he briefly reflects on the great wonder of the world—Heaven, for all it holds sun, moon, and stars, cannot support one sin, while the earth sustains a mass of them. Or he weeps over the delirium of a world which is a nurse to the wicked and to the good a torture-chamber. He addresses the vain worldling who disturbs the air with futile babblings and who, uttering only nonsense, receives the world's highest reward. He pens a stinging character of the drunkard and glutton, who makes his belly his god and is always sacrificing to it. He threatens the proud with death, and then writes with some passion of Death's terror and of repentance. Thoughts of death put worldly honours in perspective, and so another poem in scorn of them follows: the world's glittering bubble bursts as soon as seized and the horse of ambition throws its rider and breaks his skull.

The medal has both an obverse and a reverse. It was a long time before Benlowes turned it over; but at length he left off denouncing society's vices to describe the ideal life which can be lived in retirement from the world. Determining to "Waste not an other Word on *Fools*," he celebrated "the Happinesse of a Private Life" in two cantos which were numbered as the twelfth and thirteenth of *Theophila*, though to suggest that they belonged to it made *Theophila* even more unwieldy and helped still further to disguise its shape.

In Canto xii, "The Segregation," the poet leaves man's sight to view God's love. Man's world is full of war; he remembers Edge Hill and weeps for his own sin. There is division in the church. But deep in the country peace can be found. The fortune that offers it is "low-built," for

> Elm Rafters, mantled 'Ore with straws,
> Out-blesse *Escuriall* Tour's that seem Heav'ns Cupulas.

Emblems of happiness are "fragrant *Vi'lets*, blushing *Strawberies*,"

---

[1] At this date, according also to Evelyn, the painting of the face was "a most ignominious thing and us'd only by prostitutes." Under Elizabeth and James I it had been fashionable at court (of Elizabeth herself one account said, "not only all over her face, but her very neck and breast also, and... in some places near half an inch thick"—Foley, *Records of the Society of Jesus*, I, 8), but it fell into disrepute under Charles I. Within a year or two of *Theophila's* publication, however, the practice was again spreading to women of rank (Evelyn, *Diary*, II, 52).

which "Close shrouded lurk from lofty Eyes." The joys of a simple,
pastoral life, ever popular with poets, are pleasantly touched on as
Benlowes walks in meadows where at dawn dew glitters like stars
upon the grass, passes in Milton's track by "rushy-fringed Banks," [1]
and lies upon "*Earths* flow'r-wov'n Damask." There he gazes at
Nature's marvels in insect life — the society of ants and bees, the
legs of the gnat, the "*Moths* strange Teeth." By observation he discovers God in everything. Flowers and insects also remind him,
like Herrick and all the others, of earth's transience. From every
object he can take "mental Buds," and these occupy him until noon,
when he prepares to dine. A quick mental tour of the fountains and
hedgerows lists what Nature offers for man's needs, and
with a curious digression he praises her also for tobacco. The as-
ceticism of the ideal life evidently does not deny indulgence in the
"*Herb* that *Cramp* and *Toothach* drives away," "renerves slack *Joynts*,"
and with its "active Smoke" aids the poetic invention. [2] It certainly
stimulates a man's fantastic wit—the paradoxical pipe is "both
Ventiduct, & Stove." [3]

But Benlowes finds that he has "traverst *more* of *Ground* to Day"
—that he has, in fact, written 120 instead of 100 stanzas in this canto.
And so he pauses with a promise to finish the poem next day in
the thirteenth canto. This, called "The Reinvitation," contains some
of Benlowes' best writing in its charming description of the country
at midsummer. The debt to Milton is great and, as with "L'Allegro,"
the special interest here lies less in the landscape than in the country
occupations described. Into about twenty stanzas Benlowes packs
an epitome of English life. While "the merry Hamlet Bells chime
Holy Day" he watches the mower and the sheepshearer. He sees
the cattle with "galled Necks" at plough and the "wide-horn'd"
oxen trampling the grass. There are "bright-scal'd gliding *Fish*"
to be caught. On feast-days one goes to church. When harvest
comes the labourers sweat through their clothes ("through both
their Skins"). In the evening sheep are folded, men and oxen go
home tired, and milkmaids make their curtsies "to th' spungy-
teated Cow." (No subject, one sees, can fail to present an opportunity

---

[1] *Cf. Comus*, l. 890.

[2] Again he borrows something from Tomkis' *Lingua* (IV. iv). On tobacco,
see above, p. 107.

[3] This phrase had appeared in print the previous year (in the poem *News
from Newcastle*, attributed to Cleveland), but applied—surely much less neatly
—to a coal-pit.

to the fancy.) God's love for man is readily discoverable in the quiet country life, especially with the aid of Theophila, who makes a brief return to the poem to inspire the poet with *"Soul-Elevations."* Adoring God, he renounces "all Creature Love" and desires to live the life of the soul. As God made the world of nothing, he seeks to make nothing of the world. This last canto, like many of the earlier ones, is full of God's love and the power of prayer and self-dedication. It approaches its end on a high note of devotion, with the poet confidently seeking strength to live for God; and then, thinking of the day of judgment and with one last display of wit, Benlowes makes a final prayer to God to crown his end as the end of his poem crowns his work.

The composite work that *Theophila* had thus developed into was at length finished, but it had not ceased to accrete miscellaneous fragments in Latin. Benlowes could still go over again the argument of these last two cantos. So he expressed once more his joy in the countryside and his desire for a life of neither wealth nor poverty. Then, consecrating himself again to God in a final peroration, a "Peroratio Eucharistica," given both in prose and verse, he thanked God for having preserved him through a thousand perils and having brought him out of dangerous disturbances to a period of peace and pleasant leisure, such as would make a devout life possible for him. The surprising thing to notice about this is the absence of any specific reference to his part in the Civil War. The dangers Benlowes stressed were those of travel and worldly temptations of foreign lands. He briefly indicated the itinerary of his grand tour twenty years before and thanked God for bringing him safe home. He still felt what he had said to Phineas Fletcher in 1633, that to desire the grand society of courtiers was an error. But right at the end of his book came a new detail in personal revelation when Benlowes gave the first hint anywhere in his writings of an ideal other than that of the pious country gentleman. He wished to haunt the Bodleian Library, which, with its store of books, was a treasure-house second only to the Vatican in Rome. In what circumstances he came later to realize that part of his ideal the later chapters of this biography will show.

CHAPTER NINETEEN

PRAISE OF THE WORK

Eight books of exultation celebrating the soul's epic progress from repentance to the highest glory, a résumé of the theme in a ninth canto, four cantos denouncing a worldly and extolling a spiritual life, together with a host of embellishments, interludes, appendices, supplementary meditations, and Latin translations—this, then, was the somewhat unwieldy work which about the latter half [1] of 1652 was on sale to the London public. Benlowes considered it his Opus One. Nothing that he had previously done was held worthy of account, though he had dabbled in writing now for twenty years at least. He had turned out numerous complimentary verses on the works of others, and sometimes these had swelled into longish poems in themselves. Years before, he had compiled his *Sphinx Theologica* with an eye to the spiritual improvement of his young cousin, William Nevill; he had written during the Civil War in praise of peace; and he had published a diatribe against the Pope. Yet these were all trifles to the serious poet. In offering *Theophila* to God he called it his first fruits, [2] and one of its admirers spoke of it as the author's maiden work. [3]

The actual text of *Theophila* was, of course, already in part familiar to many of those who now gazed on its ornamental pages. I have already had occasion to introduce some of the privileged readers who had perused it in manuscript at some stage during its composition. Five or six years before, Clement Paman had read some of it at Spains Hall in Finchingfield and marvelled. Thomas Wincoll had praised it in 1649. In 1650 Payne Fisher had published a flamboyant poem on it. The learned Dr. Alexander Ross had liked *Theophila* so well that he had translated a canto of it into Latin.

---

[1] It was in the press in May (see below, p. 215).

[2] Canto ix, stanza 4.

[3] M.G. on page 122. This, at least, I take to be the significance of *opus virgineum*, doubtless with a play on words alluding also to the heroine of the poem.

But this was nothing to the enthusiasm of John Hall, a young scholar who had amazed the dons of Cambridge with his *Horæ Vacivæ*, a brilliant volume of essays published in 1646 when he was a student at St. John's College and only nineteen years of age. [1] Like all young men of St. John's, he could not help looking on Benlowes as a person of distinction, and he probably sent a complimentary copy of his book to him as he did to James Howell. [2] He was known as a very rapid writer, and when he read *Theophila* "his tender affections" were so "ravished with that divine piece" that he turned a whole canto into Latin in a single day. [3] The compliment of translating a canto into Latin was also paid *Theophila* by Jeremy Collier, father of the more famous Jeremy who nearly half a century later was to create a sensation in the polite world by his attack upon the stage. The elder Jeremy was another man of St. John's College who must have been taught to honour this much-celebrated college benefactor. When he translated the seventh canto of *Theophila* he was headmaster of Aldenham School. He was by that time a friend of Benlowes, perhaps a close friend and certainly one of the circle who took pleasure in the by now traditional anagram of Benlowes and "benevolus." He not only had parts of *Theophila* in his possession, but he would seem to have been consulted about the preparation of the folio; for he wrote some verses to be engraved on one of the illustrative plates. Further, he had read Benlowes' introductory poem to his Fancy and had written a poem echoing its sentiment. In it he neatly praised the poet who did not rob gardens of their flowers or strip the sea of coral to give them to his mistress's cheek and lips but preferred instead to describe the radiations of the soul.

Many other admirers also wrote poems which Benlowes could prefix to *Theophila*. Among these eulogies were three in Latin in the conventional style of much seventeenth-century panegyric. One of them was the poem which Payne Fisher had written two years before, which now appeared in a shorter version and with Benlowes modestly choosing not to print all the superlatives which Fisher had attached to his name. [4] Another was by a friend of Fisher's,

---

[1] Wood, *Athenae Oxonienses*, II, 458.
[2] Howell, *Familiar Letters*, p. 432.
[3] Wood, *Fasti Oxonienses*, II, 359.
[4] The poem is signed P.F., and Dr. Boas, taking the initials to belong to Benlowes' old friend, Phineas Fletcher, included the poem in his edition of Fletcher's works. The latest biography of Fletcher (Langdale, *Phineas Fletcher*, p. 91) has also assumed his authorship. But the presence of the poem in Payne

Peter de Cardonel, of whom little is known beyond his propensity
for writing complimentary verses to his friend in French. He spoke of
Theophila's power to make a reader love her even on a short acquaintance. The third of the Latin poems was by the renowned
John Gauden, the Dean of Bocking, Benlowes' friend and neighbour.

The authors of poems praising *Theophila* in English ranged from
an obscure relative, T. Benlowes, [1] to the poet-laureate, Sir William
D'Avenant—to give him the apostrophe which his own pretentious-
ness adopted. D'Avenant was always a literary adventurer, willing
to find a patron where he could and ever ready with glib-tongued
praise. But it was long since this dashing cavalier, who had danced
attendance for years on Queen Henrietta and been appointed lieu-
tenant-governor of a British colony by King Charles's son, [2] had
bestowed his flattery on one so little influential in state affairs as
Edward Benlowes was.

The acquaintance of Benlowes and D'Avenant may have been
of long standing; for D'Avenant had cousins in the village of Sible
Hedingham, not far from Benlowes' home. In his younger days he
used to visit these cousins of his, [3] and once, in 1633, on leaving
Sible Hedingham, he had stopped at a tavern in the neighbouring
town of Braintree, where one of the servants had been impudent
about his syphilitic nose. D'Avenant, in a sudden temper, had drawn
upon him and the man had afterwards died. [4] Even at that date
D'Avenant possessed sufficient influence at court to obtain a pardon, [5]
and his subsequent career followed a much more brilliant course
than Benlowes', along an orbit of court masques, queenly favour,
and Royalist intrigues. In the Civil War he was constantly back
and forth between England and the Continent on secret political
missions. Eventually he was captured by his enemies and imprisoned
in the Tower to await trial for his life. [6] In the Tower, it has been
said, "he tried to keep himself before his friends and possible in-

---

Fisher's volume, *Marston-Moor*, and again in his collected *Piscatoris Poemata*
leaves no doubt about the matter.

[1] My knowledge of the Benlowes pedigree, though considerable, does not
include one with this initial.

[2] Harbage, *Sir William Davenant*, p. 111; Nethercot, *Sir William D'avenant*,
p. 257. The colony was Ma yland, but D'Avenant never got there. He set
sail for America, but was captured en route.

[3] Nethercot, pp. 96, 99.

[4] *Ibid.*, pp. 101ff.; Harbage, pp. 66-67.

[5] Nethercot, pp. 103-106.

[6] *Ibid.*, pp. 263ff.; Harbage, pp. 112ff.

fluential people by inscribing copies of *Gondibert* to them or writing congratulatory verses for their books." [1] It would have been like Benlowes to come to his assistance in prison, and if D'Avenant was one of the poets to whom Benlowes was a patron, as gossip certainly said, [2] this seems the most likely time for such patronage to have shown itself. In the Tower this man of action had time to read Benlowes' *Theophila*; on May 13, 1652, he wrote a poem on it. *Theophila* was already in the press, but Benlowes rushed to have D'Avenant's poem inserted in the middle of the other complimentary verses. [3] In this poem the man who had sought the pleasures of courts bowed to one who had renounced them. An eminent literary and political figure abased himself before the retired country poet:

> Now (best *Poet!*) I Divine would be;
> And only can be so by studying Thee.

D'Avenant went on to praise Benlowes for illuminating "Heav'ns darkned Mysteries" and for an excellence so perfect that instead of encouraging others to virtue it drove them to despair. From Sir William D'Avenant, poet-laureate, author of *Gondibert*, this was high praise. But even this poem that D'Avenant wrote to Benlowes in praise of *Theophila* showed where D'Avenant's superiority lay. Its lucid, smoothly reasoned couplets looked forward to Dryden and the new age of Charles II, while Benlowes' tortured metaphors still harked back to the Elizabethan Sylvester. D'Avenant, released from the Tower, soon forgot his aim to be divine, and turned to fulfilling lowlier but more permanent ambitions. He was successfully founding a new English theatre when Benlowes, having ceased to be a subject of panegyric, was sinking into poverty and oblivion.

Another man of courts and affairs who read and praised *Theophila* was an associate of D'Avenant in the entourage of Henrietta Maria, like D'Avenant conducted secret negotiations between England and the Continent, and preceded him as a prisoner in the Tower. This was Walter Montague, son of the Earl of Manchester, a poet of the court who had once written a pastoral masque, *The Shepheard's*

---

[1] Nethercot, p. 277.

[2] Wood, *Fasti Oxonienses*, II, 358.

[3] The poem of Sir William Denny (see below) was inserted at the same time. The evidence for this is to be found in the collation of the folio. To carry these two poems, three extra leaves were interpolated, and they were not always inserted at the same place. Some copies have them after B5, others after C1, others after C6.

Paradise, in which the Queen herself had taken part. [1] Unless we are to assume that Benlowes' poem travelled to France, Montague must have read 't before 1649, the date when, along with his friend Sir Kenelm Digby, he was banished. It is odd to find this link between Benlowes and a friend of Digby's, when one remembers that Digby had been attacked by Benlowes' own friend, Alexander Ross, in a book written at the instigation of Benlowes himself. [2] This attack had been directed especially against Sir Kenelm Digby's Catholic opinions, and Montague was a Catholic too. He had even acted with Digby in collecting money from Catholics to go towards the cost of the Royalist army. So Ross and Montague found themselves strangely in one another's company when both appeared within the covers of *Theophila*. And this book by a violent hater of Catholics included a tribute from a man who ended up abbot of a Benedictine monastery in France. Nothing could better illustrate Benlowes' tolerance of religious or political opponents when religion and politics were not in question. He was never bitter against persons. A staunch King's man in the Civil War, he had yet contrived to have friends on both sides; and the contributors of prefatory verses to *Theophila* illustrate the curious diversity of his associates.

Such enterprising Royalists as D'Avenant and Montague were, for example, offset by the presence of Arthur Wilson, who belonged to the retinue of the Earl of Warwick, the Parliamentary general. Wilson had actually sought to prevent the Cavaliers, Benlowes' comrades, from plundering Warwick's armoury at the time of their march on Colchester. And his opposition was no accident of situation, for his chief literary work was a *History of Great Britain* which was principally marked by its hostility to the Stuarts. This led Anthony à Wood to suppose loftily that Wilson's talents might have seemed

---

[1] It was of Montague and this masque that Suckling wrote:

> Witty *Apollo* asked him first of all
> If he understood his own Pastoral.
> For if he could do it, 't would plainly appear
> He understood more than any man there

(*A Sessions of the Poets*). On the other hand, Carew spoke of Montague flatteringly as one who could

> *stroake great AEolus,*
> *And from him the grace obtaine*
> *To binde him in an Iron chaine.*

[2] See above, pp. 149-150.

better if he had employed them on something else. [1] Yet Benlowes was on good terms with this political opponent, and both showed themselves able to forget political and religious differences in the community of their other views. Indeed, Benlowes could not but approve the pious and unworldly disposition which had led Wilson to sympathy with the Puritans. At Oxford Wilson had hated the debauchery he saw in the university, he was "more addicted to [his] booke...than other sensual appetites," [2] and for years he lived quietly in Benlowes' vicinity on the estates of the Earl of Warwick, his patron. His poem "*For the much Honoured AUTHOR*" suggests an enthusiasm for the life of the soul, and he rivalled even Benlowes in marvelling at infinity. Further, if he had "little skill in the Latin tongue," he was at least "well seen" in poetry. [3] A conceited style which sprinkled on Theophila's sacrifice a cordial distilled from the eyes, gave perhaps an appropriate expression to his admiration for Benlowes' work.

Another small poetic satellite of Benlowes and Payne Fisher was Thomas Philipot, whom Anthony à Wood thought had been "a tolerable poet when young." [4] Like Payne Fisher, he was wont to use his talent to gain favour where he could. In one year he dedicated a volume of poems to the Earl of Westmorland, who had suffered for the King, and wrote an elegy on the Earl of Essex, who had led the Parliament's forces. One would not look for great discrimination from him, and he was rasher than most in flattery when he prophesied for Benlowes "a glorious Shrine" and an "everblooming *Name*," "free from th'*Eclipse* of *Age*." [5]

Thomas Pestell, who had himself suffered much in the Civil War,[6] was a different kind of man and perhaps less given to flattery; but he was nevertheless equally enthusiastic. He compared Benlowes to the "*Prince* of *Wits*, illustrious *Dunne*," and, beholding Theophila "Who *jemm'st* it in JERUSALEM Above," got from Benlowes a glimpse of heaven here below. Like Clement Paman, he thought Benlowes' triumph the greater in that he had composed his poem when his fellow-men were at war. Similar praise of *Theophila* for having made

---

[1] Wood, *Athenae Oxonienses*, III, 319.

[2] Wilson, *The Tract of My Life* (in Peck's *Desiderata Curiosa*, 1779, II, 470, 463).

[3] Wood, *Athenae Oxonienses*, III, 319.

[4] Wood, *Fasti Oxonienses*, I, 518.

[5] Is it very unfair to add, on the authority of Wood, that Philipot passed off a book of his father's as his own?

[6] See above, pp. 144-145.

Love's life begin in the midst of death, came from Sir William Denny, another sufferer from the times, whose career bore some resemblance to Benlowes' own. Also hailing from the eastern counties, he had been Benlowes' exact contemporary at Cambridge, he was at present meditating his own principal poem, *The Sheepheard's Holiday*, and was, a quarter of a century later, to be contemporary with Benlowes again in poverty and death. But there was one important difference: Denny's long poem remained in manuscript for over two hundred years.

CHAPTER TWENTY

PUBLICATION OF THE WORK

With tributes from such a diversity of great and small to set before his poem, Benlowes certainly did not lack encouragement in giving to *Theophila* the permanence of print. A revival in fine books (as opposed to pamphlets) occurred now that some sort of settled government had been restored to England. But there is no sign that Benlowes' elegant folio created anything of a stir among the general public when in 1652, having been printed by R.N. (that is, Roger Norton), it ornamented the shops of Henry Seile in Fleet Street and Humphrey Moseley in St. Paul's Churchyard. If it occasioned little notice, that can have been no shock, at least to Moseley, an aristocrat among publishers, who dealt in learning and culture, put out all the finest poetry of the age, and declined to accommodate baser tastes. And perhaps Benlowes himself was not disappointed. Though jealous of fame, he courted no vulgar success and had not aimed at a marketable commodity. What he did desire was the achievement of a lasting and a beautiful form for the composition which had occupied the best years of his maturity. The book might be dedicated to Christ as its patron, but its earthly format had to be such as would make it a worthy offering from a fastidious artist to a circle of the discriminating. It was something to be treasured like some rare curio and to dwell beside globes, carvings, engravings, and other *objets d'art* in the libraries of men of taste. It was a book designed, one might say, for presentation copies, and the liberal distribution of these formed the crown of Benlowes' literary career.

No pains were spared in the printing. The general decorative effect produced by a variety of lettering was one which any monkish illuminator of mediaeval manuscripts would readily appreciate, but which was somewhat rare in printed books. The title-page was well set out in black and red. The prefixed poem "To My Fancie" had the initial letter of every stanza represented by a woodcut of the human body ingeniously contorted. But the aim was not usually decoration only. A keen lover of emblems naturally sought to use the appeal to the eye in order to reinforce his message to the mind. The use of capitals and italics was accordingly prolific even for the seventeenth century. All important words—on average certainly not less than one per line—were printed in italic. For special emphasis, italic being so common, words were picked out in small capitals, and large capitals were also not infrequent. Including the Roman of the basic text, there were therefore four types, and on one occasion the need for a fifth led to the introduction of black letter. Now, these types were not used haphazardly but according to a system carefully worked out if not always adhered to with absolute consistency. [1] Large capitals, for example, were reserved for references to the deity, which, in a devotional poem on the progress of the soul, were naturally frequent. Small capitals were generally used for words relating to heavenly or spiritual things, like angels, saints, salvation, the light of the spirit, the power of God. This grading of words is well illustrated by Canto i, stanza 41:

> Had not GOD left the BEST within the Power
> Of *Persecutors*, who devoure;
> We had nor MARTYRS had, nor yet a SAVIOUR.

The supremacy of God is reflected, as usual, in the large capitals. The Best, the Martyrs, are those of His creatures in whom spirit is supreme over flesh; they rise to the dignity of small capitals. The Persecutors, as the wicked agents, need also emphasis from the voice in reading; their importance to the sense gives them italics. But that they get only italics relegates them to a lower plane: their

---

[1] A fact, unfortunately, not appreciated by Saintsbury when, in his edition of *Theophila* (*Minor Poets of the Caroline Period*, vol. I), he spoke of "arbitrary printers' caprices" and did away with the distinction in types, arguing that such an eccentricity acts as a bar to the reader in his endeavour to become acquainted with a poet already difficult. Saintsbury may have been right to do this in resurrecting Benlowes for a modern reader, though that is doubtful. But in any case, it must be observed that the eccentricity belongs to Benlowes, not to the printer; and with an eccentric poet an understanding of the eccentricity is essential to the understanding of the poetry. One cannot just ignore it. To gain acquaintance with *Theophila* by discarding the typographical arrangement which the poet very deliberately chose for it may be not to gain acquaintance with the real *Theophila* at all. Shakespeare's blank verse would no doubt be the same thing if it were set out as prose; but the reader would not see it, would not feel it as the same thing; and no editor of Shakespeare would imagine he was doing justice to it by not dividing it into lines. In Benlowes, the distribution of emphasis is almost as important as the metre itself. The distinction of type has a very real bearing on the poet's interpretation of his own lines.

status in the poet's cosmogony is apparent. This may be a fantastic interpretation, but it is not more fantastic than Benlowes' typographical method warrants. One has to remember that Benlowes is a fantastic poet.

The typography was also very subtly used to emphasize the antithesis and word-play that abounded in everything that Benlowes wrote. The favourite antithesis between world and spirit is in the following stanza pointed carefully by italics:

> Had we no *Bodies*, we were ANGELS; and
> Had we no *Souls*, we were unmann'd
> To *Beasts*: *Brutes* are all *Flesh*, all *Spirit* the *Heav'nly* BAND. (i, 31)

A similar method enforces the balance of the line,

> *Who* steals from *Time*, *Time* steals from *him* the Prey (i, 36).

And in

> With *dry* Teeth, *meager* Cheeks, *thin* Maw, & *hollow* Eyes (i, 42),

the matching of the adjectives with the type gives added weight. Italics could also be employed to rivet the attention to the development of a metaphor, when it might otherwise be missed by a careless reader, as in:

> Who bad Desires *conceive*, they soon wax *Great*
> With Mischief, then *bring forth* Deceit,
> So, *brood* They Desolation, till it *grows* compleat. (x, 55)

This elaborate letter-press was by no means all. For the man who put his thoughts in verse and then in prose, in English and then in Latin, who threaded them through a succession of conceits, who dazzled them before the eye by a rapid variation in types and stabbed them upon the ear by a plenitude of puns, there were yet other devices to employ. In the seventeenth century the different arts were more closely linked than they are now, and the cultivated gentleman was expected to know something of them all. Benlowes all his life had been keenly interested in music and in engraving. Now, when his big poem had been written, he had airs composed for it by John Jenkins, the most admired musician of the day, whose compositions—said Anthony à Wood—entered into the hands of all men. [1] And he commissioned illustrations from some of the best-known engravers. The music was not given over to the printer, and probably the airs were only privately played. But the illustrations of the 1652 folio of *Theophila* have for a long time made it a prize of book-collectors; so much so that it has been possible for bibliographers to say such things of it as that it is "more remarkable for

[1] *Life and Times*, II, 335.

its curious plates by Hollar, Barlow and other engravers, than for its literary excellences." [1]

The most important commission was for a series of engravings to be set before the eight cantos of the original poem. These may have been designed before Benlowes extended the scope of the work to thirteen cantos: though if so, it is odd that all of them do not seem to have been ready when copies of the book had begun to be printed off. Each of them represents pictorially some aspect of Theophila's story more or less appropriate to the canto which follows, and the first six are accompanied by some engraved verses in explanation. Most of them are thought to be the work of Francis Barlow. Their style is elaborately symbolical, closely following that of the emblem-books which Benlowes so greatly admired. For example, the first of these plates shows a young man with solemn countenance, but very fashionably dressed, seated at a table writing. This, as the verses underneath the picture explain, represents the author. His right foot rests upon a large globe, showing his contempt for the world, and his eye is fixed upon a somewhat matronly figure of Theophila. In her hands she holds a sphere, representing her possession of heaven. The radiance of heaven streams across the top right-hand corner of the picture, and from it a winged angel descends with a crown for Theophila's head, while to it an eagle soars bearing the author's book in its talons. For the second canto, Theophila's repentance is symbolized by a picture of her praying at an altar surrounded by wild beasts. And the same style continues in the later illustrations. At the beginning of Canto v the author gazes rapt upon Theophila as she points to an image of herself being borne aloft by angels to a heavenly palace set in a pattern of stars and cherubs' heads. Canto vii is introduced with Theophila shown above the clouds, on which the heads of cherubs float, being met by an angel holding a circle, an emblem of eternity. Subsequently two engravings were done to precede the subsidiary poems, "The Vanitie of the World" and "The Sweetnesse of Retirement," which formed the last four cantos of *Theophila* as printed. One of these engravings is a complicated piece of allegory in which the author looks upwards to a hand which holds out to him a symbol of eternity surmounted by a crown. The other is a pleasant and lightly touched engraving of the author in the company of an old shepherd in a rural landscape.

[1] Corser, *Collectanea Anglo-Poetica*, II, 250.

Benlowes had also other allegorical plates done for *Theophila* and was afterwards in some doubt about where to put them; for the engraver sought usually to suggest the whole theme of the poem rather than to illustrate a particular passage. However, one showing Theophila with a palm-branch treading on a serpent came in quite well for Canto ix. Two others proved more difficult to place. One was of a winged woman, doubtless intended to symbolize Theophila, with astronomical instruments strewn at her feet. The other was a portrait of Theophila tearfully praying, specially engraved as a decoration for the book by Pierre Lombart, a French engraver whom Benlowes, always accessible to poets, artists, and musicians in need of patronage, was one of the first in England to employ. Lombart showed an entirely different conception of Theophila from Barlow —if the principal illustrator of the book was indeed he—but it would have been unlike Benlowes to leave anything out and the engraving seemed quite good enough to use. Benlowes hesitated about inserting either that or the one with the astronomical instruments before Canto xiii, where there was no illustration, but where neither could be appropriate. Lombart's picture of Theophila at prayer was also tried opposite the author's own prayer near the beginning, and again at the point where Theophila weeps in the middle of Canto ii.

Benlowes had his portrait done by Barlow to serve as a handsome frontispiece for the volume. He also had by him a plate by William Marshall, the most prolific book-illustrator of the age, whom Benlowes had long had dealings with. Marshall had been employed on the engravings for Quarles's *Emblemes* and had first done a title-page for Benlowes nearly twenty years before.[1] The plate of his that Benlowes used for *Theophila* was a modification of one of his earlier designs and even as modified was probably not done specially for *Theophila*, since it honoured the author without making reference to the poem. At its foot were some Latin verses by one who signed himself "I.S." (could it have been John Sictor?), praising Benlowes for his benevolence to the afflicted and his hospitality to poets. Its central wreath of flowers surrounded the words, "Ludus Literarius Christianus. Anthreno-Tripsis *seu* Crabronum Tritura *Edw. Benlosij* Armig." This looks like the Greco-Latin title of some work by Benlowes which never saw the light of day: Marshall's engraving had evidently been executed with a view to a frontispiece. In copies of *Theophila* that place of honour went more fittingly to

---

[1] See above, pp. 79-80.

Barlow's portrait, though Benlowes saw nothing against inserting Marshall's design in the middle of the book.

Various other engravings were used which had not been originally intended for *Theophila*. [1] From cuts that Benlowes or his printer had access to—perhaps through the publisher Moseley, who was in the habit of employing such men as Marshall and a much more famous engraver, Hollar—it was possible to select quite a number which might come in, more or less suitably, as additional ornaments for the book. With the description of the garden of Eden in the second canto could go a large woodcut of Adam and Eve and the tree of knowledge which had first been used by Robert Barker to illustrate an edition of the Bible in 1632. Often a much scantier connection with the subject of the poem would serve to justify the inclusion of an attractive plate. For example, a woman in mask, hood, fur, and muff, adapted from one of Hollar's portraits, was felt a suitably modest study of femininity to appear opposite Benlowes' address to the Ladies. A companion portrait in Hollar's style of a lady in less wintry clothes, dressed in the height of fashion, very much *décolletée* and with generous slashings of the sleeve, did duty for the immodest woman at the end of Canto xi. To increase its aptness (see Canto xi, stanza 47), in some copies patches were inked in on the cheek, forehead, and breast. To show up the rake described as Volupto in Canto xi and railed against in some of the Latin poems which followed it, there were two small but skilfully satiric engravings, both showing a cavalier dressed quite outrageously in fashion, in one very dashing and in one very drunk. [2] These pictures no doubt every possessor of *Theophila* loved to have; but it was carrying the practice of illustration to absurdity when a passing reference to Queen Elizabeth gave excuse for a half-page woodcut of the queen at prayer, and when a denunciation of the world's licentiousness was accompanied by an engraving of the two hemispheres. Finally, there were two engraved word-puzzles on the passion of Christ devised with a seventeenth-century ingenuity and requiring in the solver a seventeenth-century zeal. One by Thomas

---

[1] Many, if not all, of the special *Theophila* plates must have belonged to Benlowes himself; but of those which I now go on to describe, most were printed on the letter-press and not on separate sheets. The originals of those would seem therefore to have been at the printing-house and I think that Benlowes kept his *own* plates at Brent Hall to be printed from by his own rolling-press. *Cf.* below.

[2] This costume is described above, p. 106. The first of these two plates, which is signed, was by Peregrine Lovell, an engraver of the school of Hollar. The second, I think, need not have been by the same hand

Cecill was dated 1632 and the other may have been equally old; but they fascinated Benlowes sufficiently to claim a leaf each at the end of his book.

To the question of illustrating *Theophila* Benlowes obviously gave enormous attention. He changed his mind about it more than once, so that almost from the beginning there were some striking differences among individual copies. A number of plates were added only after the first copies of the book had been printed off and bound, and among these were engravings specially executed for the volume. On the other hand, most of those which Benlowes merely borrowed from elsewhere—the two Hollaresque ladies, the two cavaliers, the two word-puzzles, and Queen Elizabeth—were in the book from the start. So were Theophila and the astronomical instruments, and Theophila in tears. Yet not more than half of those designed to introduce the eight cantos of the original *Theophila* were ready. In the first copies of the book, only Cantos i, ii, v, and vii possessed illustrations. The others were inserted in later copies, which also included after a bit the two plates done for "The Vanitie of the World" and "The Sweetnesse of Retirement." Some of the discrepancies between copies were therefore not due to design. But some undoubtedly were; for Benlowes hit upon a clever means of giving a distinctive form to some copies of his book and thus paying a special compliment to the friends to whom he gave them. He decided to include some of the plates only in presentation copies, which explains why they are now very rare; and of those which he bestowed only sparingly he would insert now one and now another. His own portrait was probably from the first intended only for his friends; but sometimes he would withhold it and begin with Marshall's frontispiece instead. The weeping Theophila was another possibility for a frontispiece, or the symbolic picture of the author composing might be promoted from Canto i. Other plates could also be differently placed, so that no two copies of the book needed to be alike and I think no two presentation copies were. One hopes that their recipients were aware of this peculiarity and appreciated the honour conferred on them when they were presented with a unique copy [1].

The binding of the book was another thing that needed much consideration. Here perhaps more than anywhere Benlowes could

---

[1] For a full list of plates and a further discussion of their frequency and their location in the volume, see Appendix IV.

show his esteem for those who were to be presented with his work. Again he sought to avoid standardization, and the book was bound in a number of styles. Presentation copies might be in calf, but were sometimes in brown or black or green morocco, sometimes had gilt edges, and almost always had the Benlowes arms stamped in gold both back and front. In some instances a morocco cover was further ornamented with a border of gilt lines and tooling at the corners. Benlowes might say that he did not care for a splendid cover, only for what was inside it; but that was in a Latin inscription which he wrote in copies he gave to John Selden, the great jurist, and Thomas Barlow, then a fellow and afterwards provost of Queen's College, Oxford. It was really a neat way of apologizing to Selden and Barlow for not giving them ornate copies, and even of paying them a compliment, for Benlowes hinted—and since it was not his habit to spare the cost, it was probably his sincere opinion— that they as scholars would prefer a book to have a plain exterior. Barlow's copy, which went at his death into Queen's College library [1] and which can still be seen there, had a simple calf binding with no arms of the author nor any other decoration in their place. Benlowes' more usual practice was to make the book as splendid outside as within. The expense lavished on *Theophila* was in keeping with his generous habit of mind, and the result may well have satisfied his love of beautiful things. [2]

There can be no doubt that the design of the book was largely Benlowes' own, even if part of the execution of the design took place in Roger Norton's printing-house. And part of the design— exactly how much cannot be certain—Benlowes actually carried out himself. He had his rolling-press at Brent Hall, and it would

---

[1] The residue of Barlow's books went to Queen's, after the Bodleian had taken what it did not possess already (Macray, *Annals of the Bodleian Library*, 1890 ed., p. 157). It is an interesting detail that Barlow's *Theophila* would therefore have gone into the Bodleian except that it had already been preceded by Selden's.

[2] Many of the extant copies have not, of course, retained the original binding. Specimens of the more ornate style can be seen at St. John's College, Cambridge, and the Huntington Library. The Dyce copy, which has been rebound, has the original covers mounted inside the present binding. Other copies with original bindings and the arms in gold are in the libraries of All Souls', Queen's, and Jesus Colleges at Oxford; in the Cambridge University Library; and in the Petyt Library at Skipton: though the binding of this last copy is not in good condition. These must all have been prepared as presentation copies. The absence of an inscription in two of them (Petyt and Cambridge University Library) is to be noted, but is not significant, since each of these has lost the fly-leaf.

not have been very difficult for him to have down there some of the copper plates which were specially engraved for *Theophila* and which, executed to his order, would of course be his own property. Then he could run off prints in his own house as he wanted them. So is it not most likely that some of the presentation *Theophilas* went down to Finchingfield as loose sheets from the printer's to be bound up there? This would explain how there could be so very much variation in the decoration of different copies of *Theophila*; each copy could be fondly treated as an individual book. And with the plates at hand it would have been easy sometimes to glue extra illustrations in a copy after it had been bound and before it was presented to some recipient whom Benlowes wished to do well by. This is what seems to have happened with the portrait in the copy given to Thomas Barlow and with at least two plates in the copy presented to St. John's College. This sort of thing would be Schoren's job. It was he who worked the rolling-press, and before entering Benlowes' service he had been a professional printer with the distinction of having learnt his craft in the Low Countries, where all the arts of book-production flourished. Among other things, he used, we know, to help his master with gilding, and the two of them together would certainly have been equal to the gilt ornaments which adorned the covers of *Theophila*. (Little Gidding, one remembers, could turn out very fine tooling and gilding.) It was with Schoren's trained assistance that Benlowes had designed the appearance of *The Purple Island* twenty years before. And all these years, though the motive may have been only partly conscious, Benlowes had held Schoren in reserve for his masterpiece, *Theophila*. This is partly why, even when Schoren proved dishonest and untractable, Benlowes could not willingly let him leave Brent Hall. [1]

Whatever may have been the precise details, one has a picture of Benlowes as being exceedingly busy over the printing of his book during many months. He had first to prepare the manuscript for the printer and he was most meticulous about punctuation and spelling. He had laboriously to indicate the variations in the type to be used. He had to select engravings and arrange for new plates to be designed and cut. With one thing and another he must have ridden to and fro between Finchingfield and London many times

---

[1] If Schoren was a highly skilled craftsman, he ought to have found profitable employment when he left Benlowes' service about 1642 and not to have needed to go back in poverty to Brent Hall. But that was during the Civil War, which had a very damaging effect upon the book-trade.

that spring and summer. And when the book finally left the printer's and was on sale in London, copies of it, in whatever stage of completion, surrounded Benlowes at Brent Hall. When a copy had been duly bound with the desired plates included, still he was not quite satisfied. For in spite of all the care taken, a few faults had escaped the printer, and Benlowes was too punctilious to want to let them go. Besides, as he glanced lovingly through his work, he thought now and then of tiny improvements, hesitated anew about a comma, wished to insert an accent or an apostrophe or to alter the spelling. For example, in a description of the sweetness of the countryside it seemed hardly fitting to have streams moving "in murm'ring Rage"; he would prefer to alter "Rage" to "Base." "Shew" he thought would be better spelt "show" when it had to rhyme with "to" and "woo." [1] In the line

Far fetch't, dear bought, best suits the *Apician* Appetite (xi, 18),

a syllable had to be slurred and it might be shown by an apostrophe, thus: "the' *Apician*." Benlowes therefore decided to correct the book in pen and ink. Not all, even of the presentation copies, received this final mark of his punctiliousness, but many did. It seems as though the copies which were first to be bound (identifiable because they contained only the earlier engravings) were also the first to be corrected. For Benlowes did not settle down to do a lot of copies straight off, but rather a copy—or perhaps two or three copies—at a time as he got them bound. The similarity in Selden's and Barlow's copies in the plates, the pen-and-ink corrections, and the inscription suggests that copies which were bound at the same time as one another were likely to be corrected and presented at the same time as one another too. The progress of a copy from the printing-press to the finished volume, ready for ceremonial presentation, was a long one, and everything goes to show that copies reached the final stage in turn, not all at once. So, as the process went on, the corrections made by the author's own hand fluctuated. He tired of a pedantic comma; he had a new idea for the improvement of a line, which he subsequently adopted; sometimes his memory faltered or a momentary caprice took charge. But always, as he sat at his table correcting, his pen worked with extraordinary daintiness, neatly dropping a *c* into "*Shools*," closing a *c* into an *a*, or indicating a change in the order of words by putting minute numerals above them. The passion

[1] Canto xii, stanzas 55, 70.

for accuracy which made him undertake this task was matched by the fastidious workmanship with which he did it. [1]

Illustrated, bound, and in most cases corrected, a presentation copy had still not been through all its ritual. It had first to be inscribed, and inscriptions offered fresh opportunity for some unique detail from an inventive mind or some extra decoration from a skilful pen. And Benlowes had both. Though an inscription might sometimes be repeated, there was no standard formula. Even the Latin verses by which Benlowes excused the plainness of the copies he sent to Selden and Barlow were not identical in the two copies: the outside covers *(tegmina)* which these scholars were supposed not to want were in one case beautiful *(pulchra)*, in the other bright *(clara)*. [2] The most conventional inscription would have an individual twist, showing Benlowes' sense of the occasion. To both these scholars Benlowes signed himself "Tuus Benevolus," but Selden's copy was inscribed to the well-wishing reader, without a personal address. Evidently Benlowes did not know Selden, or at least not well. It might have seemed temerity in him thus to approach a man of such distinction and such magnificent learning as Selden was; but it was Selden's habit to accept gracefully such tributes as this. In the previous year he had received the present of a copy of Hobbes's *Leviathan*, although he and Hobbes were not at that time acquainted. Selden's reply was to wish that they might be, and a friendship between Selden and Hobbes was the result. [3] Benlowes did honour to himself when he sent his book to Selden as a mark of his esteem.

The copy that went to Barlow had a more intimate inscription. It was a mark of Benlowes' *love*. Barlow was Benlowes' special *(præcipuus)* friend and was asked to keep well what a friend sent him. Benlowes did not ask for his affection to be returned, but only

---

[1] For a full list of the pen-and-ink corrections, a demonstration of their authenticity, and a discussion of their editorial importance, see Appendix III.

[2] But this is the only difference. In the Barlow copy the inscription goes:

Non opus ut Tyrio rutilent velamina Fuco,
    Aut decorent nostros Tegmina pulchra Libros;
Plana quidém facies Libri, mihi vera loquenti,
    Convenit; Interiús Splendidiora Legas.

Non Tegmen, sed Acumen, amat——
             Tuus
                 Benevolus.
Qui veniam pro Laude petit.——

[3] Aubrey, *Brief Lives*, I, 369.

that Barlow would allow him to bestow it. [1] This humility may have
been because he did not yet know Barlow as well as he hoped to
in the future. He would admire Barlow as an expert in theological
controversy and especially as one who used his learning much against
the Pope. But more than this, it is particularly interesting to find
Benlowes expressing such keen regard for Barlow at a time when he
was making up his mind that the ideal life for him would be one among
the books of the Bodleian. For Barlow had recently been appointed
librarian of the Bodleian. [2] Perhaps on some occasion when reading
there Benlowes had met him and received the kind attention which
Barlow usually gave to all who loved learning and were not alien
to his views.

Although Benlowes' eyes were already thus turned towards Oxford,
he did not forget his own university. St. John's College, Cambridge,
which had for twenty years honoured his name among its distinguished benefactors and which had only recently been presented with
his portrait, received from him another handsome volume. It was
one of the finest bound copies of *Theophila* that he now presented
to its library; and on the two leaves which preceded the title were
some of the most finished specimens of Benlowes' exquisite penmanship. Fruits of long practice and careful study of the fashionable
writing manuals, they showed him handling his pen with delightful
freedom and yet keeping a perfect symmetry, able to draw out a
flourish to fill the whole page with sheer design. [3] Pasted on to
the verso of the first leaf there is an extremely ornate design wrought

---

[1] This inscription is on the title-page, as follows:
At the top, "Clarissimo Barloo S.T.D." Below the words "Divine Poem,"
"Serva, præcipuo quæ mittit Amicus Amico." Above and below the ornament,
"Non ut me redames, sed Te patiaris amari/Postulo; sume pij Monumentu &
Pign' Amoris."
The inscription previously quoted is on the fly-leaf. And beneath the
portrait Benlowes wrote: "Pro Liberis Libros./Verè nostra quæ semper nostra."
An inscription something like this was written for the unknown recipient of
the Sandars copy now in the Cambridge University Library:

> Servet Honorando quæ donat Amicus Amico;
> Esse Ea perpetui Monumenta probantur Honoris
> Non ut me redames sed Te patiaris amari
> Sit Desiderij Meta Scopúsq[ue] mei.

[2] On April 6, 1652; see Macray, *Annals of the Bodleian Library*, p. 108.
[3] A reader not acquainted with this characteristic of seventeenth-century
penmanship may find examples of the kind of thing in Day, *Penmanship of
the XVI, XVII & XVIIIth Centuries*; see especially the flourishes of the
illustrations 103, 104, 107, and the frame of no. 95. Benlowes at his best is quite
the equal of anything here.

out of the flourishes which spring from the letters of Benlowes'
own name, and on the verso of the second leaf he wrote an inscription surrounded by an elaborate frame of intersecting curves and
twirls. Of this inscription the word "Theophila" in ornate capitals
remains to be seen, but Benlowes covered the rest of it with a piece
of paper carefully cut to fit the frame and wrote on it a second inscription to replace the first. [1] Perhaps therefore he had begun by
addressing this copy to someone else; but it may be only that what
he first wrote did not please his fastidious eye and mind. However
that may be, the final result made a suitable showpiece for a famous
library and displayed the regard which he still had for his old college.
The inscription reads:

THEOPHILA
æternum esto Monumentum Amoris mei
et Benevolentiæ in Coll: S[ti] Johañis.
EDOARDUS BENLOWES.

The most favourite words throughout the inscriptions were
monumentum et pignus amoris (varied in the case of Selden and
some others to *honoris*) to express the wish that the book should
be regarded as a monument and token of the author's love. This
was the tag that Benlowes had used in presenting copies of Fletcher's
The Purple Island, which in its smaller way was also quite a splendid
book. Benlowes' venture into book-production with that in 1633
had proved a good rehearsal for the superb production of *Theophila*
now. And the tag still served. After all the pains and art and expense
that had made his book the beautiful thing it was, Benlowes enjoyed
to the full the savour of that word *monumentum*. It had a ring of
permanence, and, delighting to honour his numerous friends and
acquaintances, Benlowes felt sure of their lasting regard.

Undoubtedly they *were* numerous, though, with just a few exceptions, one cannot now know who they were. Besides Barlow
and Selden, the recipients of *Theophila* included a number of country
gentlemen, like Walter Blount of Mapledurham, who, it seems,
was already a valued acquaintance of Benlowes. A year or two
later he became a close connection by marrying Philippa, Benlowes'
niece and only heir. Friends closer at hand to whom a copy of
Theophila went, bearing a moralizing inscription on the joys of a
writer who can touch the emotions of others, were the Barringtons

---

[1] Part of the original inscription can still be seen in a good light, as was first
noticed and pointed out to me by Col. C.H. Wilkinson. It contained Benlowes'
name and a date, but what else I do not know.

of Hatfield Broad Oak. One remembers that it was to Sir Thomas Barrington, now unfortunately dead, that Benlowes had appealed for help and protection in the Civil War when the Essex Parliamentary Committee laid too heavy a hand upon his rents. One remembers, too, that Benlowes had attributed his plight at that time to the malice of Sir Martin Lumley, and so it is a little surprising to find that Sir Martin Lumley—for the most generous baronet whose initials were M.L. could be no other than he—now also got the *monumentum et pignus* of Benlowes' affection. In the last few years, apparently, their personal and political differences had got smoothed over. They were now on good neighbourly terms and exchanged the trophies of their respective pastimes. Benlowes sent Sir Martin *Theophila* encased in leather and gilt with a Latin epigram, exhibiting his calligraphy at its most resplendent, which jocularly asked Sir Martin for a stag in return. When Benlowes went on, however, to urge him to give up hunting, [1] Sir Martin may not so easily have seen the joke. The sportsman and the poet did not quite see eye to eye, but the Civil War was over and they could now live near one another in mutual tolerance.

Many whom Benlowes found of more congenial temper and who had read *Theophila* with delight must have been presented with a copy of it too. I know of six presentation copies extant whose first recipients cannot now be identified. [2] Among the host of Benlowes' poetical acquaintance the only one I can be sure of was the Earl of Westmorland, who received it as a *monumentum et pignus* "*Honoris*" rather than "*Amoris*". This suggests that, though Benlowes admired the Earl's poetry, they did not know one another at all intimately. Perhaps they had corresponded more than they had met.

Westmorland's copy of *Theophila* was inscribed on October 17,

---

[1] See the inscription quoted above, p. 96 n. A very similar epigram, also ornately written on the verso of the fly-leaf, occurs in the Dyce copy, which unfortunately affords no clue to the original recipient. It is interesting to note that these two copies agree very closely in their pen-and-ink corrections, which points to their being corrected and inscribed at the same time. The variations in the epigram reveal, as is usual, a nice personal touch. The recipient of the Dyce copy did not get "Sit Mens larga Tibi." *His* mind was approved of as it was, and indicative could replace subjunctive. Nor was it necessary to tell him to give up sport (*fuge ludicra*). To him Benlowes said: "Est Mens larga Tibi, datur Optio."

[2] Excluding the Nassau copy, which is said to be inscribed "For the trulie Noble Tho Durham Esq", whom I have not succeeded in tracing, unless he was the Thomas Durham who became rector of Cawston (Norfolk) in 1663.

1653. [1] Since the poem had been in the press as early as May the previous year, it was taking a very long time indeed to get all the copies out. Years had gone to writing the poem to the glory of God; and many months to producing the book for the glory of man. Partly this was vanity, and partly generosity; the author was self-advertised, but the reader was honoured too. And God still was not forgotten. For I believe that Benlowes sincerely held the subject of his work to justify the richness of its presentation. His religious as well as his artistic conscience demanded that *Theophila* in thought, in phrase, and in array should be the best that he could do. It was his sacrifice to his Maker, his offering to his fellowmen, his fulfilment of himself. Think what you will of it, it is his *monumentum*.

[1] Westmorland's copy is in the Widener Library at Harvard. Of the other copies referred to above, the Barrington copy, which is badly mutilated, is along with Barlow's at Queen's College, Oxford. Oxford also has Blount's copy at Jesus, and Lumley's at All Souls'.

CHAPTER TWENTY-ONE

END OF THE LANDED GENTLEMAN

Years of war in England had not stopped Benlowes from steadily composing his poem; and the financial pressure of the times could not keep him from spending some hundreds of pounds upon its appearance. [1] To redeem his estates from sequestration he had paid a severe fine, and he had started the woeful business of mortgage. There had been heavy taxes and a steep rise in prices: in 1651, when they revised the schedule of wages for the county, the Essex magistrates took expressly into account the increased prices of "all kind of victuals and apparel, both linen and woollen." [2] Yet while his debts increased, Benlowes showed a remarkable faculty for going on his own way undeterred: he was unworldly enough to have made no serious alteration in his way of life. Very soon a major disaster was to force him to do so, and he was fortunate to have got *Theophila* out before this disaster came. Shortly after he had written the inscription in a copy for the Earl of Westmorland, towards the end of 1653, Benlowes' "Mansion house was by an unfortunate accident burned downe." [3] Whatever stocks of *Theophila* Benlowes had by him must have perished and with them went the rolling-press which had so recently accomplished its principal work. By an ironic chance a relic of Benlowes' military days, a brass blunderbuss, survived instead.

To a man of Benlowes' temper all this must have given rise in later days to a number of melancholy reflections. But these were at first submerged beneath a weight of more worldly cares. The fire seems to have started in the house, which was totally destroyed. Most of what escaped was in the outbuildings. Of furniture, books, and clothes there was hardly anything. Schoren, somewhat given

---

[1] On the cost of engravings alone, see above, p. 102.

[2] Lipson, *Economic History*, III, 260.

[3] The authority for the following account of the burning of Brent Hall rests principally in the following Chancery suits: Reynardson 31/14; Collins 28/11. There are also one or two minor details from Collins 140/147 (answer); Whittington 71/87 (answer); and Bridges 629/64.

to flying high, put his own personal losses for clothes and other property at about eighty pounds, and Benlowes lost, along with all his personal belongings and the treasures of a lifetime, many valuable documents, including some of the deeds belonging to his estates. The fire occurred, as fires will, at night, and the cause of it was never discovered. It needed a Fire of London to prompt men to devise insurance against such calamities, and Benlowes was left, quite without remedy, to lament his "extreame losse."

He was now homeless. He saw a heap of debris for the country-house where he had lived for fifty years; and there was nowhere in Finchingfield and Bardfield for him to go. A cottage with thatch and picturesque cobwebs in the rafters was all very well in a poem, but Benlowes was accustomed to the comforts of wealth and very sensible of his position as a gentleman. There was no dwelling fit for one of his quality, and he was forced to find a temporary home in London. He was settling himself in the capital about the time that Oliver Cromwell was being declared Lord Protector of the Commonwealth, and he may have seen the new master of England passing guarded through the streets or driving in state into the City to be banqueted by the Lord Mayor. All that would do nothing to console the mind of one who despised both Puritans and public pomp. Only necessity could have led him to betake himself to London at such a time. Even so, this going to London was a typical retreat from practical affairs in a time of emergency, and it was Schoren who had to manage things in Finchingfield. Benlowes, in spite of suspicions of his servant's honesty years before, put his confidence in him and left him in the country to sort out the muddle and dispose of such household goods as were salable. There was also corn and cattle in the barn and a few other items, like the blunderbuss, which was "of good vallue." Schoren managed to realize over a hundred pounds, but he cheated his master as he had done before, and never handed the money over. Benlowes later regretted that he could not prove the nature or the quality of what Schoren sold, and that he could not state in detail the sums that Schoren received. Although he entreated him in friendly manner, he never got him to render any account. He was apt himself to let things slide, and with the dissolution of his *ménage* he made no proper arrangement for paying Schoren's wages. The relationship of master and man which had existed with one break for over twenty years was not terminated: it was just allowed to lapse. And Schoren's annuity, which had caused a lot of friction in the past, was to be the cause of much more trouble in the future.

The removal to London broke up the even tenor of Benlowes' life more effectually than anything in the Civil War had been able to do. There was soon being erected a new timber-framed manor-house of Brent Hall, which, unlike its predecessor, has not yet proved true to its name. But it is not clear that Benlowes ever really settled down again at Finchingfield. His hope of continuing a life of cultured ease in a rural but elegant retirement had, with his ancestral mansion, vanished. His estates in Essex remained his source of income, but this was rather tiresome in the collecting. He was now past middle life, and he had no enthusiasm for beginning again in the new Brent Hall. He seems to have lost interest in the place—all the more because of the impossibility of ever again holding it unencumbered. What with his easy-going way with money, his patronage of the arts, his being on the wrong side in the Civil War, he had had no difficulty in getting through his income. He was already in debt and he had no margin to cope with fires and rebuild-ing. A recognizance for £1000 given to Robert Johnson on April 7, 1654, [1] looks suspiciously as though he was raising another loan; and, in fact, he soon found himself with debts approaching £3000 [2] and with mortgages on four or five of his properties. [3]

His position was then complicated further by his niece Philippa. Philippa and her mother at present lived upon Edward's bounty on the outskirts of London at St. Giles-in-the-Fields. He allowed them annually the sum of £66.13s.4d., though since they were Catholics two-thirds of that was forfeit to the state. Philippa was now being sought in marriage, and it was clearly upon Edward that the duty of providing her with a satisfactory dowry fell.

Philippa's suitor, Walter Blount of Mapledurham, was a Catholic gentleman in his early twenties. He belonged to a well-established family, older than Benlowes' own, and had inherited his Oxfordshire estates some five years before on the death of his elder brother after his father had already been killed fighting for the King. [4] The match was eminently suitable and Philippa's uncle, with his usual lavish-ness, decided to treat her handsomely. She was, after all, his only

[1] Recognizance Entry Book L.C. 4/203 fol. 280.
[2] Chancery Proceedings, Bridges 444/123.
[3] Chancery Proceedings, Collins 140/147.
[4] Burke, *Landed Gentry* (1937), p. 185.

heir. In his younger days he had looked to her father to succeed to the estates, and had taken care to have them settled upon him. But William had died twenty years ago and left no son. Since Philippa herself could not come into the estates, they must be used to provide her with a considerable fortune. So Benlowes performed one of his fine, courageous gestures. With a flourish of "haueing ever lived vnmarryed and intending soe to dye," he mortgaged his Essex lands in bulk to give Philippa her magnificent dowry. Walter Blount behaved well on his side and agreed to settle on Philippa "a Competent Joynture." He and Benlowes made a formal ratification of their agreement, each gave the other a recognizance of £10,000 on August 4, 1654, and eventually the marriage took place. On February 2, 1655, Benlowes' lands were mortgaged for the sum of £9,000 provided by an Essex gentleman called Robert Abdy and a London merchant called William Meggs. Philippa's dowry was £6,000, and the rest of the money was used to pay off Benlowes' debts. [1] The whole transaction seemed perfectly satisfactory.

In fact, as things worked out, the only sufferer was to be Edward Benlowes himself. He had had far too little experience in watching his own interests. All might have gone well if he had entered with any zest into the control of his affairs; but he was casual and improvident, and had only opened up new territories for mismanagement. For the mortgage made everything more complicated: it demanded punctual interest, at 6 per cent, but was no help with the rents. It was not his nature to live easily on margins; and in fact he was not making ends meet.

Another blow fell when Cromwell decided to lay a heavy hand on those who had formerly supported the King. Since Charles's execution there had been several plots seeking to restore the Stuarts to the throne, and in the year 1655 many Royalists were in arms. The threat of serious insurrection could no longer be ignored. So Cromwell gave order for a militia to be raised; [2] and continuing the Parliamentary tradition of making your enemies pay for the

---

[1] Chancery Proceedings, Collins 140/147; Bridges, 444/123. Deeds at the Essex County Record Office, D/DAc 65 and 109. Close Rolls, 1654, part 9, no. 16. Entry Book of Recognizances L.C. 4/204 fol. 12. Also relevant are a fine, Common Pleas 25(2)/550 A, and Recognizance Entry Book L.C. 4/204 fol. 36. It is interesting to observe that one of Benlowes' creditors acknowledged payment on March 5, 1655 (Recognizance Entry Book L.C. 4/203 fol. 137).

[2] On this and the action now taken against Royalists, see Gardiner, *Commonwealth and Protectorate*, 1903, III, 318-344; *Cal. S.P., Dom.*, 1655, p. 347.

maintenance of the force intended to suppress them, he announced
that all Royalists who had estates worth more than £100 a year
were to surrender a tenth of their annual rents. The victim usually
spoke of being "decimated." One did not need to be an active
Royalist at the time: it was enough to have once borne arms for the
King. So Benlowes was to pay his tenth. And he contemplated it
with some trembling lest worse should happen. For much more
drastic penalties were to be imposed on all concerned in plots and
rebellions, and although Benlowes was innocent of this, he was
not without fear that he might be falsely accused. Besides, he had
only to seem by word or action to "adhere to the interests of the
late King, or of Charles Stuart his son" to be in danger of imprisonment or exile. Here was opportunity for malicious informers;
and Benlowes habitually thought of the Protectorate as a "usurped
power," and John Schoren knew what his master's sentiments were.
If Schoren had been still the confidential servant who had followed
his master into battle, this might not have mattered. But although
Benlowes had resumed paying Schoren his annuity, they were in
the middle of one of their disputes about money, and Benlowes
dreaded that this servant, whom he had taken back into his employ
ten years before to have his protection against marauders, would
now be the very man who would denounce him. [1]

Benlowes' alarm was perhaps greater than his danger, though a
fellow-poet, Cleveland, was indeed imprisoned for little more than
having Royalist opinions. [2] All weapons of King's sympathizers were
confiscated; but Benlowes had already sold his blunderbuss, even
if Schoren was keeping the money for it. An order was issued ex-
pelling Royalists from London, but no action seems to have been
taken against those who were quiescent. So Benlowes was confronted
only with "decimation." But that was grievous enough when he
was already trying to maintain a precarious balance between mortgages and rents. Very soon he had contracted to sell the timber
of twenty-three acres of woodland. [3] And it was only natural that
he should by now have perceived the advantages of selling his estates
outright.

In choosing to do this, he showed for once a certain foresight.
At the same time it was a momentous decision. So long as the estates

---

[1] Chancery Proceedings, Reynardson 31/14. *Cf.* below p. 255.
[2] *Poems*, ed. Berdan, pp. 39-40.
[3] Chancery Proceedings, Bridges 444/123.

belonged to him, he was a landed gentleman, with all the prestige of vast acres of solid earth on which to rest his name. It was true that the Benlowes name would have to die out with him; but to anticipate the moment of necessity was to depart from all the traditions of his family and many of the customs in which he had been bred. Even now, in 1655, he was occupied with paying up to date Serjeant Benlowes' and his own charities. Dues for two years were outstanding since the fire had driven him from home. But the Finchingfield "Town Book" on November 9th acknowledged four pounds which the churchwarden had "recejved of Mr Bendlowes." He had always been a conspicuous local figure, well known to all the country round as Mr. Benlowes of Brent Hall—except indeed when they had called him Captain Benlowes. Could he who had led a troop of Essex horse surrender all county privileges? Could he who had watched the mower and the fish and walked the fields with his spaniel go and live in a city street? He decided that he could forgo all the charm and spaciousness of the gentleman's life if he got rid too of all its responsibilities. Probably only the burning of his mansion, which had already sent him into London lodgings and left the country-gentleman's existence without its centre, reconciled him to that choice.

Impelled by a desire "to take off that heavie burthen of interest and Taxes wᶜʰ eate vpp neere vppon the whole rent," he put the matter into the hands of Samuel Benham, of Gray's Inn; and before the end of the year Benham put him in touch with Nathan Wright, one of many London merchants who were seeking at this time to satisfy ambitions to gentility by buying up the lands of Royalists in distress. Wright, who was already settled in Essex as a country gentleman at Cranham Hall, was very willing to buy, but a difficulty arose at once. When the estates had been mortgaged, Benlowes had naturally had to give up the title-deeds, and, not having paid the interest on the mortgage, he could not now get hold of them to show to his prospective purchaser. This obstacle was only cleared when Benham remembered that Benlowes had still a few odd bits of property left out of the original mortgage. Benlowes accordingly offered those as security, and Nathan Wright himself advanced the five hundred pounds that Benlowes required. Unfortunately, Wright also had a glimpse of how needy Benlowes was and registered for his later use that Benlowes in making a bargain would have little freedom of manœuvre. Nevertheless, at the moment things went briskly. Wright saw the title-deeds on December 15, 1655, and a week later he and Benlowes signed a comprehensive agreement. It was just now that the first instalment of Cromwell's "decimation" fell due, apt, as it were, to prevent Benlowes from going back on his decision. Wright was to view the premises and decide by April 20th, and if he approved of the purchase, he was to pay eighteen times the annual rental of the estates and enter into possession by the end of the following June. He was to take over the existing mortgage as a preliminary, and it was actually transferred to him on March 3rd. At the same time he made further money advances to Benlowes, who, persecuted by debts and taxes, had now received over a thousand pounds upon account.

Benlowes' task now was to see that he got as good a price as possible. Since the price was to be calculated from the rents, it was obviously to his interest to raise these to the maximum. Having always been a bountiful landlord, he realized that a number of his farms were greatly under-rented, and he set about trying to make leases more favourable to himself. He took his agent Benham down to Finchingfield, and they were busy putting things in order for nearly two months. They had reason to be satisfied with their work; for they succeeded in getting tenants to consent to new leases which would raise the rents by a hundred pounds a year, and this looked like putting an extra eighteen hundred pounds into Benlowes' pocket.

April 20th came and Wright had viewed the estates, but he gave no word of his intention. It was not his cue now to hurry. Eventually he agreed to purchase so long as the new leases were satisfactory, but of course it was to his advantage to make difficulties. It soon became clear that Benlowes was no match for Wright and had hopelessly mismanaged things. He had not properly told his tenants that the lands were to change hands, and when they discovered it they do not seem to have enjoyed the prospect of Wright as a landlord. Wright made them afraid of his "power and greatnesse." He put it about that the lands were forfeit to him, which was hardly true; and, if Benlowes is to be believed, he browbeat the tenants and threatened them with ruin. So what happened was that they all wanted to withdraw from their agreements, and the leases which Benlowes had counted on were never signed. Having frightened the tenants out of their contracts, Wright had an excellent excuse for disapproving of the purchase, and, driving a hard bargain, proceeded to avail himself of it. Benlowes was now in a very awkward situation. He had been unwary enough to get his estates "soe secured and intangled" to Wright that it was out of the question to look for another purchaser; he could not pay back what Wright had already advanced him, and the interest on that was rapidly mounting. So he had to make concessions. He agreed to admit the old scale of rents as the basis of the valuation and to accept, for everything save one farm, seventeen instead of eighteen times the annual value. His efforts to increase his rents had therefore done much more harm than good. He not only did not get the extra eighteen hundred pounds he had tried for: Wright had forced him down by nearly nine hundred. Benlowes subsequently spoke of the "hard termes" upon which the estates had been "wrested" from him, and complained that altogether Wright had them for five thousand pounds less than they were worth. Benlowes' own computation of their value had in fact been £22,000.[1] The purchase price he had to agree to accept from Wright was £15,315.

All this dragged over a year and more, and it was not till May 11, 1657, that the conveyance of the estates was made. The purchase price of £15,315 was not of course what Benlowes was to receive. Wright had already granted him loans totalling £1,230 and had cleared off a mortgage of £9,000, with a half-year's interest on it of £270. And Wright had contrived to delay proceedings long enough to send up his own interest by £735. So Benlowes, now at the moment of alienating his family heritage, stood to have only £4,080 in pocket. That was the situation when Nathan Wright entered into possession of Brent Hall and Edward Benlowes took his final departure. Shortly afterwards he was settled again in London, having taken lodgings in St. Paul's Churchyard. [2]

Sufficient insight should by now have been got into the unscrupulous nature of Wright's dealings and the tangled state of Benlowes' affairs to warn one against supposing that even the amount now agreed on would be paid. Only two days after the deed had been signed, on May 13, 1657, Wright opened a fresh dispute and began a suit in Chancery. He found the estates heavily encumbered. Stipends had to be paid to the incumbents of Great Bardfield and Bardfield Saling; there was the jointure settled on Philippa's mother and the

[1] See a survey of his estate in the Essex Record Office, D/DAc 110.
[2] This was his address on December 15, 1657 (Chancery Depositions, C24/835/92).

annuity granted to Schoren; there were the innumerable charities imposed on the estates nearly a century before by old Serjeant William, who had provided for the upkeep of his many alms-houses and for regular gifts to the local poor. There were other charges, like the endowment of annual lectures in anatomy and odd charities of various kinds, which Edward had copied his great-grandfather in imposing. Some of these encumbrances Benlowes had declared; but others he had not sufficiently specified. And Wright further found that there had existed other charges, like the provision for a Bardfield school, which had lapsed but which might still be legally demanded. At this he got very wild and pretended that there were also annuities to be paid to some of Benlowes' relatives, even though the relatives in question had long been in their graves. But at least he had justice with him when he demanded an explicit statement of everything and the surrender of all deeds and papers. A lot of the deeds had been burnt along with Brent Hall four years before; but Benlowes had a trunkful of documents delivered over and promised others, which he admitted having, though characteristically he confessed himself vague about what they were. For his part, he was getting thoroughly exasperated. It was difficult enough to give a satisfactory account of the encumbrances, and finding Wright a grasping customer, he took the usual refuge of the weak and the defeated and adopted a policy of obstruction. There may have been some truth in Wright's assertion that Benlowes was deliberately withholding information. Even when Benlowes admitted liability, he was prone to inaction. Wright made various appointments with him at the chambers of Edward Harries in Lincoln's Inn, but every time he was disappointed: Benlowes either failed to appear or else postponed making any lucid statement. A further quarrel concerned dilapidations. Wright alleged that the farms and houses were "ruinous and in greate decay," and that Benlowes was doing nothing about it. On his side, Benlowes insisted that repairs had already cost him "a very good some of money," and he had certainly been busy cutting down timber and allotting it to farmers for the purpose of repairing their farmhouses. Perhaps he did most of what could be expected of a very peaceable person who was naturally indolent in matters of business. He did make an attempt to straighten out the encumbrances. For example, he got his sister-in-law Elizabeth to accept five hundred pounds for her jointure and to set the estate free of one of its obligations. But for particulars about old Serjeant William's charities, which he had long ceased to be clear about and some of which he had also ceased to pay, he off-handedly referred Wright to the Serjeant's will, when at length, after seven months, he put in an answer to Wright's bill of complaint on December 9, 1657. So, although Benlowes was mildly reasonable as far as he could be pinned down to anything, it was still not an altogether satisfactory statement. Benlowes had obviously no idea what sort of compensation would be proper, and his folly had been in parting with his property before so crucial a detail had been settled. The quarrel continued.

Meanwhile, Wright had handed out some further small sums, but no settlement had been reached roughly two and a half years after negotiations had been opened. Then on March 11, 1658, Wright died. It may have been some gratification to Benlowes that this hard-bargaining purchaser of his estates was spared less than a year to enjoy them; but the heir, Benjamin Wright, showed himself even more reluctant to pay than his father had been. And since he could always claim ignorance of what had passed between his father and Benlowes, there was even one more loophole for delay. [1]

It was not many years before Benjamin Wright split up the Benlowes lands. He sold one manor in 1662 and another the next year, as well as the rectory of Great Bardfield. The various charitable bequests imposed by Edward Benlowes' ancestors were again the cause of dispute and litigation, and Wright evidently found that the status of a landed gentleman carried with it difficulties as well as dignities. He finally sold Brent Hall and the remaining farms and manors in 1668. [2] Serjeant William still lay in the chancel of Great Bardfield church; but the estates which he and his father Christopher had patiently accumulated and which they had envisaged being ruled by their posterity for ever had now been mortgaged, dragged through Chancery, divided up, and twice sold in the space of a dozen years.

[1] For events leading up to the sale of Benlowes' estates and the disputes arising, the authority is again the Chancery suits: Collins 140/147; Bridges 444/123. There are also Close Rolls, 1655, pt. 24, no. 13; 1657, pt. 25, no. 22.
[2] Chancery Proceedings, Bridges 583/16; Morant, *Essex*, II, 368.

CHAPTER TWENTY-TWO

POEMS AND LAWSUITS

One of the last landowner's functions that Benlowes exercised
was to present to the rectory of Great Bardfield, the advowson
of which he, like his forefathers, held. He was lucky in still holding
it; for many Royalist delinquents had been forced to give up their
rights over ecclesiastical livings, [1] and had Benlowes taken the field
in the early part of the Civil War it is most unlikely that he would
have escaped that penalty. As it was, the Great Bardfield living was
still in his gift. It fell vacant while the negotiations with Nathan
Wright were still going on, and Benlowes was able to put in his
nominee, Samuel Hall. [2] His choice was a very significant one, for
Samuel Hall was very well known in the district. It is necessary for
a moment to have a glance at his somewhat notorious past.

In 1647 a living was vacant at the neighbouring town of Thaxted
through the ejection of the vicar; and the patroness, Lady Maynard,
insisted on nominating Hall, though his theology and his record of
having preached against the Parliament were anything but pleasing to
the Westminster Assembly, who declared that he gave them more
trouble than any other minister that had ever been referred to them.
This may well have been, for he tried to get himself inducted even
when the Assembly had six times examined him and "found him
unfit." His views were less obnoxious to the parishioners of Thaxted,
who encouraged him to take the pulpit in defiance of authority.
When the sequestrators sought to intervene, five women "fell violently upon the said Sequestratours, beat them sore, tore the haire
from some of their heads, the Bands from their neckes, their Hattes
and Cloakes off." [3] Samuel Hall was arrested by order of the House
of Lords and only released upon submitting to their judgment

---

[1] See Shaw, *English Church 1640-1660*, II, 199ff.
[2] *Transactions of the Essex Archaeological Society*, new series, VI, 132.
[3] Pamphlet, *A Great Fight in the Church at Thaxted in Essex* (1647). See also
Davids, *Evangelical Nonconformity in Essex*, pp. 490-494.

that he was not to officiate at Thaxted any more. He stayed on in Essex, however, where his friends were able to make some modest provision for him, and he is next heard of at Bardfield Saling. [1] The chapel there had, of course, been endowed by old Serjeant Benlowes, but the right to appoint the priest seems not to have stayed in the Benlowes family; [2] so there is no evidence for supposing that Edward Benlowes' influence got for Hall what was in any case a miserable preferment for an ambitious young man, and "an able preacher" to boot. But when the rectory of Great Bardfield fell vacant Benlowes was able to promote him to it. In fact, Benlowes retained the powers of a man of property just long enough to show his approval of a man whom the Westminster Assembly had six times rejected. His contempt for the Presbyterians, already eloquent in *Theophila*, could not have been better manifested. And he had the satisfaction of assisting one whom Stephen Marshall himself had denounced before the House of Lords.

The control of a rectory could never be, for a country gentleman, a wholly spiritual—or political—affair. The question of providing a barn which the new tenant wanted at the parsonage-house added its small mite to the confusion of Benlowes' estates and to the irritable dispute that the purchaser of the estates made. [3] With an offer to pay five pounds for the barn Benlowes passed out of the history of Great Bardfield rectory, and ceased to have influence upon the church where his ancestors slept and where his own crest and initials decorated corbels of the chancel roof which his money had restored. There must have been many bitter thoughts.

In London, in St. Paul's Churchyard, Benlowes missed the meadows, and the mower scything "the flowrie Tresses of the verdant Plains," and the

> *Valleyes*, by whose fringed Seams
> A Brook of liquid *Silver* streams. [4]

These he had exchanged for the air of London, which was none too sweet—"specially," by James Howell's account, "in the heart of the City, in and about *Paul's* Church, where Horse-dung is a yard deep." [5] And it is not to be supposed that he found great com-

---

[1] Davids, *Evangelical Nonconformity in Essex*, p. 284 n.
[2] *Transactions of the Essex Archaeological Society*, n.s., VI, 132.
[3] Chancery Proceedings, Collins 140/147.
[4] *Theophila*, xiii, 2-3.
[5] *Familiar Letters*, p. 542. In confirmation of the insalubrity of seventeenth-century London, if any were needed, one might cite Harvey's *Anatomical Exam-*

pensation, here beside the thoroughfare which led to the centre of the city, in the frequent spectacle of all the great going by in their coaches. It was not only that he disliked the sight of worldly great-ness, the "great" of the moment were the wrong people. Lovers of the monarchy found London unpleasant and the Royalist gentry kept mostly to the country. As Sir John Reresby found in 1658, "the citizens and common people of London had then soe far im-bibed the custome and manners of a Commonwealth that they could scarce endure the sight of a gentleman, soe that the common salu-tation to a man well dressed was 'French dog', or the like." Once Reresby actually got involved in a brawl with some workmen mending the road because of a feather in his valet's hat. [1] Benlowes' own dress could not nowadays offend, but there may have been many minor causes for irritation as he went about the streets. Yet his calm was not easily ruffled. Even the worries of his property and the equally great worry of selling it had never been able to oc-cupy all his mind. He could know other joys, which London was well equipped to minister to. He could always find his way to a bookseller's more easily than to a lawyer's office. And in St. Paul's Churchyard he was surrounded by the bookshops—among them Kirton's, familiar to all readers of Pepys, who was always in and out, buying a book to take home to his wife or pausing to look through the latest works; Thomason's, where the bookseller him-self was methodically collecting and filing all the newly published pamphlets; Moseley's, whence came most of the best poetry, as well as Benlowes' own. Overshadowing all was the famous Gothic cathedral, which, if sadly in need of repair, was able to fill Benlowes with elevated thoughts. As the temple of the true, reformed religion it was much to be preferred to the most celebrated churches he had seen, St. Mark's at Venice or St. Peter's at Rome. [2]

Here among the bookshops at the hub of England's literary world, Benlowes was able to keep in touch with some of his literary friends.

---

ination of the Body of Thomas Parr (1635). Having lived for 152 years in the "healthy region of Salop," Parr died when he went up to London, "a city whose grand characteristic is an immense concourse of men and animals, and where ditches abound, and filth and offal lie scattered about, to say nothing of the smoke engendered by the general use of sulphureous coal as fuel, whereby the air is at all times rendered heavy" (*Works*, trans. Willis p. 591). There is also plenty of corroboration for the Restoration period in Pepys. And see also, Bryant, *The England of Charles II*, pp. 16-18.

[1] *Memoirs*, pp. 21-22.

[2] *On St. Paul's Cathedrall represented by M* Dan. King.*

Among them certainly was Dr. Thomas Fuller, who had been for some years now curate at Waltham Abbey and, like Benlowes himself, had made many journeys from Essex to London to deal with publishers and engravers. He was much in London during the Interregnum and drew crowds to hear his witty preaching, though Pepys's judgment some years later could not approve the popular verdict. [1] Fuller was one who profited again from Benlowes' liberality just when Benlowes' power to be liberal was waning. Publishing his *History of the University of Cambridge* in 1655, he dedicated its sixth part to Benlowes, praised his highmindedness and unworldly wisdom, and incidentally reminded the public of his former patronage of literature and learning. [2]

Fuller specifically remembered that Benlowes had once presented St. John's College with gifts by no means to be scorned (*donaria non contemnenda*), a fact which was at this time also the subject of eager recollection on the part of the poet John Davies of Kidwelly. He had been at St. John's himself, and even though that was a quarter of a century after Benlowes' day, he did not scruple to make use of the connection. During the Commonwealth he had settled in London and made his livelihood by translating books, "and putting dedicatory and other epistles to them, gained much relief by them." [3] Whom could he find a more attractive recipient for one of his dedications than Edward Benlowes, the benefactor of the college that had trained them both and of numerous university men who struggled to make their living by the pen? In 1655 Davies was busy translating from the Latin a work called *Apocalypsis*, which contained "the Revelation of certain notorious Advancers of Heresie ...together with an account of their *Lives*, *Actions*, and *Ends*." This was the book which he now thought of dedicating to Benlowes, who was held to be an appropriate recipient—because his own principal endeavours had been displayed in the cause of religion, and because he was a great friend of Alexander Ross, who had recently, in his *Pansebeia*, added to his other *ex cathedra* pronouncements what claimed to be an authoritative survey of the world's religions and heresies. Adorned with the effigies of seventeen of the notorious heretics, the book could appeal both by its moral and its chalcography. Benlowes might be having to sell his family estates,

[1] *Diary*, May 12, 1661.
[2] *History of the University of Cambridge*, ed. Prickett and Wright, p. 179. See also above, pp. 57-58, 148.
[3] Wood, *Athenae Oxonienses*, IV, 382.

but he was still Maecenas, and no one need suppose that John
Davies lacked some personal benefit of the munificence his dedication
so warmly praised.

Benlowes was still writing poetry himself, and if this decade did
not produce another *Theophila*, that was due quite as much to the
infertility of his mind as to the discouragement of difficult circumstances. He had spoken his message, and though it could always
be used again in some new piece of verbal embroidery, he was not
averse to resting in his halo. He could not help writing, but henceforth he wrote only shorter poems.

In 1657, the very year when his mind, one might have thought,
was given over to worries about rents, leases, and encumbrances,
wrangles with Nathan Wright and apprehensions about his future
income, he had two new titles in the London bookshops. One of
these, however, did not really denote a new poem. *The Summary
of Wisedome*, a ten-leaved quarto containing a hundred stanzas of
English verse with a Latin translation, was in fact yet another of
those shoots which *Theophila*, so securely rooted in Benlowes' mind,
was constantly putting forth. The decline in his worldly position
had only deepened Benlowes' view of the world as a despicable
place of vain foolishness, and almost the same impulse that stirred
him to write prompted him to denounce again the drunkard and
the wanton, the thirsters after pleasure, fame, and wealth. He med-
itated therefore a poem on the following Biblical text, which duly
appeared on the title-page of *The Summary of Wisedome*:

> *Love not the World, neither the things that are in the World; if any Man love the
> World, the love of the FATHER is not in him: For all that is in the World, the
> Lust of the Eyes, the Lust of the Flesh, and the Pride of Life, is not of the
> FATHER, but is of the World; and the World passeth away, and the Lust thereof.
> But He that doth the Will of God abideth for ever.* 1 Joh. 2. 15, 16, 17.

But Benlowes had hardly done more than announce the subject in three
opening stanzas when he found himself slipping into phrases used
before, and the plan for the new poem soon transformed itself into a
clever scheme of bringing together all the relevant passages of *Theophila*, selecting from them, tinkering with their phraseology, and rear-
ranging them in new sequences. The sacred maiden herself no longer
appeared, but of the hundred stanzas in the now familiar metre,
hardly one sought to express a novel idea and less than twenty
failed to make use of *Theophila's* phrases. Pygmalion was so in love
with his own creation that he wanted to create it all over again.
As he had in *Theophila* echoed the phrases of a host of his

contemporaries, now he much more consistently echoed himself. But of course in thus borrowing from himself he did not intend to delude the public any more than he intended plagiarism when he borrowed from other poets. The last thing Benlowes could have wished was that readers of *Theophila* should have forgotten the striking conceits and cunning locutions that he had laboured to impress upon their brains. Perhaps he hoped with a smaller, cheaper volume to reach a public as yet unknown. But the majority of his readers were meant to recognize stones of the old building in the new house. This architectural economy was not, of course, being tried out for the first time. One or two fragments that had been used in *A Poetick Descant upon a Private Musick-Meeting* had been also intended for *Theophila*. And no doubt Benlowes himself had not forgotten how the "Quarlëis," written to promote the interests of Quarles with the dignitaries of London, had been adroitly turned to the benefit of a new protégé when parts of it had been given to John Sictor to append to an address to the Lord Mayor. Nor was Benlowes by any means a solitary player of this curious poetical game. He may easily have learned it from an earlier expert at it, his friend Phineas Fletcher. [1] The habit of using the same verses twice over perhaps began as a labour-saving device, but it developed— in *The Summary of Wisedome* at least—into a sort of refinement of writing. Benlowes made it a test of skill to transform some features without disfiguring the whole. If I have called it a game, I do not wish to suggest that it was carried out with levity. Benlowes lent himself to this intellectual exercise with all the seriousness that he and his contemporaries gave to anagrams and emblems.

When the admirer of *Theophila* recognized whole stanzas in the new volume, he would meet them often in changed contexts, and he would not find one of them that was identical in wording with

---

[1] For discussions of self-repetition in Fletcher, see *Giles and Phineas Fletcher, Poetical Works*, ed. Boas, II, pp. ix ff.; Langdale, *Phineas Fletcher*, pp. 153ff. Langdale's appendix listing Fletcher's repetitions (like his appendix on Fletcher's borrowings from other poets) is highly misleading because it includes many pairs of passages between which there is only a vague similarity. It seems proper to speak of *repetition* and *borrowing* only when passages, though not necessarily identical in all respects, are nevertheless at once recognizable as the same.

In Benlowes' poetical circle, Thomas Pestell also practised this "good husbandrie" of wit (see *Poems*, ed. Buchan, pp. xl-xli).

An interesting example by a more important poet occurs in Crashaw, who incorporated in the enlarged version of "The Weeper," with certain modifications, some stanzas which first appeared in his poem "The Teare" (*cf.* "The Teare," stanzas 4 and 5, with "The Weeper," stanzas 27 and 11).

its original in *Theophila*. For example, Benlowes was fond of his comic stanza (Canto i, stanza 20) on drinking and red noses,

> *Each Gallon breeds a Ruby*;—Drawer, *score 'um*;
> *Cheeks dy'd in* Claret *seem o'th' Quorum*,
> *When our* Nose-carbuncles, *like* Link-boyes, *blaze before 'um*,

and he used it again in the *Summary of Wisedome* (stanza 44), but gave his drunkard a "*pottle*" instead of a gallon. To make an alteration of some kind seemed a matter of principle: I suppose only in that way could a stanza merit becoming a unit in what was in one sense a new work. Usually the variation was considerably greater than here. One hopes Benlowes' readers appreciated the detail of his elegant variations when, having read, for example, in *Theophila*

> So wastful, *Us'rer*, as thy self, there's None,
> Who loosest three true *Gems* for one
> That's counterfeit; Thy *Rest, Fame, Soul* for ever gone! (xiii, 89),

they now came upon:

> So wastefull, *Usurer*, as thy self, there's none;
> Who part'st with three true *Jemmes*, for one
> Brittle as glasse;—thy Fame, Rest, Soul for ever gone!
> (*The Summary of Wisedome*, stanza 33.)

This might look like the same coin; but there had to be some pretence of its being minted afresh. Sometimes Benlowes juggled with the order of the words, often he did some trick with synonyms; frequently a thought would be repeated with a new image, or a favourite image fitted to a different thought. The result was not always better; but there is no doubt that Benlowes' finicking mind was as much eager to improve his words as it was restless to change them. He sought to make his images more vivid and concrete. Instead of sowing Sin and reaping Judgment he now sowed nettles and reaped prickles. He bribed fiends instead of Death or Vengeance. [1] His young cavalier with "all his Clothes so loosely spread" now had "fancy'd ribbands round bespread." [2] The Furies of hell, which formerly appalled him "with excessive *Frights*," came to do it much more tangibly with whips. [3] Other images were now better sustained. Gold had spotted "the dreggy *Soul*" with "*Itch*"; but the itch, now attaching itself to a specific dread disease, suggested, instead of the feeble "dreggy *Soul*," "the leprous Mind." [4] Sometimes the idea itself developed. In *Theophila* Benlowes had pictured Justice

---

[1] *Theophila*, x, 95; *Summary*, stanza 34.
[2] *Theophila*, xi, 4; *Summary*, stanza 42.
[3] *Theophila*, ii, 36; *Summary*, stanza 36.
[4] *Theophila*, x, 80; *Summary*, stanza 30.

with a "steeled *Arm*" ready to smite and had proclaimed that
Vengeance was God's; but a later and more subtle thought had
Vengeance brought down to earth to smite instead of Justice; and
found no place here for Justice, which, oppressed on earth, took
flight for heaven. [1]

One more illustration must suffice. Trying all the time for suc-
cinctness of expression and for lines packed with wit and allusion,
Benlowes would sometimes compress two stanzas into one. In *Theophila* (Canto xi, stanzas 58-59) he wrote of the gallant and his courtesan:

> On *her*, profusely now he spends his Ore;
> Scarce the *Triumvir* lavisht more
> When he did costly treat his stately Memphian *Whore*.
>
> Thou, inconsid'rate *Flash*, spend'st pretious Dayes
> In Dances, Banquets, Courtisms, Playes,
> To gain the Shade of Joy, which, soon as gaind, decayes.

This, in *The Summary of Wisedome* (stanza 53), was admirably reduced
to:

> With her profusely he mispends his dayes
> In Balls, and Dances, Treatments, Playes;
> And in his Bosome this close-biting-Serpent layes.

The main idea was retained, though Antony and Cleopatra had
gone; but from Cleopatra, through the manner of her death, came
the legacy of the serpent image which excellently suggested the
power of the courtesan's embraces to poison and destroy. [2]

In spite of the poet's careful working over his stanzas, the general
effect of *The Summary of Wisedome* is of a poem much inferior to
Theophila. Some of the diction excels in vigour, some of the lines
are very richly packed; but the general result is a row of ingenious
and conceited epigrams inadequately threaded on an argument. The
poet suffered from the loss of his heroine, who, shadowy as she
had been in *Theophila*, had been yet a unifying force throughout
the early cantos. In *The Summary of Wisedome* his satire of vanities
and his exhortation to the good life have become habitual and so
motiveless. The verbal cleverness has survived, but passion, adoration—rarely quite obscured in *Theophila*, however thick the ornament—are now absent.

One characteristic word-trick in the poem was a chronogram
such as any friend of Benlowes might by now have come to look
for; but its eccentricity was in being not in a prefixed motto, but

[1] *Theophila*, ii, 38-39; *Summary*, stanza 19.
[2] For a list of parallel passages in the two poems, see Appendix V.

within the poem itself. Benlowes dated his poem through the Roman
numerals in a prayer for the speedy destruction of the world: "thIs
year May bVrnIng CLose thy enD." He had to wait, however,
nine years before London was indeed destroyed by fire, and by that
time he was settled in the country. In 1657 London still stood,
and Benlowes had his lodgings in the middle of it in St. Paul's
Churchyard. As he went to and fro he must often have seen *The
Summary of Wisedome* on display at Moseley's, advertising itself on
the title page as by the author of *Theophila*. With it too was another
poem bearing his initials and his celebrated anagram Benevolus.
This was called *A Glance at the Glories of Sacred Friendship*, it was
printed on a single sheet, and was ready for sale at Moseley's by
August, which was when Thomason bought his copy.

A broadsheet was more flimsy and usually more ephemeral than
a book, but it did not, of course, preclude ornamental printing. On
the contrary, the layout of a complete poem on a single page was
a positive stimulus to a love of pattern, and Benlowes arranged
for the text to be printed in four columns, divided by three engraved
pillars. Unfortunately, the poem was not then big enough to fill
the frame, and various bits of Latin moralizing had to be appended.
Following his habit of using compositions twice, Benlowes included
two fragments from the *Theophila* volume. [1] A sort of symmetry
for the eye was thus maintained. The metrical form of the poem
showed him also experimenting with patterns for the ear. Discarding
now his unique three-lined stanza, he showed himself alive to current
developments in poetic form when he adopted the five-foot couplet
which was rapidly gaining ground as the fashionable metre. He
had already tried couplets in the fourth and ninth cantos of *Theophila*, but he seems to have preferred stanzaic forms. He was now
to make a compromise between the two. Aiming at pointed statement, he used the couplet, but by making every tenth line an alexandrine he preserved at the same time a stanza-unit. The new form had
an effect upon his style. The reader who looked for the excitement
of his daring epithets and concentrated metaphors might be somewhat disappointed. But there was not for long a curb upon his
fancy, and the lengthened form of stanza could not fail to invite
the working out of some elaborate comparisons.

It was not Benlowes' habit to give his mind too much to the
particular details of his theme. He sought here as usual to present

---

[1] The prose passage on p. 176 and the verse argument of Canto xii.

an ideal, and to suggest by a series of epigrams and analogies the wonders of a friendship contemplated in the abstract. He opposed the soul and the body in the manner which among followers of Donne had become conventional. Friendship was of the soul, yet was achieved by way of the body. Friends were "Although in Bodies two, in Love but one." Frequently such antitheses were combined with imagery of a typically "metaphysical" character, mixing geography with speculation about angels, drawing upon alchemy or magnetism. Friendship had an "attractive Power" which "*Heav'n* down to Earth, Earth up to *Heaven* drawes." It was one radiance coming from "two glorious Cones of Light." A more original imagination, delighting to make myth, sent Friendship riding in "*Vertues* glorious Chariot" or, in a moment of revelation, caught a glimpse of friendship as "the Realitie of *Iacobs* Dream." In some of his vaster hyperboles, Benlowes changed the Pyramids to gold and made every atom of the world a diamond bigger than Teneriffe, which was the magic mountain-island of most poets of the age. Finally, in his fancy Benlowes could see the whole of Nature shake into its original chaos, rivers stand still, and mountains "sneak away," while Friendship remained for ever "fixt in *Loves* Cœlestiall Orb."

As sometimes in *Theophila*, these images of world size tended to dazzle the reader while leaving him a little vague about the poet's actual experience. All this celebration of friendship might seem to be no more than a generalized aspiration towards some elevated but rather indeterminate emotion. Yet in the Envoy Benlowes seemed to be addressing some individual paragon whom he claimed as a friend; and it is impossible that Benlowes had not his own circumstances in mind. Long accustomed to be kind to others, he began now, as his own fortunes declined, to long for some return. So in the poem he celebrated "reciprocall Beneficence" and spoke of those whose friendship could melt the frozen zone into which "bad Times" might drive one. Read thus, the poem, for all the remoteness of its style, may yet seem a passionate affirmation of faith in friendship by a man who nevertheless dared to expect ingratitude in this world and knew that true friendship came only from above.

Benlowes' present situation certainly exhibited the irony of circumstance. He had a horror of going to law. In happier days, when he had been full of the joys of the retired life, he had said that a man who wished to improve his state by the cultivation of his mind should be careful, among other things, to shun "Prolixer Lawsuits." [1] And now he was being sued in Chancery by Nathan Wright. [2] The law had cast its net upon him, and only six days after he had put in his answer to Wright's bill of complaint, he found himself still further caught in its meshes. On December 15, 1657, a serjeant-at-mace, with his assistant—more properly called his yeoman— arrived at Benlowes' lodgings in St. Paul's Churchyard to arrest him. [3] This fresh trouble, which had been brewing for some time, all arose out of that very tiresome annuity which Benlowes had once generously established upon Schoren, which, however, he had frequently muddled the payments of, and which he had now ceased to want to pay at all.

It is necessary for a moment to go back a year or two. When Brent Hall had been burnt down, in 1653, Schoren had lost in the fire the deed which granted his annuity. He repeatedly pressed Benlowes to give him fresh security and Benlowes, notwithstanding Schoren's various acts of dishonesty, still felt it right to make provision for his servant. At length he agreed to have a new indenture drawn up, charging the annuity as before upon his Great Bardfield estates. But Schoren was still not content. In 1655 he knew that his master had got heavily into debt and had mortgaged all his lands. He may even have suspected his desire to sell his estates outright, and perhaps feared that if that happened he might have difficulty in getting his annuity paid by the new owner. At any rate, he sought a double security. On April 6, 1655, Benlowes, succumbing to pressure, gave Schoren a bond of two hundred pounds guaranteeing that the annuity should in any event be paid. Schoren could now feel that his future was secure; and hence, in spite of all their years together at Brent Hall, it hardly mattered to him when Benlowes, having decided to sell everything and give up the country gentleman's life, had no further use for him. He had his annuity, whatever happened; and he could go his own way.

When Benlowes had first granted Schoren an annuity, soon after bringing him from the Continent, he had been in a state of high religious fervour and much moved by Schoren's following him into Protestantism. He had intended it to be a condition of the annuity that Schoren should continue to conform to the doctrines of the

[1] *Theophila*, xiii, 17.
[2] See above, pp. 241 ff.
[3] Chancery Depositions, C24/835/92.

Church of England, but it had not really occurred to him that
Schoren might not want to. Nor had his unsuspecting mind thought
to have anything put in writing. Yet Schoren's Catholicism went
deep. It could be concealed as long as there was any advantage in
concealment; but when Schoren had nothing further to expect
from Benlowes, their life together being at an end, he signalized
his new freedom of action by ceasing the pretence. Benlowes at
once held himself discharged from all obligation, but the religious
stipulation could not, of course, be proved and Schoren was not
tractable. Besides, Benlowes was afraid. Cromwell had just been
taking new action against Royalists, and Schoren had a fruitful
field for blackmail. Benlowes feared him in the character of an in-
former, and having been "lately decimated for his adherency &
loyalty" to the King's cause, he dared take no risk. So Schoren's
annuity went on being paid. [1]

To some extent Schoren had Benlowes in his power. He saw
no prospect of anything to be got from resuming amicable relations,
so he cast about to see if there was anything else that he might
turn to his advantage. And then he remembered that long ago, in
1642, Benlowes had signed a bond promising to pay him £44.18s. [2]
This sum had never been paid, principally because Schoren
had made free with his master's money on his own account and
had shortly after absconded from Brent Hall. When he was taken
back into Benlowes' service it was understood between them that
all previous agreements were cancelled, but again Benlowes' open
and honourable nature never bothered to have that specifically
stated. Even when Benlowes gave Schoren the bond for two
hundred pounds in 1655 he still lightly trusted Schoren's good
faith and there was only an oral understanding that all earlier deeds
were henceforth to be void. So there was nothing in law to prevent
Schoren from trying sometime to cash in on the old bond of 1642.
And this he determined to do. [3] There was, however, one obstacle.

[1] Chancery Proceedings, Reynardson 31/14. And *cf.* above, p. 238.

[2] See above, p. 131.

[3] Schoren's persecution of his master was probably unique in its perseverance and the legality of its method, but there are several seventeenth-century
parallels to the situation of a confidential servant turning on his master. The
story that the poet Suckling was murdered by his servant's placing an open
razor inside one of his boots is now usually rejected in favour of Aubrey's account of Suckling's suicide by poison (*Brief Lives*, II, 242). But it rests upon
a long tradition and it is probable that some injury through a knife or nail in
a boot did actually take place (see *Notes and Queries*, 2d series, I, 316; and Hazlitt's
ed. of Suckling, I, lvi). The murder of Fulke Greville by his trusted body-ser-

The bond did not exist. Schoren had tried to extort money on it once before, about 1649; and on that occasion Benlowes, on finding himself suddenly confronted with a claim he thought invalid on a bond he could not dispute, had, so Schoren alleged, resorted to a trick to dispose of this very inconvenient document. [1]

Still, Schoren demanded payment and actually produced what he claimed to be Benlowes' signed bond. Benlowes, at last thoroughly disillusioned, was not amenable; whereupon Schoren sued him for the money in the City of London sheriff's court. In default of payment on an order of the court a debtor had to expect committal to prison—in this case to the Counter in Wood Street. So on December 15, 1657, Benlowes can hardly have been surprised when the serjeant and his yeoman arrived to take him into custody. In fact he knew what they had come for rather better than they did, and as they took him away he talked to them about the bond. They did not put him into the prison like any common debtor, but instead he was lodged close by at the Mitre, a tavern which, according to Pepys, writing two or three years later, was "a house of the greatest note in London."[2] It cannot, however, have been the lavish entertainment for which this tavern was noted that loosened Benlowes' tongue. His abstemiousness was known, and it must have been the nervous excitement caused by his arrest, or perhaps a sense of grievance, that made him indiscreet. The serjeant left his yeoman, William Paselew, at the Mitre to look after the prisoner, who, while they were together there, told Paselew that there had of course been such a bond as Schoren claimed. He thought it had been burnt, but he knew for a certainty that it could not be produced and boasted that he could therefore please himself whether he gave Schoren anything or not.

---

vant is fully authenticated. In a fury at being left out of his master's will, the man stabbed him while trussing up his points (Aubrey, *Brief Lives*, I, 205; Wood, *Athenae Oxonienses*, II, 432; and for other accounts, see Grosart's ed. of Greville's works, I, xcv ff.). Walter Blount, who married Benlowes' niece, only came into his estates because his elder brother had been killed by a footman (Burke, *Landed Gentry*, 1937, p. 185). In comparison, John Evelyn perhaps was lucky that his valet did nothing worse than rob him of sixty pounds' worth of clothes and plate (*Diary*, I, 295). This was at Paris; on another occasion at Tours a Spanish valet whom Evelyn had dismissed for misbehaviour had his master arrested for a hundred crowns, and when his suit failed, held a pistol to his head (*ibid.*, I, 82). These instances I find interesting in passing, but naturally I draw no general conclusion about the relations between gentlemen and their servants.

[1] See above, pp. 180-181. Chancery Proceedings, Whittington 71/87; Collins 28/11.

[2] *Diary*, Sept. 19, 1660.

Subsequently Paselew's was to be very material evidence when a court of law adjudged that Benlowes did in fact owe Schoren money on this bond, but at the moment Benlowes was right. Schoren had not got the bond and the one that he came out with was easily shown to be forged. Benlowes repudiated both signature and seal, and Schoren tacitly confessed to the forgery by abandoning his suit, as Benlowes conceived he very well might "with shame enough." [1]

Benlowes' first adventure into prison was therefore quite short. But his release did not settle matters, for Schoren was taking legal advice. He had witnesses to prove that the bond had existed, including William Tym, of Lincoln's Inn and Finchingfield, who had drawn it up. The parties had an unsatisfactory meeting on May 18, 1658, in Lincoln's Inn, where Samuel Benham, who knew them both, agreed to act as intermediary. Through him Benlowes offered Schoren a hundred pounds in full settlement of all he owed him, including the annuity. Benlowes hoped, one sees, with one stroke to quiet Schoren and to remove one of the encumbrances which were causing so much trouble with Nathan Wright. But Schoren peremptorily refused, and his wife, who seems to have been the more implacable of the two, said that she would never accept such an offer as long as she lived. Benlowes again boasted that he could not be made to pay, although Benham assured him that Sarah Schoren would never give in. Then, his good offices having failed, Benham sat himself down and would have nothing more to do with the matter. [2] In the following month Schoren brought action in Chancery. [3]

This second piece of litigation hanging over his head meant that Benlowes was very greatly harassed by the "Prolixer Law-suits" which he dreaded. The protracted nature of all Chancery actions was notorious. A Cromwellian ordinance of 1654 had made some attempt at Chancery reform, but although it had improved the organization of the law, it had not succeeded in speeding up its processes. Disputes which might in a matter of months have died a natural death were artificially stimulated when kept before a court which often took several years to settle them. Though two centuries had to pass before Dickens wrote *Bleak House*, Chancery already offered invitation to the satirist. The seventeenth century had its

[1] Chancery Proceedings, Whittington 71/87 (answer); Depositions C24/835/92.
[2] Chancery Depositions, C24/835/92.
[3] Chancery Proceedings, Whittington 71/87.

own tradition of judgments always "expected" but too often only coming when the litigant had wasted his substance and undermined his temper.

For the present, however, Benlowes was not without other interests to occupy his mind. There was always his pen, and in 1658 he had not forgotten his place in society as a patron of the arts. Since coming to London he had met the engraver Daniel King, himself a fairly new arrival, who had come up to the capital with a bit of a reputation got through a collection of engravings of his native county, Cheshire. Following a fashion set by Hollar, he gave much of his energy to topographical designs, quickly proceeded to bring out a volume describing and illustrating English cathedrals, and was then prompted by its success to undertake a series of engravings of St. Paul's. So there he was, busy depicting the cathedral in the shadow of which Benlowes had his lodging. Anthony à Wood thought King "a pitiful pretender to antiquities," [1] but he unquestionably had talent and Benlowes was naturally very interested in his project. He gave King every encouragement, perhaps helped him with money, and certainly consented to compose some verses for him. This was just what King wanted, for he had no skill himself in writing. Indeed Sir William Dugdale, who employed him to etch some plates for his *Monasticon*, told Wood that King was "a most ignorant, silly fellow," who was "not able to write one line of true English." But with some competent if rather journeymanish verses— Latin as well as English—by a poet whose name had still a great prestige within a certain circle, King could expect for his work a tolerable sale.

Benlowes' poem *On St. Paul's Cathedrall* took the form of a lament for the cathedral's ruinous condition. There had been two royal commissions to consider its repair, and the second of these had provided Inigo Jones with a splendid opportunity for self-advertisement in his classic west portico, but without doing much for the decayed fabric. The steeple, long since struck by lightning, had at length been taken down and not replaced; and the main building was, to use Evelyn's phrase, receding outwards. [2] Hence the poet's

---

[1] *Athenae Oxonienses*, III, 503.

[2] James Howell had compared "poor *Paul's*" to "a great Skeleton, so pitifully handled, that you may tell her ribs thro' her skin; her body looks like the Hulk of a huge *Portugal Carake*, that having cross'd the Line twelve times, and made three Voyages into the *East-Indies*, lies rotting upon the Strand" (*Familiar Letters*, p. 617).

fancy feared that eyes once dazzled by the cathedral's splendour would soon be blinded by the dust of its collapse. The interior had suffered Parliamentary desecration during the Civil War—the soldiers had quartered their horses in it—and Benlowes accordingly mourned "our *Augæan* Shame," [1] hoping that a future age would rebuild the church with better heart than his own had laid it waste. His wish came true, but not quite as he hoped. Within five years a third commission had been appointed; but when it had spent over three thousand pounds, the Fire of London put an end to its labours [2] and cleared a space for Sir Christopher Wren. Benlowes, in his fear that the lead of the church roof would be its own winding-sheet, had been only too prophetic.

Daniel King engraved Benlowes' verses in a pleasant cursive script, and they appeared in the centre of a large broadsheet with pictures and plans of St. Paul's placed round them. The plates had been engraved by King with some assistance from a young and as yet unknown artist called David Loggan, who had come to England a few years back after learning his art in Denmark and Holland. At the bottom, taking about two-thirds of the width of the sheet, was a general view of London from south of the river. King also found room for a tiny portrait of Benlowes (about two inches by one) three-quarters of the way down on the left-hand side. There, rather oddly among all the topographical drawings, were Benlowes' head and shoulders inside a laurel-wreath. If the portrait had any degree of likeness, Benlowes appeared before his readers considerably changed in the last six years. The rather exquisite gentleman portrayed in *Theophila* was probably a flattery of a man of fifty, but the oil-painting done in 1650 had also shown Benlowes very little lined or bowed with years. By the time King knew him he had aged a good deal. Though his eyes had the same intense look, his face had a severer cast. And his dress shows him accommodating himself to his declining years. He is now soberly dressed in black with a skull-cap on his head restraining his soft thick hair, which he still wears parted in the middle though less fastidiously groomed.

The portrait was hastily executed and not particularly skilful,

[1] Howell had already reflected "that once a *Stable* was made a *Temple*, but now a *Temple* is become a *Stable* among us" (*ibid.*).

[2] Evelyn, who was a member of the commission, records their deliberations and proposals when they went over the cathedral less than a week before it was burnt down (*Diary*, II, 199-200).

but it was, no doubt, a sincere mark of the artist's esteem. Surrounding it he put perhaps the simplest statement of thanks Benlowes ever received from all the many men he helped: "SIR, Your Merit in these Verses, & my Gratitude for your Civilities, mov'd me to joyne your Picture to this Peece, Who would also present all our other Cathedralls in this Forme, if encouraged by Such as your honoured SELFE. DAN: KING." If King got the profit of the publication, at least he made a handsome acknowledgement of Benlowes' gift, even while begging for more gifts like it. The broadsheet was sold in London for a shilling. Anthony à Wood got a copy of it, which is now preserved at the Bodleian.

This was not the only publication with which Benlowes associated his name in 1658, for he wrote a tiny poem for his old acquaintance Payne Fisher. Fisher had first had complimentary verses from Benlowes to introduce his poem on Marston Moor in 1650, when Benlowes helped him market that product of his Civil War experience. Since then he had gone on making literary capital out of public events, though he had changed his point of view to conform to the change of government. He had got as far as celebrating the generals of the army he—and Benlowes too—had fought against. He had written, among other things, an elegy on Ireton, who had put to death at Colchester the leaders of the rebellion which Benlowes had supported. He was fawning upon those who had taken from Benlowes a tenth of his income. Benlowes not only cannot have sympathized with this part of his friend's career, but must have seen in it ample confirmation for his views on the world and its vanities. Fisher had made of himself an unofficial poet-laureate, and kept turning out odes and addresses on Cromwell's anniversaries. It is true that once, when attempting to recite one of his numerous elegies at Christ Church, he had been howled down by the Oxford undergraduates; but he had become quite a popular poet with those as fickle as himself. In 1658 he found it obviously his task to celebrate the capture of Dunkirk by French and British troops fighting against Spain—a victory through which Dunkirk was ceded to the British. He addressed a high-flown "Epinicion vel Elogium" to Louis XIV, and Benlowes, along with one or two others, was given it to read. Evidently their acquaintance had survived a difference of party, but Benlowes wrote only a somewhat meagre tribute, more complaisant than enthusiastic. Still, there were seven lines of Latin verse, to go with some in French by Peter de

Cardonel and other specimens of the usual sort of compliments, when Fisher had his poem published in an elaborately adorned and slender folio, with the French king's portrait at the beginning and an engraving to embellish the margins of every page. I suppose that, whatever one's views of the Protector, one could quite properly celebrate a victory of British arms; and glowing praise of a monarch —even a foreign one—had a tinge of Royalism. This, evidently, was the view of Fisher, who selected this from all his works as the one to flourish when a Stuart king was again on the English throne. It was when he sought to curry favour with the new office-holders and was actually projecting a panegyric on Charles II himself that he presented a copy of it to Samuel Pepys, who described it as "a book in praise of the King of France, with my armes, and a dedication to me very handsome." [1]

The pleasure of Benlowes at the return of Charles II was likely to have been more sincere. For although he had made peace with some former opponents, he had not confused the meanings he attached to words like "loyalty" and "usurpation." When most Englishmen, in their eagerness to acclaim the new King, were hurriedly forgetting the Protectorate—it was months before they thought to dig up Oliver's body and hang it—Benlowes also raised his voice in praise of "liberty restored."

It was on May 29, 1660, that Charles II entered London "with a triumph of above 20,000 horse and foote, brandishing their swords and shouting with inexpressible joy; the wayes strew'd with flowers, the bells ringing, the streets hung with tapissry, fountaines running with wine." Evelyn "stood in the Strand and beheld it," and knew that this brightest and most joyful day in all the nation's history, which it was "past all human policy" to effect, "was yᵉ Lord's doing." Benlowes no doubt shared his sentiment, though it is difficult to imagine him in the midst of that pushing throng of "myriads of people flocking." Yet he must have seen his Majesty "go with as much pompe and splendour as any earthly prince could do" to a great feast at the Guildhall on July 5, when "the streetes were adorn'd with pageants at immense cost"; and have shared in the general regret about "the exceeding raine which fell all that day" and "much eclips'd its lustres." [2] During the summer he made one personal contribution—a very characteristic one—to the general

---

[1] *Diary*, July 14, 1660.
[2] Evelyn, *Diary*, II, 112-115.

rejoicing. He had composed his own triumph-song, his *Threno-Thriambeuticon*, in a series of Latin poems, and he had it printed with engraved portraits of Charles I and Charles II. And in spite of his dwindling resources he had his own pageantry with a little luxury in printing. Some copies were done on white satin, and one such copy, in a suitable frame, he gave to the Bodleian. At the Bodleian another change of government was at this time taking place; for Charles II's return brought promotion to Benlowes' good friend Thomas Barlow, who had been librarian for eight years. He resigned in September when he was appointed professor of divinity.[1] But Benlowes' gift nevertheless retained an honourable place in the librarian's study, where Anthony à Wood—and I suppose Benlowes himself—used to see it, in Thomas Hyde's time, hanging on the wall. [2]

Public celebrations were not, of course, much to Benlowes' taste. In the moment of victory as well as during the war he preferred as far he could to stay in the solitude of his study and give his thoughts to books of poetry or devotion. A favourite at this time was a series of disquisitions upon "the Feasts and Fasts of the Christian Church," each being accompanied with a poem and most of them with an engraving. It was by Edward Sparke, one of the ejected Royalist clergy, who, punning on his own name as a seventeenth-century author would, called his book *Scintillula Altaris*. It had first been published in 1652. Benlowes had often turned its pages, and he wrote a poem in honour of the author, "*Historian, Poet*, Orthodox *Divine*," which joined tributes by Fuller and others in the second edition in 1660. [3] He extolled the book for having helped him to direct his course "through the *Zodiack* of th'*APOSTLES Light*" and thereby to "Antedate *ANGELLICK Bliss*." The sentiment of Benlowes' poem, its imagery of gems and spouses, and, by no means least, its typography stiff with capitals and italics, mark the author of *Theophila*, which, though it could not rival the popularity of the *Scintillula Altaris*, did, like it, provoke an occasional belated tribute.

One such tribute came from Benlowes' old acquaintance James Howell, who, though he cannot have missed hearing talk about

[1] Macray, *Annals of the Bodleian Library*, p. 127.

[2] That is, after 1665. See Wood, *Fasti Oxonienses*, II, 359; *Life and Times of Anthony Wood*, II, 361.

[3] Six more editions before the end of the century offer evidence of the book's continued popularity with a less pious age.

Theophila, seems not to have written on it before its publication. He had since rectified the omission, and, disdaining lyrics, pastorals, and war-songs, had praised a muse which mounted to the skies and produced hymns fit for the angels to sing in heaven. His verses "Upon Mr. Benlowes Divine Theophila" were published when his poems were collected by Payne Fisher in 1663. While in the Fleet, Howell had kept himself for eight years by his pen, and he had since done a great deal of the sort of pamphleteering which brought him into favour first with Cromwell and then with Charles II. He could by this time be referred to by Payne Fisher as an eminent author whom not to know would be ignorance beyond barbarism. So the inclusion of a poem on *Theophila* in a collection of his works would be perhaps a useful reminder of Benlowes' existence when his friends were in danger of forgetting him and when in his own life legal documents threatened to usurp the place that his preference would have given to manuscripts of poems.

CHAPTER TWENTY-THREE

IN CHANCERY

One of the big disadvantages of Chancery litigation is its habit-forming propensities. Benlowes was not only sued both by Nathan Wright and Schoren, but after a little while he was bringing a suit in Chancery himself. Yet he can hardly be accused of overhastiness in trying to recover the money owing him on the sale of his family estates, for over four years had passed since the estates changed hands and he had still not been paid in full.

Benlowes had not in fact derived great benefit from parting with his lands. He had been able to provide Philippa with a handsome marriage portion, he had cleared off all his debts and freed himself from the perpetual persecution of having to find the interest on various loans and mortgages. But he had received very little into his own pocket at the time when he relinquished possession of Brent Hall, with £4080 still owing to him. [1] After that Nathan Wright had let fall a few dribbles of money most exasperating to a recipient who all his life had been accustomed to wealth. And then Benlowes' difficulties had been increased by Nathan Wright's death. For Nathan Wright had at least come into Chancery to try to get the disputes about encumbrances cleared up. Now with his death his lawsuit lapsed, and his son Benjamin adopted the simpler procedure of doing nothing at all. Benlowes approached him "in freindly manner" and got a fair reception but no money. Benjamin Wright was secure in possession of the property, which he "quietly held and enioyed" without troubling whether he ever finished paying for it or not. At length, eighteen months after he had inherited, in September 1659 he paid £40 and followed this up with £10 three months later and another £10 the following April. These small sums were insulting to a man who had enjoyed a thousand a year, and it argues a good deal of need on Benlowes' part that he should be reduced to accepting his money in such pitiful instalments. After this, payment stopped again, and Benlowes' further appeals were met only with a reminder that the matter of repairs and encumbrances had

[1] See above, p. 241.

not yet been settled and a claim to deduct for these on what Benlowes called Wright's "owne vnreasonable Termes." Wright, according to Benlowes' firm conviction, was seeking "to defraude" him and availing himself of every possible excuse for delay. Sometimes he said that he was waiting for particulars from his father's executors, sometimes he pretended that he had already paid all that was owing. And Benlowes suffered the additional indignity of finding Wright in control of lands which he intended to exclude from the sale, so that Wright was unjustly receiving rents of £37 a year which Benlowes now could well have done with. Benlowes' troubles eventually found expression in a bill of complaint which was lodged in Chancery on November 26, 1661. [1]

The policy of Sir Benjamin Wright (he had recently been made a baronet) was all the time one of obstruction. Fifteen months after Benlowes' suit had been entered he had not put in an answer, and he did not do so until the court had given order for his arrest. [2] When at length the case was argued in court, it was admitted that the parties were in dispute about the amount of money due. So the court made an arrangement which Wright and Benlowes, had they been either more business-like or more amenable, ought to have been able to come to for themselves years before. The dispute was referred to two arbitrators, who were to assess the amount of compensation for repairs and encumbrances that the purchaser might be allowed to deduct from the purchase price. It was six years since Benlowes had been so refractory about meeting Nathan Wright to discuss encumbrances. Now, in 1663, he had to have several meetings with Wright's son and the arbitrators; but with two such dilatory parties, perhaps it is not surprising that the time allotted by the court was exceeded. Eventually, on June 5th, a decision was reached, and five months later the court ratified it. Of the price originally agreed on the amount still unpaid was now £3315; yet Benlowes was awarded only £990. [3] This meant that Benjamin Wright was allowed well over £2000 in compensation for the encumbrances. But in spite of having done so well out of the arbitration, he placed every possible obstacle in Benlowes' way and only £290 was paid.

[1] Chancery Proceedings, Bridges 444/123.

[2] Chancery Decrees and Orders, 1662 A fol. 330.

[3] The arbitrators' award is preserved in the Chancery Reports and Certificates (C38), vol. 146. See also Chancery Decrees and Orders, 1662 A fol. 623; 1663 A fol. 206; Chancery Proceedings, Bridges 44/89.

Some new financial entanglements of Benlowes' only made things
more complicated. He had had to borrow more money and had
apparently done so on the strength of his expectations from Wright.
The result was that he owed £166 to Thomas Colwell and £171
to Edward Nash, who, now that he had got his judgment, together
descended on him for the money. But he could not pay, and preferred, as often, to hide from an awkward situation rather than
face it. He proceeded to make himself inaccessible to his creditors.
Colwell and Nash complained that he "had and did obscure and
obscond his p[er]son and Concealed his Estate," so that they "could
not in any wise speake with him... or take any legall course against
him or his Estate." They therefore sued him in the Lord Mayor's
Court in London on December 5, 1663. But despairing of ever
getting anything out of Benlowes himself, they sought to get satisfaction from Wright, out of the £700 which Wright still owed
Benlowes. Wright, not unnaturally, resented this, especially as
Benlowes was at the same time trying to recover the full £700 himself. Finding himself assailed on two sides, Wright sought relief
in a new Chancery action in May 1664. [1] Things were therefore effectively held up again, and it was now seven years since Benlowes
had sold his estates to Wright's father. Eventually Wright paid
another £400, but this apparently went to Colwell and Nash, while
Benlowes again got nothing. [2] That still left £300 owing to Benlowes.
And in the end he never got even that. In 1666, three years after
Benlowes had secured his judgment, Wright had shown not the slightest sign of paying it.

During all this time the action brought by Schoren against Ben-

---

[1] Chancery Proceedings, Bridges 44/89. What happened was that when
Colwell and Nash sued Benlowes in the Lord Mayor's Court, they joined Wright
with him in the action. Wright had been warned to appear as garnishee, but
with the obstinate nature and obstructive tactics so frequently met with in
seventeenth-century litigants, he defaulted. Judgment was given against him
in his absence, and it was on this judgment that Colwell and Nash were now
proceeding against him. But Chancery refused to let Wright deduct from the
£990 which he was to pay to Benlowes the sum claimed by Colwell and Nash
(Decrees and Orders, 1663 A fol. 410). So Wright in his Chancery suit pleaded
that if he was to pay Benlowes in full, he should be granted an indemnity against
Benlowes' creditors. On June 10, 1664, he obtained an injunction staying the
proceedings of Colwell and Nash (Decrees and Orders, 1663 B fol. 760). And
there, for the moment, the matter seems to have rested.

[2] In 1666 Wright swore to having paid £690 of the sum awarded to Benlowes
(Chancery Proceedings, Collins 28/75), and he must therefore have paid out
in the meantime another £400. This was the precise amount that Colwell and
Nash were suing him for; so it looks as if their claim ultimately succeeded.

lowes in 1658 was dragging on. Benlowes for a long time held a position between a battering-ram and a stone wall. On the one side was Schoren constantly pressing him for money, on the other was Wright refusing to pay. For example, Schoren's by now notorious annuity was tied to lands in Great Bardfield and had to be paid by the owner, who was now Wright. It was in fact paid by Wright for a year or two, but in 1660 it suddenly stopped. Wright was refusing to pay this charge any more until Benlowes, who had imposed it on the estates, allowed him compensation for it; and this of course seemed reasonable to anyone who did not know that Wright was at the same time withholding over £3000 of Benlowes' money largely to cover charges of this kind.

Schoren had no better success than Benlowes in his attempts to wring money from Wright; but he was a much less patient man and lost little time in bringing an action—in May 1661—to force Wright to pay the annuity. Wright as usual delayed about answering, and Schoren had to drop his proceedings for lack of funds. [1] It was then that Schoren turned to account the canny foresight he had displayed years before when, not content with having his annuity charged on the Great Bardfield lands, he had got Benlowes to give a personal bond that the annuity would be paid. This bond, dated 1655, was for £200, and this amount Schoren attempted to recover from Benlowes by an action in the Court of Common Pleas in the Michaelmas term of 1662. For Benlowes this was desperate, and for once he took prompt action. He tried to frustrate Schoren by bringing a suit in Chancery on November 21, 1662. [2] He acknowledged his bond, but his plea was that Schoren's first claim was upon the estates, which now belonged to Wright. He insisted, moreover, that Schoren had forfeited his right to the annuity when he "changed his Judgment in matters of Religion," as the Court of Chancery would have it phrased. Benlowes' own phrase was expunged from the record as being scandalous. [3] This case was heard while Benlowes was very much occupied with Sir Benjamin Wright and the arbitrators in the dispute about the purchase price—Benlowes certainly led a harassed existence in the summer of 1663—and early in July a typical Chancery compromise was achieved. Benlowes need not forfeit the £200 of the bond so long as he paid Schoren's annuity

[1] Chancery Proceedings, Bridges 629/64; Reynardson, 31/14 (answer).
[2] Reynardson 31/14.
[3] *Ibid.*, and Reports and Certificates, vol. 146.

up to date. Nothing had been paid for three years, so that meant £40, and Benlowes paid it. [1] Thus at the very time when he had to admit compensation to Sir Benjamin Wright because of this wretched annuity, he also had to pay the annuity himself. And he went on paying it until Schoren's death. The satisfaction he got was that he did obtain on July 8, 1663, an injunction barring Schoren's claim for £200, which the Common Pleas had in the meantime upheld. But Schoren persisted in spite of this, had writs delivered on Benlowes and his agents, tried to get the injunction cancelled, and when he failed disobeyed it. [2] So various legal squabbles carried on until the end of the year, and by December, of course, Benlowes was involved also in the Lord Mayor's Court, where he was being sued for debt.

In the midst of these appalling annoyances Benlowes nevertheless could at the end of the year look back and reckon up some small gains. Sir Benjamin Wright had not yet paid in full, but he had paid something, and the amount he *was* to pay had at last been fixed. Schoren might be getting his annuity, but he had been checked over the bond. Action, it seemed, was sometimes profitable. So action was called for in the other lawsuit which still had Benlowes in its toils. This was Schoren's Chancery suit begun in 1658 demanding payment on the old bond of 1642, over which Benlowes had already been arrested once, which he now tried to pretend had never existed, and which was certainly not extant. [3] It appears that during five whole years this matter had never got to the stage of being argued in court. But Benlowes occasionally heard rumblings in the distance and sought to put a stop to them.

What he did was to open yet another suit in Chancery on November 25, 1663, [4] and in it he claimed that when Schoren's annuity had been re-granted in 1655 (and guaranteed by the £200 bond which Schoren had just been suing upon), there had been an oral agreement effectively annulling all outstanding debts. He sought, therefore, to have Schoren's proceedings stopped. Schoren's persecution had at length driven him to an orgy of recrimination, and in his bill of complaint he recapitulated all the transactions between himself and his servant. He recalled how Schoren had once defrauded him

---

[1] Decrees and Orders, 1662 A fols. 731, 856. Depositions C24/896/13.

[2] Affidavits, Trinity 1663, no. 454; Michaelmas, 1663. nos. 831, 832. Decrees and Orders, 1663 A fols. 274, 563. Depositions C24/896/13.

[3] See above, pp. 255-257.

[4] Collins 28/11.

and run away from Brent Hall; how, during the Civil War, he had once entrusted thirty pounds to Schoren and never got it back; how Schoren had sold goods saved in the Brent Hall fire and never handed over the money. He decided suddenly to demand this money, and he allowed himself one further satisfaction when he had Schoren's wife, who he knew egged her husband on, dragged into the case. Sarah Schoren, however, could easily show that she had nothing to do with all these matters, and Schoren himself repudiated his debts to Benlowes by pleading the Statute of Limitations—which he could do successfully since it was now over six years after the sale of the goods for which Benlowes was demanding an account.

There remained then the dispute over the bond of 1642. Benlowes' intervention had at least succeeded in having this matter heard by the deaf ears of Chancery, but it now only began a very tortuous journey through the courts, attended by many legal quibbles on both sides. The whole of this litigation is an excellent example of the law's delays and of the steadfast determination of the parties to obstruct each other as much as possible. Schoren's very clever counsel, Rich, sought to wreck Benlowes' suit by submitting that his bill of complaint contained scandalous matter. Investigation was called for, the scandal was cut out, and Benlowes had to pay Schoren £2.6s.8d. costs. [1] Rich also made use of a demurrer, claiming that Benlowes' bill contained nothing new for his client to answer. The demurrer was dismissed, but Schoren of course appealed and it had to be twice reheard because first one side and then the other was not represented in court. Eventually, on May 12, 1664, it was referred for decision to Sir Justinian Lewin, one of the Masters of the Court. [2]

The final result of all this was that Benlowes did not succeed in stopping Schoren's action on the bond of 1642. That case therefore went forward and was argued in court on June 17, 1664. [3] On June 10th the court was occupied with the case in which Sir Benjamin Wright sought an injunction against Benlowes and his creditors; so Benlowes obviously had a trying and exacting month. This summer, like the last, found him constantly in demand at lawyers' chambers and having to haunt the hated corridors of law-courts. His life was coloured with parchment, he was chased by writs and duns. And in retaliation, once at the law's mercy, he got a certain jaded pleasure

[1] Decrees and Orders, 1663 A fol. 169. Reports and Certificates, vol. 146.
[2] Decrees and Orders, 1663 A fols. 421, 572, 751.
[3] Decrees and Orders, 1663 B fol. 874.

out of using legal intricacies against his opponents and obstructing
all his creditors and suitors. It was a sad state for an idealistic poet
who had won extensive admiration for his worship of the soul.

As between Schoren and Benlowes on June 17, 1664, a fairly disinterested observer in full possession of the facts, as disinterested
observers very rarely are, would probably, I think, have decided:
first, that Benlowes had behaved throughout his transactions with
his servant with considerable generosity and with moral if not legal
justice; and secondly, that the deed of 1642 had in fact if not in
law been many times superseded. But that was exactly what Benlowes
could not prove. The case therefore turned on Schoren's ability to
prove the authenticity of a bond on which he sued but which he
could not produce. Benlowes no doubt felt justified in denying it
altogether; but that the bond had in fact existed was just as clear
as that it ought to have been considered obsolete. It would seem
therefore as though a very knotty problem in equity had been presented. The court's decision was a master-stroke of irony, worthy
of Gilbert at his most fantastic and outdoing anything Dickens
thought of for *Bleak House*. The Chancery hearing of the case took
place exactly six years after Schoren had begun it; and it was then
decided that the issue was not one for Chancery, the court of equity,
at all, and that the case must be dismissed.

Schoren, as usual, appealed and got a rehearing on condition
that he paid Benlowes' costs. [1] There was an interval of five months
before the case was heard again, and then again it was decided that
the issue was not one for Chancery but must be judged by a
court of common law. By now it was evidently thought that a little
dispatch would be advisable, and a special arrangement was made
for the case to come before Lord Chief Justice Bridgman at his
next sitting for him to decide the question of fact which was in
dispute — whether or not there had ever been such a bond as Schoren
alleged. It hardly needed the acumen of a Lord Chief Justice to
pronounce upon that, and although there was a long debate of
counsel, the inevitable verdict in Schoren's favour was given. So
back the case came into Chancery early in the new year of 1665,
and Benlowes was ordered to pay the debt for which he had given
his bond as long ago as 1642. The debt itself was £44.18s., but interest for twenty-three years came to £67.2s.6d. And Benlowes

---

[1] Benlowes estimated his costs at £30.2s. Schoren had to pay £8.15s. of
this (Reports and Certificates, vol. 153).

also had to pay Schoren's costs, which were assessed at £45. So the final award which was given against Benlowes on April 15, 1665, was for £157.0s.6d. [1]

The case was by no means ended, for Benlowes did not pay. On the contrary, he obstinately ignored all attempts to make him do anything in the matter at all. Whereas in earlier days he had been too susceptible to Schoren's importunity, he now became adamant, though hardly more business-like. But it is difficult to see how he could have paid if he would. His debts had been chronic for years, and the remaining crumbs of his fortune must have been swept up in his own legal costs. He had never received satisfaction of his claims upon Sir Benjamin Wright, and his only other asset was his claim upon the gratitude and affection of his one surviving relative, the niece whom in happier days he had so handsomely dowered.

Benlowes now gave up his London lodgings and went to live with this niece and her husband, Walter Blount, at their home at Mapledurham in Oxfordshire. There, close beside the Thames, he was back amid the sights and sounds of the country, in which his mind had always been able to find peace. He missed all the dignities of status that he had formerly enjoyed among his own tenantry, but after almost ten years of the noise and filth of London, which he had never liked and now had come to loathe, he found at Mapledurham a place of safe retreat. He moved there in time to avoid dying in the Great Plague.

Schoren was less fortunate and died within the year, possibly from the plague, but perhaps merely from the old age of which he had been complaining for some time. [2] In seven years of unrelenting agitation in the law-courts he had succeeded in winning one suit, but he did not live to enjoy one penny of the award. He died, in fact, in complete poverty, [3] but persisting to the end. Benlowes did "so abscond himself" in Walter Blount's house that Schoren, having got his verdict, could not serve Benlowes with a writ of execution and had to be content with having it taken in at the door. Then after Schoren's death his wife took a hand, but neither she

[1] The relevant decrees and orders in the case are: 1663 B fols. 832, 874, 880, 883; 1664 B fols. 170, 215, 269, 270, 323, 473. The computation of the sum to be paid may be found among the Chancery Reports and Certificates, volume 153.

[2] Chancery Proceedings, Bridges 629/64; Reynardson 31/14 (answer).

[3] He had obtained leave on February 7, 1665, to continue his action *in forma pauperis* (Decrees and Orders, 1664 B fol. 269).

nor others whom she employed had any better success. Benlowes refused to speak with them. By the beginning of 1666 he had made no move, and one writ after another was ignored. At length, on February 9th, a subpoena was issued commanding him to appear in court. On the morning of the 12th, between nine and ten o'clock, an officer succeeded in serving this on Benlowes in person; but it made no difference. Benlowes was to come into court that very day, but he paid no attention to the order at all. [1]

Then Mrs. Schoren, in despair of ever getting the money from Benlowes, tried to get it from Sir Benjamin Wright. She opened proceedings against him on February 13, 1666, [2] recklessly accusing him of conspiring with Benlowes to defraud her. She tried to pretend that the £157.0s.6d. that had been awarded to her husband represented arrears of his annuity, which was charged upon property belonging to Wright. This led Benlowes to intervene. For the first time for over a year he showed a sign of life and awareness, and succeeded in thwarting his adversary. On May 21st the court had ordered Wright to pay her out of the £300 that he still owed Benlowes; [3] but on July 4th Benlowes got the order rescinded. At the same time Benlowes was warned that if he continued to act in contempt of all the orders of the court, the £300 in Wright's hands would be confiscated to satisfy Mrs. Schoren's claim. [4]

This further legal development drew Benlowes out of his seclusion. He went up to London, and about the 6th or 7th of July he was seen in Whitefriars, where no doubt he was visiting Richard Tovey, who had recently been his agent in paying instalments of Schoren's annuity. [5] Benlowes was believed to be still about in London on July 12th, but he was not long before going back to his retreat at Mapledurham. There he did "very much secret himselfe" in Walter Blount's house, so that he was "very hard to bee spoaken withall." But Mrs. Schoren was a determined woman. On August 2nd she appeared at Mapledurham herself to serve a writ upon him. He refused to see her unless she would first promise that she had nothing against him. She knew that he was in the house, but he "kept himselfe in a Roome the door being made fast." Her persistence eventually

---

[1] Decrees and Orders, 1664 B fol. 570; 1665 B fols. 125, 308. Affidavits, Easter 1665, no. 337; Easter 1666, no. 552.
[2] Collins 28/75.
[3] Decrees and Orders, 1665 B fols. 222, 316. For the £300, see above, p. 266.
[4] Decrees and Orders, 1665 B fols. 308, 561.
[5] Affidavit, Trinity 1666, no. 862; Depositions C24/896/13.

wore him down, but when she demanded her money he flatly refused to pay. And she had no hope of repeating her achievement.
When there was a new decree issued on August 7th, the Master of
the Rolls had to consent to its merely being left at the house instead
of being served on Benlowes in person. It was delivered at Mapledurham by a porter, but Benlowes still held out. Then came a public
proclamation that he would be attached, but that too—so the Sheriff
of Middlesex reported on October 6th—had no effect. According
to the usual procedure, a Commission of Rebellion was next appointed and also had to report failure. Benlowes could not be found.
So on November 5th a serjeant-at-arms was commanded to appre-
hend him and bring him into court that he might be charged with
contempt. Committal to the Fleet prison was to be expected in such
cases, but eleven days later the serjeant reported without his prisoner
and said that Benlowes did "soe hide and abscond himselfe" that
he could not lay hands on him. The order was then given for the
sequestration of Benlowes' personal estate. [1]

Throughout these proceedings Benlowes behaved with greater
firmness than at any other time of his life. He had always been open-
handed, and readily responsive to persuasion; the Schorens had
driven him to be the hardest of skinflints. He sat out all the processes
of the law against him, and although Mrs. Schoren got her money
in the end—in 1667—Benlowes derived great satisfaction from
keeping her out of it for about two years. He could not frustrate
her further, or oppose the sequestration of his estate. For his estate
consisted of £300 owed him by Sir Benjamin Wright, who was
ordered to pay Mrs. Schoren her £157.0s.6d. Benlowes' obduracy
had been expensive: the delay in paying the Chancery award called
for interest of over £17 and Mrs. Schoren had incurred fresh costs
of over £23. All this Benlowes had to pay. So that left about £100
to come to him from Wright, and when Wright had complained
of the expenditure to which he had been put and had been given
leave to recoup himself also, there can have been little left of that.
In fact, Wright never bothered to make a statement of his costs:
it was simpler to keep the whole £100 and do nothing. [2]

Thus vanished in the summer of 1667 the last remnant of the

---

[1] Affidavits, Trinity 1666, nos. 833, 860, 861. Decrees and Orders, 1665 B
fols. 433, 631; 1666 B fols. 25, 53. For the order of procedure, *cf.* Wood,
Institute of the Laws of England, 1720, II, 795-796.

[2] Decrees and Orders, 1666 B fols. 540, 689; Affidavits, Easter 1667, no.
256; Reports and Certificates, vol. 161.

money for which Benlowes had sold his family estates ten years
before. The expense of ten years at law finally overwhelmed him.
Without that, no doubt he would have preserved a precarious in-
dependence. Yet even all this litigation was only the last straw of
the camel's load. Without it he would still have fallen, though he
might not have broken his back. Anthony à Wood has always caused
it to be believed that Benlowes frittered away his large fortune by
his extravagance and his foolish acts of benevolence. [1] But these
are now seen to be only one item in his downfall. It was the Civil
War as much as any other single cause that led to his ruin. Its de-
vastating taxation first put him into money difficulties. On top of
that, his property was sequestrated and had to be expensively redeemed; when his affairs were already seriously embarrassed he
was again "decimated" under the Protectorate. To meet all these
demands of the state he had to have recourse to borrowing, and
this always led to interest and more borrowing to pay it. This in
turn led to sale, entanglements, and lawsuits. Ultimately there was
nothing left at all.

Benlowes' friend Quarles had died in distress in the early years
of the Civil War. Thomas Pestell had been eleven times plundered,
and forced to surrender his benefice. [2] Who shall say that Benlowes
fared better through the war than either of those, or than the fair
gentlemen of England who had left their bones at Edge Hill, where
Benlowes had sorrowfully imagined them whitening the land? [3]

Sooner or later the sale of his estates would have become inevitable. But Benlowes' distresses were undoubtedly aggravated by
his own mismanagement. What principally he saved from the wreckage
was the portion he gave to Philippa. In counting on some kind
return from her, he failed to allow for the possibility of his surviving
her, a failure in which Anthony à Wood shared when he insinuated
against Philippa a charge of ingratitude. [4] This was a grave error
of judgment. Similarly, if Benlowes' adventures in the law had not

---

[1] *Fasti Oxonienses*, II, 358.

[2] See Chapter 12.

[3] *Theophila*, xii, 59.

[4] Wood, *Fasti Oxonienses*, II, 358. Wood has been too uncritically followed
here by later writers — for example, Barrett, *Essex*, II, 31. (This is a very inaccurate account: "In his old age Benlowes deserted Catholicism," and Philippa
"had the ingratitude to desert him upon the score of creed.") For a correction,
see *Life and Times of Anthony Wood*, II, 362. But it does not seem to have been
previously observed that Philippa's husband did make a small provision for
Benlowes in his will. (See below, p. 279).

been of his own seeking, they had resulted from bad handling of his affairs. He allowed both Nathan Wright and Schoren to secure the better bargaining position, apparently without realizing the power he was giving them or ever dreaming they would use it. He allowed Schoren to badger him into establishing an annuity upon him, without insisting on any conditions. While Schoren was as astute as he was plausible in always obtaining a tangible security for every promise or obligation, Benlowes was easily contented with a sort of gentleman's agreement. He let his estates get so entangled that Nathan Wright could dictate his own terms of purchase. In the Wrights, it is true, he met with cunning and exacting customers; in Schoren he had a grasping and unscrupulous servant. But the weakness of his own unworldliness combined with them to get the better of him. Altogether, Benlowes' career had its own conspicuous *hamartia*. The degree by which his ruin exceeded his culpability is the measure of his tragedy.

CHAPTER TWENTY-FOUR

OXFORD

Tragedy has usually been held to involve a descent from great prosperity to dire ill fortune. Such a descent Benlowes certainly accomplished. But his fall had no dramatic rapidity. There was not the sudden plunge into the abyss which may give to catastrophe a certain dread nobility. For all the elegance of his early days at Brent Hall, Benlowes never lived on a heroic scale and his character did not lend itself to the heroic in disaster. There is only pathos—but of that plenty—in the long years of slipping slowly into poverty.

For a time the process was arrested; for one must suppose Benlowes to have enjoyed some gentlemanly comfort after he had found a refuge at Mapledurham. Philippa and Walter Blount received the ageing man in his distress and let him bar the door against the Schorens and the officers of the law. They must at least have connived at his continued evasion of justice. But he cannot have been an easy guest in that household, for the constant worry of his lawsuits had tended to embitter him and he had become set in his ways, not easily adapting himself to changing times. The poetry that he wrote in later life shows small development over twenty years, and the poet was unaware that in English literature and society a new age had dawned. His continued taste for Latin composition showed him not appreciating that Latin was now in England a dying language, and his favourite poets were still his contemporaries of twenty or thirty years before.

The most rigid of his views were, as was to be expected, on matters of religion. Since the time of his becoming a Protestant he had never shown the slightest sympathy for his earlier creed, never relented in his animosity towards the Pope and his adherents. Nor could he "endure any person that seemed to favour the opinions of Arminius or Socinus." [1] Such people were too tolerant of the

---

[1] Wood, *Fasti Oxonienses*, II, 358.

unorthodox to appeal to his rigid mind. These were subjects on which he had always argued hotly, and his wrath did not decrease with age. On the contrary, as his interests narrowed his fanaticism not unnaturally intensified. Anything might release the spring of his passion. In 1658 he could not write his verses on St. Paul's without making the dilapidated building he lamented outshine the Catholic cathedrals of St. Peter and St. Mark. It is easy, therefore, to imagine what his feeling would be in the 1660's when the king whose restoration he had himself joined in applauding showed strong Catholic leanings and allowed papists to flaunt themselves at court.

Religious differences, it is true, had occasioned no break with his family and had not hampered his lordly treatment of Philippa. But that she and her husband were Catholics was harder to ignore when Benlowes came to share their home. On their side they owed him gratitude and respect, but to manifest kindness continually in all the little acts of daily routine is the hardest form that gratitude can take. They might well have exhausted their patience in seeking to accommodate the caprices of a difficult old man. And indeed they did, if Anthony à Wood is here to be believed. Wood made Benlowes' acquaintance shortly after the departure from Mapledurham, and could perhaps speak from personal knowledge when he said that Benlowes' habit of disputing frequently against papists and their opinions "was not at all acceptable to his nephew and niece Blount." [1] The state of affairs in England was likely to exacerbate their religious quarrel. It was already being said that papists were governing the country from Whitehall—and not without some truth, for among the King's advisers Clifford, at least, was an ardent if secret Catholic, whose policy was to culminate in the secret Treaty of Dover (1670), by which Louis XIV promised aid to Charles II in his attempts at the reconversion of the country. Wilder rumours even charged Catholic plotters with responsibility for the Fire of London. [2]

Benlowes attacked the matter with a good deal of fervour. In his attempt to convert his niece to his own religion he wrote a poem in a hundred couplets called *Truth's Touchstone*. He had it printed on one long sheet of paper and dedicated it to Philippa. Even this was not enough. He added to it some *Annotations for the better con-*

[1] *Ibid.*, II, 359.
[2] Trevelyan, *History of England*, pp. 455-456.

firming the several Truths in the said Poem. [1] Far from persuading, this only gave annoyance to Philippa and her husband, and eventually relations between them and Benlowes became so strained that, as Wood puts it, "his room rather than company, was desired by them."

It was only a year or two that they had to endure his company. After that he was rounded up by the law and taken off to prison in Oxford. Exactly how and why this happened cannot be ascertained. If the serjeant-at-arms who had been ordered to arrest him had at last succeeded, the prisoner should have been taken to London and not thrown into the Oxfordshire county gaol. But though his being taken into custody was not, then, the aftermath of his defiance of the Court of Chancery, the coincidence of dates makes it impossible not to suspect a connection between the Chancery judgment in Mrs. Schoren's favour and Benlowes' subsequent imprisonment. [2] What is more likely than that Mrs. Schoren, having got it pronounced by Chancery that Benlowes owed her £157, had somehow

---

[1] Wood, *Fasti Oxonienses*, II, 359. Dr. Andrew Clark suggested a date of about 1658 for *Truth's Touchstone* (*Essex Review*, XVIII, 23), but there is no evidence at all for this, and in the light of Wood's remark about Benlowes giving offence to his niece by anti-Catholic arguments when he lived with her, the poem seems more appropriately dated at that period. Some of Clark's dates —for example, 1664 for Benlowes' imprisonment at Oxford—are undoubtedly wrong.

[2] The relevant dates are these: In August 1666 Mrs. Schoren was attempting to have several writs served on Benlowes, who was then at Mapledurham. On November 16, 1666, the serjeant-at-arms announced that Benlowes could not be found. On June 14, 1668, Anthony à Wood records the lending of a book to Benlowes (*Life and Times*, II, 139), whose acquaintance he had made in Oxford. This was clearly after Benlowes' imprisonment, "which was the matter that first brought him thither" (Wood, *Fasti Oxonienses*, II, 358). Between November 1666 and June 1668, therefore, Benlowes had been arrested, imprisoned, and released. Now, Wright started paying Mrs. Schoren the money awarded her by Chancery in the Easter term of 1667 (Affidavit, Easter 1667, no. 256), though he did not pay in full before July (Decrees and Orders, 1665 B fol. 689). I suggest therefore that Benlowes may have been arrested at the end of 1666 or the beginning of 1667 and released when Mrs. Schoren's debt was paid. This is at least a possible interpretation of what facts there are. Unfortunately, the Oxfordshire records do not include particulars of prisoners for debt before 1691.

One other consideration supports the view that Benlowes' imprisonment was the result of his quarrel with Schoren. One cannot understand why the Blounts did not come to his aid. They had given him shelter in his need, and whatever the friction between them and him, might have been expected to give him help with his debts. But the Schoren debt was a matter in which he would refuse help. It was a debt which his outraged sense of justice would not rather than could not pay. There is little doubt that he would choose to go to prison sooner than pay Mrs. Schoren anything.

succeeded in getting him arrested for the debt? Anthony à Wood's impression was that Benlowes got himself into prison through having "very imprudently entred himself into bonds for the payment of other men's debts"; [1] and though this puts a different colour on events, it is not really inconsistent with the situation which made Benlowes, through his luckless bond guaranteeing Schoren's annuity, responsible for paying what ought to have been paid by Sir Benjamin Wright.

It was Benlowes' committal to prison, whatever may have been its cause, that first brought him to lodge in Oxford. In this the fate that played so heartlessly with Benlowes' life showed another of its little ironies. For fifteen years Oxford had been the cynosure towards which his eyes were drawn in longing. Now when at last he came to dwell there it was not to pursue his ideal life among the treasures of the Bodleian, but to be the inmate of the debtors' prison in Oxford castle.

By this unhappy route Benlowes did, however, attain his goal. Once in Oxford, he stayed there. When he was released from prison there was little incentive to go back to Mapledurham. Philippa died in 1667 and Benlowes was left quite solitary. Walter Blount soon married again, and must have been only too pleased not to have his first wife's uncle back. He survived Philippa only four years, dying in 1671, a year after he had made over the succession of his estates to his seventeen-year-old cousin. [2] Of Benlowes' once large fortune, even the dowry he had bestowed upon Philippa was now gone almost without trace. Almost—for Walter Blount had not forgotten old Edward Benlowes' claim upon him. It was his charity that kept Benlowes going during these years, and on his deathbed in April 1671 he remembered to put Benlowes in his will. It was not exactly a generous settlement when one thinks of Philippa's marriage-portion of £6000 and discovers that, apart from the Mapledurham estates, which went to the cousin, Blount had extensive property in the Hundred of Hoo area of Kent. This was to be sold for the benefit of Blount's second wife and her unborn child. Yet £300 could be spared for his eldest niece, while Benlowes, who was nearly seventy, had a legacy of £20 a year for the rest of his life. [3] It was more than the annuity Benlowes

---

[1] *Fasti Oxonienses*, II, 358.

[2] Burke, *Landed Gentry* (1937), p. 185.

[3] The relevant part of the document, which is preserved at Somerset House, directed Blount's trustees to "pay yearely to my uncle Edmund [*sic*] Bendlowes

himself had bestowed on his servant Schoren, but if you allow for board and lodging, rather less than Schoren had had in the Brent Hall days. Benevolus, who had known what it was to spend a thousand a year, had become a poor relation.

Still, Benlowes' poverty was not abject. He managed to provide for his personal needs, and when he resumed writing poems he could afford to have some of them printed at his own expense.

The closing years of his life had few comforts—strange alteration from the days when he was a Maecenas and a rural magnifico—but he had come to ask for few. Food and shelter, paper and ink—these were his necessities. And in the Bodleian Library was one of the greatest luxuries mind could desire. So it was not with a sense of hardship, but rather with a feeling of ease, of a man entering into a state of repose after a greatly troubled life, that Benlowes on his release from prison found himself some lodgings in what, though a sinister chance had taken him there, was nevertheless the city of his choice.

There he spent his time, as Anthony à Wood has told us, "in the public librar , and conversation with ingenious scholars." [1] For Benlowes was not without friends in the university city. Indeed, one of his friends, the "learned Dr. Barlow" — as Evelyn always called him — was one of its most noted figures. Barlow had the reputation of always offering kindness and encouragement to men of learning. Long ago Benlowes had inscribed a copy of *Theophila* to him in terms of warm affection, and it had added to the attraction of the Bodleian that Barlow was its librarian. He was librarian no longer, but as the Provost of Queen's College and Archdeacon of Oxford he wielded tremendous influence in the university. His patronage was certainly an asset to any needy scholar in and about the city. The danger in being friends with him was that his dogmatic temper was irritable of any opposition and might make great demands upon his adherents. But from Benlowes Barlow was unlikely to get anything but warm approval, for he had a violent bias against Catholics and was capable of identifying the Pope and antichrist. [2]

Esqr dureing his life the annuall sume of twenty pounds of lawfull English money at the two ffeasts of St Michaell the Archangell and the Annunciacõn of the blessed virgin Mary by equall porcõns the first payment thereof to begin at such of the said ffeasts as shall next happen after my death."

[1] *Fasti Oxonienses*, II, 358.

[2] Though Wood charges him with having been "a seeming friend to the papists" until the Popish Plot of 1678 made it expedient to become their "bitter enemy" (*Athenae Oxonienses*, IV, 335).

Barlow on his side might have a special interest in one who had been brought up a Catholic and then become a staunch Protestant.

One of the Oxford men who owed much to Barlow's assistance was Anthony à Wood, whose "sedulous and close studying" in the Bodleian had impressed Barlow at the time of his librarianship. [1] Barlow had been generous in providing him with books and bookish information. [2] Yet later on they fell foul of one another and Wood took revenge in what is perhaps his masterpiece in malice. He decided that his former friend was a time-server (which perhaps was true), "a person of no sincerity, of little religion, and not... that scholar that common fame reports him to be." [3] This, however, was years after Benlowes had taken up his abode in Oxford, [4] and it may have been through Barlow's kind offices that Wood and Benlowes met. Certainly Barlow would be useful in commending Benlowes to the new librarian and introducing him to other regular readers.

There is such scanty reference to Benlowes among Anthony à Wood's voluminous papers that it is difficult to think of these two as ever becoming friends. Wood's autobiographical notes, strewn though they are with names of Oxford notables, suggest that he had few real intimates. Though he contrived to know all the gossip and scandal of the university, Wood had, by the time Benlowes knew him, become very much of a solitary. He spent long hours in the garret study opposite the gate of Merton College into the privacy of which he was extremely reluctant to admit anybody at all. In the afternoons he prowled the bookshops and in the evenings sat in a tavern, where Benlowes is unlikely to have followed him. Intercourse with him was made difficult by his deafness and his peevish temper. All the same it is clear that he and Benlowes must have seen a good bit of one another about the Bodleian, and they were soon on fairly good terms. They sometimes saw one another outside Bodleian hours, and there might now and then be the loan of a book. One Sunday in June 1668, for example, Wood lent Ben-

[1] *Life and Times of Anthony Wood,* I, 189. For Barlow's assisting Wood, see also *ibid.,* II, 109, and the next note.

[2] *Ibid.,* I, 50, 142, 144, 189, 190; II, 175, 312; IV, 144-145, 189.

[3] *Ibid.,* I, 364-365.

[4] Wood, as a member of Merton, was very angry at Barlow's intrigues to get Thomas Clayton appointed to the wardenship of that college in 1661 (*ibid.,* I, 383, 394-395, 471); but he was on good terms with him for years after that and, as the above references will show, received from him many favours in the way of access to his valuable library and other assistance with his research.

lowes a copy of Brian Twyne's *Apologia*. [1] This book contained the earliest attempt at a history of the university, and it was extensively used by Wood in his own work on Oxford's antiquities. Evidently Benlowes—and what could be more natural for a man so academically minded?—was taking an interest in Wood's researches. When in 1670 the University Press was contemplating publishing Wood's book on *The History and Antiquities of the University of Oxford*, Wood's labours were such that "his life, day and night, was in a continual agitation," and it was long since he had been able to spare much time "from his beloved studies of English history, antiquities, heraldry and genealogies." [2] So these topics no doubt formed the staple of discourse when Wood and Benlowes talked together. Occasionally their conversation would be enlivened by a discussion on religious matters, in which Wood's tolerance towards Roman Catholics was always liable to provoke violent outbursts from Benlowes. On one occasion Benlowes was moved to show Wood a manuscript copy of Crakanthorpe's "Popish Falsifications," a work in which a famous Puritan controversialist had confuted the treatise of a "Popish Recusant." [3] Benlowes' respect for Crakanthorpe probably dated from the time of his youth, when Crakanthorpe had been rector of Black Notley, not very far from Benlowes' Essex home. No doubt Crakanthorpe's treatise had enjoyed some circulation in manuscript in that part of the country and Benlowes had come across it. Whether he had treasured a copy of it all these years, or whether he had somehow procured another, it is interesting to find him in his old age still going over its arguments.

Although Wood wrote patronizingly about Benlowes and the improvidence which had brought him to his present "mean condition," he admired and enjoyed his conversation and he easily recognized in it the marks of Benlowes' education. In the decrepit bookworm there was still visible the accomplished gentleman who had travelled on the Continent forty years before. Benlowes' mind now dwelt quite a little on his adventurous days, and allusions to his travels had now a way of getting into his verse. Wood heard something of them, and that incorrigible scandalmonger ferreted out the bits about Benlowes' previous life which formed the basis of the account he subsequently put into his *Fasti Oxonienses*. [4] Yet, prone to jump

---

[1] *Ibid.*, II, 139.
[2] *Ibid.*, II, 187; I, 273.
[3] Wood, *Athenae Oxonienses*, II, 363.
[4] Vol. II, pp. 358-359.

to conclusions, he could not but get some of it wrong. He knew of the unfortunate manner of Benlowes' arrival in Oxford and his former life with the Blounts; but the details of Benlowes' early career he could only conjecture. Benlowes never moaned to him about his troubles at the law nor about what he had suffered through taking the King's side in the Civil War. So Wood could only conclude that Benlowes had squandered his vast fortune on poets, flatterers, and buffoons. Even more significant was Wood's assumption that Benlowes got "tinged with romanism" when he travelled on the Continent. He understood somehow that Benlowes had not always been the zealous Protestant he now saw him to be; but Benlowes had carefully concealed from him the Catholic upbringing which he never willingly avowed.

Anthony à Wood had by his own account a "genuine skill in musick" [1] and certainly a great love of it. This would be another bond between him and Benlowes, who could find in Oxford's colleges and churches plenty of opportunity to indulge what was with him a passion. There was also in the university a great vogue for chamber-music. In the years before the Restoration, when music was severely discountenanced by the Puritans, many distinguished musicians had gathered in Oxford, and weekly musical evenings used to be held at the house of William Ellis in Broad Street and in some of the colleges, in the rooms of such enthusiasts as Narcissus Marsh at Exeter College and Thomas Janes at Magdalen. When King Charles was restored and episcopacy and cathedrals with him, "the masters of musick were restored to their several places that they before had lost" in cathedrals and collegiate choirs; but the traditions remained. [2]

Nor was Oxford barren of another art in which Benlowes took delight — that of engraving, in which the most distinguished performer was a man who reappeared out of Benlowes' London years. This was David Loggan, whose reputation as an engraver had been growing since the time when he had assisted Daniel King in the illustrations of St. Paul's Cathedral that Benlowes himself had sponsored. Loggan had been settled in Oxford for some years, and in 1669 he became official engraver to the university. [3] During the succeeding years he worked steadily on the views of the colleges

---

[1] *Life and Times*, I, 204.
[2] On music at Oxford, see *ibid.*, especially I, 204-206, 212, 257, 273-275.
[3] *Ibid.*, II, 153.

and other buildings which made up his *Oxonia Illustrata*. He was in constant touch with Wood and intended his series of engravings as a companion volume to Wood's *History and Antiquities*. Benlowes was able to watch the progress of both works. [1]

A few friends, then, and a great deal to interest him Benlowes had in Oxford. But on the whole he did not much seek society so long as he had books. The Bodleian, with its staff of four, [2] was by our standards still only a small library; but Benlowes loved the

> *Thirty Thousand* Books *in Order'd Rows,*
> *The* Generall Councel *of* Fames Priests,

including the "*Heap of* Wonders" left by Selden, [3] whose scholarship he had so much esteemed. There were only a handful of regular readers. Benlowes, daily flitting in and out, was soon a familiar figure. He had now become one of those studious recluses who find in study a substitute for experience. Yet it was only late in life that he thus completely turned his back on the world and buried himself in books. Such a prospect had always attracted him; but he was not one to renounce all and enter a monastery in youth. Born to a responsible station in the world, he had had to grapple with its problems and only entered his monastery when the world finally defeated him. Defeated but not disposed of, he was one of those human derelicts—so their fellows tend to look on them— who haunt all the great libraries, creeping past the shelves to esconce themselves in corners piled with books, forgetting all about the life that still calls men to activity outside, hiding their old age between the leaves which drily crackle as their fingers slowly turn them. Yet Benlowes did not see himself as a derelict. He was enjoying an exquisite feast of philosophy and poetry, and believed that those live greatly who banquet with the Muses. [4] His life was therefore one of fulfilment, not frustration, though one may think that his personality had become much shrunken if it could fulfil itself entirely within such narrow limits. He was still the man of devout soul. A life of study, he thought, was one dedicated to God, for the

---

[1] After a great deal of squabbling with the delegates of the University Press, and especially with Fell, who was the book's principal sponsor and who made so many alterations that in the end Wood "would scarce owne it" (*ibid.*, II, 243), Wood's book, by Fell's insistence translated into Latin, came out in 1674. Loggan's followed it from the University Press the next year.

[2] The librarian, his deputy, an assistant, and a janitor (Macray, *Annals of the Bodleian Library*, pp. 124, 133).

[3] "On Oxford, the Muses Paradise," stanzas 6 and 4.

[4] *Oxonii Encomium*, "In Florentissimam Oxonii Academiam."

way to God lay through learning.[1] The professors in the university
had learning—the massive weight of it they bore on their
shoulders made them compared to Atlases—and they thus were
Heaven's envoys. [2] Sometimes Benlowes attended their lectures, [3]
and from them he got a double satisfaction—that of indulging
his own taste and of believing that what he did was good and
right conduct in the eyes of his Maker. He liked to think of the
Sheldonian (the opening of which with a big musical festival in
1669 must have been a great event in Benlowes' Oxford life) as
always resounding to the applause which the eloquence of the
learned merited. [4] Without a trace of cynicism in his make-up,
he persuaded himself that all people (except Catholics) were what
he would have them. Thus the professors pursued an ideal of knowledge and the undergraduates venerated them for it. Yet in 1673,
the very year when Benlowes pictured Oxford in this perfection,
Anthony à Wood complained how only the poor studied hard, while
noblemen's sons got their M.A. for nothing. [5] John Eachard, though
a Cambridge don, had obviously both universities in mind when
he scorned the lack of discrimination with which boys were admitted.
Many who were unfit for serious study were allowed to attempt
it instead of being returned home by the next carrier. [6] Wood,
lamenting how times were changing, described the "great rudeness"
at Trinity and Wadham when the undergraduates "came up into
the hall; scrambled for biskets"; and ran off with bottles and glasses. [7]
Benlowes shut his eyes to such incidents, and to what Wood called
the "discomposures between the scholars and townsmen" when
the mayor of Oxford was elected. One Brasenose man had his
arm broken, another his head; and brawling went on for a week. [8]

[1] *Ibid.*, "Academicis Serenitatem."
[2] *Ibid.*, "Celeberrimae Oxoniensi Academiae," stanza 8.
[3] *Ibid.*, "On Oxford, the Muses Paradise," stanza 6.
[4] *Oxonii Elogia.*
[5] *Life and Times*, II, 276-277.
[6] Eachard, *The Contempt of the Clergy*, in Arber, *An English Garner*, VII, 256.
[7] *Life and Times*, II, 261-262.
[8] *Ibid.*, II, 270-271.

CHAPTER TWENTY-FIVE

LAST POEMS

The life that Benlowes led was by no means one of indulgence —certainly not in winter. Books could not be removed from the library—Barlow had stopped that—and the Bodleian was unheated. Muffled up in winter clothes, Thomas Hyde, the librarian, worked on at cataloguing the books and boasted of not shrinking from the inclemency of the weather. [1] For a regular reader the spiritual elevation was accompanied with some mortification of the flesh.

Yet this was the life that Benlowes desired above everything. If he had to be a prisoner, he said (borrowing a conceit from James I), he would choose to be one of the chained captives of the Bodleian. [2] But of course he felt himself to be, almost for the first time in his life, free; and above all, happy. Happy, of course, in the way of one who believed that "*Happinesse* consists not in the Affluence of Exorbitant Possessions, nor in the Humours of fickle Honour" and who held that nothing was "so great in humane Actions as a pious knowing *Minde*, which disposeth great Things, and may yield such permanent *Monuments*, as bring *Felicity* to Mankinde above the Founders of Empires." [3] After four or five years of continued happiness, his enthusiasm for this way of life moved him to pen a set of eulogies upon it, and he had these printed by Henry Hall, one of the printers to the university, under the title of *Oxonii Encomium*, in 1672. [4] The Latin, no doubt, was frigid; but throughout the composition, though it gave few precise details and instead took refuge in generalized emotion, the poet struck not a note of doubt that here, at last, was man's best life.

Once Benlowes had cultivated a peaceful existence at Brent Hall and in the fields round about it; but his leisured ease had not been able to shut out the noise of battle and the wranglings of men. Now at last, in Oxford, when the war had long been over, he found the

---

[1] He was working on the catalogue during the years 1668-1674 (Macray, *Annals of the Bodleian Library*, pp. 139-140).

[2] *Oxonii Encomium*, "In Florentissimam Oxonii Academiam."

[3] Preface to *Theophila*.

[4] See Madan, *Oxford Books*, no. 2915.

true peace of retirement that he had set as his ideal. Books and manuscripts did not entirely cloud his vision; he loved to walk in Oxford's gardens and meadows and to feast his eyes and rest his mind with the country scenes around. His "encomium," while it praised the Bodleian and its books, never forgot to celebrate the Oxford landscape. It *began* by describing the surrounding hills and the rivers running through flowered pastures.

After the opening address to the university, which praised it as the laboratory of knowledge and—still in the old vein—prophesied disaster for those who preferred foolish pleasures to study, there followed three poems in Latin and one in English which together made up a slender volume of eight leaves. There is in them perhaps less of the startling phrase than in earlier poems; the style is diffuser and ingenuity a little waning. But throughout one meets the unrestrained hyperbole which was familiar in most seventeenth-century panegyrics and which always characterized compliments from Benlowes' pen. A poem of ten stanzas embroidered the idea that at Oxford the monuments of ancient Athens rose up from their ruins to enjoy a new and greater glory. The hundred eyes of Argus could not spy out a superior situation for the arts. So a second poem, on this splendid site, sketched the idyllic landscape where the mind could be safe, free from care, and full of God. How Benlowes' mind remained young and earnest for God's truth, though he was now over seventy years old, was then the theme of a third poem, on the serenity of academic life.

The English poem appended, "On Oxford, the Muses Paradise," again extolled the Oxford landscape, a region of immense fertility, where was

> *All that may invite*
> *A longing* Eye, *or craving* Appetite" (stanza 4).

Some return to his youthful fancy told how "Fœcundity *it self had sign'd the* Lease" (stanza 1), and how "Summer, *what each* Spring *engag'd for, payes*" (stanza 3). The Elysium of the poets was a foolish boast, which Oxford, however, now made good for those who dwelt there. In this Elysium grew the Tree of Knowledge, on which the finest fruit of Beauty hung; and the learned dons were radiant stars whose "refulgent Constellation" lit the way "*To th'*EMPIRE *of* ETERNAL DAY." They had the "*twofold* Excellence" of knowing and acting wisely and in their victory the "*Rude* World," which Benlowes had spent so much of his life despising and denouncing, finally was vanquished.

When Benlowes spoke of his seventy years, he lamented too that he had little skill in verse. For one who had been accustomed to have his poems extravagantly praised by friends and to print their fulsome tribute with no sign of embarrassment, this little touch of humility was surely more than a formal modesty. It breathed a hint that with all his confidence about the excellence of his way of life, he was becoming aware of declining powers. Yet in his old age he had set himself down again to composition, and once more he gave himself the pleasure of putting out a volume of his poems and—tiny offering though it was beside the *Theophila* of twenty years before—presenting it to his friends.

The volume sold at the booksellers' for fourpence. [1] But Benlowes did not seek remuneration for his poems any more than in his wealthier days, and for the most part—as with *Theophila*—copies of *Oxonii Encomium* were privately bestowed. One of them naturally went to Anthony à Wood, and is now among his books in the Bodleian. In all, the Bodleian has three copies—a proud solace, one may fancy, to Benlowes' ghost. Retaining his pride in an elegant format, Benlowes had a few copies done on large paper for some specially honoured recipients. One was given to Corpus Christi College—it would be interesting to know what this college had done to gain this mark of esteem. [2] There was a Latin inscription in which Benlowes praised three former worthies of Corpus Christi —Jewell, Reynolds, and Hooker—and those who through the example of these might be inspired towards things sublime. All later members of the college who might read Benlowes' book were thereby exhorted to emulate their distinguished predecessors. The inscription was in Benlowes' most ornate handwriting with some very well executed and elaborated majuscules, showing that though the author might feel a decline in poetic facility he had lost none of his skill in penmanship. His misfortunes had not frustrated his love of decoration, and this was still the fastidious creator of *Theophila* with all his little pedantries intact. One valued possession fate had left him—his eyesight was still obviously good. Nor did his hand shake unduly as, sitting solitary in his Oxford lodgings, he went laboriously through his presentation copies, marking them

[1] See the Balliol copy for a note to this effect by the college librarian. Incidentally, this is only half a copy, wanting sigs. A1, C1, C2, D1.

[2] The college librarian tells me that there is no record of the presentation, but agrees with me that the inscription addresses the members of the college as a body.

in pen and ink—correcting misprints, making minute alterations in punctuation, inserting accents. If anything, he grew fussier in his old age. With his devotion to even the trivial sorts of beauty, his pen curled out to an exaggerated length the tails of a number of capitals. And since Hall's old, worn type did not come up to his exacting standard, he also touched up a number of defective letters. [1] In the colophon, which gave the date, he added to the year 1672 the precise day and month—July 27th.

Having ventured again into publication, Benlowes resolved on continuing an author. In 1673 he brought out two publications, each consisting of a handful of Latin poems set out on a single sheet. [2] He had little new to say, but he was still in love, as he had been all his life, with the idea of being a poet; he enjoyed fussing with manuscripts and with sheets from the printer's; and though he was quite content to address himself to a small group of Oxford readers, he could not forbear to satisfy his vanity by presenting ornamental sheets of paper to his dwindling circle of friends. If he had had any copies of *Theophila* by him instead of having lost them all, as I think, in the Brent Hall fire, one can imagine his cherishing them to bestow occasionally upon privileged acquaintances. Barlow at Queen's still had his copy, but Anthony à Wood and the rest of Benlowes' newer acquaintance had to be content with the smaller offerings of his old age.

The one new experience his old age offered him—a taste of the delights of Oxford—had already been made use of in *Oxonii Encomium*. But that was a book, and there seemed no reason why he should not use the same material for a broadsheet. He had long ago shown his skill at tying up the same thoughts in a variety of different parcels, and *Oxonii Encomium* itself adapted the passage praising Oxford in *Theophila*. [3] In pretty much the same way as selected passages of *Theophila* were reintroduced to the public in *The Summary of Wisedome* in slightly different dress, so now the Latin portions of *Oxonii Encomium* turned out in a new costume and called themselves *Oxonii*

---

[1] The author's punctilio in these things is seen at its maximum in the Corpus Christi copy and in the Bodleian in Arch. Bodl. C. Infra II. 4. Wood's copy had only a few of the author's improvements. Copies offered for public sale, of course, had none. Madan is in error in supposing there to be pen-and-ink correction in all copies.

[2] Although *Magia Coelestis* is actually on two sheets, these are intended to be fastened together to make one.

[3] *Cf.* the "Peroratio Eucharistica" of *Theophila* and, in *Oxonii Encomium*, "In Florentissimum Bellositum."

Elogia.[1] Benlowes' mastery of Latin synonyms made him always able to knock out any given noun or epithet and put a new one in its place. Or if there was not a synonym, a slight modification of the thought would achieve the trick of elegant variation just as well. That sort of verbal jugglery never deserted him. What had before been referred to as the finely situated theatre could now be called the Sheldonian, and the full-stuffed *(tumens)* library—perhaps it had not been a very successful epithet—could now become stupendous *(stupenda)*. The author was equally clever at manipulating the syntax to accommodate his new phrases to the metre. To illustrate the degree to which Benlowes frequently altered the details of his text while keeping it essentially the same, I quote what is in each case the second stanza of the opening poem. In *Oxonii Encomium* it reads like this:

> *Cernimus antiquæ redivivas cernimus Arces*
> Cecropiæ; *lætis florent fælicius Arvis*
> Aönidum Tempe; *Non unquàm* Oracula Delphis
> *Tàm sacra, quæ dubiis effusa fuere sub umbris,*
> Enthea *quum tumuit vento distenta* Sacerdos;
> Scripta *nec hîc volitant rapidis Ludibria ventis,*
> *Qualia bacchantes eructavere* Sibyllae;
> *Clarior extinctis* ACADEMIA *fulget* Athenis
> *Edita ab* Æterno *emanant* Oracula VERBO.

And in *Oxonii Elogia*:

> Ecce (DEO sit Honos) rediviva *Lycea*, Sepultis
> *Cænobiis*; plusquam *Veterum* celebrantur *Athenæ*
> OXONIDUM *Tempe*; Non unquam *Oracula* Delphis
> Tam rata, quæ dubiis latuere dolosa sub umbris,
> Enthea quùm tumuit *Flatu* distenta *Sacerdos*:
> Scripta nec hîc rapidis volitant Ludibria Ventis,
> Qualia dementes eructavere *Sybillæ*;
> Hîc fixus *Pietatis* Honos, hîc Norma *Salutis*,
>   Edita ab *Æterno* emanant *Oracula* VERBO.

The working out of such airs and variations was of course interspersed with passages of original composition. The Oxford landscape could be sung at length; Benlowes lingered, for instance, over a panegyric on Oxford's more ornamental trees—the cherry-tree and the almond, the ilex and the tamarisk. But on the whole he was too preoccupied with his books or with his spiritual life to notice the external world at all minutely. The plants were mostly those his mind saw as fitting to a seat of learning, and his laurels and his myrtles seem of very literary inspiration. Nevertheless, this pro-

---

[1] Described in Madan, *Oxford Books*, no. 2968.

duction found favour with the committee which controlled printing in the university, chief of whom was Fell, the Dean of Christ Church, who took a kindly interest in the activities of the poor poet. [1] Fell had had much to do with the arrangements for printing provided in the Sheldonian: he had purchased extra presses and brought compositors from France to work them. It must have given Benlowes great delight to have his poems printed in the new Theatre. [2]

The eyes of the old are turned towards the past, and in the rather faded poems of his old age Benlowes made more allusion to the doings of his youth than he had ever done before. In his English poem, "On Oxford, the Muses Paradise," he thought of the sunny flowered valleys he once had seen in Italy (stanza 3) and recalled how he had heard lectures at famous Continental universities (stanza 6). Conservative, timid, unenterprising, he had never wanted to repeat his travels; but so long as they were behind him he valued the experience they gave. What a man has done once he feels excused from exerting himself to attempt again. The mind justifies its present inertia by taking credit for its past activity. Perhaps something in Benlowes' subconscious did not find the ideal life altogether satisfying, and his sense of it as feeble sought compensation in mild hints about what he had once achieved.

With all his veneration for Oxford, Benlowes felt something of an outsider with Wood and all the dons of a university to which he did not, after all, belong. So in the *Oxonii Encomium* he added to the anagram Benevolus, which he still in his poverty was pathetically proud to use, the statement that he had once been a fellow-commoner of St. John's College, Cambridge. When he gave a copy of his *Magia Coelestis* to Wood, the chronicler of Oxford's fame, he could not resist asserting that he had a university too. So he added to the signature "Benevolus" the word "Cantabrigiensis." In the *Oxonii Elogia* he could not celebrate Oxford's men of learning without extolling one of the Cambridge dignitaries of his own college. He told how Dr. John Williams, whom he commended for his intellect and lofty aspiration, rose to be both Lord Keeper of England and Archbishop of York. And him he offered as an example to the young minds of the day. In exhorting them to learning he proposed to them authors whom he had been put to study when an undergraduate himself. In these last years his present meant

---

[1] Perhaps it is not irrelevant that the University Press was short of matter for printing in 1673 (Madan, *Oxford Books*, III, xlii).

[2] For an account of printing in Oxford at this period, see *ibid.*, III, xiii ff.

little to him and his mind was incapable of freeing itself from its own past. In the city which Robert Boyle had recently put in the van of modern science, at the beginning of the era of Newton, a dozen years after the founding of the Royal Society, more than twenty after the death of Descartes, Benlowes could think of nothing better to recommend than Aristotle and Scotus.

His mind ran, too, upon his earlier writings. He not only recast in 1673 his Latin poems of the year before, but he rewrote a Latin poem that he had composed nearly thirty years ago. *Oxonii Elogia* was designed to be a sheet of poems in four columns, but the Oxford group of poems occupied only two and a half of them. On the rest of the sheet was printed a poem called *Echo Veridica*, which may not have been recognized by any of its readers in 1673, but was in fact not very much more than a new version of the *Papa Perstrictus* of 1645. There was, however, good reason why this of all his publications should afford the model for a new poem by Benlowes now. *Papa Perstrictus*, into which had been concentrated, in the gibes of the Echo, all Benlowes' anti-papal venom, came to light again when the Catholic danger to the realm of England seemed greater than it had ever been as far back as Benlowes could remember.

The pro-Catholic policy of Charles II, supported by an unpopular French alliance, had become increasingly detested. It made Charles's opponents sink their differences, so that in March 1673 it seemed clear to Burnet that "all were united against popery." In what Burnet called a memorable Parliamentary session, "the church party shewed a noble zeal for their religion" [1] and succeeded in passing the Test Act. This act was the kind of thing that would arouse great enthusiasm in Benlowes' Oxford circle. It demanded that all who held office under the Crown should take the sacrament according to the rites of the Church of England, and called on them to renounce the doctrine of transubstantiation. The sponsors of this measure were fishing in the mightiest waters of the kingdom, and they got their desired catch when not only Clifford, the Lord Treasurer, but James, the Duke of York and heir to the throne, refused to take the test. James was commanding the British fleet in the middle of a war against the Dutch, but "after the session was over the duke carried all his commissions to the king, and wept as he delivered them up." [2] The good Protestants of England knew not whether

---

[1] *History of My Own Time*, ed. Airy, II, 8, 17.
[2] *Ibid.*, II, 17.

to be horrified at the revelation that the heir to the throne was a
Catholic or relieved at the avowal of what had for some time been
suspected. Horror triumphed when it was known that not only was
James a Catholic himself but that negotiations were afoot for his
marriage to a Catholic princess, the fifteen-year-old Maria d'Este, sister
of the reigning Duke of Modena. Rome was demanding that Maria
"might have a public chapel," but the English attitude to such things
had changed a great deal since James's mother had come from France
with twenty-eight priests, and this was something the negotiators
"would not hearken to." [1] After many difficulties marriage by proxy
took place on September 30th, to be followed by angry protests
in the House of Commons. There were attempts to stop the match
even when the lady was already at Paris on her way to England.
Feeling ran very high and Guy Fawkes' Day, with its memories of
other popish plots, was a sinister occasion that year. The wildest
stories went round. "Should shee arrive tonight," it was said, "shee
would certainly bee martyr'd, for the comon people here and
even those of quallyty in the country beleeve shee is the Pope's eldest
daughter." [2] Even without her the London mob showed its rage
with the Duke of York "for altering his religion and marrying an
Italian lady," and the youths of the city "burnt the Pope in effigie,
after they had made procession with it in great triumph." [3]

Meanwhile, in Oxford, Benlowes had been moved to let off his
own squib. It must have met with approval in university circles,
though it was not easily heard amid the general noise. For Oxford
had been thrown into great consternation, and there was much search-
ing out of Catholics. Richard Reeve, who was said to have "a
stipend from the Catholicks yearly to pervert or reconcile
others," was expelled from the mastership of Magdalen College
School; and Anthony à Wood had new troubles to add to his
deafness and his indigestion when he was rumoured for a
papist himself. [4]

As in the *Papa Perstrictus*, Benlowes in the *Echo Veridica* told
how the Pope one day heard an echo beside the Tiber which argued
with him and threatened him with ruin. The pattern of the poem
was the same, and so were a great many of the echoes. As before,

---

[1] *Ibid.*, II, 20-22.
[2] Letter of Thomas Derham to Sir J. Williamson, *Letters to Sir Joseph
Williamson* (Camden Soc.), ii. 63.
[3] Evelyn, *Diary*, II, 298.
[4] *Life and Times*, II, 275-276.

the Pope was afraid *(vereor)* but the Echo did not spare its accusations *(reor)*. Asking where the greatest vice was to be found, the Pope begged the Echo, "Tell me" *(prome)*; and got for his pains the answer, "In Rome" *(Romae)*. He claimed that Rome was a refuge for the good *(hospitium)* and was told that it was pitch-black *(piceum)*. If anything, this poem was more abusive than the earlier one, which had at least left the Pope praying for salvation. By now Benlowes gave the Catholics no hope of repentance. At the end the Pope asked, "What dost thou advise?" *(quid indè mones?)* and got only the echo, *Daemon es*, "Thou art a devil." This sort of bitter jesting was not to Benlowes' mind unseemly, for he did not think it jesting at all. Even at the moment of inventing his echoes, he did not find it incongruous to accuse the Catholics of joking about religion. They had suffered more from Erasmus' levity than from Luther's rage. Himself in deadly earnest, he heard his echo as a true voice; and he could tell, for had he not once himself been snatched from popish fire? This was almost the only time he referred to his earlier heresy.

His religious faith was simple and unquestioning. He read his Bible as devoutly as he always had, and for the other verses he was working on at this time he had decided on nothing more than a catalogue of some of the wonders the Bible recorded. He had these poems printed by Leonard Lichfield, one of the university printers, under the title of *Magia Coelestis*. [1] First, a general argument gave typical illustrations of what God's marvels were: manna rained from the clouds, rocks melted like wax, a withered twig put forth shoots, rivers turned back in their courses; the blind got back their sight, the dead and buried were restored to life. Then followed the miracles, neatly touched off in Latin elegiacs, beginning with the creation of Adam, and passing by way of Lot's wife, the waters of the Red Sea, and Daniel's den of lions, to Jonah and the whale. There were a hundred couplets in two columns for the Old Testament, and then the poet began again for the New. In the miracles he found plenty of material for the epigrammatic utterance he loved. The Virgin Mary was praised as the mother of her parent; she gave life to Him who first gave life to her. [2] But the epigrams of a pious writer were not the self-indulgence of a wit. All through the seventeenth century

---

[1] In Madan's *Oxford Books*, no. 2967.

[2] These epigrams are no newer than many of the thoughts in Benlowes' Oxford poems. They are variations on the address he made to the Virgin in English in the sixth canto of *Theophila* (see especially stanzas 25, 30).

there had been men who found the most sublime truths in those miracles which suspended the operation of natural laws. The Christian faith itself meant a belief in truths which sprang out of contradictions. Red blood washed as white as snow, and through death one came to life. The discovery of God's mysterious order made one write in paradox; and to do so was to honour God by imitation. In such a poet as Benlowes this "metaphysical" method survived well into the Restoration. By now Hobbes and Newton had exalted reason and natural law; but Benlowes still retained the earlier mind which, instead of looking for a lucid system of things, thrilled to a mystery inexplicable on earth.

Magia Coelestis has been disparaged, [1] and certainly it was not a distinguished work of literature. But it hardly pretended to be that. It was not a book to be read and pondered, but a "table" to be taken in quickly at a glance. It was now beyond Benlowes' resources to provide printing on satin or many ornaments by well-known engravers. But at the foot he had an engraved signature, "Benevolus," in the best writing-master's style. It gave a flourish to what he had designed as a useful decoration to be hung up on the wall, where it would be a perpetual reminder of the facts that every Christian cherished. The four columns of verse provided an index to God's glorious works, with scriptural references in the margin, and the whole was produced by the same spirit of pious industry as had made the harmonies of the gospels at Little Gidding earlier in the century. Benlowes' mind still gave itself with childlike application to a long but simple task in a way that after the Civil War had generally ceased to appeal. Perhaps not many people treasured Benlowes' tabulation of the miracles. There seems, as with the *Oxonii Elogia*, to be only one copy extant. Anthony à Wood, who would keep anything, kept the copy of each that Benlowes gave him, and they are now in the Bodleian. The big world did not bother itself with such things. Latin was out of fashion outside the universities; and even at Oxford it was spoken in hall much less than it used to be. Even so, John Eachard of Cambridge thought the universities had far too much of it and longed for the youths to be given more instruction and practice in their own language. [2] He ridiculed also the quibbling and punning in which Benlowes delighted, and looking for *The Grounds and Occasions of the Contempt of the Clergy and Religion*

---

[1] Madan, *Oxford Books*, III, 279.
[2] *The Contempt of the Clergy*, in Arber's *English Garner*, VII, 262-265.

(in 1670) he found one of the reasons in the habit of loading sermons with absurd metaphors and conceits. [1] The immediate popularity of his pamphlet is a clear indication of a change in taste to which Benlowes never sought to accommodate himself and of which he was probably unaware. Another change was the growing secularity of culture. Yet this hardly applies beyond the literary coteries and that fashionable world which Benlowes had always despised. Any work which would treat a theme of simple, homely piety with genuine imagination had waiting for it throughout the country hosts of God-fearing, if unlettered, men and women. It was not to them, who knew nothing of art's foibles and read no word of Latin, that Benlowes from his cloistered, bookish world would ever speak. But over in Bedfordshire a village tinker and wayside preacher was just getting ready to write the *Pilgrim's Progress*.

[1] *Ibid.*, pp. 265ff., 271ff.

CHAPTER TWENTY-SIX

PAUPER

Books and poetry continued to be Benlowes' one delight until the end of his life, to an extent that caused the university bigwigs to marvel at his simplicity and unworldliness. Poetry stuck to him as closely as his poverty, said Dr. Fell of Christ Church;[1] and it was certain that nothing Benlowes did on his own initiative would ever separate him from either. Gradually he spent up his scanty means, and by 1674 he was in danger of destitution. It does not look as if even the small annuity left him in Walter Blount's will was paid to the end. He was still a dignified if pathetic figure, and even the most notable men in Oxford did not ignore his presence in their midst. On the contrary, their amiable condescension was not untinged with respect. But they thought of him as one remote from the busy world that they inhabited, as "poor Mr. Benlowes," who was "well nigh fourscore."[2] As such he was a worthy object of charity, and it was upon their generosity that he came to depend even for the means of his livelihood. This was the one thing that mitigated for him the cruelty of the world: Benevolus, when he became a pauper, had one or two kind friends himself.

Chief among them were the heads of two Oxford colleges, Thomas Barlow and John Fell, two of the busiest and most important men in the university. With Barlow at Queen's was his great friend, Timothy Halton, who was soon to succeed him as provost; and associated with Fell was Richard Allestree, the erudite professor of divinity, canon of Christ Church and Provost of Eton. Benlowes was fortunate in enjoying the kind regard of Dr. Fell, whose zeal in university matters was only matched by his energy in directing the affairs of anyone he took an interest in. He was just as likely to pay a needy man to give free education to poor children as he was to discipline incompetent university examiners or to tour the chambers

---

[1] Letter of Fell to Sir Joseph Williamson, S.P, Dom., Chas. II, 408/184.
[2] *Ibid.*

of the Christ Church students to test them in their studies. "He was also a person of a most generous spirit, undervalued money, and disburs'd it so freely upon learned, pious and charitable uses, that he left sometimes for himself and his private use little or nothing." His "just and generous designs" were so many that they were "the chief reason of shortning his days." [1]

Between Fell and his distinguished associates the plight of "poor Mr. Benlowes" was more than once discussed. Barlow, in particular, finding Benlowes to be in gravest poverty, busied himself in his affairs and succeeded in discovering that Benlowes had some assets by way of unpaid debts. There were certain bonds which Benlowes held but which he had become too helpless to do anything about. What they were can only be conjectured; but I suppose them to have been the last relics of the days when he was a man of property, perhaps including the bond for £1800 by which Sir Benjamin Wright had guaranteed the final payment for Benlowes' estates. [2] Even after all the litigation in the matter Wright had defaulted of £300, and though most of this had been seized and swallowed up by Chancery, [3] no final settlement had ever been made. Doubtless injustice still rankled, and Benlowes could not help thinking what might be if he had his rights. He must on one occasion have said something of the sort to Barlow.

Whatever the bonds in question were, Barlow saw them and decided to take action. He had very powerful friends and was not the man to fail for want of pulling strings. He thought at once of Sir Joseph Williamson, who had once been a fellow of the college of which Barlow was provost, but who had now recently (in 1674) bought for £6000 the exalted office of Secretary of State. He was a man of considerable, if capricious, benevolence, and had little scruple in using his office to the advantage of his friends, of whom Queen's College men in particular expected to benefit by his appointment. It did seem that if so important an ear could be whispered into, Williamson might be able to do something in the little matter of Benlowes' bonds.

At Queen's College Barlow broached the matter to Halton, who was also a great friend of Williamson. Halton was going up to London and he interviewed Williamson while he was there. Williamson may already have known Benlowes and the panegyrics Benlowes

[1] Wood, *Athenae Oxonienses*, IV, 196-197.
[2] Chancery Proceedings, Bridges 44/89; Reports and Certificates, vol. 146.
[3] See above, p. 273.

had written on Oxford, for he had always been in close touch with
Oxford affairs and had been one of the committee controlling the
University Press when it had printed some of Benlowes' poems.
He behaved with all the graciousness expected, and Halton
was able, when he went back to Oxford, to tell Barlow "how
willingly" his suggestion had been "imbrac'd." One wonders whether
Benlowes was in a flutter to find these great ones moving in his
behalf. Barlow himself was, and on February 28, 1675, he wrote
Williamson a special note of thanks [1] for the way in which he "vnder-
tooke the trouble." He added a hope that through Williamson's
"prudence and authority" the money, which was "certainely and
justly due to the poore Gentleman," would be recovered. Benlowes
would never get the money otherwise, so it would be "an act of
great charity" to him. Queen's College was also going to benefit
—how Barlow did not say; but since he obviously referred to something more than the spiritual comfort the fellows would have in
knowing that Benlowes would not starve, presumably Benlowes
was to express his gratitude by leaving some of the money to the
college when he died. Is that, then, why Barlow bestirred himself
so anxiously?

There is no record of what steps Williamson took, but they did
not get anywhere. Barlow became Bishop of Lincoln and Halton
succeeded him as Archdeacon of Oxford. In January 1676 Fell was
made Bishop of Oxford. But Benlowes only got poorer. Yet Fell,
to whom he confessed his poverty, nevertheless found him "as
little disturbd as if he were master of the Indies." [2] It is not every
man who has both opportunity and character to practise what he
preaches. But Benlowes was able to do it better than the friends of
his wealth could have surmised. He now in his life showed that
contempt of worldly possessions which he had always proclaimed
in his verse. Bred in luxury, accustomed to ease and extravagance,
he achieved his greatest content when he had nothing. He was
happy as a bird; but it was a bird that had got used to its cage. He
might go on singing; but it was a quarter of a century since he had
attempted any ambitious flights. The ecstasy of *Theophila* was long
past.

Though Williamson had been able to effect nothing about the
bonds, he did not forget Benlowes' need. On one occasion he sent

[1] S.P., Dom., Chas. II, 368/134.
[2] Fell to Williamson, S.P., Dom., Chas. II, 408/184.

five pounds to Fell to be given to the poor poet, and it was just when Benlowes had only four shillings left that this money providentially arrived. Fell took the money to him and Benlowes "was exceedingly surpriz'd at so unexpected a releif," as Fell reported when he wrote to give Williamson "an account of the disposal of [his] Charity" to "the poor man" whom he took "to be the most helpless creature in the world." Fell sent his letter by Allestree, who was going up to London, and Benlowes would have sent "his thankfull acknowledgments" by the same hand if Allestree had not set out earlier than was expected. He was therefore waiting for the next opportunity, and Fell expected that Williamson would then receive "an heroical Epistle."

Benlowes was beyond heroics, and no epistle was written; but he did not neglect a becoming acknowledgement. In May 1676 he sent his thanks in a Latin couplet which, with charming simplicity, reported receipt of the money and prayed that the donor might be eternally happy. [1] Benlowes still loved a gesture, and the prettiness of this one was completed by the characteristic flourishes of a handwriting which, arranging the couplet like an ornament on the page, introduced into the State Papers an unwonted decoration.

These distinguished friends of Benlowes' exercised their minds with other projects for his welfare, and Fell had to sound Benlowes about them. He quickly found that "tho one in his condition ought not to be a chuser," yet the poor man had "no kindness for London, and had rather hazard the starving in the Country, then live there." [2] Benlowes had found a haven in Oxford and showed himself no more pliable than of old in refusing at all costs to return to the city of his troubles. So Fell had to report that "it would be a very acceptable as well as necessary provision for him to be one of the poor knights of Windsor."

This famous charitable institution had been established by Edward III and it was of course in the gift of the sovereign, so that a friend like Williamson at court was likely to prove a great blessing. Evidently Williamson proposed to use his influence to put Benlowes in when a vacancy occurred. But that might easily not be soon, since there was provision for only eighteen "poor knights," who dwelt, as their successors still dwell,

[1] S.P., Dom., Chas. II, 381/203: "Quinq[ue] Libras à Te, Vir Præclariss^me, cæpi:
Ex animo, fœlix sis sine Fine, precor."
[2] Fell to Williamson, S.P., Dom., Chas. II, 408/184.

in an alms-house built for them in the time of Mary Tudor in the precincts of Windsor Castle opposite St. George's Chapel. Once, when his own house got burnt down, Benlowes had found no dwelling in the country fit for one of his quality. But that was twenty years ago; and this one-time splendid gentleman was now ready to don the red gown and blue mantle of a soldier of charity. Edward III had founded this charity "out of the great Regard he had to military Honour" and the poor knights had to be, by a decree of Elizabeth, "Gentlemen...that have spent their Time in the Wars, or other Service of the Realm." [1] Benlowes had the necessary status and had reason to be glad of the little soldiering experience that made him eligible. But he had loathed war passionately, and it was a crowning irony that when this man of almost proverbial benevolence was in need of alms himself, what was proposed for him was a military charity. The only other condition was extreme poverty. [2] Any "knight" who acquired property of as much as twenty pounds had to resign. [3] Nothing could make it clearer that Williamson had given up hope in the business of the bonds.

A "poor knight" could not want. His annual allowance, as fixed by James I, was £36.10s. So Benlowes looked like ending his days, after all, in ease; but it was a pathetic thought that the last survivor of a family who had regularly been prayed for by their almsfolk in Great Bardfield church should come to earn his own charitable allowance by the regulation daily prayers for his benefactor. Nashe's gibe at Gabriel Harvey would have done for Benlowes' epitaph: "A smudge peice of a handsome fellow it hath beene in his dayes, but now he is olde and past his best, and fit for nothing but to be ...a Knight of *Windsor*." [4]

Benlowes was eligible for the place, his friends sought it for him, and he had no pride left to keep him from it. But even this last solace he was not to enjoy. Before a vacancy occurred winter came on.

---

[1] Particulars of the Knights of Windsor are taken from Ashmole, *The History of the most Noble Order of the Garter* (I quote from the 1715 ed., pp. 95ff.), which see for a full account.

[2] By order of the founder the Knights of Windsor were to be "real Objects of Charity....*viz.* poor Knights, infirm in Body, indigent and decay'd, or... such as thro' adverse Turns of Fortune were reduced to that Extremity that they had not wherewithal to sustain themselves."

[3] Which seems to show that Benlowes was not getting the twenty pounds a year that Walter Blount had bequeathed him.

[4] *Have with You to Saffron-Walden*, Nashe's *Works*, ed. McKerrow, III, 94.

And it was not the sort of winter that Benlowes had pretended when he had told in his poem "On Oxford, the Muses Paradise" how there winter was like spring. [1] On the contrary, Anthony à Wood found it sensationally severe. That winter many university men died of fever. In November there was frost for almost three weeks. A week's relaxation, and then on December 2nd another three-week spell began. The 8th, a Friday, was a bitterly cold day, and on the Saturday it snowed. [2] Over at Deptford, just out of London, John Evelyn was kept that Sunday from going to church because the snow was so deep. [3] The only entries that he made in his diary for over a month were to report the snow. He was able to go to London on the 12th, but there was more snow than he remembered ever having seen. In Oxford, that day and the two following were —in Wood's words—"bitter cold, rimy, and misty." On the Sunday it snowed again. Again Evelyn had to stay away from church. And in this appalling weather Benlowes was in "want of conveniences fit for old age as clothes, fewell, and warme things to refresh his body." He became ill and was taken to the house of an apothecary, Nicholas Maund, and there, on Monday the 18th, about eight o'clock at night, he died. [4] In this extraordinary winter the rivers were all frozen up. Carts and coaches could cross the Thames at London on the ice. Snow-huts were built on the river and brandy sold from them. Wood lamented the abundance of fish and fowl that perished through the frost. [5] Benlowes, as helpless as they, had preceded them.

His burial, however, was more august than theirs. He found a grave, if not a house, fit for his quality. The dons suddenly realized how worthy he was to be respected and whipped up a collection for his funeral. His friends at Queen's College were agitated, and John Mills, one of the fellows, gave forty shillings. He was buried on December 21st [6] in Oxford at St. Mary's Church, and, according to the growing custom, inside the building—"under the north wall of the body, his head neare to the entrance of the vestry where the Drs. put on their robes." Some of the doctors of the university followed his corpse and there was a fair gathering of Masters

[1] Line 13.
[2] *Life and Times of Anthony Wood*, II, 359, 363.
[3] *Diary*, II, 323.
[4] *Life and Times of Anthony Wood*, II, 360-362.
[5] *Ibid.*, II, 363.
[6] Church Register of St. Mary the Virgin, Oxford.

of Arts and others to do honour to one who had "died poore, for want of fire to keep him warme and hot things."

The Benlowes arms made their last appearance on his hearse.[1]

---

[1] *Life and Times of Anthony Wood*, II, 360-361.

APPENDICES

AND

BIBLIOGRAPHY

APPENDIX I

FROM BENLOWES' NOTEBOOK
(See Chapter 11)

The following lines and phrases occur on the verso of the first leaf of an exercise-book of Benlowes which is now in the Bodleian. It is MS. Rawlinson D.278. The page in question is divided in two by a vertical line, and the writing occupies very little more than the top half of the first column, the rest of the page being blank. All the passages, except those here marked with an asterisk, are crossed out by a series of oblique or vertical strokes. What is illegible in the manuscript I indicate by square brackets.

*blus[t]ring [1]. poure flux of Teares amain
    The poysnous Dragons Thou dost slaue
                                raue
And makst Hyrcani[ā] [2] hungry Tigers cease to

---

*The sun beam prints yᵉ houre

---

come let us glut oʳselves wᵗʰ rampant wine
    & let sweet oyntmᵗˢ on us shine
             Heads   pine
& let us crown oʳselves wᵗʰ Rosebuds ere they

---

enrobed in yᵉ []es[] of []am[] [3]

They pillowe stone to vice & virtue quell
    Turn Moses into machivel [4]   Hell
Devious to peace & Truth they lead to war &

To peace run counter, in yᵉ braud high way to

[1] t invisible beneath a blot.

[2] The last letter, presumably a, invisible beneath a blot.

[3] This line is so crossed out as to be hardly legible. There is one letter before the es and one after it, one letter before the am and one or two after it. I think the letter which precedes am and of which the tail is visible is S, and the word may be Samit.

[4] machivel. The i is written over another letter, possibly a.

In amplitude penuriously scant
The more they haue yᵉ more they want

---

couldst monarchize yᵉ Globe [1]

---

*In tyme past time this Being may not be at all

---

not Aristotles eye   unbounded
yᵗ Ipse of Philosophy   learning
who into Natures Mysteries did pry   had

Him need compels not, nor disasters sad
Disturb nor joyfull things make glad
Oblivion takes not nor to Him cā Mem'ry adde

---

[1] The *G* of *Globe* is written over another letter, I think a *W*, as though the original intention was to write *World*.

APPENDIX II

BENLOWES' BORROWINGS FROM MILTON

I can hardly hope to have detected every passage in which Benlowes imitated Milton, but the following list presents the evidence I have collected to show how very extensive Milton's influence on him was. It is reprinted, by kind permission of the editors, from my article "Benlowes and Milton" in the *Modern Language Review*, vol. XLVIII (April 1948). In each instance the Milton passage, as the original, is placed first. References to Milton's poems are always to the line. All the Benlowes passages are taken from *Theophila*, which is referred to by canto and stanza.

ON THE MORNING OF CHRISTS NATIVITY

1. M.   he wont at Heav'ns high Councel-Table,
To sit the midst of Trinal Unity   (10-11)

    B.   THOU, *sitting in the Midst of* TRINAL-UNITY
At Heav'ns High Councel-Table   (vii, 64-65)

2. M.   Ring out ye Crystall sphears   (125)

    B.   *Chime out, ye* Crystal Sphears   (v, 53)

3. M.   Time will run back, and fetch the age of gold   (135)

    B.   listning *Time* runs back to fetch the Age
Of *Gold*   (xiii, 95)

4. M.   the tissued clouds   (146)

    B.   we the blew-ey'd *Skie* in Tissue-Vest behold   (xiii, 1)

5. M.   The wakefull trump of doom   (156)

    B.   His wakefull *Trump* of Doom   (vi, 79)

6. M.   The dreadfull Judge   (164)

    B.   th' dreadfull JUDGE   (vi, 80)

7. M.   Trampling the unshowr'd Grasse with lowings loud   (215)

    B.   wide-horn'd Oxen, trampling Grass with Lowings loud (xiii, 9)

8. M.   Bright-harnest Angels   (244)

    B.   Bright-harnessed INTELLIGENCIES   (vi, 72)

Psalm 136

9. M.   caus'd the Golden-tressed Sun,
                 All the day long his cours to run
                            · · · · ·

                 The horned Moon to shine by night   (29-33)

    B.   Whose *Cone* doth run
                 'Bove th'horned *Moon*, beneath the golden-tressed *Sun* [1]

                                                                (iii, 39)

On Time

10. M.   thy [*i.e.* Time's] greedy self   (10)
    B.   Times greedy Self   (xi, 91)

11. M.   Then long Eternity shall greet our bliss
                 With an individual kiss   (11-12)

    B.   Passe on to Blisse,
                 That with an individual *Kisse*
                 Greets Thee for ever!   (v, 69)

L'Allegro

12. M.   Where the nibling flocks do stray   (72)
    B. While nibling *Ewes* do bleat, & frisking *Lambs* do stray
                                                                (xiii, 5)

13. M.   The up-land Hamlets will invite,
                 When the merry Bells ring round,
                            · · · · ·

                 And young and old com forth to play
                 On a Sunshine Holyday   (92-93, 97-98)

    B. And all the merry Hamlet Bells chime *Holy Day*   (xiii, 8)

14. M.   The hidden soul of harmony   (144)
    B.   most harmonious *Musicks* mystick Soul   (iii, 52)
                 [folio, "mosts"]

15.   [The above examples are not the extent of Benlowes'
                 debt to *L'Allegro*. That he had Milton in mind during his tour
                 of the rural landscape in Canto xiii is clear from the country
                 figures that he introduces—the mower (stanza 2), the shepherds
                 (5), and then in the evening-scene the ploughman and the milk-
                 maid (82. *Cf. L'Allegro*, lines 63-67). An interesting reminis-
                 cence occurs in the description of the ploughmen ceasing work.
                 Elegant variation demanded an alternative name for them and
                 Benlowes, instead of something ordinary like "labourers,"

---

[1] Both of these epithets came out of Sylvester, who in the *Devine Weekes*,
I, 4, referred to the moon as the "Horned Queene" and the sun as having "golden
tresses" (1605, pp. 130, 135; 1641, pp. 35, 36). But "golden-tressed" as an epithet
for Phoebus goes back to Chaucer (*Troilus and Criseyde*, book v, line 8), and
was already a stock adjective in Elizabethan times.

rather surprisingly chose *"Whislers."* The one thing *L'Allegro* tells us about the ploughman is that he "whistles."][1]

IL PENSEROSO

16.	M.	rocking Winds	(126)
	B.	rocking Windes	(xii, 54)
17.	M.	bring all Heav'n before mine eyes	(166)
	B.	*Bring down all* HEAV'N *before the Eyes o'th'* HEAV'NLY LOVER	
			(vi, 1)

ARCADES

18.	M.	shallow-searching *Fame*	(41)
	B.	[see below, no. 20]	

LYCIDAS

19.	M.	What time the Gray-fly winds her sultry horn	(28)
	B.	Soon as the Sultrie *Month* has mellow'd Corn,	
		Gnats shake their Spears, and winde their Horn	(xiii, 14)
20.	M.	*Fame* is no plant that grows on mortal soil	(78)
		[with which take also no. 18 above: "shallow-searching *Fame*".]	
	B.	*Fames* Plant takes Root from *Vertue*, grows thereby;	
		Pure *Souls*, though Fortune-trod, stand high,	
		When mundane shallow-searching *Breath* It self shall die	
			(xiii, 107)
21.	M.	to scramble at the shearers feast	(117)
	B.	Scramblers at the Shearing Feasts	(xii, 12)

COMUS

22.	M.	Swift as the Sparkle of a glancing Star,	
		I shoot from Heav'n	(80-81)
	B.	*I did attain,*	
		Swift as a glancing Meteor *to th'* Aerial Plain.	(v, 42)

---

[1] The imitation of *L'Allegro* in the pastoral scene did not prevent Benlowes from echoing several other poems at the same time. The description of the mower comes actually from Tomkis' *Lingua*. (see above, p. 121) As we have seen above, the sky's "Tissue-Vest" (stanza 1) and the oxen "trampling Grass with Lowings loud" (9) are from the Nativity ode. The gnats "winde their Horn" (14) like the grayfly in *Lycidas*. The ox goes "in loose Trace home" (83) as in *Comus*, which also suggested "the folded *Flocks*." The sand seemed like gold and the pebbles like gems (3) because that was how Sylvester had already seen them (*Devine Weekes*, II, 1, part 1—1605, p. 289; 1641, p. 85). The description of Winter (54) is imitated from both Sylvester and William Browne. The less pastoral parts of the canto have also echoes of Donne and Randolph. (See above, pp. 113-116).

23. M. The Sounds, and Seas with all their finny drove (115)

   B.   from Air, Earth, Seas,
     The wing'd, hoof'd, finnie *Droves* [1]   (x, 10)

24. M.   O theevish Night
     Why shouldst thou, but for som fellonious end,
     In thy dark lantern thus close up the Stars (195-197)

   B.   theevish *Night* had *stole*, and *clos'd* up quite,
     In her dark *Lantern*, starrie *Light*   (v, 27)

25. M.   a strong siding champion Conscience   (212)

   B.   *Conscience*, that strong Champion   (xii, 29)

26. M.   the labour'd Oxe
     In his loose traces from the furrow came (291-292)

   B.   the tir'd *Ox* sent
     In loose Trace home   (xiii, 83)

27. M. Unmuffle ye faint stars, and thou fair Moon
         . . . . .
     Stoop thy pale visage through an amber cloud,
     And disinherit *Chaos*
         . . . . .
     Or if your influence be quite damm'd up
     With black usurping mists   (331-337)

   B. Unmuffle, ye dim Clouds, and disinherit
     From black usurping Mysts his Spirit (xi, 72)

28. M. The folded flocks pen'd in their watled cotes (344)

   B.   the folded *Flocks* are pent
     In hurdled Grates   (xiii, 83)

29. M.   or village cock
     Count the night watches to his feathery Dames (346-347)

   B. Before the *Cock*, Lights Herald, *Day-break* sings
     To's Feathr'ie *Dames*   (viii, 76)

30. M. 'gainst the rugged bark of som broad Elm
     Leans her unpillow'd head   (354-355)

   B.   In guiltlesse Shades, by full-hair'd Trees,
     Leaning unpillow'd Heads   (xii, 72)

31. M.   Wisdoms self
         . . . . .
        lets grow her wings
     That in the various bussle of resort
     Were all to ruffl'd   (375-380)

   B.   *Fancie*, keep up thy *Wings*,
     (Ruffled in *Bussle* of low Things   (iii, 18)

---

[1] But "finny drove" goes back to Spenser (*Faerie Queene*, book III, canto viii, stanza 29).

32.	M.	the unsun'd heaps Of Misers treasure	(398-399)
	B.	thy [*i.e.* Avaro's] unsunn'd *Hord*	(x, 76)
33.	M.	Tell her of things that no gross ear can hear	[(458)
	B.	Such no gross *Ear* can hear	(vi, 66)
34.	M.	night-founder'd	(483)
	B.	*Night-founder'd*	(ii, 99)
35.	M.	this cordial Julep here That flames, and dances in his crystal bounds	(672-673)
	B.	Sparkling 'bove *Nectar* which i'th' *Crystal* skips	(ix, 53)
36.	M.	She hutch't th'all-worship ore	(719)
	B.	Now *chest* th'all worshipt *Ore* with rev'rend Awe	(x, 81)
37.	M.	vermeil-tinctur'd lip	(752)
	B.	*Vermeil-tinctur'd* CHEEK	(i, 11)
38.	M.	*The loose train of thy amber-dropping hair*	(863)
	B.	Whose Amber-curling *Tresses* were unbound	(v, 37)
39.	M.	diamond rocks	(881)
	B.	Diamond *Rocks*	(vii, 22)
40.	M.	*By the rushy-fringed bank*	(890)
	B.	By rushy-fringed Banks	(xii, 68)

In the above list I have not included such parallel passages as make use of stock seventeenth-century images, when no direct borrowing is likely—as, for example, the comparison involving the *"duskie atoms in the* Suns *embrightning* Ray" (*Theophila*, v, 95). This, it is true, is common to *Theophila* and *Il Penseroso* (lines 7-8: "As thick and numberless/As the gay motes that people the Sun Beams"); but, like so many other things in seventeenth-century poetry, it had already occurred in Sylvester and had been popularised in other places, inc'uding Browne's *Britannia's Pastorals* (book II, 1, 853-855) and Randolph's *A Pastorall Courtship* (lines 118-119).

List of copies of the 1652 folio of *Theophila*
used as evidence for Appendices III and IV

(Of the copies listed below I have myself examined all except the three American copies. For information of those I am indebted to the librarians of the Huntington Library and the Harvard College Library. I have not attempted anything like a complete census of copies. While *Theophila*, 1652, is a recognized collector's piece, it is not in the strictest sense a rare book, and my primary aim in studying Benlowes has not been bibliographical. But I think I may claim to have examined enough specimens for my observations to be worth recording and to justify certain tentative conclusions.)

The copies marked with an asterisk are those which have pen-and-ink corrections.

*A	All Souls' College, Oxford
*B	Blount (Jesus College, Oxford)
*C1	Cambridge University Library, Sandars copy (SSS.28.2)
C2	Cambridge University Library, Syn. 4.65.1
*D	Douce (Bodleian Library)
Du	Dulwich College
*Dy	Dyce Collection (Victoria and Albert Museum)
G	Grenville (British Museum)
*H	Harvard, Widener Library
H2	Harvard, copy presented by Rev. J. Barnard, *c*. 1764
Hn	Huntington Library (Hoe copy)
*J	St. John's College, Cambridge
Je	Harold Jenkins
M	British Museum, C.30.m.8
*P	Petyt Library, Skipton
*Q1	Queen's College, Oxford, 88.I.13 (Barlow)
*Q2	Queen's College, Oxford, 507.F.20
*S	Selden (Bodleian Library)
T	Trinity College, Dublin
U	University College, London
W	Col. C. H. Wilkinson
Wo	Worcester College, Oxford

There are also copies of *Theophila* at Williams College (the Chapin Library), Williamstown; Columbia University; the Newberry Library, Chicago; Wellesley College; and Yale. I am informed by the respective librarians—to all of whom I offer my grateful thanks for that kindness and courtesy which American libraries invariably show to the inquirer—that none of these copies has any pen-and-ink corrections. And the only one that seems to be of any particular interest is the first, which is a presentation copy (recipient unknown) in the original binding, with Benlowes' arms.

PEN-AND-INK CORRECTIONS IN *THEOPHILA*

The existence of pen-and-ink corrections in some copies of *Theophila* and their importance for an editor of the text was pointed out by Geoffrey and Arthur Tillotson in an article in the *Library* in June 1933. The number of corrections, however, is considerably greater than has been previously observed, as is also the number of copies in which corrections occur. Of the nineteen copies which I have myself examined (see list on opposite page), ten have authoritative corrections in pen and ink. For particulars of similar corrections in H I am indebted to the Harvard librarian. Q2 is so very imperfect that it can offer no kind of evidence more than sporadically.

Apart from corrections of erroneous pagination, which I have not thought worth recording, the following is a complete list of the pen-and-ink corrections that I have observed. In each case the reading of the printed text (1652) is given first, followed by the corrected reading.

Page Sig.	Line	Correction	Copies
A2	1	*Shools* *Schools*	S Q1 C1 B J A Dy H P
	19	her Her	J A Dy
A2ᵛ	10	*Money,* *Money;*	J A Dy
¶ 2	10	intemperate intemperate,	S Q1 C1 B J A Dy H P
¶¶¶ 2	16	prudenr prudent	S Q1 C1 H
B2ᵛ	4	of on through	A J Dy

EDWARD BENLOWES

Page Sig.	Line	Correction	Copies
B3ᵛ	20	*Ecacsties* [1]	
		Ecstasies	J A Dy
B4ᵛ	st. 5, line 3	Which	
		Which,	J A Dy
B6ᵛ	21	frame	
		frame,	J A Dy
	22	*Cormorant*	
		Cormŏrant	J A Dy
(c)1ᵛ	17	Widwife	
		Midwife	S Q1 C1 B J A Dy H D P
(c)2ᵛ	7	Twas	
		'Twas	J A Dy
	8	Which	
		Which,	J A Dy
	9	Twas	
		'Twas	J A Dy
(d)	22	Course	
		Course,	J A Dy
C1ᵛ	17	EXCELLENCE.	
		EXCELLENCE:	J Dy
		EXCELLENCE;	A
C3ᵛ	5	Chymistrie,	
		Chymistrie	J A Dy
	8	sprinkle it on th'	
		sprinkle 't on the	C1 B J A Dy H D P
		sprinkle'it on the	S Q1
C4ᵛ	4	Poetarum	
		Pöetarum	J A Dy
	13	PERGE	
		PERGE,	J A Dy
	15	*CEOLI* [2]	
		COELI	S C1 B J A Dy H D P
	16	*Et quæ densa tegit Nubes*	
		Et, quæ densa tegit Nubes,	J A
C6ᵛ	15	*profit*	
		profit,	J A Dy
	22	She thus cuts	
		thus She cuts	J A
		She cuts thus	Dy

[1] Correctly printed *(Ecstacies)* in some copies.
[2] Correctly printed in some copies, including Q1.

Page	Stanza and Line	Correction	Copies

Canto i

Page	Stanza and Line	Correction	Copies
1	1, iii	STRIANS STRAINS	S Q1 C1 B J A Dy H D P
2	8, iii	*Sols* *Sol's*	H D P
3	19, iii	*yore* *yore.*	J A Dy
4	21, i	*Catches* *Catches,*	J A Dy
5	30, iii	*Man* 'twixt them *Both* *Man,* 'twixt them *Both,*	J A Dy Q2
	32, i	One thus, One, thus; One, thus,	J A Dy Q2
	32, iii	*Sin* *Sin,*	J A Dy
6	36, iii	*Few* like the *blessed Thief* *Few,* like the *blessed Thief,*	J A Dy
	37, iii	*Antidate* *Antedate*	Q2
	39, iii	*Bethesda* *Bethsaida*	Q1 C1 B H D P Q2
7	47, i	Thunder Thunder,	J A Dy H D P
	50, iii	own black	Q2
8	54, i	There There,	J A Dy
	55, i	There There,	J A Dy
	56, i	There There,	A
	59, iii	nam'd nam'd.	J A Dy H P
10	70, iii	And Thou	Dy
	71, i	Thee Thee,	J A Dy
	72, i	*Arts* *Arts,*	J A Dy
	74, iii	*Presidents* *Precedents*	H D P

Page	Stanza and Line	Correction	Copies	
11	80, iii	*Elf.* *Elf,* *Elf;*]	J A Dy	H D P
12	84, i	That display, That, display;	J A Dy	
	Line			
15	11	CRIST CHRIST	S Q1 C1	J A Dy H D P
16	16	*She* *She,*	J A Dy	
	19	that that,	J A Dy	
	26	him Him	J A Dy	
	28	him Him	J A Dy	
	29	And by *all these* And, by *all these,*	J A Dy	
17	8	*Impotencie:* *Impotencie!*	J A Dy	
	23	therefore therefore,	J A Dy	
	25	*Wine:* *Wine!*	J A Dy	
	26	*Judgements:* *Judgements!*	J A Dy	
18	12	*Sacriledge* *Sacriledge,*	J A Dy	
20	20	let me let me,	J A Dy	
21	19	*Europ* *Europe*		D P
22	2	Wнoм Wнoм,	J A Dy	
	4	UNITIE UNITIE,	J A Dy	

Canto ii

23	Argument, line 7	*CHISTS* *CHRISTS*		

Q2

Page	Stanza and Line	Correction	Copie	
23	1, i	POWER, / POWER, / POWER!	J A Dy	Q2
	2, i	Blisse, / Blisse!	J A Dy	
24	7, i	Who / Who,	J A Dy	
	10, ii	*Beasts* / *Beasts,*	J A Dy	
	10, iii	*Fish* / *Fish,*	J A Dy	
25	13, ii	Earth, / Earth;	J A Dy	
27	29, iii	*Core.* / *Core;*	J A Dy	
30	59, iii	Snuffs / Snuffs,	J A Dy H D P	
31	66, i	Judgement / Judgement,	C1 J A Dy H D P Q2	
32	73, iii	Stange / Strange	B J A Dy H D P Q2	
	75, ii	till'd / till'd,	C1 J A Dy D P	

Canto iii

Page	Stanza and Line	Correction	Copie
39	16, i	*Ascendant*'s: How / *Ascendant*' is	D P
42	39, iii	*Sun.* / *Sun;*	H D P
44	52, iii	mosts / most	S Q1 C1 B J A Dy H D P Q2
	53, i	*tast.* / *tast*	Q2
	56, i	*traceless;* / *traceless*	S Q1 C1 B A H D P Q2
	59, iii	they / the	S Q1 C1 B J A Dy H D P Q2
45	60, i	[Wrong indentation corrected by two horizontal strokes] / ZEALS burning Feaver, / (ZEALS burning Feaver)	B H D P / Dy
	64, i	Yes. / Yes;	D P

Page	Stanza and Line	Correction	Copies
		Canto iv	
52	4, iii	*pas'd*	
		pass'd	H D¹ Q2
53	16, ii	rejoyce,	
		rejoyce	Q2
54	23, iii	Condescend	
		Condescent	J A Dy H
58	50, iii	SPIRITS	
		SPIRITS	H D P
	52, iii	Up	
		Up,	Q2
61	75, i	Soul,	
		Soul	Q2
66	engraving, line 5	THEOPHLA	
		THEOPH'LA	D P
		Canto v	
76	71, iii	*Unboundless*	
		Unbounded	J A Dy H D P Q2
80	100, i	SPIRITS	
		SPIRITS	H D P
		Canto vi	
81	3, ii	unpolish	
		unpolisht	J H D P
		unpolish'd	Q2
84	25, iii	*the*	
		thee	J A Dy
		Thee	Q2
90	68, iii	EXCES	
		EXCESSE	Q2
	69, iii	THAT	
		THAT.	J A Dy D P
91	79, ii	to th'	
		to'h'	D²
		Canto vii	
103	64, i	ESSENCE, One	
		ESSENCE One,	D P
106	86, iii	*most* It self *most doth*	
		most It self *doth most*	J A Dy H D P
		most most doth It self	B
		most, most doth It self	Q2

¹ D lacks the corroboration of P, with which it usually agrees, because this page in P is badly mutilated.

² The correction is probably an error.

Page	Stanza and Line	Correction	Copies
106	88, ii	*wast* *waste*	H D P
107	96, iii	IMMORTALITIE. IMMORTALITIE!	H D P
	98, ii	IRRESISTABILITIE IRRESISTIBILITIE	J　Dy H D P Q2
108	Envoy, line 2	Portum Portus	J A Dy H　　P Q2
		Canto viii	
110	11, iii	*Pow'r;* *Pow'r,*	H　　P
112	21, iii	CREATOR CREATOR,	J A Dy
113	29, i	INDENTITIE IDENTITIE	J A　　H D P Q2
	30, iii	SPIRIT SPIR̂IT	H D P
	31, i	FATHER FAT̂HER	H D P
116	56, iii	*This* *This*!	H D P Q2
117	67, i	LOVE, LOVE!	H D P
119	81, iii	Frequents Frequent	J A Dy H D P Q2
121	96, i	*Fortune* trod *Fortune*-trod	J A Dy H D P Q2
		Canto ix	
126	2, i	*accuminat* *acuminat*	B J A Dy H D P Q2
130	28, i	[Wrong indentation corrected by two horizontal strokes]	H D P
132	31, i	*nou* *non*	J A Dy H　　P
133	30, ii	our *Church* new Kirk(e)	J　　H D P Q2
144		[Wrong numbering of stanzas corrected] [partially corrected]	J　Dy A
		Canto iii (*Latin version*)	
165	28, iii	*praeslorida* *praeflorida*	H D P Q2

EDWARD BENLOWES

Page	Stanza and Line	Correction	Copies		
169	60, i	*repugnat*			
		repurgat	B J A	H D P	
173	90, iii	exersis			
		eversis	J A	H	Q2
174	95, i	*tacuit,*			
		tacuit;	J A		

Canto x

Page	Stanza and Line	Correction	Copies		
183	34, iii	*Bloud,* like the *Red Sea,* with Lust			
		Lust, like the *Red Sea,* with *Bloud*	S Q1 C1 B J A	H D P Q2	
191	92, i	Sruck			
		Struck	J A	H D P Q2	
	94, iii	begits			
		begets	J A		

Canto xi

Page	Stanza and Line	Correction	Copies		
195	18, ii	spice			
		spicie	J A	H D P Q2	
	18, iii	the *Apician*			
		the' *Apician*	J A		
196	24, i	Ill			
		Ill,	J	H D P	
202	75, i	Soul,			
		Soul		Q2	
	75, iii	*Despair;*			
		Despair,		H P	
203	82, ii	Foe			
		For	J A	H D P Q2	
204	91, i	*That*			
		That,		H D P	
207	Title	lenocitantes			
		lenocinantes	S Q1 C1	H D Q2	

Line

Page		Correction	Copies		
207	10	Minioq;			
		Minióq;		H D P	
208	2	colas			
		colis	J A	H D P Q2	
	20	Metamorphosis			
		Metamorphôsis (ō in P)	J A	H D P	
	21	Metamorphosin			
		Metamorphôsin (ō in P)	J A	H D P	
209	10	*peccatum*			
		Peccatum	J A Dy H D P		

Page	Line	Correction		Copies
213	19	*Poclis*		
		Poĉlis		H D P
214	12	Examines		
		Exanimes	J A	H D P Q2
	17	*difficile*		
		difficilè		P
	24	*teterrimi,*		
		teterrimi	Q1 C1 J	H D P
217	7	splendit		
		splendet	J A Dy	H D P Q2

Stanza and Line		*Canto xii*		
226	53, iii	do *These*		
		These do		H D P
	55, iii	Rage		
		Base	A	H D P Q2
227	67, iii	plaies.		
		plaies,		H P
228	70, iii	shew		
		show	A	H D P Q2
231	98, ii	remaning		
		remaining		Q2
232	103, ii	*Canzons,*		
		Canzons;	J	

		Canto xiii		
239	29, i	dist		
		didst	J A Dy	D P Q2
240	38, i	*His Command*		
		His high *Command*	J A Dy	
		His blest *Command*		H D P Q2
241	41, i	*Deliccaies*		
		Delicacies		A Dy H D P Q2
246	79, iii	defeat.		
		defeat!	J A Dy	

Line				
252	9	Navis		
		Navis,		H D P
253	20	cui		
		tibi		H D P
	25	Amico		
		Amico.		P
		Amico~	Q1	
268	25	Mectare		
		Nectare	S Q1 C1 B J A Dy H D P Q2	

It is not possible for me to claim that the list of pen-and-ink corrections that I have set out is an exhaustive one. It will be seen at once that the corrected copies show considerable variation and it would be necessary to examine every copy of the book with laborious minuteness to determine exactly how many corrections were made in printed copies of the poem. It is possible that there may be copies extant which contain corrections not found in any of those I have seen. But since the number of corrections found in one only of these eleven specimens is relatively very small, I do not think many significant alterations can have been made beyond those which have come to my notice. Even in the copies that I have examined I cannot swear that there may not be other corrections, though I think I can say that there are not in those copies any striking or important alterations that I have not observed. Many of the corrections are extremely minute—the addition of an accent; the insertion of a comma; the scratching out of the point of a semicolon to change it into a comma; the closing up of a *c* to give an *a*; the alteration of long *s* to *f* by a horizontal stroke. Some of these are impossible to detect except by a careful collation of copies. In order to be sure that there are not other delicate corrections of this kind one would have to make a complete collation of all the copies. I have myself collated the Petyt copy against the Grenville copy in the British Museum (a copy which has no pen-and-ink corrections at all) and also against the St. John's College copy. Each of the other copies I have examined with the results of this collation in mind. A further search for possible additional corrections in them has revealed occasional alterations not present in P or J, but, except in Q2, these are extremely few.

It should perhaps be stated that some of the unasterisked copies in my list (see p. 314) have alterations; but these are not authoritative. U, for example, has two minor corrections in pen and ink which are also made in the officially corrected copies. The punctuation is corrected at vii, 64, i; and at ix, 2, i, *accuminat* is corrected to *acuminat*. But these are both obvious misprints and have been rectified by an independent hand. Seventeenth-century readers tended to obey quite simply the author's instructions to correct a list of typographical errors, and the errors recorded in the Errata were obediently corrected through the text by the owners of M, H2, and Je. M, however, has three additional corrections, all on p. 208, which match corrections in some of the eleven copies now under review and therefore may well have been made by the hand that corrected these eleven. "Metamorphosis" and "Metamorphosin" each have a circumflex accent on the second o, and "colas" is altered to "colis." These three minute alterations are made in a pale brown ink quite different from that found elsewhere in this copy and similar to that generally used in the ten corrected copies that I have myself examined. The circumflex accents at least are details which would hardly suggest themselves to an independent corrector. It is also noteworthy that the engraved portrait on p. 206 (*i.e.* on the same *sheet*) has patches inked in in this copy, as in other copies corrected in pen and ink. But except on this one sheet there is no trace of the authorized corrector here. This makes the whole problem more puzzling than ever, for I do not think the corrections can have been made as a rule in the unbound sheets: all the other evidence goes to suggest that the corrector worked straight through complete copies two or three at a time.

In Chapter 20 above, I have taken the pen-and-ink corrections to be Benlowes' own work. I shall now give the evidence which leads to that conclusion. There cannot be the slightest doubt that the corrections made in the eleven copies listed above proceed from one central authority. There are individual variations, but there are also very striking similarities, not only in the corrections made, but in the way in which they are executed. Very few corrections are confined to one copy, and most of the alterations are found in at least three copies. A few are found in all eleven. Among the alterations found in as many as ten is the transposition of the words "Lust" and "*Bloud*" at x, 34, iii, which the corrector has indicated in each instance by writing a minute 1 over "Lust" and a minute 2 over "*Bloud*." The correction of "STRIANS" to "STRAINS" in the first stanza of the poem goes through all ten copies which have evidence to offer here, Q2 being mutilated; and always the I is made to serve for one arm of the required A, a second arm and a horizontal stroke being added, while one of the arms of the A in the type is inked over. The very neat insertion of a *c* to correct the misprint "*Shools*" in the first line of the Address to the Ladies is found in nine out of ten copies. In the Summary of the Poem (line 11) "CRIST" has been corrected to "CHRIST" in nine copies and in five of these the H is written, not between the C and R, but inside the curve of the C. Such peculiarities in execution might of course have been copied; but the correction of *Theophila* cannot have been carried out by a scribe working from a specimen copy or from instructions supplied him, for along with striking similarities, there are divergences far greater than could have been achieved by even the most inefficient of scribes. The corrector did not work from instructions, but was himself the authority for the corrections he made. He must therefore have been the author himself. Who indeed, other than the author, would trouble with the introduction of accents and the fastidious alteration of punctuation? Who other than Benlowes would ink over defective letters, as has been done in several copies, or add with the pen to the ornate curl of a capital?[1] This peculiar treatment was also accorded to the large paper copies of Benlowes' *Oxonii Encomium* when that was published twenty years later. And finally, who but the author himself would, when altering *"Bethesda"* to *"Bethsaida"* at i, 39, iii, add in the margin a note explaining that the name means in Hebrew "The House of Hunting"? This has been done in two copies, B and C1.[2]

It is perhaps fortunate that one has no need to resort to handwriting to show that the corrections were made in all copies by the same hand and that the hand was Benlowes' own. There is not much individuality about a neatly inserted comma, or even a succession of commas, or in the occasional interpolation of a *c* or *r*. But the handwriting expert would not find himself entirely without evidence. Sometimes the corrector has had to write a whole word, and there is also the specimen of his handwriting provided by his one marginal note. In J what seems to be the same hand has called attention to the transposition in that copy of signatures I2 and I5 and has given direction for the astronomical engraving (*i.e.* plate no. 12—see Appendix IV) which faces p. 122 to be placed before p. 125. It is this hand, too, which has written a Latin motto in S and Q1 beneath the first of the two word-puzzles at the end of the book (*i.e.* plate no. 24); and this in turn is certainly the hand which wrote some of the presentation inscriptions. These one would naturally suppose to be by Benlowes himself and the handwriting clearly resembles acknowledged specimens from Benlowes' pen. Though his use of a number of different styles and the segregation of small fragments of writing in different libraries makes comparison unusually difficult, I have myself no doubt in the matter.

---

[1] These "improvements" are commonest in J. I have not recorded them here since my concern is rather with corrections of the text.

[2] C1 also notes that Bethany is the "House of mourning."

If Benlowes had corrected the book in loose sheets it is inconceivable that some corrected sheets would not have found their way into every copy, since a study of the typographical variants, of which there are a number, indicates quite clearly that the earlier and the later sheets to come from the press were not kept separate but were mixed together when the edition was bound. And in spite of the considerable divergence between some copies—between, for example, J and B—there will be observed in some cases a remarkable degree of conformity between two or more copies, showing that they were corrected as completed copies, perhaps together, but certainly at approximately the same time. Even more conclusive proof that the bound copy and not a bundle of loose sheets was the unit for the correction is forthcoming when it is observed that some of the pen-and-ink corrections have left a blot on the opposite page. [1] Examples will be found—there are however several others—in P in the corrections at i, 39, iii; iii, 16, i; xi, 82, ii; in D also at iii, 16, i; in C1 at x, 34, iii; and in Q2 at ix, 2, i.

One of the most interesting things revealed in a study of the pen-and-ink corrections in eleven copies is that the copies tend to fall together in twos or threes. A cursory glance at the list set out above shows H, D, and P agreeing in the main, though P is slightly more fully corrected than either of the others; J, A, and Dy in close conformity, though Dy is less fully corrected than the other two after the middle of the book and each has one or two corrections not found in the others; Q1 very closely matching S; [2] and B on the whole following C1, though there is here rather more discrepancy. There is also a smaller degree of conformity in Q1 and S, B and C1 considered together: each of these four is much less fully corrected than the group made by the trios H, D, P and J, A, Dy. Q2 stands by itself; although it has at some time been very seriously mutilated, it is important in having several corrections which do not appear in any of the others. P and D, and then H, are the copies showing the most careful correction throughout. If numerically their emendations fall below those in J, A, and Dy, that is because this latter group was corrected at a time when Benlowes' fastidiousness about punctuation was more than usually acute; it manifests itself especially

---

[1] This detail has been already pointed out by Geoffrey and Arthur Tillotson in their *Library* article.

[2] It should be noted that these two copies also resemble one another in the plates they contain (see Appendix IV), and that they also have similar inscriptions.

in a small shower of commas over the preliminaries and the first two cantos. Through the later cantos J and A, and especially Dy, show much less thorough correction.

The pen-and-ink corrections present several problems to an editor of *Theophila*. Which of them is he to adopt? With considerable variation between individual corrected copies, how can he know what readings the author finally came to prefer? Can one know that in a corrected copy *all* corrections are the author's own? I take the last question first. If we leave aside Q2 for the moment, and consider the other ten copies, there are less than half-a-dozen minor corrections in the whole list which I have found in one copy only. And all are precisely the kind of correction which there is abundance of evidence to show that Benlowes was himself likely to make. I think an editor careful for Benlowes' authoritative text should have no hesitation in adopting all the pen-and-ink corrections contained in these ten copies.

There remains to be considered the copy Q2. This has a sufficient number of corrections identical with those in other copies for there to be no doubt that it was corrected by the same authority. But it has also a number of corrections not found elsewhere, and it is important to decide whether these are the author's own, or whether a second corrector is to be detected here. Now in those instances where Q2 follows the corrections of some or all of the other copies it usually shows the correction made in exactly the same way. But occasionally the same correction is made in a different way. At ix, 2, i, for example, *accuminat* is corrected to *acuminat*, but whereas in the other copies which show this alteration, one or other of the two *c*'s has been struck through with the pen, in Q2 the *a* has been blacked out and the first *c* closed to make an *a*. In other instances the corrector's pen has altered the same words or phrases as in other copies, but has made a slightly different correction. If these instances merely showed the correction of a misprint, one might naturally suppose that an independent corrector was at work. But some of them are textual emendations the need of which would hardly seem pressing except to the author himself. In correcting Q2 he felt the need for emendation just as when he corrected other copies, but now—on a different occasion and perhaps after a considerable lapse of time—a different emendation suggests itself to him. So, in the line printed "At first GOD made them One thus, by subjecting" (i, 32, i) he inserts a comma after "One," but the comma already present after "thus" is not changed to a semicolon, as it is in J, A, and Dy. Line vii, 86, iii he again finds an unsatisfactory one: "*Whose* STORE, *when empty'd most* It self *most doth advance*!" In correcting J, A, Dy, H, D, and P he was content to transpose the words "*most doth*," but in Q2 he changes to "*Whose* STORE, *when empty'd most, most doth* It self *advance*!" The authenticity of this new arrangement is vouched for by B, which has the same order as Q2, but does not insert the comma.

The variations in Q2 in instances where the author is thus admittedly the corrector prepare one not to be surprised if Q2 shows a few alterations which are not in the other corrected copies. And these alterations, while different individually, are usually of the same kind as the corrections that Benlowes has made elsewhere. Once a comma is inserted (iv, 52, iii); three times one is deleted (iv, 16, ii; iv, 75, i; xi, 75, i). One misprint is corrected—in the Argument of the second canto, line 7—and there are three alterations of spelling, emending "*Antidate*" to "*Antedate*" (i, 37, iii), "EXCES" to "EXCESSE" (vi, 68, iii), "remaning" to "remaining" (xii, 98, ii). In the first line of the second canto, "POWER" is altered to "POW'R," a most characteristic emendation, since the apostrophe is much used by Benlowes and some other seventeenth-century writers as a metrical device to denote a slurring of syllables. And lastly, at i, 50, iii "her own cursed *Gore*" has been altered to "her black cursed *Gore*." Here the handwriting at least does not prohibit the view that the correction was made by Benlowes himself. On the whole, then, while the editor would naturally be more chary of accepting all the Q2 corrections, I certainly think he should do so.

The variation in the corrections made in the different copies of the book must, I think, be due to the fact that they were corrected at different times. It is a matter of some interest and a great deal of difficulty to determine the order in which the copies were brought to the operating-table; but it is possible to form some theory. The group of copies, Q1, S, C1, B, I take to have preceded the others. They have many fewer corrections, and while this might be attributed to a certain perfunctoriness in the author after his original ardour had cooled, the nature of the corrections made in these four copies leads one to the alternative view. If Benlowes had begrudged the labour required for a thorough correction, he would, one imagines, have selected the most important alterations of the text, neglecting small matters of punctuation and leaving a few trivial misprints to correct themselves. There are *some* corrections of importance like the transposition of "*Bloud*" and "Lust" at x, 34, iii; and some of significant interest like the alteration of the second line in the last paragraph of Arthur Wilson's complimentary poem (sig. C3ᵛ, line 8), and the displacement of "*Bethesda*" by "*Bethsaida*" at i, 39, iii (not in S). The first of these, it is true, is not in Dy, and the last not in any of the group J, A, Dy; but otherwise they run through all corrected copies. That is to say, any really significant corrections found in Q1, S, C1, and B continue in the other copies. But on the other hand, some highly important alterations in the other group are not found here. None of these four copies has, for example, the substitution of "Base" for "Rage" at xii, 55, iii; or the alteration of "our *Church*" to "new Kirk" at ix, 30, ii; or the insertion of the missing epithet which the metre demands at xiii, 38, i; or various minor improvements of punctuation.

For similar reasons I take J, A, and Dy to have been corrected next. When an occasional correction is missing from this group, it may be due to an oversight. But none of them has the alteration, metrically important, of iii, 16, i; or the undoubted improvement effected by the transposition in the rather weak half-line at xii, 53, iii; or the necessary correction of punctuation at vii, 64, i. Only the second of these examples is found in H, which may therefore have preceded D and P. It certainly seems unlikely that Benlowes would not have kept these corrections in later copies (except perhaps in copies corrected much later, when they may have slipped his memory). But one can easily understand his not retaining the commas that he sprinkled so lavishly on J, A, and Dy. They were part of a scheme of heavier punctuation which he temporarily adopted. He seems to have abandoned it even in this group after correcting as far as Canto ii, [1] so that one is quite prepared to find the lighter pointing frequently kept in H, D, and P.

An editor arrived at this conclusion would be faced with a further problem. Since he believes H and D and P to be later than J, A, and Dy, is he to suppose that Benlowes subsequently rejected the heavier punctuation? Does its absence from H, D, and P denote a deliberate reversion to the text as printed? Or is it merely that so thorough a revision of the punctuation of the book involved a

---

[1] Note that this suggests that these three copies were actually corrected page by page simultaneously. This, however, as far as Dy is concerned, seems not to have continued after Canto ix.

labour, enthusiastically begun, which was found too arduous to carry through? A scrutiny of the relevant passages shows that while few of the commas added in J, A, and Dy are strictly necessary for grammar or sense, they are often helpful in pointing a phrase and emphasising the poet's meaning. At least they are valuable as showing how the author himself would have read certain lines, and if occasionally pedantic, they are in harmony with the nice standards of correctness that Benlowes constantly sought in the presentation of his work in print. I myself believe that the heavier punctuation superimposed upon the earlier part of *Theophila* in these three copies represents the poet's ideal and that only the weakness of the flesh prevented its introduction more consistently in other copies. No editor would have the right to ignore it unless he were convinced that its omission from H, D, and P denoted that the poet was actively discarding it, and I do not believe that there was in Benlowes' mind a deliberate intention to revert to the original form. The fact that in two instances at least the commas introduced in J, A, and Dy also appear in Q2 lends a crumb of support to this view. I think, then, that an editor should accept all the corrections of punctuation in these three copies. Only by adopting all the author's corrections in all the copies could he hope to approach the poet's ideal text. He could then at least claim to render what was at some time the author's expressed intention, even if it is just possible that this intention subsequently changed.

The relation of Q2 to the other copies in point of time has still to be considered. This copy obviously belongs to the more thoroughly corrected group which I hold to be the later. It is closer to D and P than to any of the others. It is characteristic that it has at xiii, 38, i "*His* blest *Command*" rather than the "*His* high *Command*" of J, A, and Dy or the obviously defective "*His Command*" of the uncorrected copies. It unfortunately lacks one or two important metrical alterations found in D and P; and it may therefore have preceded them. On the other hand its own original divergences give it a place by itself, and it may equally have been corrected later than all the others when the author had but an imperfect memory of corrections previously made. Against this is the fact that this copy was formerly in the possession of the Barrington family, and it is natural to infer that Benlowes himself presented it to one of the Barringtons. He was on good terms with the Barringtons many years before the publication of *Theophila*, and one would not have expected a presentation copy to them to be given later than the others. Further, this copy cannot have been presented much later than H, which went to the Earl of Westmorland, as its inscription indicates, on October 17, 1653. For by the end of 1653 Brent Hall had been burnt down and whatever stock of *Theophila* Benlowes had there must have perished. Probably copies were still obtainable from the booksellers, but the destruction of Brent Hall would undoubtedly put an end to presentation bindings and gilt armorial decorations such as the Q2 copy has. This still need not mean that Q2 was not *corrected* later than H, which may of course have been corrected some time before it was ultimately presented. But this can only be conjectural, and on what evidence there is, Q2 remains a puzzle.

A note on Saintsbury's copy of "Theophila" and his edition of the poem

Some pen-and-ink corrections are recorded by Saintsbury as having been in the copy which was in his possession and upon which he based his text of the poem in his *Minor Poets of the Caroline Period*, volume I. (See, for example, his footnotes on pp. 322, 373, 428, 449, 457.) But Saintsbury did not adopt these corrections in the text even though he regarded some of them as obviously right. Clearly it did not occur to him that they were of any particular authority. This is unfortunate, since it meant that he did not trouble to record them all; there is not the slightest doubt that his copy contained many corrections beyond those he has described. He looked upon them as the conjectures of an intelligent reader, and sometimes he has proposed as his own an emendation which was almost certainly suggested to him by a pen-and-ink correction in his own copy. (See his notes on vi, 3, ii and xi, 18, ii.) At other times he has introduced into the text without comment of any kind readings which are found only in pen-and-ink corrections. In Arthur Wilson's introductory poem, for instance, he prints the line "And we must sprinkle't on the sacrifice." It is hardly conceivable that the change from "And we must sprinkle it on th' *Sacrifice*"—a change made quite consistently in the corrected copies of the 1652 folio—should have been made by Saintsbury independently. Similarly, at vii, 86, iii he reads "doth most" with J, A, Dy, H, D, and P instead of "most doth" as in the printed text. In the matter of accents and punctuation he frequently followed the correction rather than the printed version. His practice is very inconsistent and his handling of the punctuation throughout is very free; so that one cannot assert dogmatically what corrections were or were not in his copy. But some facts are clear. Nowhere, save in correcting one or two trivial and obvious misprints, does he introduce an emendation not found in the group J, A, Dy but present in other copies. At xiii, 38, i, the defective line is emended by the insertion of "high" as in J, A, and Dy, not "blest" as in H, D, P, and Q2. And Saintsbury's punctuation, for all its vagaries, has many resemblances with the heavier pointing adopted by Benlowes at the time of the correction of J, A, and Dy. Of 46 alterations in punctuation made by this group of copies, Saintsbury adopts 27. Some of these could easily be improvements made independently, but many of the alterations are by no means obvious. There is quite adequate evidence to show that Saintsbury's copy belonged to the same group of copies as J, A, and Dy.

APPENDIX IV

ENGRAVINGS AND DECORATIONS IN *THEOPHILA*

(For reference list of copies discussed, see p. 314)

The 1652 folio of *Theophila* has always been a bibliographical puzzle because of the great variation in the number and position of the plates included in different copies. There are twenty-five [1] which it is generally held should be present in perfect copies, but additional plates are also found in rare copies; as many as eleven extra ones were to be found in the Inglis copy described by Lowndes. I am not aware that any of these extra plates are found in copies which still preserve the original binding, and they were, I think, later additions. Each of the other twenty-five is found as part of the original make-up of at least one copy, and forms part of the author's design for the book. But few copies, if any, had all twenty-five. Even when a copy has less than half that number, it should not be described as imperfect unless there is clear evidence that it once possessed plates which now it lacks.

The six plates on the letter-press must always have been present: nos. 8, 17, 18, 19, 20, and 23. In addition, the most regular plates seem to have been 3, 7, and 10, with perhaps 2, 12, and 22. The position of 12 and 22 was several times changed. No. 7, though certainly intended for Canto iv, seems to have been used in early copies to precede Canto ii, being transferred to Canto iv when plate 4 was added along with 6, 9, and 11. But a plate once introduced was not necessarily inserted in all subsequent copies. Each copy when it was bound was illustrated with a number of plates selected from those listed below. It is clear that when the earlier

---

[1] Lowndes lists twenty-four, omitting from his enumeration the engraved verses on p. 123, though he mentions these in his collation of the book. The verses accompanying nos. 3, 4, 6, 7, 8, and 9 were engraved separately from their illustrations, but it seems convenient in these cases to regard picture and verses together as one plate.

copies were being bound only some of these were available, but
it by no means follows that a copy necessarily included all the plates
which were available at the moment when it was bound. I think
the author never intended all his illustrations to appear in any one
copy, and that he tried to make each presentation copy unique.
It would be easier to demonstrate this if more of the copies
now extant had escaped having extra plates inserted or original
plates torn out.

I have seen only three copies with all twenty-five plates: the Grenville copy in the British Museum, the Douce copy in the Bodleian,
and the Dyce copy at South Kensington. All are copies in which
extra plates have been inserted in rebinding. In their passion for
accumulating as many plates as possible in a single copy the quondam
owners of these must have ravaged a number of other copies. The
Dyce copy has no fewer than 22 of the plates in duplicate, the exceptions being no. 13 (the engraved verses on sig. O2, for although
the leaf is duplicated, it lacks the verses in one instance) and the
very rare 16 and 21. Even so, the want of a second specimen of
no. 16 is supplied by a traced copy of it. The Grenville has four
plates in duplicate: nos. 3, 8, 24, and 25. The Douce has extra copies
of nos. 3, 5, and 8 pasted in at the beginning and has also no. 15
in duplicate and no. 22 in triplicate. Douce himself admitted that
some plates were lacking when he bought the book and took pride
in the fact that, apart from the portrait of Benlowes (which, cut
from another copy, he was able to add subsequently) his copy had
as many plates as the Bindley copy; and this, when it was sold in
1819 (for fourteen pounds), was supposed to have more plates than
any other copy extant. When Douce obtained his copy it lacked,
besides no. 1, plates 2, 16, and 25 at least. In G no. 12 is an example
of a later insertion. Another copy which contains all twenty-five
plates is that in the Huntington Library, formerly in the possession
of Mr. Robert Hoe. A full bibliographical description of it by Miss
Carolyn Shipman may be found in *The Bibliographer*, II, 12-14. I
have not myself seen this copy, but apparently it is not, any more
than the other three, a copy with twenty-five original plates. An
official of the Huntington Library, to whose courtesy I am indebted, reports to me that, while the copy has its original binding,
"the body of the work has every appearance of having been removed
from the binding at some time or other, and plates inserted." The
Sandars copy in the Cambridge University Library, which contains

22 of the 25 plates, as well as 8 of the extra ones, also shows clear signs of having been made up. The copies, then, which contain most plates are not the most reliable in indicating the position plates were intended to occupy. In this respect a copy like C2, with the original binding and with no sign of any attempt to "improve" it by the addition of plates which it was not originally intended to possess, is much more important, even though it had but 15 plates. Other seemingly reliable copies are P, with 22 plates, A with 12, and—in some ways the finest of all—B, a copy which was only discovered by the librarian of Jesus College in 1935, although it is believed to have been in the possession of the college since the end of the seventeenth century. It has consequently escaped both the "improvements" and the ravagings of eighteenth and nineteenth-century collectors. It does seem, however, to have lost one or two plates at some time or other. Two copies—Wo and U—should be ruled out altogether (although U has a fairly early binding); their plates have been inserted quite haphazardly, and apart from those on the letter-press, every one occupies a position in the volume not paralleled in any other copy I have seen.

I have found only two copies agreeing exactly in the number and location of their plates. Not only did the number of plates vary from copy to copy, but the plates were not always intended to be inserted in the same places. A few plates had engraved [1] on them the numeral of the cantos they were intended to accompany, but even these could vary their position in the book. Of many plates, therefore, it is not possible to speak of the "correct" position. The subjoined list gives merely the most usual one, and no copy I have seen conforms to the list in every detail. (Dy comes nearest.) There is, however, considerable agreement between Du, S, Q1, Je, and C2 as far as they go, [2] none of them having more than 15 plates. None of them has the engraved verses on p. 123 (no. 13). A blank space was left at the foot of the page to receive the verses, and copies without the engraving must, I think, have been among the first to be bound. It is worth observing, too, that none of the rarest, and presumably the latest, plates occurs in these five copies. S and Du have 14 plates—nos. 2, 3, 7, 8, 10, 12, 17, 18, 19, 20, 22, 23, 24, and 25

---

[1] I emphasise "engraved," since sometimes one sees numerals which have been added at some time in pen and ink and to which naturally no significance attaches whatever.

[2] Except that Du has the last plate upside down, the first two of these agree exactly.

—and I take these to be the ones included in the first-finished copies. Je agrees, except that it now lacks, though it probably did not always lack, no. 12. C2, with some variations in position, has the same 14 plates, plus no. 6. Q1 agrees with Du and S in everything except the presence of no. 1 in Q1, where it was pasted in after binding.

If these copies were indeed among the earliest copies to be bound, then that would provide a little corroboration for my suggestion that S and Q1 were among the first copies to be corrected with the author's pen (see pp. 329-330).

In considering the plates, it is also to be observed that there are slight but significant resemblances in detail between J and A and Hn, even though A has only a dozen plates. Here again the similarity between the first two matches a striking similarity in their pen-and-ink corrections. The same is true of P and D. This corroborates the suspicion that *some* of the variations in the occurrence and the positions of the plates are capable of being reduced to a chronological system, which would indicate how Benlowes changed his mind about their insertion.

The list of plates is as follows:

1. Frontispiece, facing title-page. Portrait of Benlowes within a wreath of laurel enclosed in an ornamental frame. Said to be by Francis Barlow. In J and Hn this follows the title-page and faces sig. A1. It is perhaps odd, but I think significant, that these two copies also agree in unusual positions for nos. 14 and 22. In J nos. 1 and 14 at least have been glued in after binding, and both of them are unusually tall so that they have to be folded to fit the book. It is probable that they were inserted by Benlowes just before the copy was presented to St. John's College, just as no. 1 seems to have been inserted in Q1 when that copy was to be presented to Thomas Barlow.

2. Facing sig. A2. An engraving of a lady in a mask, with fur and muff. It is copied from Hollar's 1643 engraving of a lady in winter dress with Cornhill in the background ("Winter", but not the same as "Winter" in the group of the Four Seasons).

3. Preceding Canto i, facing p. 1. The author writing at a table, with his foot on a globe, gazing at Theophila, on whose head an angel is placing a crown. Beneath it verses beginning "The Author musing here survay." Found in all good copies. Corser (*Collectanea Anglo-Poetica*, II, 250) had seen this plate used as a frontispiece. For lengthier description, see p. 222.

4. Preceding Canto ii, facing p. 23. Theophila praying, surrounded by wild beasts. Subscribed verses beginning "Satan caus'd Eves, Eve Adams Fall." This is only fairly common. In some copies, including Du and S, Q1, and Je, its place is taken by no. 7. These all lack nos. 4, 9, and 11, which usually go together.

5. Facing sig. F1, p. 25. A large woodcut, representing Adam and Eve and the tree of knowledge. This was not specially designed for *Theophila*, but had already been used to illustrate Barker's *Bible* (1632).

There it is considerably larger, having an elaborate framework for which there was not room on the smaller page of *Theophila*. In a number of instances this plate, while occupying the same position in the order of the leaves, faces p. 24 instead of p. 25 (J, G, Hn). In M it has been bound up facing p. 23, in place of the missing no. 4.

6.   Preceding Canto iii, facing p. 37. An allegorical design representing man penitent and showing also David with his harp and Theophila honoured by angels with wreaths. Subscribed verses beginning: "Here Angels tender from the Skie." C2 has this plate without the verses.

7.   Preceding Canto iv, facing p. 51. Theophila with a shield and a flaming sword fighting against a throng of temptations symbolically represented. Subscribed verses beginning: "The Soule against Temptations fights." Found in all good copies, though it sometimes appears before Canto ii, when no. 4 is absent. A figure 4 engraved on the plate leaves no doubt about which canto it was intended for. An interesting thing about this engraving is that it is in reverse, so that Theophila and at least two of the other figures (one flourishing a whip) are shown left-handed. This of course suggests that it is a copy of something else.

8.   Preceding Canto v, on p. 66. The author (with cat and dog and owl) looking at Theophila (with an eagle), who stands pointing upwards to a symbol of herself being borne by angels up to heaven. Subscribed verses beginning: "View here the Authors high Designe." This plate, being on the verso of sig. I3 and not on a separate leaf, should be present in all unmutilated copies. But in some cases (including Du and Je and a duplicate in T) the picture has been printed separately and then glued on to the page. One may infer that it was not ready until after some copies had been bound up.

9.   Preceding Canto vi, facing p. 81. Groups of figures of prophets, martyrs, apostles, angels, etc. Subscribed verses beginning: "Here Abraham, David, Daniel stand." Only fairly common, but found usually in copies which have nos. 4 and 11.

10.   Preceding Canto vii, facing p. 95. An angel bending down to Theophila, offering her an emblem of eternity. Heads of cherubs floating on the clouds. No verses. Found in all good copies.

11.   Preceding Canto viii, facing p. 109. On the left Theophila borne aloft by angels, on the right the wicked falling into hell-mouth. No verses. Usually found along with nos. 4 and 9.

12.   Following Canto viii, facing p. 122. A winged woman leaning against a globe, with astronomical instruments strewn around her feet, and pointing up to the heavens. Lowndes took this to be "an emblematical female figure of Astronomy," but it was presumably intended to symbolize Theophila. This, though missing from some copies, including the excellent B, is not a rare plate. In P, C2, and D it precedes Canto xiii, this and no. 22 having been transposed. It is bound here in J, A, M, W, Dy, and Hn, and I have no doubt that the variation in position is the responsibility of the author himself and one instance of the flexibility of his scheme of illustration. In J and A a pen-and-ink note in Benlowes' hand directs that this plate should be put before p. 125. In Du, S and Q1 it precedes Canto x, facing p. 179, where it was afterwards superseded by no. 16. Je, which agrees elsewhere with these, lacks this plate, but it probably once had it, since it has clearly lost something before p. 179.

13.   On sig. O2, p. 123. At the foot of the page, an engraving of twelve lines of Latin verse, beginning: "Vos sacra Progenies CŒLI, celsiq[ue]

capaces." When these engraved verses are not found the space is left blank. It seems likely that those copies which lack them were the first to be bound up. They include Du, S, Q1, C2, and Je. But the verses are not as rare as Lowndes believed, and I think he was also mistaken in stating in his collation of the folio that pp. 123-124 appeared twice. The leaf appears in duplicate only in made-up copies, a specimen with the verses having been sometimes inserted by an enthusiastic collector whose copy in its original form had a blank at the foot of p. 123.

14. At the beginning of Canto ix, facing p. 125. Theophila leaning against a pedestal, treading on a serpent, holding a palm-branch and a book in her right hand, pointing upwards with her left, faced by another female figure with a palm-branch. Attributed to Barlow. In some copies this plate is too large for the dimensions of the book and has to be folded. In others there is a slightly shorter print of it, Theophila being deprived of her left forefinger. This is the location usually assigned to this plate, and it seems natural to put it here to provide an illustration for Canto ix. Yet Canto xi is not preceded by a plate (except in G, which uses a duplicate of no. 3 here, and M and W, which have supplementary plates inserted here). And the very naturalness of the position may be against it, since it would explain why the plate was inserted here in made-up copies. I have seen it here only in copies which have been rebound—Dy, W, G, and C1 (where it faces p. 124). It is a rare plate and one cannot properly speak of a "usual," much less a "correct," place for it. In J and Hn it rather unaccountably faces p. 60. In P and D it comes immediately after the title, facing sig. A1.

15. Facing sig. R3, p. 161. A small plate engraved by William Marshall. A large wreath surrounding the inscription "Ludus Literarius Christianus. Anthreno-Tripsis *seu* Crabronum Tritura *Edw. Benlosij* Armig." Beneath are a winepress and beehives, and at the foot are engraved seven lines of Latin verse signed with the initials I.S. The general design of the plate Marshall took from his own frontispiece for Benlowes' "Quarlëis," which has the winepress and beehives, but in reverse. There the wreath is smaller, and the upper part of the two plates is quite different. This is a very rare plate, but will be found here in B, G, Hn, Dy, and D. The last two even have duplicates. In P it serves instead of the portrait of the author as a frontispiece, for which Marshall probably designed it (though not for *Theophila*).

16. Preceding Canto x, facing p. 179. The author looking up to the heavens, and over his head a hand descending with a crown and the emblematic ring of eternity. A female figure on either side and two men in the foreground, one in armour and wearing a crown with swords and other weapons in it, the other with a pack on his back. This is extremely rare. It was evidently added at the same time as no. 21. It is contained in B, G, Hn, Dy, and D; Douce, who took pride in acquiring this plate for his copy, unfortunately bound it to face p. 178 instead of p. 179.

17. On sig. X1ᵛ, p. 206. Occupying the lower two-thirds of the page and occurring in all unmutilated copies, an engraving of a lady holding a fan, done in the style of Hollar. But Lowndes (followed by the Grolier Club Catalogue) is wrong in describing it as Hollar's Spring, and a pencilled note in G calling it Hollar's Summer is also wrong. The plate is intended to illustrate the "Dame of Pleasure" who is satirized in Canto xi; in some copies the patches which should adorn the wanton to make an adequate illustration have been distributed over the face and neck with pen and ink—for example, in P, D, J, and A—presumably

by the hand that made the pen-and-ink corrections in the text of these copies. Saintsbury's copy also had patches in ink. In M they have less claim to have been done by Benlowes himself. (But see above, p. 325.)

18. At the top of sig. Y1, p. 209. An engraving of the two hemispheres: "Typus Orbis Terrarum." This and the two following, being on the letter-press, are necessarily found in all unmutilated copies.

19. On sig. Y1^v, p. 210. A small square engraving showing a fashionable gallant of the time, signed, by Peregrine Lovell.

20. On sig. Y2^v, p. 212. A companion picture of a toping cavalier. Although a companion picture, this is not signed like the other and may not have been by Lovell, for it is in my view inferior to the preceding, which it seems to have imitated. For a description of the costume in these two engravings, see above, p. 106.

21. Preceding Canto xii, facing p. 217. A rural scene with an elegantly dressed young man (presumably intended for the author) talking to an old shepherd in the foreground. Extremely rare; found, along with no. 16, in B, D, Hn, Dy, and G, in the last two of which it is bound up to face p. 218. A different engraving on the same subject—no. 32—is occasionally found substituted for this plate, as in W, M, and C1.

22. Preceding Canto xiii, facing p. 235. A tearful woman, intended for Theophila, praying. At the top a symbolic heaven from which light shines on the woman's brow. On the left a ladder with angels ascending and descending. In the bottom left-hand corner a scroll with the inscription: "THEOPHILA'S LOVE SACRIFICE. WRITTEN BY. EDW BENLOWES ESQ^v" and signed by the engraver, Pierre Lombart. Below are verses in Latin and English, signed by Jeremy Collier. This plate, though wanting in B, is found in most copies, but its location varies a great deal. It is found here in C1, G, W, Dy, T, and M, all of them copies which have been rebound. Perhaps it should be transposed with no. 12, as in P and C2. Douce thought this the proper place for it, but the original copy of it in D seems to have faced p. 17. In Du, S, Q1, and Je also the plate faces p. 17—that is, where the Author's Prayer begins. But since the engraving is of Theophila, perhaps it is more fittingly situated in J, A, and Hn, opposite p. 30, where Theophila is described weeping. Saintsbury (*The Bibliographer*, II, 6) seems to have seen it also used as frontispiece, for which it may well have been designed.

23. On sig. Hh1, p. 245. On the top half of the page, a woodcut of Queen Elizabeth kneeling to pray, encased between lines of English prose, running vertically, eulogizing her life. Necessarily found in all unmutilated copies.

24. Following the text, but preceding plate 25. An engraved Latin word-puzzle fitted into a design of the crucifixion, signed by Thomas Cecill and dated 1632. In S Benlowes has written below this plate, "Hic Oedipus esto, nam Labyrinthus inest, & Labor intus adest," and in Q1 "Et Labyrinthus inest, & Labor intus adest."

25. At the end, immediately following plate 24. A similar, but less elaborate, Latin word-puzzle on the passion and the resurrection. Signed with a monogram of the initials M.R.D., which have been conjectured to be those of Martin Droeshout.

There are still the eleven extra plates listed by Lowndes from the Inglis copy. I have not seen any of these in copies which have not been rebound, and it is possible, even probable, that all of them are spurious. Benlowes may have had some or all of them bound up in a few odd copies; it would have been perfectly in character. But they may equally well have been inserted by some possessor of the book who thought them appropriate. It is clear that they appear today in *some* copies where they did not belong originally. Bibliophiles who had seen them in one copy of *Theophila* concluded that their own copies were imperfect and strove to fill the gaps. But note, on the other hand, that Dy, D, and G, although they all show the delight of their owners in collecting duplicate copies of plates, have no sign of an attempt to procure more than the twenty-five indubitably authentic decorations.

26. An etching illustrating Matthew xxi : 28. This does not appear in any copy I have seen.

27, 28, 29, 30. The Four Seasons, by Hollar. These are the commonest of the supplementary plates; they are found in C1, W, M, and Hn. In M they occur in the order Spring, Summer, Autumn, Winter, following sig. A1, but preceding plate no. 2. In W they are found in the same position, but in the reverse order. In C1 they face respectively B1ᵛ, B2ᵛ, B4ᵛ, and B5ᵛ. In Hn they are found as follows: Autumn facing ¶¶¶ 2ᵛ, Winter facing B4ᵛ, Summer facing (d)ᵛ, Spring facing C1ᵛ.

31. An engraving of the day of judgment. In the bottom corner the text "Vanitas vanitatum, omnia Vanitas." This plate is not in any copy I have seen.

32. A country scene with an elegant youth talking to a shepherd. A plate on the same subject as no. 21, which it replaces in C1, M, and W, in each case facing p. 218. This engraving properly belongs to Davies' *The Extravagant Shepherd*, where it is prefixed to book i.

33. Described by Lowndes as "a curious emblematical engraving allusive to the vanity of the world; being the bust of a female, a Cupid issuing from the forehead, the breast formed by globes." It faces p. 175 in C1, p. 179 in M (that is, in place of no. 16), and p. 193 in W. This plate also belongs to *The Extravagant Shepherd*, where it is prefixed to book ii.

34. An engraving inscribed in the upper left-hand corner, "THE EXTRAVAGANT SHEPHERD," and used as the frontispiece of Davies' book. Facing sig. (c)1 in C1, p. 109 in M (replacing no. 11), and p. 203 in W.

35. A large engraving which has to be folded to fit the size of *Theophila*, inscribed at the lower left-hand corner, "IANBATTEST IASPERS IN ET FE." This also belongs to *The Extravagant Shepherd*, where it appears between sigs. I1 and I2, illustrating the banquet of the gods, which forms part of book iii. It is found both in C1 and M between pp. 192 and 193.

36. An engraving entitled "A curious piece of antiquity on the Crucifixion of our Saviour and the two Thieves." I have not come across this plate in any copy.

PARALLEL PASSAGES IN *THEOPHILA* AND *THE SUMMARY OF WISEDOME*

The Summary of Wisedome in its English version consists of a hundred stanzas, of which most are repetitions, with more or less variation, of stanzas in *Theophila*. The following is a list of the parallel stanzas I have detected. The stanzas are never identical; the closest parallel admits an alteration of one word. But the resemblance is in all cases close and immediately recognizable, unlike the very *recherché* parallelisms which have sometimes been listed as a poet's "self-repetitions." Sometimes two lines from *Theophila* are coupled with one which is new. But when the resemblance does not extend beyond one line or less, the bulk of the stanza being different, I have placed the number of the *Theophila* stanza in parenthesis. In those cases the resemblance is still close as far as it goes; there are always identical phrases. When a numeral in parenthesis is added to the number of a stanza it refers to a neighbouring stanza from which some significant detail of vocabulary has been borrowed; for example, stanza 42 of *The Summary of Wisedome*, describing the gallant, largely follows *Theophila*, xi, 4, but incorporates also the word "modish" from xi, 8.

The Summary of Wisedome Stanza	Theophila Canto & Stanza	The Summary of Wisedome Stanza	Theophila Canto & Stanza
1		15	viii, 88
2		16	x, 34
3		17	xi, 98
4	x, 7	18	x, 42
5	x, 8	19	ii, 38
6	x, 10	20	xi, 100
7	i, 35	21	x, 76
8	x, 44	22	x, 78
9	x, 26	23	
10		24	(x, 81)
11		25	x, 82
12	(xii, 16) (17)	26	viii, 64
13	xii, 7	27	viii, 65 / x, 83
14	x, 31		

The Summary of Wisedome Stanza	Theophila Canto & Stanza	The Summary of Wisedome Stanza	Theophila Canto & Stanza
28	x, 85 (86)	65	x, 47
29	(x, 92)	66	x, 62
30	x, 80	67	(x, 63)
31	x, 90	68	x, 57
32	x, 96	69	x, 58
33	xiii, 89	70	
34	x, 95	71	
35	x, 97	72	x, 69
36	ii, 36	73	x, 70
37		74	xii, 90
38	viii, 56	75	xii, 91
39	viii, 62	76	x, 60
40	ii, 45	77	i, 46
41	xi, 6	78	x, 66
42	xi, 4 (8)	79	(ii, 43)
43	xi, 12	80	(ii, 44)
44	i, 20	81	ii, 81
45		82	xii, 48
46	xi, 16 (19)	83	
47	xi, 25	84	xiii, 7
48	xi, 20	85	xiii, 18
49		86	
50	xi, 44	87	
51	xi, 47	88	viii, 90
52	i, 6	89	xiii, 24 (22)
53	xi, 58, 59	90	
54		91	viii, 49
55		92	
56	i, 37	93	xii, 94
57	xi, 79	94	
58	xi, 80	95	vi, 60
59	xi, 81	96	iii, 12
60	xi, 94	97	v, 84
61	x, 48	98	v, 100
62	xi, 5	99	vi, 44
63		100	xiii, 120
64			

BIBLIOGRAPHY AND SOURCES

A. LIST OF BENLOWES' WORKS

1. *Lusus Poëticus Poëtis*. (Containing "Quarlëis.") London, 1634. Octavo. Latin verse. Intended to be appended to, and usually found with, the first edition of Quarles's *Emblemes* (1635). But also found bound separately. The Bodleian has it in both forms, but the copies listed by *S.T.C.* as in the British Museum and at St. Edmund's College, Ware, are the normal appendix to the *Emblemes* and not instances of the separate item.

2. *Sphinx Theologica* seu Musica Templi, ubi Discordia Concors. Cambridge, 1636. Octavo. A devotional work in Latin prose and verse. Copies at the British Museum, the Bodleian, and at Cambridge at St. John's College (two), Trinity College, and Emmanuel College.

3. *De celeberrima & florentissima Trinobantiados Augustæ Civitate*. A Latin poem appended to John Sictor's *Panegyricon Inaugurale. . . Richardi Fenn*. London, 1638. Copies at the British Museum; the Guildhall Library; the Bodleian; the Huntington Library; Trinity College, Dublin.

4. *Honorifica Armorum Cessatio*, sive Pacis et Fidei Associatio Feb. 11. An. 1643 (*i.e.* 1643/44). Octavo. Not extant.

5. *Papa Perstrictus*. London, 1645. Broadsheet. A Latin echo-poem. Copy in the British Museum, dated by Thomason August 20, 1646.

6. *A Poetick Descant upon a Private Musick-Meeting*. [1649.] Broadsheet. No imprint. Thomason dates it November 1649. English verse. Copy at the British Museum.

7. *Theophila*, or Loves Sacrifice. London, 1652. Folio. An English poem in thirteen cantos, with parts translated into Latin and incidental prose and verse in English and Latin. For copies, see list on p. 314.

8. *The Summary of Wisedome*. London, 1657. Quarto. An English poem with a Latin translation face to face. Copies at the British Museum, the Bodleian, and the Huntington Library.

9. *A Glance at the Glories of Sacred Friendship*. London, 1657. Broadsheet. A poem in English with addenda in Latin prose and verse. Copy at the British Museum, dated by Thomason August.

10. *On St. Paul's Cathedrall represented by Mr Dan. King*, and *Threnodia Ædis Paulinæ de Seipsâ*. London, 1658. Two poems forming the central part of a broadsheet of engravings of St. Paul's by Daniel King. Two copies in the Bodleian.

11. *Threno-Thriambeuticon*. London, 1660. Broadsheet. A few copies printed on white satin. Latin poems on Charles II's Restoration. I have not traced a copy of this, though Hazlitt saw one in the last century (*Hand-book*, p. 36).

12. *Truth's Touchstone*. [*circa* 1665-66.] Broadsheet. A poem in a hundred distichs, dedicated to Philippa Blount. Not extant.

13. *Annotations for the better confirming the several Truths in the said Poem*. [*circa* 1665-66.] Not extant.

14. *Oxonii Encomium*. Oxford, 1672. Folio. Latin prose and verse, concluding with the English poem, "On Oxford, the Muses Paradise." Large paper presen-

tation copies at the Bodleian and Corpus Christi College, Oxford—dated in ink July 27th. Other copies are at the Bodleian (two); the British Museum; the London Library (two); Balliol College, Oxford (imperfect); Yale University.

15. *Oxonii Elogia*. [Oxford, 1673.] Broadsheet. In Latin, principally verse. No imprint, but the Bodleian copy is dated in a contemporary hand, presumably Anthony à Wood's.

16. *Echo Veridica*. An echo-poem in Latin. On the same sheet as *Oxonii Elogia*.

17. *Magia Coelestis*. Oxford, 1673. Broadsheet. A Latin poem. Copy at the Bodleian.

Nos. 6, 7, and 8 are reprinted in Saintsbury, *Minor Poets of the Caroline Period* vol. I (Oxford, 1905).

Five stanzas from *Theophila* (Canto i, stanzas 63-7) are included in Ault, *Seventeenth Century Lyrics* (London, 1928).

In the above list, I thought it convenient to indicate where copies might be found, but I make no claim to list all copies. The items which are not extant are included on the authority of Wood (*Fasti Oxonienses*, ed. Bliss, II, 358-359).

Benlowes has also complimentary poems in Payne Fisher's *Marston-Moor* and *Epinicion vel Elogium...Lodovici XIIII[u] Galliae...Regis*; in Phineas, Fletcher's *The Purple Island*; in Francis Quarles's *Emblemes*, and *Hieroglyphikes of the Life of Man*; in Richard Sibbs's *The Soules Conflict* (2d ed.); in Edward Sparke's *Scintillula Altaris* (2d ed.); in Ralph Winterton's *A Golden Chaine of Divine Aphorismes* and in his edition of the aphorisms of Hippocrates. There is also a poem of his quoted in Fuller's *Church-History of Britain* (1655), book x, pp. 103-104.

B. MANUSCRIPT SOURCES

1. LETTERS

John Fortho to Robert Cecil, Earl of Salisbury. April 11, 1611. S.P., Dom., Jas. I, 63/26.

Edward Benlowes to Sir Thomas Barrington. October 11, 1643. Brit. Mus. MS. Egerton 2647, fol. 312.

Clement Paman to Edward Benlowes. [*circa* 1646.] Bodleian MS. Rawlinson D. 945, fols. 29-32.

Dr. Thomas Barlow to Sir Joseph Williamson. February 28, 1674/75. S.P., Dom., Chas. II, 368/134.

John Fell, Bishop of Oxford, to Sir Joseph Williamson. [1676.] S.P., Dom., Chas. II, 408/184.

Edward Benlowes to Sir Joseph Williamson. May 1676. S.P., Dom., Chas. II, 381/203.

2. PERSONAL AND FAMILY MANUSCRIPTS

Exercise-book of Edward Benlowes. Bodleian MS. Rawlinson D. 278.

Case-book of Serjeant William Benlowes (Edward's great-grandfather). Bodleian MS. Rawlinson C. 728.

Thirteenth-Century Psalter of William Benlowes (Edward's grandfather). Bodleian MS. Douce 131.

3. CHURCH AND PARISH RECORDS

The "Town Book" of Finchingfield, Essex. (The original is in the church at Finchingfield; there is a transcript in the Essex County Record Office at Chelmsford.)

Register of St. Mary the Virgin, Oxford.

4. STATE PAPERS

(For personal letters included in the State Papers, see above, under 1).
S.P., Dom., Eliz., 276/109.
>Jas. I, 63/26.
>Chas. I, 358.
>Interregnum, G95/422-445; G158/307-318; G248/12, 14, 31; G252/136; G261; G262.
Docquets, vol. VIII (1607).

5. LEGAL DOCUMENTS, ETC.

a. Wills and Administrations (P.C.C. At Somerset House).
Serjeant William Benlowes (Edward's great-grandfather). November 17, 1584. Brudenell 10.
Mary Benlowes (Edward's sister). January 8, 1630. Administration Act Book 1630, fol. 144.
William Benlowes (Edward's brother) (nuncupative). August 1633. Russell 111.
Francis Benlowes (Edward's uncle). April 1, 1647. Fines 81.
Walter Blount, of Mapledurham. April 26, 1671. Duke 86.

b. Inquisitions Post Mortem (P.R.O.)

Chancery Series II, 207/59. William Benlowes (Edward's great-grandfather)' died November 19, 1584.
Chancery Series II, 343/137. William Benlowes (Edward's grandfather), died November 18, 1613.

c. Court of Wards (P.R.O.)

Wards 9/162. Grant of Edward Benlowes' wardship, 1614.
Wards 5/13, no. 2066. Feodary's survey.
>53, no. 229.

d. Deeds and Property Conveyances

Deeds at Essex County Record Office, Chelmsford: D/DAc 65, 109, 110.
Close Rolls (P.R.O.):
>11 Charles I, part 1, no. 17.
>21 Charles I, part 1, no. 31.
>22 Charles I, part 8, no. 41.
>1649, part 10, no. 18.
>1649, part 46, no. 23.
>1654, part 9, no. 16.
>1655, part 24, no. 13.
>1657, part 25, no. 22.

Fine (P.R.O.): Common Pleas 25(2)/550 A. Hilary, 1654/5. Robert Abdy and William Meggs *v.* Edward Benlowes, etc.
Recovery (P.R.O.): Common Pleas 43/73. Easter, 1601. Edward Gage, etc. *v.* William and Andrew Benlowes.

e. Recognizances (P.R.O.)

Recognizance Entry Books, L.C. 4/200 (f. 470), 201 (f. 119), 203 (ff. 137, 280), 204 (ff. 12, 36).

f. Recusant Rolls (P.R.O.)

E377. *Temp.* James I and Charles I. (References to members of the Benlowes family occur on nos. 14, 15, 19, 26, 28, 29, 35.)

g. *Essex Quarter Sessions Rolls* (Chelmsford).

References to members of the Benlowes family occur on nos. 86, 94, 96, 117, 151, 171, 177, 180, 189, 190, 191, 192, 193, 199, 207, 211, 217, 219, 232, 233, 235, 237, 245, 246, 250, 251, 255, 263, 264, 268, 269, 272, 273, 274, 280, 284, 293, 294, 298, 301, 304, 307.

h. *Chancery Proceedings* (P.R.O.)

Bills and Answers
Nathan Wright *v.* Edward Benlowes, etc. 1657. Collins 140/147.
John Schoren *v.* Edward Benlowes. 1658. Whittington 71/87.
John Schoren *v.* Sir Benjamin Wright. 1661. Bridges 629/64.
Edward Benlowes *v.* Sir Benjamin Wright, etc. 1661. Bridges 444/123.
Edward Benlowes *v.* John Schoren. 1662. Reynardson 31/14.
Edward Benlowes *v.* John and Sarah Schoren. 1663. Collins 28/11.
Sir Benjamin Wright *v.* Edward Benlowes, etc. 1664. Bridges 44/89.
Sarah Schoren *v.* Sir Benjamin Wright and Edward Benlowes. 1666.
  Collins 28/75.
Sir Benjamin Wright *v.* Edmund Plumer, etc. 1669. Bridges 583/16.

Depositions (connected with the second and sixth of the suits listed above)
C24/835/92.
    896/13.

Decrees and Orders
1660 B 586.
1661 A 572.
1662 A 330, 623, 731, 856.
1663 A 169, 206, 274, 410, 421, 563, 572, 721, 751.
1663 B 378, 431, 760, 832, 874, 880, 883, 979.
1664 B 170, 215, 269, 270, 323, 473, 570, 626.
1665 B 125, 222, 308, 316, 433, 561, 609, 631.
1666 B   25, 53, 540, 689.

Reports and Certificates: Volumes 146 and 153.

Affidavits

Trinity, 1663.	312, 454, 505.
Michaelmas, 1663.	831, 832, 851.
Hilary, 1664.	167, 770.
Easter, 1665.	337.
Easter, 1666.	552.
Trinity, 1666.	833, 860, 861, 862.
Easter, 1667.	256.

The above all relate to suits in which Edward Benlowes and/or his estates were involved. Chancery proceedings relating to other members of the family include

Bills and Answers

First Series, Elizabeth, B 26/26.
        Charles I, B 36/66.
                 J 7/23.
                 J 24/37.
                 J 33/106.

There are also *Depositions*
C24/129/13
    129/22
    288/82
    291/6
    etc.

6. MISCELLANEOUS MANUSCRIPTS

Bodleian MS. Rawlinson Essex 1. (William Holman on Benlowes.)
British Museum, MS. Harleian 5846 (fol. 12) (Benlowes arms.)
          Stowe 692 (fol. 12)
          Additional 5505. (Survey for Sequestrations.)
Cole, W. Athenae Cantabrigienses. British Museum, MS. Add. 5863 (fols. 61 ff.).
Hasted, E. The Original Papers, Letters and Accounts of the Committee of Sequestrations. British Museum, MS. Add. 5491.

C. PRINTED DOCUMENTARY COLLECTIONS

Acts of the Privy Council.
Arber, E. A Transcript of the Registers of the Company of Stationers of London; 1554-1640 A.D. 5 vols. London. 1875-1894.
Bland, A. E., P. A. Brown, and R. H. Tawney. English Economic History. Select Documents. London. 1914.
Dyson, Humphrey. A Booke containing all such Proclamations, as were published during the Raigne of the late Queene Elizabeth. (A bound collection of the original proclamations.) London. 1618.
The Douay College Diaries—Third, Fourth and Fifth, 1598-1654. Ed. E. H. Burton and T. L. Williams. 2 vols. (Publications of the Catholic Record Society, vols. X-XI.) London. 1911.
Ellis, Henry. Original Letters illustrative of English History. 3 series. 11 vols. London. 1824-1846.
Eyre, G. E. B. A Transcript of the Registers of the Worshipful Company of Stationers; from 1640-1708 A.D. 3 vols. London. 1913-1914.
Firth, C. H., and R. S. Rait. Acts and Ordinances of the Interregnum, 1642-1660. 3 vols. London. 1911.
Gardiner, Samuel R. The Constitutional Documents of the Puritan Revolution, 1625-1660. 3d ed. Oxford. 1906.
Historical Manuscripts Commission, 10th Report, Appendix, part 4. Westmorland MSS. London. 1885.
Historical Manuscripts Commission, 12th Report, Appendix, part 9. Beaufort MSS. London. 1891.
Husband, Edward. A Collection of all the publicke Orders, Ordinances, and Declarations, of both Houses of Parliament, from March 9th 1642, untill December 1646. London. 1646.
[Lincoln's Inn.] The Records of the Honourable Society of Lincoln's Inn. Vol. I. Admissions from A.D. 1420 to A.D. 1799. London. 1896.
Metcalfe, Walter C. The Visitations of Essex. (Harleian Society Publications, vol. XIII.) London. 1878.
[Royal College of Physicians.] A Descriptive Catalogue of the Legal and Other Documents in the Archives of the Royal College of Physicians of London. (Typescript.) [London.] 1924.
State Papers, Domestic. Calendars. Elizabeth, James I, Charles I, Interregnum, Charles II.

The Statutes of the Realm (1101-1713). 11 vols. London. 1810-1828.

Steele, Robert. Tudor and Stuart Proclamations, 1485-1714. Vol. I. England and Wales. Oxford. 1910.

D. SEVENTEENTH-CENTURY WORKS

I have not included here every book to which incidental reference may have been made.

My practice is to give the first publication, except that when a collection of poems is cited, it may happen that single items in it have had previous publication individually. I give also those later editions which are standard or which I have found helpful, distinguishing with an asterisk those which have been used for quotations and page-references.

(Anon.) The Godly Man's Legacy to the Saints upon Earth, exhibited in the Life of that Great and Able Divine, and Painful Labourer in the Word, Mr. Stephen Marshal, sometime Minister of the Gospel at Finchingfield in Essex. London. 1680.

———A Great Fight in the Church at Thaxted in Essex, between the Sequestrators, and the Minister... London. 1647.

Ashmole, Elias. The Institution, Laws & Ceremonies of the most Noble Order of the Garter. 2 vols. London. 1672.

　　　*Continued by Thomas Walker as *The History of the most Noble Order of the Garter*. London. 1715.

Aubrey, John. Lives of Eminent Men. (In *Letters Written by Eminent Persons in the seventeenth and eighteenth Centuries*, vol. II.) London. 1813.

　　　*Ed. Andrew Clark ('Brief Lives'). 2 vols. Oxford. 1898.

Bacon, Sir Francis. Of the Proficience and Advancement of Learning. London. 1605.

　　　*Works, ed. Spedding, Ellis, and Heath, vol. III. London. 1857.

Beaumont, Joseph. Psyche: or Loves Mysterie. London. 1648.

　　　Complete Poems, ed. A. B. Grosart. 2 vols. Edinburgh. 1877-1880.

Benlowes, Edward. (See above, Section A).

Brathwait, Richard. The English Gentleman. London. 1630.

Browne, Sir Thomas. Religio Medici. [London.] 1642.

———Pseudodoxia Epidemica. London. 1646.

　　　Works, ed. Charles Sayle. 3 vols. Edinburgh. 1904.

　　　*Works, ed. Geoffrey Keynes. 6 vols. London. 1928-1931.

Browne, William. Britannia's Pastorals. London. 1613-1616.

　　　Poems, ed. G. Goodwin. (Muses' Library.) 2 vols. London. [1891.]

Buckler, Edward. A Buckler against the fear of Death. Cambridge. 1640.

Burnet, Gilbert. History of His Own Time. 2 vols. London. 1724-1734.

　　　*Part 1. The Reign of Charles II, ed. O. Airy. 2 vols. Oxford. 1897-1900.

Burton, Robert. The Anatomy of Melancholy... Oxford. 1621.

Butler, Samuel. Hudibras. 3 parts. London. 1663-1678.

　　　Ed. A. R. Waller. Cambridge. 1905.

———Characters. (In *The Genuine Remains in Verse and Prose*, ed. R. Thyer.) London. 1759.

　　　*Characters and Passages from Note-books, ed. A. R. Waller. Cambridge. 1908.

Carew, Thomas. Poems. London. 1640.

　　　Ed. R. Dunlap. Oxford. 1949.

Clarendon, Edward Hyde, Earl of. The History of the Rebellion and Civil Wars in England, Begun in the Year 1641. 3 vols. Oxford. 1702-1704.

　　　*Ed. W. D. Macray. 6 vols. Oxford. 1888.

Cleland, James. Ἡρω-παιδεια, or The Institution of a Young Noble Man. Oxford·
1607.

Cleveland, John. The Character of a London-Diurnall with severall select Poems.
London. 1647.

———News from Newcastle. London. 1651.

———Poems. London. 1651. (For first appearance of "Fuscara.")

———(attrib. to.) J. Cleaveland Revived. London. 1659.

　　　　Poems, ed. J. M. Berdan. New York. 1903.

　　　　In Saintsbury, *Minor Poets of the Caroline Period*, vol. III. Oxford. 1921.

Coryat, Thomas. Coryats Crudities, hastily gobled up in five moneths travells
in France, Savoy, Italy... London. 1611.

　　　　*Reprint. 2 vols. Glasgow. 1905.

Crashaw, Richard. Steps to the Temple... with other Delights of the Muses.
London. 1646.

———Carmen Deo Nostro. Paris. 1652.

　　　　*Poems, ed. L. C. Martin. Oxford. 1927.

[Crosby.] Crosby Records: A Chapter of Lancashire Recusancy. Ed. T. E.
Gibson. (Chetham Society Publications, new series, vol. XII.) Manchester.
1887.

D'Avenant, Sir William. A Discourse upon Gondibert... with an Answer to
it by M^r. Hobbs. Paris. 1650.

　　　　Also as The Preface to Gondibert... Paris. 1650.

　　　　Prefixed to *Gondibert: an heroick Poem* (The author's Preface). London.
1651.

　　　　Reprinted in Spingarn, *Critical Essays of the Seventeenth Century*, vol.
II. Oxford. 1908.

Davies, John (of Kidwelly). The Extravagant Shepherd. Or, the History of
the Shepherd Lysis. London. 1653. (Translated from the French of C. Sorel.)

———Apocalypsis; Or, The Revelation of certain notorious Advancers of
Heresie. London. 1655. (Dedicated to Benlowes.)

D'Ewes, Sir Simonds. The Autobiography and Correspondence of Sir Simonds
D'Ewes, Bart., during the Reigns of James I. and Charles I., ed. J. O. Halliwell.
2 vols. London. 1845.

———The Journal... from the beginning of the Long Parliament to the
opening of the Trial of the Earl of Strafford, ed. W. Notestein. New Haven.
1923.

———The Journal... from the first recess of the Long Parliament to the
Withdrawal of King Charles from London, ed. W. H. Coates. New Haven.
1942.

Donne, John. Poems. London. 1633.

　　　　*Ed. H. J. C. Grierson. 2 vols. Oxford. 1912.

Drummond, William, of Hawthornden. A Cypresse Grove. (Appended to
Flowres of Sion.) [Edinburgh.] 1623.

　　　　* The Poetical Works, ed. L. E. Kastner. 2 vols. Edinburgh and
Manchester. 1913.

Dryden, John. Of Dramatick Poesie, an Essay. London. 1668.

　　　　*Essays, ed. W. P. Ker. 2 vols. Oxford. 1926.

Du Bartas, Guillaume de Saluste. (See Sylvester, Joshua.)

Eachard, John. The Grounds & Occasions of the Contempt of the Clergy and
Religion enquired into. London. 1670.

　　　　*Reprinted in E. Arber, *An English Garner*, vol. VII. Birmingham. 1883.

Evelyn, John. Sculptura: or the History, and Art of Chalcography and Engraving
in Copper. London. 1662.

　　　　Ed. C. F. Bell. Oxford. 1906.

———Memoirs, Illustrative of the Life and Writings of John Evelyn, Esq. F.R.S. ...comprising his Diary, from the year 1641 to 1705-6... ed. W. Bray. 2 vols. London. 1818.

> The Diary, ed. Austin Dobson. 3 vols. London. 1906.

> * The Diary, ed. H. B. Wheatley. 4 vols. London. 1906.

Feltham, Owen. Resolves Divine, Morall, Politicall. London. [1620?]

> Ed. O. Smeaton. (Temple Classics.) London. 1904.

———Lusoria, or Occasional Pieces. (Appended to 8th ed. of the *Resolves*. London. 1661.)

Firmin, Giles. A brief Vindication of Mr. Stephen Marshal. (Appended to *The Questions between the Conformist and Nonconformist*.) London. 1681.

Fisher, Payne. Chronosticon Decollationis Caroli Regis. London. 1648 (*i.e.* 1648/49).

———Marston-Moor. London. 1650.

———Piscatoris Poemata. London. 1655-56.

———Epinicion vel Elogium... Lodovici XIIII^{ti} Galliæ... Regis... pro nuperis passim victoriis, in Flandria... [London? 1658.]

Fletcher, Giles. Christs Victorie, and Triumph in Heaven, and Earth, over, and after death. Cambridge. 1610.

> Giles and Phineas Fletcher, *Poetical Works*, ed. F. S. Boas, vol. I. Cambridge. 1908.

Fletcher, Phineas. Locustæ, vel Pietas Jesuitica. Cambridge. 1627.

———Sicelides. London. 1631.

———The Purple Island, or The Isle of Man: together with Piscatorie Eclogs and other Poeticall Miscellanies. Cambridge. 1633. (Dedicated to Benlowes.)

———Sylva Poetica. Cambridge. 1633. (Dedicated to Benlowes.)

> The Poems, ed. A. B. Grosart. 4 vols. (Fuller Worthies' Library.) 1869.

> Giles and Phineas Fletcher, *Poetical Works*, ed. F. S. Boas. 2 vols. Cambridge. 1908-1909.

Fuller, Thomas. A Pisgah-sight of Palestine. London. 1650.

———The Church-History of Britain. London. 1655.

———The History of the University of Cambridge since the Conquest. (With *The Church-History of Britain*.) London. 1655. (The sixth section dedicated to Benlowes.)

> * Ed. M. Prickett and T. Wright. Cambridge. 1840.

———The History of the Worthies of England. London. 1662.

> * Ed. J. Nichols. 2 vols. London. 1811.

Gauden, John (attrib. to.) Εἰκὼν Βασιλικὴ: the Pourtraicture of His Sacred Maiestie in His Solitudes and Sufferings. [London.] 1648 (*i.e.* 1648/49).

Guise, Sir Christopher and Sir John. Memoirs of the Family of Guise of Elmore, Gloucestershire, ed. G. Davies. (Camden 3d series, vol. XXVIII.) London. 1917.

Habington, William. Castara. Parts 1 and 2, London, 1634. Part 3, London, 1640.

> Ed. E. Arber, English Reprints. London. 1870.

> Poems, ed. Kenneth Allott. Liverpool. 1948.

Harvey, William. Anatomia Thomæ Parri. (Written 1635.) Published in John Betts, *De Ortu et Natura Sanguinis*. London. 1669.

> * Works, translated Robert Willis. London. 1847.

Herbert, Edward, Baron Herbert of Cherbury. Occasional Verses. London. 1665.

> Poems English and Latin, ed. G. C. Moore Smith. Oxford. 1923.

———The Life of Edward Lord Herbert of Cherbury, written by himself. (Written *circa* 1643.) Strawberry-Hill. 1764.

> * Autobiography, ed. Sidney Lee. 2d ed. London. [1906.]

Herbert, George. The Temple. Cambridge. 1633.

———A Priest to the Temple, or, The Countrey Parson His Character, and Rule of Holy Life. (In Herbert's *Remains*.) London. 1652.

    * Works, ed. F. E. Hutchinson. Oxford. 1941.

Hobbes, Thomas. The Answer of Mr Hobbes to Sr Will. D'Avenant's Preface before Gondibert. (See above, under D'Avenant.)

———Leviathan, Or the Matter, Forme, & Power, of a Common-wealth Ecclesiasticall and Civill. London. 1651.

    Ed. A. R. Waller. Cambridge. 1904.

Howell, James. Instructions for Forreine Travell. London. 1642.

    * Ed. E. Arber, English Reprints. London. 1869.

———Epistolae Ho-Elianae... Familiar Letters Domestic and Forren. 4 books. London. 1645-1655.

    * Ed. J. Jacobs. 2 vols. London. 1890-1892.

    Ed. O. Smeaton. (Temple Classics.) 3 vols. London. 1903.

———Poems on several Choice and Various Subjects, ed. Payne Fisher. London. 1663. (Includes *Upon Mr. Benlowes Divine Theophila*.)

Hutchinson, Lucy. Memoirs of the Life of Colonel Hutchinson... with original anecdotes of many... of his contemporaries, and a summary review of public affairs... Published from the original manuscript by... J. Hutchinson... London. 1806.

    * Ed. C. H. Firth (new ed., revised). London. 1906.

Lovelace, Richard. Lucasta. London. 1649.

    Poems, ed. C. H. Wilkinson. 2 vols. Oxford. 1925.

Markham, Gervase. Countrey Contentments. London. 1615.

Marvell, Andrew. Miscellaneous Poems. London. 1681.

    Poems and Letters, ed. H. M. Margoliouth, vol. I. Oxford. 1927.

Milton, John. The Reason of Church-governement Urg'd against Prelaty. London. 1641.

———Areopagitica; a Speech... for the Liberty of Unlicenc'd Printing. London. 1644.

———Of Education. [London. 1644.]

———Poems... both English and Latin. London. 1645.

    Type-facsimile. Oxford. 1924.

———Εἰκονοκλάστης, in Answer to a Book Intitl'd Εἰκὼν Βασιλικὴ. London. 1649.

———Pro Populo Anglicano Defensio Secunda. London. 1654.

———Epistolarum Familiarium Liber Unus: quibus accesserunt... Prolusiones Quaedam Oratoriae. London. 1674.

    * Works. 18 vols. (Columbia University Press.) New York. 1931-1938.

More, Henry. Ψυχωδια Platonica: or A Platonicall Song of the Soul. Cambridge. 1642.

    Philosophical Poems, ed. G. Bullough. Manchester, 1931.

Moryson, Fynes. An Itinerary. London. 1617.

    * Reprint. 4 vols. Glasgow. 1907-1908.

Nalson, John. An Impartial Collection of the Great Affairs of State, from the Beginning of the Scotch Rebellion... to the Murther of King Charles I. 2 vols. London. 1682-83.

Ogilby, John. The Fables of Æsop Paraphras'd in Verse. London. 1651.

[Oxinden, Family of.] The Oxinden Letters 1607-1642, ed. Dorothy Gardiner. London. 1933.

———The Oxinden and Peyton Letters 1642-1670, ed. Dorothy Gardiner. London. 1937.

Peacham, Henry. The Compleat Gentleman, fashioning him absolute in the most necessary & commendable Qualities concerning Minde or Bodie that may be required in a Noble Gentleman. London. 1622.
> 2d ed., enlarged, 1634.
> *Reprint of 1634 edition, ed. G. S. Gordon. Oxford. 1906.

Pepys, Samuel. Memoirs... comprising his Diary from 1659 to 1669... ed. Lord Braybrooke. 2 vols. London. 1825.
> *The Diary, ed. H. B. Wheatley. 10 vols. London. 1893-1899.

Pestell, Thomas. Poems, ed. Hannah Buchan. Oxford. 1940.

Prynne, William. The Unlovelinesse, of Love-Lockes. Or, a Summarie Discourse, prooving: The wearing, and nourishing of a Locke, or Love-Locke, to be altogether unseemely, and unlawfull unto Christians. London. 1628.

Puttenham, George. The Arte of English Poesie. London. 1589.
> *Ed. G. D. Willcock and A. Walker. Cambridge. 1936.

Quarles, Francis. Sion's Elegies, Wept by Jeremie the Prophet, and periphras'd. London. 1624.

————Divine Poems: containing the history of Jonah, Esther, Job, Sions Sonets. London. 1630.
> Newly augmented. London. 1633.

————The Historie of Samson. London. 1631.
> Included in the *Divine Poems*, 1633.

————Divine Fancies; digested into epigrammes, meditations, and observations. London. 1632.

————Emblemes. London. 1635. (Dedicated to Benlowes.)

————Hieroglyphikes of the Life of Man. London. 1638.

————Enchyridion. London. 1640.

————The Whipper Whipt. London. 1644.

————The Loyall Convert. Oxford. 1644.

————Solomons Recantation, entituled Ecclesiastes, Paraphrased. London. 1645. (Containing "A Short Relation of the Life and Death of M^r. Francis Quarles, by Ursula Quarles, his sorrowfull Widow.")
> Collected Works in Prose and Verse, ed. A. B. Grosart. 3 vols. Edinburgh. 1880-81.

Quarles, John. Fons Lachrymarum, or a Fountain of Tears; from whence doth flow Englands Complaint....and an Elegy upon that Son of Valor, Sir Charles Lucas. London. 1648.

————Regale Lectum Miseriae; or, a Kingly Bed of Miserie... with an Elegy upon the Martyrdome of Charles, late King of England... London. 1649.

————Gods Love and Mans Unworthiness. London. 1651. (Dedicated to Benlowes.)

Randolph, Thomas. Poems. Oxford. 1638.
> *Ed. G. Thorn-Drury. London. 1929.

Raymond, Thomas. Autobiography, ed. G. Davies. (Camden, 3d series, vol. XXVIII.) London. 1917.

Reresby, Sir John. The Memoirs of the Honourable Sir John Reresby, Bart. London. 1734.
> *Ed. A. Browning. Glasgow. 1936.

Reynolds, Henry. Mythomystes wherein a short Survay is taken of the Nature and Value of true Poesy and Depth of the Ancients above our Moderne Poets. London. [1632?]
> *Reprinted in Spingarn, *Critical Essays of the Seventeenth Century*, vol. I. Oxford. 1908.

Ross, Alexander. Medicus Medicatus: Or The Physicians Religion Cured, by a Lenitive or Gentle Potion: With some Animadversions upon Sir Kenelme

Digbie's Observations on Religio Medici. London. 1645. (Dedicated to Benlowes.)

————The New Planet No Planet, Or, the Earth no wandring Star; Except in the wandring heads of Galileans. London. 1646.

————Arcana Microcosmi: or, the hid Secrets of Man's Body disclosed... with a refutation of Dr. Browns Vulgar Errors, and the ancient opinions vindicated. London. 1651.

————Πανσεβεια, or, a View of All Religions in the World... together with a Discovery of all known Heresies. London. 1653.

Sandys, George. A Relation of a Journey Begun An. Dom. 1610. London. 1615.

————Ovid's Metamorphosis Englished by G.S. London. 1626.

————A Paraphrase upon the Psalmes of David. London. 1636.

————A Paraphrase upon the Divine Poems. London. 1638.

   Poetical Works, ed. R. Hooper. 2 vols. London. 1872.

Sibbs, Richard. The Soules Conflict with it selfe, and Victory over it selfe by Faith. London. 1635.

Sictor, John. Panegyricon Inaugurale Honoratissimi & Amplissimi Domini Prætoris Regii, sive Majoris, Nobilissimæ & Florentissimæ Reipublicæ Londinensis, Richardi Fenn, sub finem Anni Christi 1637. London. [1638.] (Includes Benlowes' *De celeberrima & florentissima Trinobantiados Augustæ Civitate*.)

————Compendium Religionis Christianae his turbulentis temporibus Magnae Britanniae. Cambridge. 1644.

Smectymnuus (*pseud*.) An Answer to a Booke entituled, An Humble Remonstrance. London. 1641.

Smith, John. Select Discourses. London. 1660.

Sparke, Edward. Scintillula Altaris, or, A Pious Reflection on Primitive Devotion. London. 1652.

   2d ed. London. 1660. (Containing a complimentary poem by Benlowes.)

Suckling, Sir John. Fragmenta Aurea. A Collection of all the Incomparable Peeces written by Sir John Suckling. London. 1646.

   The Poems, Plays and other Remains, ed. W. C. Hazlitt. Revised ed. 2 vols. London. 1892.

   Works, ed. A. Hamilton Thompson. London. 1910.

Sylvester, Joshua. (trans.) Bartas his Devine Weekes and Workes. [London. 1605.] (Parts from 1592 onwards.)

   7th ed. London. 1641.

Tomkis, Thomas. Lingua: or the Combat of the Tongue, and the five Senses for Superiority. London. 1607.

   Dodsley's *Old English Plays*, ed. W. C. Hazlitt, vol. IX. London. 1876.

   Tudor Facsimile Texts. London. 1913.

Vaughan, Henry. Silex Scintillans 2 books. London. 1650-1655.

   * Works, ed. L. C. Martin. 2 vols. Oxford. 1914.

Walton, Isaak. The Lives of Dr John Donne, Sir Henry Wotton, Mr. Richard Hooker, Mr. George Herbert... London. 1670.

   * The Lives. (World's Classics.) Oxford. 1927.

   The Compleat Walton, ed. G. L. Keynes. London. 1929.

Westmorland, Mildmay Fane, Earl of. Otia Sacra. London. 1648.

   Poems, ed. A. B. Grosart. Manchester. 1879.

Wilson, Arthur. Observations of God's Providence, in the Tract of my Life. (In Peck, *Desiderata Curiosa*, vol. II.) London. 1735.

   * Revised ed. London. 1779.

Wincoll, Thomas. Plantaganets Tragicall Story: or, The Death of King Edward the Fourth: with The unnaturall Voyage of Richard the Third, through the

Red Sea of his Nephews innocent bloud, to his usurped Crowne. Metaphrased by T. W. Gent. London. 1649. (Dedicated to Benlowes.)

Winterton, Ralph. (trans.) A Golden Chaine of Divine Aphorismes Written by John Gerhard... [Cambridge.] 1632.

———(trans.) The Considerations of Drexelius upon Eternitie. London. 1632. 2d ed., Cambridge, 1636. (Dedicated to Benlowes.)

———... Hippocratis Magni Aphorismi, Soluti & Metrici. Interprete Joanne Heurnio... Metaphrastis, Joanne Frero... et Radulpho Wintertono... Cambridge. 1633.

Wood, Anthony à. Athenae Oxonienses. An exact history of all the Writers and Bishops who have had their education in the... University of Oxford, from... 1500 to the end of... 1690... To which are added, the Fasti or Annals of the said University, for the same time. 2 vols. London. 1691-92.
*Ed. P. Bliss. 4 vols. London. 1813-1820. (The *Fasti*, with separate pagination, appended to vols. II and IV.)

———The Life and Times of Anthony Wood, antiquary, of Oxford, 1632-1695, described by Himself, ed. Andrew Clark. 5 vols. Oxford. 1891-1900.

ADDENDA.

List of some of the books presented to St. John's College (Cambridge) by Benlowes in 1631.

Becan, Martin. Opera Omnia. 2 vols. Mainz. 1630-31.

Bedell, William, and James Wadsworth. The Copies of Certaine Letters which have passed betweene Spaine and England in matter of Religion... London. 1624.

Bell, Thomas. The Anatomie of Popish Tyrannie. London. 1603.

Bernard, Richard. Rhemes against Rome. London. 1626.

Davenant, John. Praelectiones de Duobus in Theologia Controversis Capitibus. Cambridge. 1631.

Epithalamium... Caroli regis et H. Mariae reginae a Musis Cantab. Cambridge. 1625.

Fletcher, Giles. Christs Victorie, and Triumph in Heaven, and Earth, over, and after death. Cambridge. 1610.

Gordon, John. Antitortobellarminus, sive Refutatio calumniarum, mendaciorum, et Imposturarum Laico-Cardinalis Bellarmini... London. 1610.

Ledesma, Pedro de. Theologia Moralis. Douai. 1630.

Leius, Matthias. Liber de Triumphata Barbarie. [?] 1621.

Montaigne. Essayes. Translated Florio. 3d. ed. London. 1632.

Nicrina ad Heroas Anglos. Heidelberg. 1620.

Saravicto. Querelae Saravictonis et Biomeae. [?] 1620.

Valacrius, Joannes. Spectacula Veneta. Venice. 1627.

Weever, John. Ancient Funerall Monuments within the United Monarchie of Great Britaine and Ireland, and the Ilands adjacent... London. 1631.

E. LATER WORKS

Again in this section the reader will not generally find books mentioned which have been cited in the text once only on some point of incidental interest but which have no direct bearing on the subject of this biography or on seventeenth-century life and literature.

Addison, Joseph. The Spectator, nos. 58-63. London. 1711. Ed. G. A. Aitken, vol. I. London. 1898.

Ashton, Harry. Du Bartas en Angleterre. Paris. 1908.

Ault, Norman. (ed.) Seventeenth Century Lyrics. London. 1928.

Bailey, John E. The Life of Thomas Fuller. London. 1874.

Baker, Thomas. History of the College of St. John the Evangelist, Cambridge, ed. J. E. B. Mayor. 2 vols. Cambridge. 1869.

Barrett, C. R. B. Essex: Highways, Byways and Waterways. 2 vols. London. 1892-93.

Barwick, G. F. "Impresas," The Library, 2d series, vol. VII. April 1906.

Bateson, F. W. (ed.) The Cambridge Bibliography of English Literature. 4 vols. Cambridge. 1940.

Beachcroft, T. O. "Quarles—and the Emblem Habit," Dublin Review, vol. CLXXXVIII. January 1931.

———"Crashaw—and the Baroque Style," The Criterion, vol. XIII. April 1934.

Blackstone, Bernard. "Story-Books of Little Gidding," Times Literary Supplement, March 21, 1936.

———(ed.) The Ferrar Papers. Cambridge. 1938.

Brook, Benjamin. The Lives of the Puritans... 3 vols. London. 1813.

Bryan, Michael. Dictionary of Painters and Engravers. 4th ed., revised by G. C. Williamson. 5 vols. London. 1903-04.

Brydges, Sir Samuel Egerton. Restituta: or, Titles, extracts, and characters of old books in English literature, revived. 4 vols. London. 1814-1816.

Buckler, W. H. "Edward Buckler (1610-1706) Poet and Preacher," The Library, 4th series, vol. XVII. December 1936.

Burke, Sir Bernard. Genealogical and Heraldic History of the Landed Gentry. 15th ed., ed. H. Pine-Gordon. London. 1937.

Bush, Douglas. English Literature in the Earlier Seventeenth Century, 1600-1660. (Oxford History of English Literature, vol. V.) Oxford. 1945.

———Mythology and the Renaissance Tradition in English Poetry. Minneapolis. 1932.

The Cambridge History of English Literature, ed. A. W. Ward and A. R. Waller, vol. VII. Cambridge. 1911.

Campbell, Mildred. The English Yeoman under Elizabeth and the Early Stuarts. New Haven. 1942.

The Catholic Encyclopaedia. 16 vols. New York. 1907-1914.

Clark, G. N. The Seventeenth Century. Oxford. 1929.

Collier, John Payne. A Bibliographical and Critical Account of the Rarest Books in the English Language. 2 vols. London. 1865.

Colvin, Sir Sidney. Early Engraving and Engravers in England (1545-1695). London. 1905.

Cooper, Charles H. and Thompson. Athenae Cantabrigienses. 3 vols. Cambridge. 1858-1913.

Corser, T. Collectanea Anglo-Poetica. (Chetham Society.) 11 vols. Manchester. 1860-1883.

Cory, H. E. Spenser, the School of the Fletchers and Milton. (University of California Publications in Modern Philology, vol. II, no. 5.) Berkeley. 1912.

Courthope, W. J. A History of English Poetry, vol. III. London. 1903.

Davids, T. W. Annals of Evangelical Nonconformity in the County of Essex.... London. 1863.

Davies, Godfrey. The Early Stuarts, 1603-1660. Oxford. 1937.

Day, Lewis F. Penmanship of the XVI, XVII, & XVIIIth Centuries. London. [1911.]

Dictionary of National Biography, ed. Leslie Stephen and Sidney Lee. 63 vols. London. 1885-1900.

Eliot, T. S. Homage to John Dryden. London. 1924.

Encyclopaedia Britannica. 14th ed. 24 vols. 1929.

The Essex Review. Chelmsford, afterwards Colchester. From 1892. In progress.

Fletcher, William Y. English Bookbindings. London. 1896.

Freeman, Alexander. Our Portrait Pictures. (A descriptive list of the Portrait Paintings in St. John's College, Cambridge.) [Cambridge. 1880?]

Freeman, Rosemary. English Emblem Books. London. 1948.

Gardiner, Samuel R. A History of England, from the Accession of James I to the Outbreak of the Civil War, 1603-1642. 10 vols. London. 1883-84.

————History of the Great Civil War, 1642-1649. Revised ed. 4 vols. London. 1893.

————History of the Commonwealth and Protectorate, 1649-1660. Revised ed. 4 vols. London. 1903.

"A Gentleman". A New and Complete History of Essex. By a Gentleman. (Preface by Peter Muilman.) 6 vols. Chelmsford. 1770-1772.

Gosse, Sir Edmund. Sir Thomas Browne. (English Men of Letters.) London. 1905.

Grierson, Sir Herbert J. C. The First Half of the Seventeenth Century. (*i.e.* Periods of European Literature, ed. Saintsbury, vol. VII.) Edinburgh and London. 1906.

————Cross Currents in English Literature of the XVIIth Century. London. 1929.

[Grolier Club.] Catalogue of Original and Early Editions of some of the Poetical and Prose Works of English Writers from Wither to Prior, vol. I. New York. 1905.

Grove, Sir George. Dictionary of Music and Musicians. 3d ed., ed. H. C. Colles. 5 vols. London. 1927-28.

Haight, Gordon S. "The Publication of Quarles' *Emblems*," *The Library*, 4th series, vol. XV. June 1934.

————"The Sources of Quarles's *Emblems*," *The Library*, 4th series, vol. XVI. September 1935.

————"Francis Quarles in the Civil War," *The Review of English Studies*, vol. XII. April 1936.

Harbage, Alfred. Sir William Davenant, Poet Venturer, 1606-1668. Philadelphia. 1935.

Hazlitt, William Carew. Hand-book to the Popular, Poetical, and Dramatic Literature of Great Britain, from the Invention of Printing to the Restoration. London. 1867.

————Collections and Notes. Four series. London. 1876-1903.

Hilton, James. Chronograms. 3 vols. London. 1882-1895.

[Hoe, Robert.] A Catalogue of Books by English Authors who lived before the Year 1700 forming a part of the Library of Robert Hoe (prepared by J. O. Wright and Carolyn Shipman). 1903.

Houghton, Walter E. "The English Virtuoso in the Seventeenth Century," *Journal of the History of Ideas*, vol. III. Jan.-April 1942.

Jenkins, Harold. "Towards a Biography of Edward Benlowes," *The Review of English Studies*, vol. XII. July 1936.

————"A Poet in Chancery: Edward Benlowes," *Modern Language Review*, vol. XXXII. July 1937.

————"Benlowes and Milton," *Modern Language Review*, vol. XLIII. April 1948.

Johnson, Francis R. Astronomical Thought in Renaissance England. Baltimore. 1937.

Johnson, Samuel. Life of Cowley. (In *Prefaces Biographical and Critical to the Works of the most Eminent English Poets*. London. 1779. Subsequent editions, *The Lives of the English Poets*.)

       Ed. G. Birkbeck Hill, vol. I. Oxford. 1905.

Langdale, A. B. Phineas Fletcher, Man of Letters, Science and Divinity. New York. 1937.

Leishman, James B. The Metaphysical Poets: Donne, Herbert, Vaughan, Traherne. Oxford. 1934.

Lipson, Ephraim. The Economic History of England, vols. II and III. The Age of Mercantilism. 3d ed. London. 1943.

Lodge, Sir Richard. The History of England from the Restoration to the Death of William III (1660-1702). (*i.e. The Political History of England*, ed. Hunt and Poole, vol. VIII.) London. 1910.

Lowndes, William T. The Bibliographer's Manual of English Literature. New ed. 11 vols. London. 1857-1864.

McColley, Grant. "The Ross-Wilkins Controversy," *Annals of Science*, vol. III. April 1938.

McKerrow, R. B. A Dictionary of Printers and Booksellers in England, Scotland and Ireland, and of Foreign Printers of English Books, 1557-1640. London. 1910.

Macray, William D. Annals of the Bodleian Library, Oxford. 2d ed. Oxford. 1890.

Madan, Falconer. Oxford Books. 3 vols. Oxford. 1895-1931.

———A Chart of Oxford Printing, '1468'-1900. Oxford. 1904.

Marshall, L. Birkett. (ed.) Rare Poems of the Seventeenth Century. Cambridge. 1936.

Masson, David. The Life of John Milton: Narrated in Connexion with the Political, Ecclesiastical, and Literary History of His Time. 7 vols. Cambridge. 1859-1894.

Mathew, David. The Social Structure in Caroline England. Oxford. 1948.

Mayor, J. E. B. (ed.) Nicholas Ferrar. Two Lives by his Brother John and by Dr. Jebb. (Cambridge in the Seventeenth Century. Part 1.) Cambridge. 1855.

Mead, H. R. "Three Issues of *A Buckler Against the Fear of Death*," *The Library*, 4th series, vol. XXI. September 1940.

Meyer, A. O. England and the Catholic Church under Queen Elizabeth. Trans. J. R. McKee. London. 1916.

Miller, Perry. The New England Mind. The Seventeenth Century. New York. 1939.

Montague, Francis C. The History of England from the Accession of James I to the Restoration (1603-1660). (*i.e. The Political History of England*, ed. Hunt and Poole, vol. VII.) London. 1907.

Moore, C. A. "Midnights Meditations (1646). A Bibliographical Puzzle." *Modern Language Notes*, vol. XLI. April 1926.

Moorman, F. W. Robert Herrick. London. 1910.

Morant, Philip. The History and Antiquities of ... Colchester. London. 1748.

——— The History and Antiquities of the County of Essex. 2 vols. London. 1768.

Mullinger, James B. The University of Cambridge. 3 vols. Cambridge. 1873-1911.

Nethercot, Arthur H. "The Literary Legend of Francis Quarles," *Modern Philology*, vol. XX. February 1923.

———Sir William D'avenant. Chicago. 1938.

Niemeyer, Carl. "New Light on Edward Benlowes," *The Review of English Studies*, vol. XII. January 1936.

Nicolson, Marjorie. "The 'New Astronomy' and English Literary Imagination," *Studies in Philology*, vol. XXXII. July 1935.

Peckard, Peter. Memoirs of the Life of Mr Nicholas Ferrar. Cambridge. 1790.

Plomer, Henry R. A Dictionary of the Booksellers and Printers who were at work in England, Scotland and Ireland from 1641 to 1667. London. 1907.

Pollard, Alfred W. Fine Books. London. 1912.

Pollard, A. W., and G. R. Redgrave. A Short-Title Catalogue of Books Printed in England, Scotland, and Ireland and of English Books Printed Abroad, 1475-1640. London. 1926.

Pope, Alexander. The Dunciad. London. 1728.
———— Ed. J. R. Sutherland. London. 1943.

Praz, Mario. "The English Emblem Literature," English Studies, vol. XVI. 1934.
————Studies in Seventeenth-Century Imagery. 2 vols. London. 1939-1947.

The Retrospective Review. 16 vols. London. 1820-1828.

Robbie, H. J. L. "Benlowes: A Seventeenth-Century Plagiarist," Modern Language Review, vol. XXIII. July 1928.

Rogers, J. E. Thorold. Six Centuries of Work and Wages. London. 1884.

Royal Commission on Historical Monuments, Essex, vol. I.

Saintsbury, George. "Edward Benlowes's 'Theophila,' " The Bibliographer (New York), vol. II. January 1903.
————(ed.) Minor Poets of the Caroline Period. 3 vols. Oxford. 1905-1921.

Sharp, Robert L. From Donne to Dryden. Chapel Hill. 1940.

Shaw, W. A. A History of the English Church during the Civil Wars and under the Commonwealth, 1640-1660. 2 vols. London. 1900.

Smith, Logan Pearsall. The Life and Letters of Sir Henry Wotton. 2 vols. Oxford. 1907.

Spingarn, J. E. (ed.) Critical Essays of the Seventeenth Century, vols. I and II. Oxford. 1908.

[Stanley, Family of.] The Stanley Papers. Part III, ed. F. R. Raines. (Remains Historical and Literary....published by the Chetham Society, vols. LXVI, LXVII, and LXX.) Manchester. 1867. (This work is listed in this section as being largely a memoir by a modern hand.)

Stopes, Charlotte C. The Life of Henry, Third Earl of Southampton, Shakespeare's Patron. Cambridge. 1922.

Thieme, Ulrich, und Felix Becker. (ed.) Allgemeines Lexicon der Bildenden Künstler. 32 vols. Leipzig. 1907-1938.

[Thomason Tracts.] Catalogue of the Pamphlets, Books, Newspapers, and Manuscripts relating to the Civil War, the Commonwealth, and Restoration, Collected by George Thomason, 1640-1661. 2 vols. London. 1908.

Thoms, William J. (ed.) Anecdotes and Traditions, illustrative of early English History and Literature. (Camden Society Publications, vol. V). London. 1839.

Thomson, Gladys Scott. Life in a Noble Household, 1641-1700. London. 1937.

Tillotson, Geoffrey. On the Poetry of Pope. Oxford. 1938.

Tillotson, Geoffrey and Arthur. "Pen-and-ink Corrections in Mid-Seventeenth-Century Books," The Library, 4th series, vol. XIV. June 1933.

Tillyard, E. M. W. Milton. London. 1930.

Traill, H. D., and J. S. Mann. (ed.) Social England, vol. IV. London. 1895.

Transactions of the Essex Archaeological Society. 5 vols. Colchester. 1858-1873. New series. Colchester. From 1878, in progress.

Trevelyan, George M. England under the Stuarts. Revised ed. London. 1925.
————History of England. London. 1926.
————English Social History. London. 1944.

Tuve, Rosemond. Elizabethan and Metaphysical Imagery. Chicago. 1947.

Ustick, W. Lee. "Changing Ideals of Aristocratic Character and Conduct in Seventeenth-Century England," Modern Philology, vol. XXX. November 1932.

Vaughan, Eliza. Stephen Marshall, a forgotten Essex Puritan. London. 1907.
————The Essex Village in Days Gone By. Colchester. 1928.

Venn, John. Early Collegiate Life. Cambridge. 1913.

Venn, John and J. A. Alumni Cantabrigienses. Part 1. From the Earliest Times to 1751. 4 vols. Cambridge. 1922-1927.

Warren, Austin. Richard Crashaw. A Study in Baroque Sensibility. Baton Rouge. 1939.

Wheatley, H. B. Of Anagrams. Hertford. 1862.

White, Helen C. The Metaphysical Poets: A Study in Religious Experience. New York. 1936.

Willey, Basil. The Seventeenth Century Background. London. 1934.

Williamson, George. "Three Thefts from Cleveland," *Modern Language Notes*, vol. XLIV. June 1929.

——The Donne Tradition. Cambridge (Mass.). 1930.

Wing, Donald. Short-Title Catalogue of Books Printed in England, Scotland, Ireland, Wales, and British America and of English books printed in other countries 1641-1700, vol. I. New York. 1945.

Wood, Thomas. An Institute of the Laws of England. London. 1720.

Woolrych, Humphry W. Lives of Eminent Serjeants-at-Law of the English Bar. 2 vols. London. 1869.

Wright, Thomas. The History and Topography of the County of Essex. 2 vols. London. 1836.

Young, Robert F. A Czech Humanist in London in the 17th Century. Jan Sictor Rokycanský (1593-1652). London. [1926.]

INDEX